Ultimate Parallel and Distributed Computing with Julia For Data Science

Excel in Data Analysis, Statistical Modeling and Machine Learning by Leveraging MLBase.jl and MLJ.jl to Optimize Workflows

Nabanita Dash

www.orangeava.com

First published: January 2024

Published by: Orange Education Pvt Ltd, AVA™

Address: 9, Daryaganj, Delhi, 110002

ISBN: 978-93-91246-86-0

www.orangeava.com

Dedicated To

My beloved Parents:

Mr. Bimal Kumar Dash

Mrs. Sakuntala Dash

My sibling

Bikash Ku. Dash

and

My grandparents

Lt. Bichitra Nanda Dash

Lt. Sebati Dash

Lt. Sukadeb Pati

Sandhya Rani Pati

About the Author

Nabanita Dash is a dynamic and results-driven Research Engineer with a robust academic foundation and a passion for technology. She earned her Bachelor of Technology in Computer Science and Engineering from the prestigious International Institute of Information Technology in BBS, India, in 2021. Throughout her academic journey, Nabanita showcased not only her technical prowess but also her leadership skills as the Head of the Programming Club, emphasizing her commitment to collaborative projects and technological innovation.

Her educational journey began at Ispat E. M. School in Rourkela, India, where she built a solid foundation in Mathematics, Physics, Chemistry, English, and Computer Science. This comprehensive education laid the groundwork for her future success in the tech industry.

Currently serving as a Research Engineer at Antimodular Research in Montreal, QC, Nabanita specializes in creating artworks using deep learning and analyzing voice, text, and 2D/3D data and models. Her innovative contributions to the intersection of technology and art showcase her creativity and technical prowess.

Nabanita's commitment to the broader tech community is evident in her roles as a remote volunteer Research Engineer for MLPack and OpenMined. In these positions, she demonstrated her expertise in C++ by developing data management functions, troubleshooting installations, and contributing to research on differential privacy algorithms. This experience reflects her dedication to pushing the boundaries of knowledge and contributing to the open-source community.

Earlier in her career, Nabanita showcased her versatility as a Full Stack Developer at Julia Computing Incorporation. This role allowed her to refine her skills and gain hands-on experience in various aspects of software development, contributing to her well-rounded skill set.

Her technical proficiency spans Machine Learning, Deep Learning, Computer Vision, and expertise in tools and frameworks such as TensorFlow, PyTorch, Flux, NumPy, Pandas, Scikit-learn, Hugging Face, Linear Algebra, Natural Language Processing, and Parallel Computing. Nabanita's ability to seamlessly integrate diverse skills with a dynamic approach positions her as a valuable and well-rounded professional in the field of research and technology. As she continues to make strides in her career, Nabanita Dash remains at the forefront of technological innovation, leaving an indelible mark on the intersection of art and artificial intelligence.

About the Technical Reviewers

Chayan Datta is a versatile Software Engineer with nearly 5 years of experience across healthcare, Ed-tech, FinTech, and scientific computing. He excels as a full-stack developer creating robust applications, blending technologies like Python, Django, Vue.js, JavaScript, Julia, and Go. His leadership is evident in his past roles, contributing significantly to the success of various platforms.

Chayan is deeply involved in DevOps, system design, and scalability. His expertise lies not only in building robust applications but also in orchestrating seamless integration between development and operations. With a keen eye for system design, Chayan envisions and implements architectures that prioritize efficiency, reliability, and scalability. His practices ensure smooth collaboration between development and IT operations, fostering a streamlined and agile development pipeline. His commitment to scalability extends beyond individual projects, encompassing a holistic approach to designing systems that can adapt and grow with evolving business needs.

Adhering to coding practices, he ensures project longevity. Understanding front-end and back-end synergy, he crafts user-friendly applications. He understands the crucial interplay between front-end design and back-end functionality, ensuring that the user interface is not only visually engaging but also seamlessly integrated with the underlying system architecture. His holistic approach to software development encompasses a keen awareness of the end-user experience, resulting in applications that not only meet technical requirements but also delight users with their usability and design aesthetics.

Besides work, Chayan contributes to open-source projects and maintains a technical blog, showcasing his commitment to knowledge-sharing and community engagement. He brings a well-rounded perspective to his work, fueled by his avid reading habits and a constant desire to stay updated on the latest industry trends and technologies.

Venkateshprasad Bhat is an electronics engineer and an avid Julia developer. He specializes in developing modeling and simulation tools, along with improving package tooling in Julia. He frequently contributes to open-source software. Additionally, he enjoys building robots, especially working on computer vision and electronic circuitry.

He is deeply committed to writing highly performant and readable Julia packages.

Acknowledgements

To my parents, whose unwavering encouragement and belief in my abilities kept me going through the late nights and countless revisions. Your support was the foundation on which this book stands, and I am forever grateful.

I extend my thanks to the educational institutions and companies that played a pivotal role in my journey of learning data analysis, machine learning and Julia language. The tools and knowledge acquired from your courses and collaborations have been invaluable, shaping the very core of this book.

A special shout-out to the unsung heroes–the ones behind-the-scenes offering hidden support. Your contributions have not gone unnoticed, and I appreciate the collective effort that made this book possible.

I want to express my sincere gratitude to the technical editors who meticulously combed through the manuscript, ensuring it reached the readers in its best form. Your attention to detail and dedication to perfection did not go unnoticed.

Thanks to my incredible team for their unwavering support and understanding. The flexibility you provided allowed me ample time to complete the book. It's a reflection of your commitment to delivering quality content in the dynamic field of data analysis and machine learning.

Preface

Welcome to the fascinating world of machine learning and data analysis in Julia! In this book, we embark on a journey that explores the powerful intersection of Julia, a high-performance programming language, and the transformative fields of machine learning and data analysis. As technology continues to evolve, the ability to harness and interpret vast amounts of data becomes increasingly crucial. Julia, with its speed, simplicity, and expressive syntax, emerges as an ideal language for tackling the challenges posed by the ever-growing datasets and complex algorithms in these domains.

This book is designed to be a comprehensive guide for both beginners and experienced practitioners seeking to master machine learning and data analysis using Julia. Whether you are a seasoned data scientist or a curious enthusiast, the content here will equip you with the tools and knowledge to navigate the dynamic landscape of modern data science.

The Journey unfolds...

Chapter 1: Julia in ML Fields

In our opening chapter, we lay the foundation by introducing readers to Julia as the optimal language for machine learning. We delve into the essence of data science, elucidate the necessity of data analysis, and showcase Julia's prowess in the realm of machine learning. While extolling the virtues of Julia, we candidly explore its strengths and acknowledge its limitations, culminating in a thoughtful conclusion.

Chapter 2: Get Started with Julia

This chapter serves as your gateway into the Julia ecosystem. We guide you through the installation process, introduce various Julia Integrated Development Environments (IDEs), and delve into the essentials of Julia's package management system. Building a solid foundation, we cover topics ranging from basic variable declarations to defining functions and navigating the intricate rules of variable scope.

Chapter 3: Features Assisting Scaling ML Projects

Discover how Julia's unique features enhance the scalability of machine learning projects. We explore the type system, multiple dispatch, and the intricacies of working with packages, modules, and macros. This chapter equips you with the tools needed to harness Julia's full potential for robust and scalable machine learning endeavors.

Chapter 4: Working with Julia Arrays

Delve into the world of Julia data structures. From arrays and tuple structures to advanced concepts like broadcasting and integration with Python/R, this chapter ensures a comprehensive understanding of Julia's array capabilities.

Chapter 5: Working with Datasets – A Data Science Problem

In this chapter, we tackle real-world scenarios, guiding you through the process of obtaining, inspecting, and handling diverse datasets. Learn to manipulate numerical, textual, and temporal data effectively, setting the stage for more advanced analyses.

Chapter 6: Basics of Statistics – StatsBase.jl

Unlock the power of statistics in Julia with a focus on fundamental statistical concepts. Covering scalar stats, distance methods, counts, and sampling, this chapter ensures a solid understanding of the statistical principles essential for data analysis.

Chapter 7: Probability Data Distributions – Distributions.jl

Navigate the world of probability distributions using Julia's Distributions.jl package. From common functions to univariate, multivariate, and matrix-variate distributions, this chapter delves into the mathematical underpinnings essential for probabilistic modeling.

Chapter 8: Framing the Data in Julia – DataFrames.jl

Introduce yourself to DataFrames.jl, Julia's premier package for working with tabular data. From fetching and inspecting data to manipulating columnar data and indexing, this chapter provides the skills needed to wield DataFrames effectively.

Chapter 9: Working on Data from DataFrames

Explore the myriad functionalities of DataFrames, including creating and converting dataframe objects, grouping and mutating dataframes, and applying transformative operations.

Chapter 10: Visualizing Data in Julia - Plot.jl

Unleash the power of data visualization in Julia with Plot.jl. Dive into plotting techniques, themes, colors, and layouts, mastering the art of making data come alive through compelling visuals.

Chapter 11: Introducing Machine Learning in Julia - MLBase.jl

Embark on the exciting journey of machine learning in Julia using MLBase.jl. From selecting and training models to evaluating loss and comparing metrics, this chapter demystifies the machine learning process.

Chapter 12: Data Modeling - GLM.jl and MixedModels.jl

Delve into data modeling with GLM.jl and MixedModels.jl, empowering you to construct statistical models efficiently. Gain insights into various GLM models and understand the essentials of mixed-effects modeling.

Chapter 13: Bayesian Inference - Turing.jl

Take a deep dive into Bayesian inference using Julia's Turing.jl libraries. Explore probabilistic modeling and learn practical applications for Bayesian workflows in machine learning.

Chapter 14: Parallel Computation in Julia

Master the art of parallel computation in Julia, leveraging multi-threading capabilities to speed up data science workflows. Discover the potential of JuliaHub and conclude with insights into optimizing code execution.

Chapter 15: Distributed Computing within Julia

Explore distributed computing in Julia, focusing on scaling data science and machine learning problems on CPUs. Dive into Dagger.jl, drawing parallels with Dask, and gain an introduction to CUDA.jl and CuArrays for GPU programming.

This book is designed to be a comprehensive and accessible companion for anyone eager to excel in machine learning and data analysis using Julia. Whether you are a novice or an experienced practitioner, the knowledge and skills imparted within these pages will empower you to navigate the complexities of modern data science. Let the exploration begin!

Get a Free eBook

We hope you are enjoying your recently purchased book! Your feedback is incredibly valuable to us, and to all other readers looking for great books.

If you found this book helpful or enjoyable, we would truly appreciate it, if you could take a moment to leave a short review with a 5 star rating on Amazon. It helps us grow, and lets other readers discover our books.

As a thank you, we would love to send you a free digital copy of this book, and a **30%** discount code on your next cart value on our official websites:

www.orangeava.com

www.orangeava.in (For Indian Subcontinent)

☑ **Here's how:**

Leave a review for the book on Amazon.

Take a screenshot of your review, and send an email to **info@orangeava.com** (it can be just the confirmation screen).

Once, we receive your screenshot, we will send you the digital file, within 24 hours.

Thank you so much for your support – it means a lot to us!

Downloading the code bundles and colored images

Please follow the links or scan the QR codes to download the **Code Bundles and Images** of the book:

https://github.com/ava-orange-education/Ultimate-Parallel-and-Distributed-Computing-with-Julia-For-Data-Science

The code bundles and images of the book are also hosted on ***https://rebrand.ly/6f7ebd***

In case there's an update to the code, it will be updated on the existing GitHub repository.

Errata

We take immense pride in our work at **Orange Education Pvt Ltd,** and follow best practices to ensure the accuracy of our content to provide an indulging reading experience to our subscribers. Our readers are our mirrors, and we use their inputs to reflect and improve upon human errors, if any, that may have occurred during the publishing processes involved. To let us maintain the quality and help us reach out to any readers who might be having difficulties due to any unforeseen errors, please write to us at :

errata@orangeava.com

Your support, suggestions, and feedback are highly appreciated.

DID YOU KNOW

Did you know that Orange Education Pvt Ltd offers eBook versions of every book published, with PDF and ePub files available? You can upgrade to the eBook version at **www.orangeava.com** and as a print book customer, you are entitled to a discount on the eBook copy. Get in touch with us at: **info@orangeava.com** for more details.

At **www.orangeava.com**, you can also read a collection of free technical articles, sign up for a range of free newsletters, and receive exclusive discounts and offers on AVA™ Books and eBooks.

PIRACY

If you come across any illegal copies of our works in any form on the internet, we would be grateful if you would provide us with the location address or website name. Please contact us at **info@orangeava.com** with a link to the material.

ARE YOU INTERESTED IN AUTHORING WITH US?

If there is a topic that you have expertise in, and you are interested in either writing or contributing to a book, please write to us at **business@orangeava.com**. We are on a journey to help developers and tech professionals to gain insights on the present technological advancements and innovations happening across the globe and build a community that believes Knowledge is best acquired by sharing and learning with others. Please reach out to us to learn what our audience demands and how you can be part of this educational reform. We also welcome ideas from tech experts and help them build learning and development content for their domains.

REVIEWS

Please leave a review. Once you have read and used this book, why not leave a review on the site that you purchased it from? Potential readers can then see and use your unbiased opinion to make purchase decisions. We at Orange Education would love to know what you think about our products, and our authors can learn from your feedback. Thank you!

For more information about Orange Education, please visit **www.orangeava.com**.

Table of Contents

1. Julia In Data Science Arena **1**

Introduction 1

Structure 1

Introducing Data Science 2

Defining Data Science 2

The need for Task Automation 3

Introducing Statistics 3

Introducing machine learning 4

Drawing Correlations from Raw Data 4

Explaining the Need for Data Analysis 6

Introducing Julia 6

Astounding Julia language!! 8

Julia: Ideal for Data Analysis 10

Limitations of Julia 13

Conclusion 13

Points to Remember 14

References 15

2. Getting Started with Julia **16**

Introduction 16

Structure 16

Installing and setting up Julia 17

Working with Julia IDEs 18

Using Julia REPL 19

Using IDEs 19

Using Notebook 19

Julia package manager: Pkg 20

Project environments 20

Working in Pkg REPL mode 22

Handling project environments 24

Numerical Data Handling in Julia 26

Declaring variables 32
Acceptable variable names in Julia 36
Bound vs Copy in mutable variables 37
Constructing control flows 39
Evaluation under conditions 40
Evaluating short circuits 42
Handling exceptions 44
Loops (Repeated evaluation) 45
Expressions in compound form 47
Defining functions 48
Conclusion 49
Questions 49
3. Features Assisting Scaling ML Projects 50
Introduction 50
Structure 50
Revisiting Functions in Julia 51
The function-end keyword 51
The name of the function 52
The Arguments Used in the Function 54
The Body of the Function 54
The return Statement of the Function 55
Positional and keyword arguments 55
Passing arguments in Julia 57
Short Syntax for Writing Functions in Julia 58
Type System in Julia 58
Hierarchy in Julia's Type System 62
Various Data Types in Julia 70
Multiple Dispatch in Julia 73
Managing code structure in Julia 77
Using Macros 80
Conclusion 85
Questions 86
4. Data Structures in Julia 87
Introduction 87
Structure 88

Arrays in Julia 88
Tuple Data Structure in Julia 94
Mapping Value to its Keys 97
Set Data Structure in Julia 102
Operations on Julia's Data Structures 103
Arrays 103
Tuples 104
Dictionaries 104
Sets 104
Map 105
Reduce 106
Filter 107
Broadcasting 108
Example of Module Subtyping 109
Integrating with Python 110
Integrating with R 113
Conclusion 114
Questions 115
5. Working With Datasets In Julia 116
Introduction 116
Structure 117
Getting and Inspecting Data in Julia 117
Acquiring Data from Julia 118
Accessing Data from a Database 122
Inspecting Data in Julia 125
DataFrames in Julia 126
Saving text files 128
Packages for Text Analysis 130
Visualizing the DataFrame 131
Working with Strings 132
Reading from a Text File 134
Splitting Text String 135
Regular Expressions 137
Temporal Data 138
Handling missing Data 139

Handling Temporal Data 140
A Data Science Problem 143
Conclusion 145
Questions 145
6. **Basics of Statistics** **147**
Structure 148
Statistics in Julia 148
Descriptive Statistics and its purpose 149
Overview of the main descriptive statistics measures 149
Outlier detection and treatment in data analysis 156
Distance methods in StatsBase.jl 158
Sampling and counting methods 161
Counting methods 161
Sampling methods 164
Relationship between various features in the dataset during data analysis 165
Miscellaneous statistical functions that aid in data analysis 172
Observational estimation in data analysis 175
Conclusion 179
Questions 179
7. **Probability Data Distributions** **181**
Structure 181
Introduction to probability 182
Introducing probability package in Julia 183
Introducing the Distributions.jl package 185
Common functions in distributions 186
Type hierarchy 186
Parameter retrieval 188
Sampling 189
Computation of statistics 190
Estimating probability 192
Dimension inspection 194
Univariate probability distribution 195
Censored probability distribution 196
Truncated probability distribution 197

Difference between censored and truncated probability distributions 198

Multivariate probability distribution 199

Matrix-variate probability distribution 200

Mixture models in Distributions.jl 202

Mixture models and convolutions in Distributions.jl 204

Fitting a probability distribution 205

Conclusion 207

Questions 207

8. Framing Data in Julia 209

Structure 210

Introducing DataFrames.jl package 210

Setting up the environment 210

Constructing DataFrame objects 211

Fetching data 215

Inspecting data 217

Major data manipulation frameworks in Julia 230

DataFramesMeta.jl 230

DataFrameMacros.jl 232

Query.jl 232

Comparing with other language frameworks 234

Comparing with pandas - a Python framework 234

Comparing with dplyr - an R framework 235

Conclusion 235

Questions 236

9. Working on Data in DataFrames 238

Structure 239

Missing data in DataFrames 239

Missing values in Julia 240

Sorting data in DataFrames 244

Sorting a Vector 244

Sorting a DataFrame 245

Reshaping data in DataFrames 248

Reshaping data in Julia 249

Categorical data in DataFrames 253

Joining data in DataFrames 255
Split-apply-combine data in DataFrames 262
Conclusion 269
Questions 269
10. Visualizing Data in Julia 271
Structure 272
Introducing Plot.jl 272
Installing Plots.jl 273
Plots.jl package 274
Attributes in plotting 277
Scatter plots in Plots.jl 279
Plotting backends 281
Subplots in Plots.jl 284
Recipes in Plots.jl 286
Using Statsplots.jl recipes 286
Contour plots 289
Histograms in Plots.jl 293
Weighted histograms 295
Stacked histograms 297
Overlaid histograms 298
Cumulative histograms 299
2D histograms 300
Conclusion 302
Questions 302
11. Introducing Machine Learning in Julia 305
Introduction 305
Structure 306
The need for machine learning 306
Introducing machine learning 307
MLJ.jl - the machine learning library of Julia 308
Specialties of MLJ.jl 308
Handling data in MLJ.jl 309
Data containers and Scitypes 310
Handling 2D data in MLJ 311
Scitypes of data 313

Generating data....315
Regression data....316
Categorical data....318
Handling categorical data....319
Correct data scientific type for categorical data....320
Changing the incorrect scitype of categorical data....320
Tracking all various categories....321
Preparing data....323
Splitting data....323
Addressing the mismatched scitype of data-model....324
Weights....325
Models....325
Unsupervised Learning Models:....326
Model search....327
Model queries....328
Models matching....329
Loading models....331
Revisiting weights....333
Data preprocessing using transformers in MLJ....334
Conclusion....335
Questions....336
12. Data and Models....337
Introduction....337
Structure....338
Model interface in MLJ.jl....338
Model representation....339
Supervised model....341
User-defined models in MLJ....342
Deterministic regressor....343
Probabilistic regressor....344
Fitting a model....347
Predict method....347
Training losses....349
Feature importances....350
Update! Method....350

Transform method ... 352
Models with a probability distribution ... 352
Serialization ... 353
The need for a data frontend for MLJ ... 353
Data frontend for MLJ ... 354
Machines in MLJ ... 355
Model composition ... 356
Performance measures in MLJ.jl ... 357
Built-in performance measures ... 358
Custom performance measures ... 358
Model evaluation measures ... 358
Evaluating model performance on a hold-out set ... 359
Evaluating model performance over time ... 360
Model tuning ... 360
Common stopping criteria ... 362
Regularization ... 362
Interpreting learning curves ... 363
Using learning curves to improve models ... 364
Conclusion ... 364
Questions ... 365
13. Bayesian Statistics and Modeling ... 366
Introduction ... 366
Structure ... 367
Bayesian inference ... 367
Difference between Bayes' theorem and Frequentist statistical methods ... 368
Basic concepts of Bayesian statistics ... 369
Calculating the posterior distribution ... 370
Making inferences from the posterior distribution ... 371
Bayesian models ... 372
Various Bayesian models ... 373
Bayesian linear regression ... 375
Bayesian logistic regression ... 376
Bayesian networks ... 377
Gaussian processes ... 379

Bayesian neural networks.......... 380
Building a Bayesian model.......... 381
Bayesian modeling in Julia.......... 383
Manipulating discrete data with Bayesian approach.......... 385
Manipulating categorical data with Bayesian approach.......... 388
Gaussian Process Latent Variable Model.......... 391
Other Bayesian models.......... 394
Conclusion.......... 396
Questions.......... 396

14. Parallel Computation in Julia.......... 398

Introduction.......... 398
Structure.......... 399
Parallel computation in Julia.......... 399
Asynchronous programming.......... 400
Asynchronous tasks in Julia.......... 401
Task operations.......... 402
Yieldto function in tasks.......... 404
Scheduler in Julia.......... 405
Connecting via channels in Julia.......... 406
Multi-threading.......... 408
Multiple threads in Julia.......... 409
ThreadPools.......... 411
Communication and synchronization in Julia.......... 412
@threads macro.......... 413
Atomic Operations.......... 415
Per-field atomics.......... 417
Side Effects of using threads.......... 418
@threadcall.......... 419
Task migration.......... 420
Use of finalizers.......... 421
Speeding up data science workflows.......... 422
Using the power of JuliaHub.......... 423
Conclusion.......... 424
Questions.......... 425

15. Distributed Computation in Julia **427**
Introduction 427
Structure 428
Distributed computation in Julia 428
Harnessing the Strength of Many 429
A Fresh Take on Message Passing 429
Remote References: Bridging the Gap 429
Remote Calls: Executing from Afar 430
Process Identity and Worker Model 430
Embracing Parallelism: A Practical Guide 430
Asynchronous Execution and Cooperative Task Scheduling in Julia ... 432
The Magic of Future Caching 432
Cooperative Multitasking: The @async and @sync Approach 432
Feeder Tasks and @async 433
@sync: Coordinated Synchronization 433
Sharing State and Cooperative Multitasking 433
Mindful Context Switching 433
Preparing for Future Innovations 433
Loading packages in Distributed Computing 434
Managing processes 435
Data transfer in distributed computing 436
Variables in distributed computing 438
Maps and Loops 441
References and Channels 442
Distributed Garbage Collection 444
Local Invocations in Distributed Computing 445
Shared Arrays 447
Cluster Managers 449
Conclusion 452
Questions 452
Index **454**

CHAPTER 1

Julia In Data Science Arena

Introduction

This chapter acts as an insight into the buzzwords such as Julia, data science, and machine learning in the title of the book. We will discuss data science, machine learning, and the need for data science and machine learning in today's world to solve and automate challenging problems. We will learn about technologies that will help us tackle these problems. You will gain an accurate and deep understanding of Julia programming language and the reason for using Julia in addressing all data-related issues. Julia is a new and actively developing language. Every programming language has some lacunae. Most of the time, Julia's numerous advantages surpass its flaws. In the end, we will go through some shortcomings of Julia language.

Structure

In this chapter, we will discuss the following topics:

- Introducing data science
    - Defining data science
    - The need for task automation
    - Introducing statistics
    - Introducing machine learning
- Drawing correlations from raw data
- Explaining the need for data analysis

- Introducing Julia
    - Astounding Julia language!!
- Julia: ideal for data analysis
- Drawbacks of Julia

Introducing Data Science

Data is everywhere and abundantly available and more so in the near future. According to a late-2012 assessment, the quantity of digital data saved would increase by a factor of 300 between 2005 and 2020. The total digital data saved would be approximately 130 exabytes to 40,000 exabytes (Gand & Reinsel, 2012). Total digital data saved equates to 40 trillion gigabytes, which is more than 5.2 terabytes for every individual! The rising availability of data and the value of data will have an influence in every industry (Chen et al., 2014; Khan et al., 2014). We need data to understand the process and make decisions based on it. We must learn skills that will assist us in better interpreting the data cheaper and faster. A data scientist/data analyst/researcher is familiar with fundamental data management techniques. *Figure* 1.1 paints quite a picture of all the fundamental data management techniques.

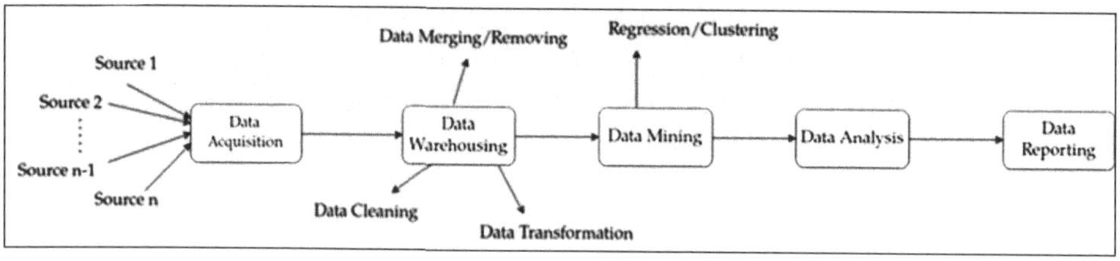

Figure 1.1: *The data science workflow*

Defining Data Science

Data science is the study of massive data using advanced tools and methodologies to discover previously unknown patterns, extract valuable information, and make better decisions. We employ science and math to help us use data to make better decisions. We can safely say that data science is a culmination of data acquisition, data warehousing (maintaining data by cleaning, processing, and creating an architecture), data mining (clustering/modeling), data analysis and data reporting techniques. It is quite humanly impossible to browse through the entire dataset and derive any useful insights from it. We use various statistical techniques to gain an understanding from our data. We use advanced technologies such as machine learning to analyze the data and automate the entire process. Although most of you are familiar with the concepts of machine learning and statistics, let me refresh those concepts again. Before going into machine learning, let us see why we need to automate all the data processes.

The need for Task Automation

Artificial intelligence was created in the 1950s by computer scientists who were interested if computers might be programmed to **think on their own**—a dilemma that is still being debated and looked into today. Artificial intelligence may be defined as a machine's ability to accomplish activities that would normally need human-level intelligence and judgment. We should keep in mind that AI is a fairly wide science that covers not just machine learning and deep learning but also various approaches that do not involve learning.

One of the first significant results of AI algorithms was successfully implemented in chess competitions. Deep Blue (https://www.chess.com/terms/deep-blue-chess-computer) was created to compete with humans in chess. It had 8,000 handmade elements. In 1997, the Deep Blue program defeated former chess champion, Gary Kasparov. For a long time, most academics and scientists felt that achieving human-level intelligence required handcrafting a sufficiently wide set of specialized instructions.

The disadvantage of employing handmade characteristics is that only game professionals (checkers or chess) can build computer algorithms. Even professionals might fail to manufacture characteristics for complex tasks like image classification, speech recognition, natural language translation, and so on. Analyzing huge amounts of data and figuring out the apt algorithms is humanly impossible. We need some kind of automation tool that will solve our problem. In the next part, we will discuss machine learning, which is a subset of artificial intelligence.

Introducing Statistics

Statistics is a highly diverse research discipline. Statistics study has applications in almost all scientific research domains. Scientific research and data analysis, in fact, drives the development of novel statistical methods. Statistics is the branch of science that deals with creating and researching ways to gather, analyze, interpret, and display empirical data. Statistics aids in gaining a better understanding of the facts from raw data. Statisticians use a range of mathematical and computational techniques to develop procedures. Statistical computations demand an easy-to-read language with high-scaling features that can help Statisticians to focus only on developing theories rather than worry about the computational aspect of the data as in computing or testing or verifying the data.

It is humanly impossible to formulate a statistical equation for every set of inputs and outputs in a case where the data is large. Here, machine learning, a paradigm that devises statistical equations between outputs and inputs on its own, comes to our aid. A simple machine learning system is shown in *Figure* 1.2. The machine learning system in *figure* 1.2 shows that multiple inputs and outputs are fed into the machine and the machine devises an algorithm or model on its own. The model shows a correlation between the inputs and outputs of data. This correlation is further used for test inputs to find the outputs predicted.

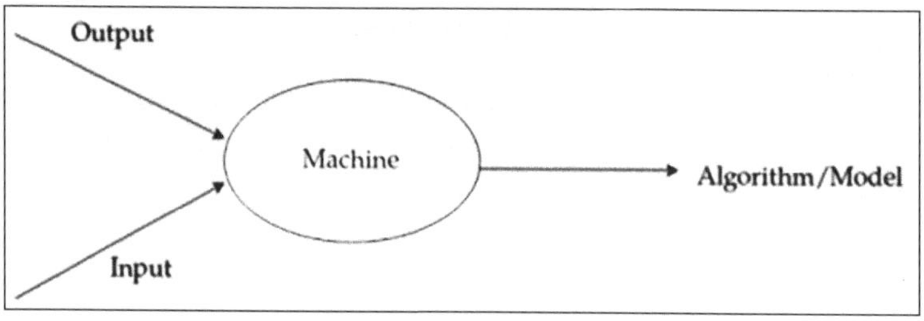

Figure 1.2: *Basic machine learning workflow*

Introducing machine learning

Machine learning, a novel programming method, takes in input data and correlates it with answers, then deciphers the rules that link the inputs to their corresponding responses. The machine is given different samples and their related outputs while attempting to comprehend the statistical association between the samples and their outputs on its own. To categorize photographs of cats and dogs, we input different images of cats and dogs that have previously been tagged by humans, and the system will learn the statistical relationships between the images and their related labels. Machine learning is closely connected to computational statistics, which is the fundamental goal of making the machine properly predict the consequence. Now that we know we can use data science to derive insights, let us go step by step to understand how data is analyzed to derive meaningful information.

Drawing Correlations from Raw Data

Before collecting or processing data, we will understand the problem at hand. If we face a complex problem, then we can divide it into smaller subproblems and solve them one at a time. We will examine the subset of data pertaining to the smaller problem we are attempting to address. Otherwise, if our initial problem is not that complex, we will use the entire data for addressing the issue. While solving a real-world problem, we don't get a customized dataset. We have to figure out the variables concerning the problem that can provide us valuable information about the data. We have to curate and create our own data pertaining to the problem. We compile data from numerous sources to create a unified dataset.

After collecting the data, we need to process the raw data into a format that is suitable for performing data analysis. At this stage, we delete any misplaced or incorrect data. If necessary, we will consolidate some data or eliminate all unneeded data.

1. The raw data is processed so that we can easily make correlations from it.
2. The second step is to create a machine learning or statistical model which will learn the data correlations on its own.
3. The third step encompasses interpreting the acquired information from the data. At this stage, we find the solution to our problem. Otherwise, we will keep on changing metrics and techniques till we find a proper solution to our desired problem.
4. The fourth step is to prepare the results and summarize the insights to share.

Figure 1.3 shows a pictorial description of the steps to follow while drawing correlation from raw data.

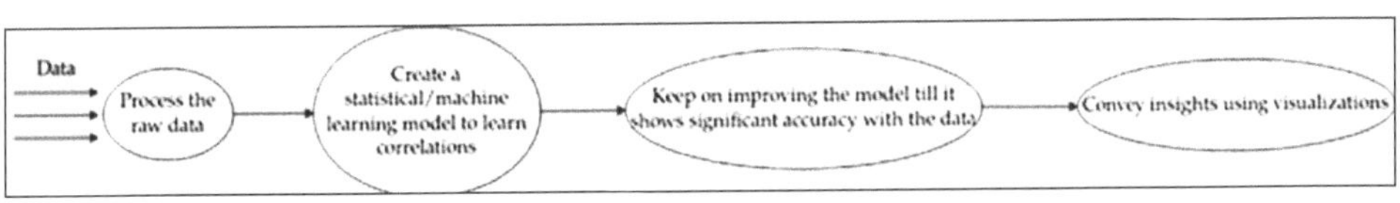

Figure 1.3: *The process of drawing correlations from the raw data*

A data scientist gets insights and finds patterns and trends in datasets by making data models and forecasting algorithms. These algorithms are written using machine learning techniques on the data. The product is improved consistently by sharing ideas with other teams and upper management. We use several data analytics tools such as SAS, SQL and various programming languages like R, Python, and Julia leading developments in the field of data science. Some of these tools have a graphical interface and are thus simple to use. But they typically have constraints on how they are used. The wide diversity of jobs that a data scientist must perform points to the fact that some programming language is essential to accomplish maximum flexibility and clarity.

Explaining the Need for Data Analysis

Data analytics is critical since it allows firms to improve their performance. Companies that include it in their business models can assist cut expenses by discovering more efficient methods of doing business. Data analytics may also help a firm improve its business decisions and assess consumer patterns. Let's see some features of data analysis:

- Data analysis is a simple approach to check on the research topic and provides the reader with information on what upgrades have been acquired in the whole data and interpretation process.
- You can understand your clients, tailor the model according to your client and support their specific needs.
- Data analysis aids in the reduction of enormous datasets via the application of new tools and technologies.
- Sellers rely on a large quantity of data to deliver their worth in the study and exploration of information via data mining.
- Data analysis entails comprehending and interpreting data in the form of data analysis without any human bias.
- Data analysis increases the legitimacy of existing data or the latest research by providing solid references that depend on a conceptual framework.
- Data analysis enables you to adapt your approach and technique, focus on saving money, and improve your initial research.

Introducing Julia

Julia is a fast, dynamic, high-level dynamic programming language widely developing and a huge number of machine learning libraries and frameworks are being developed which are being used by data analysts, data scientists, and machine learning researchers both in industry and academics. Julia is a free and open-source programming language that was created in 2012 by MIT. It is extensively used in statistical computing, data analytics, scientific research, data modeling, graphical representation, and reporting. Julia includes statistical modeling, plotting, and modeling libraries required for data science.

Julia is a huge ecosystem consisting of several libraries that are focused on many machine learning-related areas. This book will give a broad overview of the libraries and their functions along with hands-on exercises and code so that readers can directly start working on their own model with Julia. This book is aimed at creating interest in readers to contribute to various Julia libraries. This chapter aims to give an overview of the use and efficiency of Julia in handling Statistics, Data Science, and Machine Learning. *Figure* 1.4 shows a comparison of the speed of execution time of various languages including Julia with respect to a static language C.

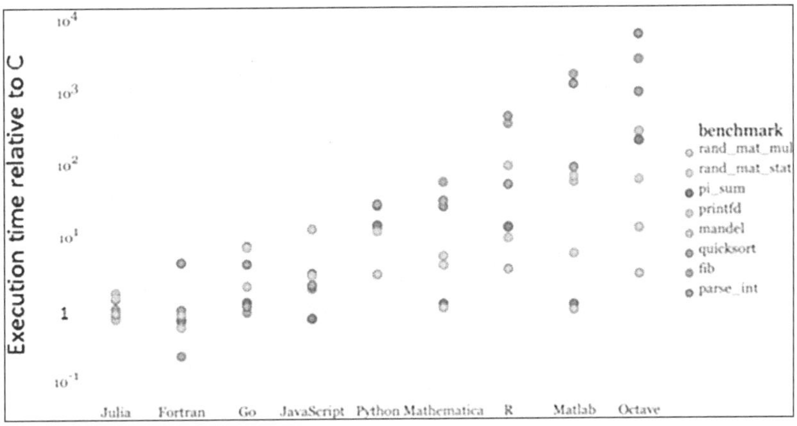

Figure 1.4: *Comparison between speeds of various languages with Julia*

In this book, we are going to focus mainly on the use of Julia in machine learning and data science fields. Since Julia is open source, a lot of packages and libraries are developed for the use of data science and machine learning. We are going to cover the most important and recent development packages for both data science and machine learning. This book focuses mainly on machine learning, different packages that are designed for classical ML are thoroughly explained in the book. Statistical analysis and its use in data science in Julia are also visited. A few bonus chapters such as an introduction to parallel and distributed computing in Julia are well explained. This book can assist data scientists and analysts who desire to transition to Julia for their daily data science job. This book will demonstrate how and why using Julia will be a game-changer for them. Let us look at some of the major functionalities of Julia language that make it stand out. *Figure* 1.5 shows some of the important features of Julia language.

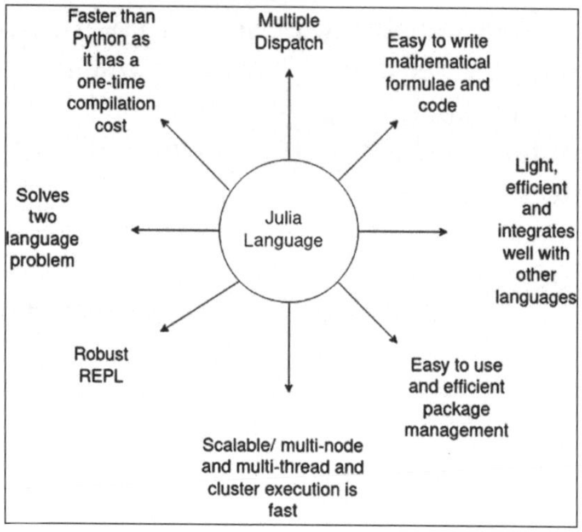

***Figure* 1.5:** *Features of Julia language*

Astounding Julia language!!

Julia was designed to combine multiple performance measures from different languages into a single language. Julia was originally designed to have scientific computing in consideration. As a result, it began as a competition between languages such as Python, R, and MATLAB to employ the most effective metrics of such languages and achieve greater performance than other languages.

Machine-learning programmers and scientists want a language that can do quantitative, probabilistic, differentiable, tree-structured, and parallelized calculations. Julia is a functional programming language that employs the LLVM compiler framework with just-in-time compilation, making it possible to perform complex deep learning tasks quickly. In contrast to verbose C++ code, Julia is dynamically typed, making it perfect for designing, training, and tweaking data-related code.

There are several tools that you can use to write Julia code. You can use Julia REPL (read-eval-print-loop) which is a command line built into Julia executable or Pluto notebooks which are like Jupyter notebooks with additional functionalities for code execution and sequencing. If you have installed Julia (we will learn about it in the next chapter), you can open your terminal and type in **`julia`**. A Julia prompt will appear on your terminal screen. *Figure* 1.6 shows the Julia prompt.

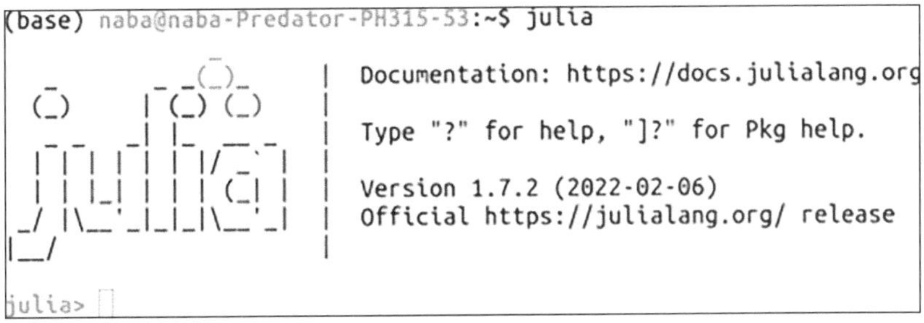

Figure 1.6: *Julia prompt in REPL*

Let us look at a sample function written in Julia that returns an integer raised to the power of 7. We can measure the performance of our code using @time macro and pay attention to the memory allocation. Generally, Julia runs faster after the first iteration.

```
julia> x = 7

7

julia> @time x->x^7

0.008357 seconds (977 allocations: 62.519 KiB, 66.14% compilation
time) #1 (generic function with 1 method)
```

Julia is open source and widely available, making it simple to examine high-level code rather than delving into low-level abstractions. Julia is quicker than other dynamic languages like Python and similar to static ones.

Now, let us look into some of the main features of Julia language.

- Julia includes all features for complicated mathematical computations, so you can immediately write your mathematical equations into code. Julia syntax is close to that of MATLAB, making the transition to Julia easy for MATLAB users. This feature allows you to create mathematical equations in Julia while utilizing the same mathematical operators and expressions as you would in Julia code.
- Julia and Python are both dynamic-typed languages with similar-looking and easy-to-write prototype code. Julia's Python interface is available at JuliaPy/pyjulia for Python developers. Julia, like Common Lisp, is easy to write and executes almost as quickly as C. Julia adheres to the majority of Lisp's programming paradigms and components. Julia executes with a speed equivalent to FORTRAN.
- When you compile your program in Julia, all data types are moved from dynamic to static code, which takes some time but is afterwards super-fast. Julia has been a member of the petaflop club since 2020, which means it can execute one petaflop of instructions in one second.

This minimizes compile time delay while also making it easier to write code in Julia without having to define the same object numerous times.

- As Julia's code is written in Julia, programmers may simply make modifications or rectify problems. There is no need to install anything or bother about package linking services or different environments.
- Since Julia is a new language, numerical computing libraries in C and FORTRAN outperform Julia language libraries. Julia makes it simple to call C and FORTRAN functions, allowing you to reuse existing code. To call such functions, no in-between code, code creation, or compilation is required; instead, a regular call using **`ccall`** syntax from an interactive Julia prompt is sufficient.
- Julia dynamically dispatches functions and values based on the object's run-time type. This entails leveraging the combined attributes of one or more function parameters to implement functions or values. When developing idiomatic Julia, type stability and memory allocation are taken into account. This functionality allows Julia code to be reused across many packages.
- Julia's programming language enables coroutines, multi-threading, distributed computing, and GPU computing. Julia provides a message-passing multiprocessing environment that enables programs to run in many memory domains at the same time. Julia's message-forwarding technique is distinct from those used in other contexts such as MPI. This functionality enables the CPU to accelerate deep learning job execution.
- The REPL (read-eval-print loop) is an interactive command-line interface that is built into the Julia executable. REPL provides simple and quick execution, a searchable history, tab completion, various handy key bindings, help, and shell mode. This feature makes it easier to write and run Julia code in the interactive Julia shell.
- Julia's package manager **`Pkg`** can add packages quicker than the library equivalent since it does not have to recompile a stale cache file. **`Pkg`** handles package dependencies entirely on its own. While utilizing a package in a project, it downgrades and upgrades package dependencies. **`Pkg`** also manages project environments by utilizing two files, **`Project.toml`** and **`Manifest.toml`**, to keep track of package versions and dependencies in a specific project context. You may easily reproduce the full project procedure on your machine.

Julia: Ideal for Data Analysis

The most important feature of every language is its extensibility. The language should be designed in such a way that programmers may simply add new necessary functionality. Julia's open-source machine learning frameworks make it simple for programmers to utilize and build specialized functionality as needed. Flux is a machine learning package that is intended for use in high-performance application pipelines. Flux is able to meet high-performance expectations because of a combination of current and novel compiler designs. The Flux framework is used to write all differentiable algorithms in Julia. Plots and graphs, as well as Flux, may be used to visualize data in **`Pluto.jl`**, a basic reactive notebook for Julia. **`CUDA.jl`** is used in Julia to communicate with NVIDIA CUDA GPUs, including array abstraction, CUDA kernel development in Julia, and wrappers for other CUDA libraries. The development and application of numerical computation libraries, such as differential solvers like **`SciML`** and optimization libraries like **`JuMP`**, have made it feasible to address complicated real-world problems with ease. Programmers can only view a restricted range of mathematical operations and cannot directly operate the GPU when training machine learning algorithms in parallel. Julia GPU programming allows you to work directly with CUDA kernels produced and executed from a script or notebook. This entire Julia GPU architecture contributes to boosting machine learning capabilities such as scalability because frameworks supply kernels.

Julia contributes to the development of many tools and technologies. Many major institutions, both technical and academic, employ Julia to perform various tasks more efficiently and quickly. You can go to https://juliahub.com/case-studies/ to learn about more use cases of Julia. You can see some of the major use cases of Julia in *Figure 1.7*.

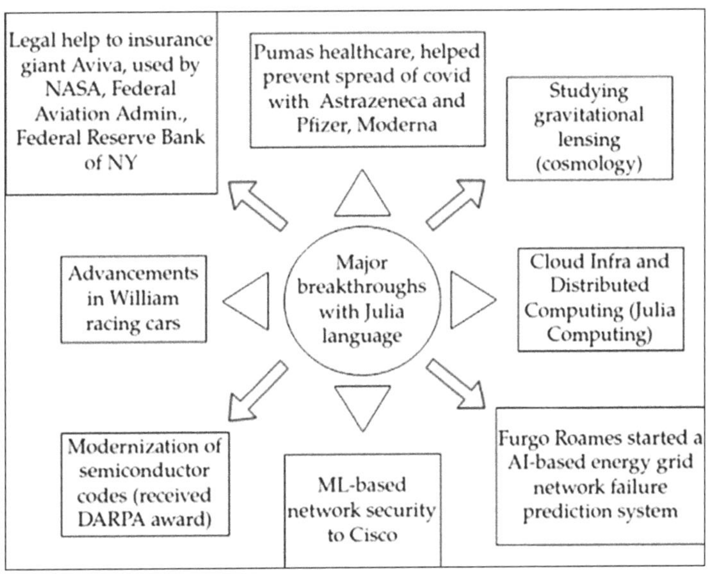

Figure 1.7: *Break-throughs in various fields using Julia language*

Some of the industrial and academic real-world use cases of Julia and its related libraries and frameworks are:

- Apart from these classical libraries and packages, Julia is progressing in the fields of modeling and simulation, which has aided Pumas' predictive healthcare analytics. Pumas is a comprehensive platform for pharmacological modeling and simulation from Julia Computing and Pumas.ai. It is a tool for the whole drug development pipeline.
- Raj Dandekar, Chris Rackauckas, Emma Wang, and George Barbastathis of MIT devised a model to help reduce and stop COVID-19's spread.
- Marius Millea, a cosmologist, used Julia to study gravitational lensing in the Cosmic Microwave Background from the South Pole Telescope.
- Jean-Christophe B. Loiseau uses Julia and highly recommends it for modeling turbulence because of the ability to write only fewer lines of code in Julia.
- JuliaHub is the simplest way to use the cloud to scale enormous, distributed Julia jobs.
- Julia Computing's JuliaHub makes it easy for Julia users to manage their packages, locate documentation, contribute to open-source projects, and run large compute intensive workloads.
- Julia is taught at many institutions, including MIT and Stanford.
- Stipple is a new tool for developing, deploying, and scaling Julia applications. Stipple is a reactive UI library for building interactive data applications in pure Julia.
- JuliaTeam from Julia Computing allows your organization to collaborate, build, and manage private and public packages, manage open-source licenses, and take advantage of Julia's continuous integration, deployment, security, indemnity, and enterprise governance capabilities.
- We at Julia are trying to heal the planet together. `JuliaClimate` is devoted to climate research and solving climate change problems utilizing Julia tools.
- Pfizer and Moderna have used Julia Computing to simulate new pharmaceuticals.
- `JuliaComputing` helps AstraZeneca with AI-based toxicity prediction.
- `JuliaComputing` aids European insurance giant Aviva in compliance issues.
- `JuliaComputing` has provided energy provider Fugro Roames with an AI-based grid network failure prediction system and the FAA with its airborne collision prevention program.

- `JuliaComputing` helped Cisco with ML-based network security and several national labs and academic institutions with ML-based network security research programs.
- Julia Computing also made headlines because of a DARPA award to modernize semiconductor codes for more efficient, current simulation codes.
- The language is used by over 10,000 firms throughout the world, including AstraZeneca PLC, BlackRock, and Microsoft Corp. Julia is also used by NASA, the Federal Aviation Administration (FAA), and the Federal Reserve Bank of New York.
- JuliaHub has also helped in the advancements in Williams racing cars.
- `JuliaComputing` team will be designing digital phased array systems using Julia and GPUs. Eventually, Julia is expected to become an integral part of next-generation wireless systems.

Limitations of Julia

Julia's code pre-compilation and dynamism are certainly noteworthy, but as with any other advantage provided by the language, Julia has its own limitations related to code pre-compilation and dynamism. Julia's REPL takes a long time to start any Julia process for the first time.

This is due to Julia taking longer to compile the many available data types when the program is initially started. Although the compilation time delay has decreased with each subsequent Julia version, it remains relatively considerable. This is quite inconvenient when compiling a large complex machine learning program for the first time. When an executable is built from Julia code, Julia consumes extra RAM which makes it inconvenient to run complex data science or machine learning problems. As Julia is a functional programming language, integrating it into other languages is tricky. Static languages like C/C++/Rust are easier to incorporate since they generate binaries that can be compiled by other languages. Since the Julia environment is less developed than those of other languages, it is prone to a few common issues. There are several packages in Julia that cannot be used in production. To access R and Python libraries in Julia, use packages such as RCall.jl or PyCall.jl. Only production-ready libraries will be covered in the book.

Conclusion

Machine learning and data analysis lay the ground for data science tasks. Julia is a high-level and general-purpose language that is used to construct code for scientific computations which are quick to execute and simple to implement. The language is intended to address all of the requirements of scientific researchers and data scientists in order to maximize experimentation and design execution. You've probably heard of Julia, the future programming language of data science if you're a data aficionado. There are speculations that Julia will eventually replace Python and R in the data science arena due to considerable improvements in performance, efficiency, and usability.

In the next chapter, we will learn to install Julia on our system. We will learn about various tools and technologies to write Julia code. We will learn to write basic Julia code in Pluto notebooks. We will go through the fundamentals of programming such as using data types, writing loops, functions and some other functionalities in Julia language.

Points to Remember

- Data science is the study of massive data using advanced tools and methodologies to discover previously unknown patterns, extract valuable information, and make better decisions.
- Artificial intelligence uses computers and technology to emulate humans' problem-solving and decision-making skills.
- Machine learning is the usage and development of computer systems that can learn and adapt without explicit instructions, by analyzing and drawing conclusions from data patterns utilizing algorithms and statistical models.
- Statistics is the branch of science that deals with creating and researching ways to gather, analyze, interpret, and display empirical data.
- Julia is a high-level dynamic programming language. Julia is known for its high speed and performance compared to other languages used for machine learning, such as Python.
- Julia is an open-source language which was mainly designed for scientific computing but Julia also supports web development, database, gaming and so on efficiently.
- Julia's package manager and REPL are robust. Julia supports multiple-dispatch.
- Julia uses the LLVM compiler with just-in-time compilation and is dynamically typed which makes it ideal for writing, training and tuning machine learning programs.
- Julia's extensibility of code which makes it flexible to use and write various Julia programs and simplified design of the machine learning framework in Julia makes it the ideal machine learning language.

References

1. Gand and Reinsel, 2012:

   https://datastorageasean.com/sites/default/files/idc-the-digital-universe-in-2020.pdf

2. Chen et al., 2014:

   https://www.sciencedirect.com/science/article/abs/pii/S1551741113001277

3. Khan et al., 2014:

   https://link.springer.com/book/10.1007/978-3-319-06710-0

Chapter 2
Getting Started with Julia

Introduction

This chapter will walk you through installing and configuring Julia on your PC. We will practice coding on several Julia IDEs (integrated development environments). We will learn about package management in Julia. We will define Julia environments and use them to develop project code. If you are new to the Julia language, this chapter will teach you the basic syntax and most significant ideas. Even if you are previously acquainted with Julia, we recommend that you rapidly review the offered subjects to ensure that you have a thorough knowledge of the fundamental principles. In this chapter, we will go through the fundamentals and basic functionalities of Julia. We will learn how to express values, variables, loops, functions, and so on. For a thorough introduction to Julia programming, we recommend the books mentioned at https://julialang.org/learning/books/ or the Julia guide at https://docs.julialang.org/en/v1/.

Structure

In this chapter, we will discuss the following topics:

- Installing and setting up Julia
- Working with Julia IDEs
- Julia package manager: Pkg
- Handling numerical data in Julia
- Declaring variables
- Constructing control flows

- Defining functions
- Scope rules for variables

Installing and setting up Julia

Let us go through the process of downloading, installing, and configuring Julia environments on our own PC. These steps can be replicated in your own system. Once you have correctly configured Julia in your system, it will be simple to follow along with the examples in the chapters.

To begin, visit the website https://julialang.org/downloads/ to download Julia on your local PC. There are numerous operating systems and Julia versions available at the site. You can get Julia for your operating system by downloading the correct version. There are operating system specific instructions to set up Julia in your system.

We use Julia version 1.7 throughout the book because it's the most recent one. However, you can read the book while using version 1.7 or above (if available). Using Julia versions greater than 1.7 will not cause problems, while using Julia versions less than 1.7 may cause problems. Version 1.7 was used to test the code in this book. However, the code will basically operate as expected for any Julia 1.x version. Higher versions may include minor modifications to execution or output. If you need Julia 1.7, go to the older unmaintained releases page (https://julialang.org/downloads/oldreleases/).

Follow the instructions for your operating system at https://julialang.org/downloads/platform/ to load the Julia executable on your system. Linux users can use Julia Installer (https://github.com/abelsiqueira/jill) to download and install Julia on their machine, or they can follow the platform-specific methods.

```
sudo bash -ci "$(curl -fsSL
```

https://raw.githubusercontent.com/abelsiqueira/jill/main/jill.sh)"

You can download Julia using the above code with the help of the jill package. It is an unofficial Julia Linux downloader.

After loading Julia, make sure to add Julia to the PATH environment variable. There are various methods for adding Julia to the PATH variable, each operating system has its own download and installation requirements along with adding the executable to the PATH. This makes it simple to start the Julia executable by entering `julia` followed by Enter keypress in a terminal.

Figure 2.1 depicts a basic Julia session running on the terminal.

- Launch your system's terminal.
- The $ sign symbolizes the command prompt in the operating system. Along with the $ sign, enter the `julia` command.
- A Julia session will begin, and you will see the Julia logo, as well as links to assistance, such as documentation, help, and the official release repository.
- Below the Julia logo, you can notice the $ prompt change to `julia>` prompt. This implies
- that you can execute Julia instructions.
- To return to the terminal prompt and exit the Julia prompt, use the Julia command `exit()` on the terminal. The $ prompt has returned to your terminal screen.

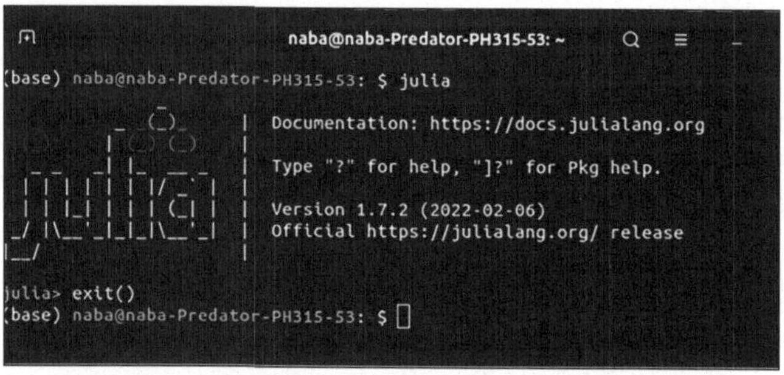

Figure 2.1: *The Julia prompt in the Linux terminal*

Working with Julia IDEs

We learned how to install and configure Julia locally using our terminal in the previous part. In this part, we'll look at different ways to run Julia commands locally. You can use any of the techniques listed to write and execute Julia commands locally.

We'll take a quick look at the many ways to run Julia commands. Throughout the book, we've used Julia's REPL to write the code examples. It is up to you where you want to run the Julia code. The output will be the same in all three modes. An integrated development environment (IDE) offers robust technological facilities for software development. Programmers who use IDEs can edit code, and build and debug the code simultaneously. To recapitulate, some typical methods for creating and modifying Julia code include:

- using Julia read-evaluate-print-loop (REPL)

- using an integrated programming environment (IDE) like Visual Studio Code (VSCode) or Atom
- using notebooks like Jupyter Notebook or Pluto notebook

Using Julia REPL

After adding the Julia executable to the PATH environment variable, you will just type *julia* commands directly into the terminal. There are two methods to access the terminal to execute Julia commands. To begin, you can employ the Julia executable's in-terminal interactive session. Julia read-evaluate-print-loop is yet another name for the terminal with Julia prompt (REPL).

Julia REPL is the code editor for Julia command line programming.

In the previous unit, we explored how to use Julia REPL to run Julia commands. We used Julia's `exit()` command in the previous section. You can apply any Julia command line options in addition to interactive Julia sessions https://docs.julialang.org/en/v1/manual/command-line options/#command-line-options.

Julia scripts can also be executed from the terminal. You can write Julia code in a ***.jl** file, where

* is the filename. You may run the file by typing julia *.jl into the terminal. This will execute the file's code and then exit at the completion of the code in the file.

Using IDEs

Aside from the Julia REPL, we can create and execute Julia code in any integrated development environment (IDE). To see the results, we may write a `.jl` script in the IDE and then execute it on the terminal. The Julia plugin may be added and installed on any IDE of your choosing, such as Atom or VSCode. You may learn how to access and configure all settings by consulting the instructions for VSCode or Atom. You can refer to https://code.visualstudio.com/docs/languages/julia and https://docs.junolab.org/stable/man/installation/ for assistance. The VSCode add-on contains capabilities such as integrated interactive autocompletion, embedded REPL, inline solutions, code tracking, plot panel, debugger, and many more.

Using Notebook

Pluto (https://github.com/fonsp/Pluto.jl) is a reactive notebook designed by Julia developers that includes capabilities not found in Jupyter notebooks. Being reactive implies that if you update a variable, Pluto will run all the cells that reference the variable after the change.

Because it automatically discovers relationships between cells, you can arrange them in whatever order you like. Pluto understands which packages are required in the project and installs and handles them automatically.

Julia can be composed and performed in notebooks as well. In the notebook, you must switch to the Julia executable and then type Julia commands in the cell. Both Jupyter and Pluto notebooks include output as well as graphical visualizations. The concept of a notebook, which incorporates code, arithmetic, graphs, prose, and other multimedia in a single prepared document, simplifies project collaboration.

Text, programming, arithmetic, and other graphical information can be written in the Jupyter or Pluto notebook. More installation options are available in the documentation at https://julialang.github.io/IJulia.jl/stable/. Launch your Jupyter notebook and change the kernel to Julia by choosing it from the drop-down menu.

You may also use IJulia to write Julia code in Jupyter notebooks by launching the IJulia notebook in your browser with the IJulia.jl package (https://julialang.github.io/IJulia.jl/stable/). Participate in the Julia interactive session. Then, in the REPL, enter the following code to open a notebook with Julia kernel in your browser.

Pluto makes it easy to develop and manage project environments. If we use the terminal to execute Julia code, we will learn how to establish and maintain project environments in the following section.

Julia package manager: Pkg

Julia has built-in package management. It allows you to install, manage, and use a wide range of dependent and independent packages in your projects. In this part, we'll go through the most important components of package management in Julia. More thorough explanations may be found at https://pkgdocs.julialang.org/v1/.

Project environments

Julia has an in-built package manager - Pkg. Pkg handles packages, registries and artifacts. Pkg is based on "environments," which are discrete groups of packages that can be local to a single project or shared and accessed by name.

Pkg maintains packages in /.julia/environments/v1.6, registries in /.julia/registries, and artifacts in /.julia/artifacts in the local machine if the Julia executable is running in the home directory. You can alter the locations by establishing new environments, registries, or artifacts. We will just learn how to set up and oversee new project environments in this segment. You can learn more about managing registries at https://pkgdocs.julialang.org/v1/registries/ and about artifacts at https://pkgdocs.julialang.org/v1/artifacts/.

When you create a new project environment, you will see two new files created, that is, **manifest.toml** and **project.toml**. The **manifest.toml** file captures the detailed collection of packages and versions in an environment, which is then checked into a project repository and managed under version control, considerably increasing project reproducibility.

Figure 2.2: *The manifest.toml file which contains information about all the packages*

A ***project.toml*** is a file in the root directory of a project that contains metadata about the project, such as its name, UUID (for packages), authors, license, and the names and UUIDs of the packages and libraries on which it depends.

```
[deps]
Flux = "587475ba-b771-5e3f-ad9e-33799f191a9c"
```

Figure 2.3: *The project.toml file collects details about the packages in the project environment*

Note If you've ever tried to execute old code only to realize that it no longer works because you've changed or deleted some of the packages in your project. Pkg has its own set of package versions, and it updates the packages and dependencies by locating the needed version for the time being, while older packages and their dependencies are garbage-collected.

Pkg, the project manager, provides two interfaces via which you may interact with it locally. Pkg may be interacted with via REPL when writing code interactively and using APIs when executing Julia code scripts via the terminal. The commands used in REPL mode and API mode differ depending on how they are written. Throughout the book, we shall use REPL mode. To use these commands in API mode, go to https://pkgdocs.julialang.org/v1/api/.

Working in Pkg REPL mode

To enter package management mode, press the] key after beginning your Julia session. The prompt julia> will be replaced by pkg>, indicating that you are now in package management mode. By default, this prompt will appear like this - (@ v1.7) pkg>.

Figure 2.4: *Pkg mode in REPL with pkg> prompt*

It is advised that you use the **manifest.toml** and **project.toml** files to manage your project environment. We will use the repository https://github.com/dnabanita7/DataScienceWithJulia that comes with this book. As in the examples that follow, store this repository under the */DataScienceWithJulia$* folder.

Otherwise, you may generate a new project environment in Pkg mode by entering a new package name.

```
pkg> generate new_package_name
```

The *DataScienceWithJulia* repository contains its own **manifest.toml** and **project.toml** files. These two files are created automatically when you add a package or dependency to your project environment.

Figure 2.5: *isfile() function checking if manifest.toml and project.toml files are present*

You can check if the project has those two files by using the `isfile(filename)` function where the filename is the name of the file.

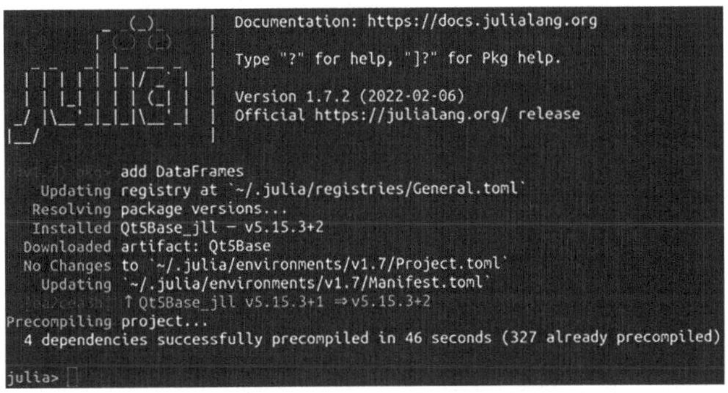

Figure 2.6: *Adding a package "DataFrames" to the project environment through interactive REPL mode*

You can add a package such as `DataFrames` by writing

```
pkg>add DataFrames
```

in Pkg mode. Now, if you use the `isfile()` function on those two files, it will return true.

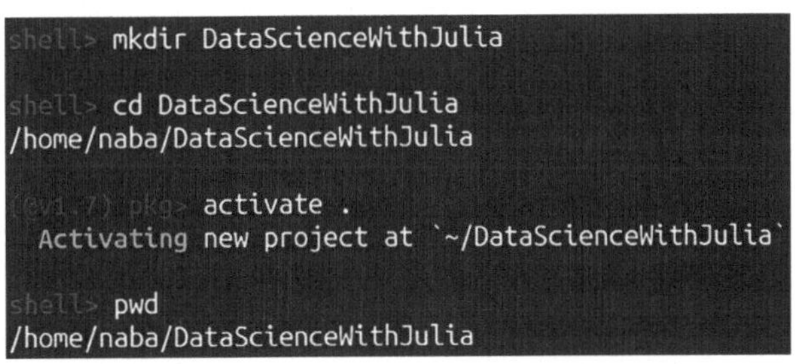

Figure 2.7: *Activating the project environment*

To activate the project environment, execute the `activate.` command and the prompt will change to the repository name, which is now "DataScienceWithJulia". Julia's existing work directory is represented by the dot following the activate command. Rather than changing the working directory, simply type `activate ~/DataScienceWithJulia`.

If you are employing a project environment for the very first time, you must `instantiate` it to ensure Julia receives all required web packages. By using the backspace key, you can quit the package manager.

Note Entering shell mode allows you to see what directory you are in. You may write shell commands from the REPL by pressing ; (semicolon).

Handling project environments

Once you have activated and instantiated your project environment, you will start building Julia applications that use the environment's packages. Meanwhile, you can modify the existing packages. Pkg provides the most common package management activities including displaying available packages, adding packages, removing packages, and updating packages.

You may use `add` to add new packages, `update` to update the package's version, and `status` to determine the version compatibility of your packages in the environment.

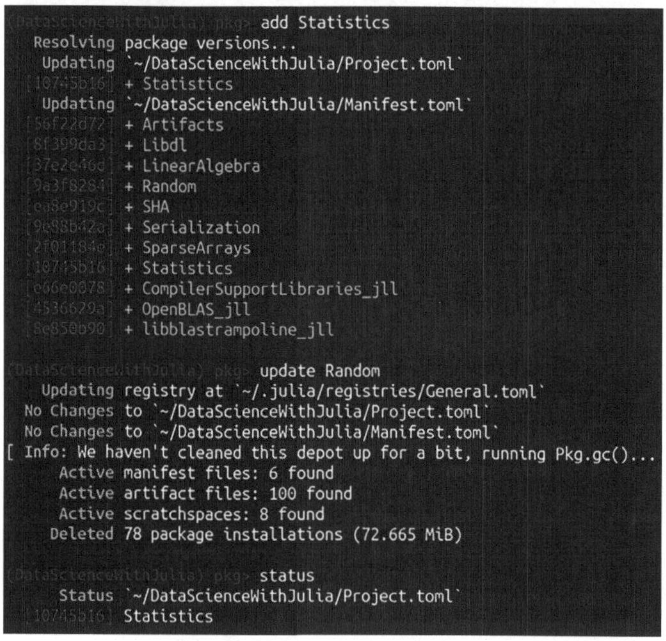

***Figure 2.8**: Trying out a few commands such as add, update, and status on the packages in this environment*

Here, we are adding a package `Statistics` and updating a package `Random` in the project environment. If you are starting from scratch, you can follow the instructions. Otherwise, clone the repository and proceed with the instructions.

- You can verify the directory you are in by using the `pwd()` function in Julia prompt and changing to `~/DataScienceWithJulia$`
- Enter Pkg mode by pressing `]`
- Using the `activate.` command, activate the environment.
- You can use `status` in Pkg mode to verify the project's status.
- Then, in Pkg mode, add the **Statistics.jl** package to this environment by the command `add Statistics`
- In Pkg mode, you can update any package in the project environment such as Random.jlby using the command `update Random`
- You can check the status of any particular package or all packages in your project environment by using the command `status`

When you add **Statistics.jl**, several more packages and dependencies are automatically added. **Statistics.jl** gets included in the **project.toml** and **manifest.toml** files. If someone else wishes to recreate the environment, they can do so straight from the repository. You can now view the status to see which version of Statistics has been added to the project repository.

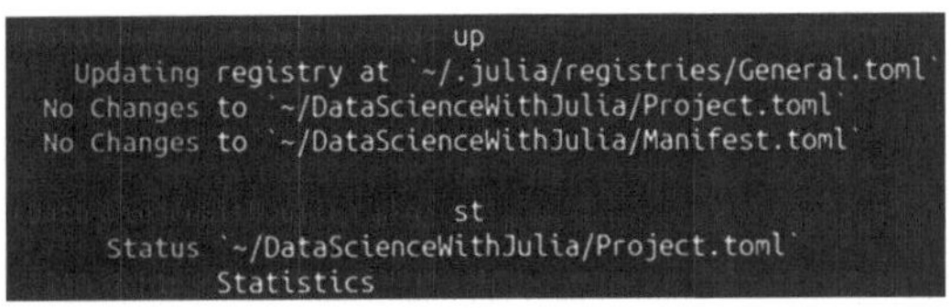

Figure 2.9: *You can use short forms of update as up and status as st to perform the desired tasks*

After a new release, simply type `update` in Pkg mode to update the packages. All packages and their dependencies will be updated accordingly. It might delete some outdated dependencies or introduce some new ones. Pkg is intelligent enough to update the packages on its own.

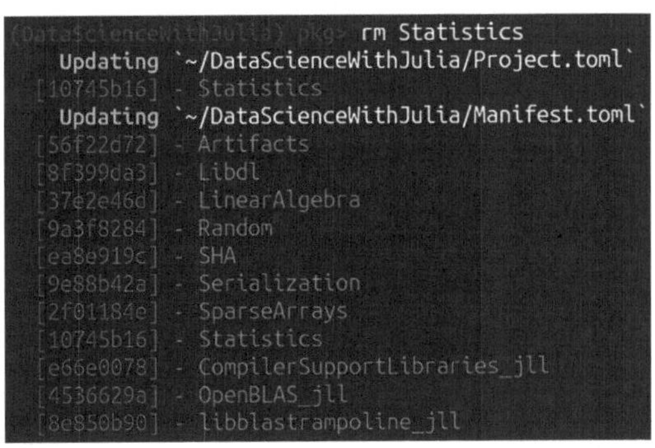

Figure 2.10: *Removing a package from the environment manually*

You can remove the package by using the command `remove Statistics` in Pkg mode. This will delete any dependencies associated with Statistics.jl as well as remove it from the project.toml and manifest.toml files as required.

Now that we have installed Julia on our system, let's learn to code in Julia. Julia is highly suited for scientific computing. We will go through numbers, variables, loops, functions and other error-handling techniques used in Julia in this chapter.

Numerical Data Handling in Julia

In general, we need to understand how Julia handles ***values***. A value is a representation of some type of data that the Julia program can modify. Every value is the result of a Julia expression being evaluated. Let's understand how values are represented in Julia.

```
julia> 7 # integer value
7

julia> 7.4 # floating point value
7.4

julia> false # boolean value
false

julia> Inf # infinity
Inf

julia> "Hello World!" # string value
"Hello World!"

julia> [4.3, 5, 0] # single dimensional array
3-element Vector{Float64}:

4.3

5.0

0.0

julia> [4.3, "Hello", 0, 7] # single dimensional array
4-element Vector{Any}:

4.3

"Hello"

0

7
```

The values in listing 2.3 are an integer 7, a floating point value 7.4, a boolean value false, an infinity value representation Inf, a string value "Hello World!", a 3-element vector [4.3, 5, 0] and another 3-element vector [4.3, "Hello", 0, 7].

You can see that although I used both integer and floating point values in the same array, it didn't give any error, rather it converted integers to floating point values. This is called implicit type casting. Generally, when more than one type is present, the compiler can convert the type of the value to a higher data type which is known as implicit type casting. You would have noticed the Float64 data type in the Vector{Float64}. This means the value takes up 64 bits of memory. In the second vector, the type is set to Any. Julia can hold any data type in its array.

Any data type is hierarchically at the top of the type graph in Julia.

```
julia> [1;; 2;; 3;; 4] # 2 dimensional matrix
1×4 Matrix{Int64}:
1 2 3 4
julia> [[1, 2] [3, 4]] # 2 dimensional matrix
2×2 Matrix{Int64}:
1 3
2 4
```

In Julia, a vector is a one-dimensional array. `Vector{Float64}` is the same as `Array{Float64, 1}`. `Array{Float64, 1}` indicates that the value is of Array type. `{Float64, 1}` indicates that the values are of type Float64 and the number 1 represents the dimension of the array. One-dimensional arrays are otherwise termed vectors, while more than one-dimensional arrays are otherwise termed matrices. We represent a single-dimensional array as a single column having the total number of rows equal to the size of the vector. A two-dimensional matrix has both defined rows and columns. A three-dimensional matrix has its 3 dimensions or axes defined and so on. There are various ways of defining matrices in Julia. Some of the ways are using semicolon(s), commas, spaces or a combination of all three. You can look into https://docs.julialang.org/en/v1/manual/arrays/ to get a better idea.

```
julia> typeof(Inf) # finding the data type of Infinity defined in
Julia Float64
```

You can get the data type of the value by using `typeof()` in Julia. `typeof(Inf)` is Float64. In Julia, Inf is defined as an infinity value. Although Julia has a dynamic type system (see Chapter 1) you can still define types while writing the values except on global variables.

```
julia> reshape([1, 2, 3, 4], (2, 2)) # resizing a matrix to a
defined
size 2×2 Matrix{Int64}:
```

```
1 3

2 4
```

`reshape()` function in Julia returns an array with the provided modified dimensions. While working with mathematical operations on arrays, it becomes necessary to reshape the matrix or vector to perform certain computations such as vector dot products.

```
julia> arr = [1, 2, 3, 4]
4-element Vector{Int64}:

1

2

3

4

julia> arr + arr # addition operation on two arrays
4-element Vector{Int64}:

2

4

6

8

julia> arr - arr # subtraction operation on two arrays
4-element Vector{Int64}:

0

0

0

0

julia> arr * reshape(arr, (1, length(arr))) # multiplication
operation 4×4 Matrix{Int64}:

1 2 3 4

2 4 6 8

3 6 9 12

4 8 12 16

julia> arr / arr # division operation
4×4 Matrix{Float64}:

0.0333333 0.0666667 0.1 0.133333

0.0666667 0.133333 0.2 0.266667

0.1 0.2 0.3 0.4
```

```
0.133333 0.266667 0.4 0.533333
```

As you can see, we can perform various basic mathematical operations such as addition, subtraction, multiplication and division with arrays. Manipulating arrays in programming is similar to array manipulation in mathematics. Arrays perform various mathematical operations when inputs have the same dimensions. While vector addition, subtraction and division don't need to change the dimensions of the arrays in Julia, we need to reshape our second array during multiplication to match the dimensions of the first array. `reshape(arr, (1, length(arr)))` is similar to transpose operation in mathematics. The dimensions of the resulting array depend on the dimensions of the input arrays. It can be a single-valued array or a multidimensional array.

```
julia> Float32.([4.3, 5, 0]) # type-casting of an array to floating
point 3-element Vector{Float32}:

4.3

5.0

0.0
```

You can convert the type from Float64 to Float32 in Julia by using `Float32.([4.3, 5, 0])`. The vector is now a 3-element `Vector{Float32}`.

You must have noticed a dot after the type declaration. That dot is a dot operator. The dot operator is designed to be applied element-wise with collections of values such as a vector or matrix. In programming, this technique is known as broadcasting. If we want to apply specific functions over single or multi-dimensional arrays, then usually we go for a loop, that is, `if-else-end`, `while-end`, or `for-end` loops. But it is lengthy for typing out. In Julia, we can apply the same function across all elements of the array by using a *dot* notation after the function's name. Let's see an example.

```
julia> func(x) = 7x^2/(4+5x^3) # defining a function in Julia
func (generic function with 1 method)

julia> x = [2π/n for n=1:3]
3-element Vector{Float64}:
6.283185307179586

 3.141592653589793

 2.0943951023931953

julia> y = func.(x)

3-element Vector{Float64}:

 0.22210061177582122
```

```
0.43442513879920297

0.6149053316945388
```

In the example, `func.(x)` shows that it is applied across all elements of the three-element Vector. Dot notation can be used with binary operators, functions, data types, and so on. `julia> x = [2, 4, 5]`

```
3-element Vector{Int64}:

 2

 4

 5

julia> y = 5x.^3 + 6x.^5
3-element Vector{Int64}:

 232

 6464

 19375

julia> y = sin.(x) # using sine operation over all values in
array 3-element Vector{Float64}:

0.9092974268256817

 -0.7568024953079282

 -0.9589242746631385
```

Note: π is a Unicode representation of the value pi=3.141592653897... in Julia. Julia supports many other symbolic Unicode representations. You can get the π Unicode in Julia REPL or notebook via TeX completion *pi followed by a tab*. You can also access the pi value by writing just pi in the Julia console. In Julia, the π value is stored as irrational rather than rounded to the nearest floating-point value.

While working on any deep learning problems, we generally work with arrays of numerical data. It is impossible to write huge arrays of numbers by hand, hence, we use a function `rand` which generates the desired number of random numbers. For example,

```
julia> example = rand(5, 7) # defining an array with random floating
values 5×7 Matrix{Float64}:

        0.84574 0.394717 0.317663 0.0265575 0.154856 0.180189

        0.865816 0.251014 0.256149 0.557439 0.814052 0.607115 0.173

        0.265682

        0.265331  0.439098  0.786905  0.310021  0.441693  0.407871
```

```
0.145327  0.269942  0.992338  0.044133  0.493182  0.424494

0.869254  0.319185  0.300924  0.117598  0.250328  0.863686

0.351836  0.163491  0.617714

julia> example1 = rand(Int64, 5, 7)#Random Integer values in
array 5×7 Matrix{Int64}:

          -7854820187046981395 671422092392350264 …

-8797921353975463297 1190311527666160570 -2999535863210223006

1196246067491248664  4090788726465192959 -5805998217061788037

-6607041929927670283 -3603700130076647610 4972624035219583797

                     907458187756625011

-6979151765419648327 8824871015523778106 -1654918304789514935
```

You can see the rand function creates a two-dimensional array with 5 rows and 7 columns as specified in the `rand(5, 7)` function. By default, the data type is set to `Float64`. But you can change that as shown in the second example. The data type is changed to Int64. Some other useful functions while dealing with numerical data are `randn, ones, zeros, size, length,` and so on which we will be using throughout the book. Let's see how these work. `julia> length(example) # finding total elements in the array`

```
35

julia> size(example) # finding the size/no. of dimensions of the
array (5, 7)

julia> typeof(example) # finding data types of values in the
array Matrix{Float64} (alias for Array{Float64, 2})

julia> zeros(5, 4) #creating an array with defined size filled only
with 0
5×4 Matrix{Float64}:

 0.0  0.0   0.0   0.0

 0.0  0.0   0.0   0.0

 0.0  0.0   0.0   0.0

 0.0  0.0   0.0   0.0

 0.0  0.0   0.0   0.0

julia> ones(4) #creating an array with defined size filled only
with

1 4-element Vector{Float64}:

 1.0
```

```
 1.0
 1.0
 1.0
julia> randn(5, 2) # defining an array with random floating
values 5×2 Matrix{Float64}:
 -0.221947 -0.462047
 1.00376 0.775232
 -0.870823 -1.34012
 -0.0373757 -1.26907
 -0.155329 1.46971
```

`length(example)` returns the total number of elements in the array. `size(example)` returns the size of the array. `randn(example)` works similarly to `rand()` with more variables, one for the number of rows and the other one for the number of columns. For more information on these functions, you can always go to help mode in REPL by typing **?** on the console. In help mode, the prompt will change from `julia>` to `help?>`. Press Backspace to exit the help mode. Apart from the above operations, Float64, Float32, ComplexF64 and ComplexF32 support some linear algebraic operations such as dot product, vector addition, deep copying, finding maximum absolute value and so on. Basic Linear Algebra Subprograms (BLAS) is a design that defines a set of low-level routines for executing standard linear algebra operations such as vector addition, scalar multiplication, matrix multiplication, linear combinations, and dot products.

By default, BLAS is the standard low-level operation for linear algebra libraries. Heavy linear algebra operations in Julia are based on the LAPACK library, which is constructed on top of fundamental linear-algebra building blocks known as the BLAS. There are highly optimized BLAS implementations available for every computer architecture. It is convenient to invoke the BLAS functions directly in high-performance linear algebra routines. You can look into https://docs.julialang.org/en/v1/stdlib/LinearAlgebra/#BLAS-functions for more information on LAPACK/BLAS support in Julia. BLAS functions perform way faster than naive implementations of algorithms.

Declaring variables

We understand the meaning of a value be it numeric or textual. Now we will learn about variables. A program is typically made up of instructions that tell the computer what to perform and the data that the program needs while executing. A variable in programming is a value that may vary depending on the conditions or information provided to the program. Simply put, a variable is a name that is associated with a value. The assignment operator = (equal sign) is the easiest technique to associate a value with a variable name.

```
julia> n = 1
1

julia> a = 7
7
julia> t = false
false

julia> yt = [2, 4, 56.7]
3-element Vector{Float64}:
  2.0
  4.0
  56.7
```

In this code sample, n, a, t and yt are all variables. The values 1, 7, false and [2, 4, 56.7] are the values contained in the respective variables. If we want to use the value, we can simply use the variable associated with the value instead.

```
julia> a+1
8

julia> a+1
8

julia> a+1+1
9

julia> ~t
true

julia> t
false
```

As you can see, we can use the variable a to represent 7 instead of writing 7. The variables are useful when writing expressions and manipulating them. Another thing you can see is that the original value of the variable is not changed when you try to manipulate it. A variable can retain a location in one form of memory known as the "heap." The heap variables have an address that corresponds to the place in the memory that they inhabit, and so the value that they represent can be altered by updating the content of that location in memory. Heap is the location of mutable variables.

There are other fast-tracked memory locations such as stack or processor cache and most immutable variables are stored, altered and manipulated by the compiler according to the instructions. In this code sample, you can see the value of a or t is not altered, hence these variables are stored in the heap with a memory address.

Julia has a highly flexible variable naming mechanism. Variable names have no semantic value and are case-sensitive. Unicode names (encoded in UTF-8) are also supported.

```
julia> udhr = "在尊严和权利上一律平等"
"在尊严和权利上一律平等"


julia> 하세요 = "Yellow"
"Yellow"


julia> σ = 0.003
0.003
```

You can't redefine variables with the already defined constant values or functions in Julia. You will get errors if you try defining the built-in variables again in the same Julia session.

```
julia> length = 3
3


julia> string = 5
5


julia> sqrt = 3
```

```
3

julia> string(4)
ERROR: MethodError: objects of type Int64 are not callable
Maybe you forgot to use an operator such as *, ^, %, / etc. ?
Stacktrace:
[1] top-level scope
@ REPL[17]:1

julia> string(4.6)
ERROR: MethodError: objects of type Int64 are not callable
Maybe you forgot to use an operator such as *, ^, %, / etc. ?
Stacktrace:
[1] top-level scope
@ REPL[18]:1

julia> null = 9
9

julia> Inf = 8
8

julia> pi = 3
3
julia> pi
3

julia> sqrt(100)
ERROR: MethodError: objects of type Int64 are not callable
Maybe you forgot to use an operator such as *, ^, %, / etc. ?
Stacktrace:
[1] top-level scope @
REPL[23]:1
```

In general, `sqrt()` and `pi` would act as square root functions and the value of pi should be shown as we saw earlier. But since here, we defined variables sqrt and pi initially, they are treated as variables now and their values can't be altered.

In short, they won't be overwritten by the in-built value of a function or constant respectively. If initially, we would have used sqrt as a function and pi as its in-built constant, then we can't use those as variables in the same Julia session.

Acceptable variable names in Julia

As we learnt that we can't have generic in-built predefined constants or function names as variables in a single Julia session, let us see what characters and names are acceptable to use in Julia.

- Variable names must begin with a letter (A-Z or a-z), underscore, or a subset of Unicode code points greater than 00A0; specifically, the Unicode characters, currency and other symbols, and a few other letter-like characters are permitted.
- The following characters may contain ! and digits (0-9), as well as additional Unicode code points, certain punctuation connectors, primes, and a few other characters.
- The variables shouldn't be in-built keywords like `if`, `for`, `else`, `try`, and so on.

```
julia> else = false

ERROR: syntax: unexpected "else"
Stacktrace:

[1] top-level scope
@ none:1


julia> if = true

ERROR: syntax: unexpected "="
Stacktrace:

[1] top-level scope @ none:1


julia> catch = "HEllo"

ERROR: syntax: unexpected "catch"
Stacktrace:

top-level scope
@ none:1


julia> for = 75.4
```

```
ERROR: syntax: unexpected "="
Stacktrace:
[1] top-level scope
@ none:1
```

As you can see, when you use predefined keywords as variables, Julia's compiler will generate problems.

There are some specific styling conventions that are used for declaring variables in Julia which are encouraged to follow but that's not bound.

- Variable names are in lowercase.
- Underlines ('_') can be used to denote word separation, although they are discouraged unless the name would be difficult to read otherwise. Functions and macro names are in lowercase, with no underscores.
- Type and Module names begin with a capital letter, and word separation is represented with upper camel case rather than underscores.
- Function names that end in! are those that write to their arguments.
- These are sometimes known as "mutating" or "in-place" functions since they are meant to induce changes in their parameters after the function is called rather than just returning a value.

Bound vs Copy in mutable variables

A value is bound to a variable if we use an assignment operator such as "=". A value is copied to a variable if we use the `copy()` function. Let us understand this through the example. `julia> a = 4`

```
4

julia> b = a

4

julia> n = copy(a)

4

julia> a = 6

6

julia> b

4
```

```
julia> n
4
```

No changes happened as numerical values are not associated with multiple variables. All the variables are independent of each other. But let us see where values such as arrays and tuples are mutable and dependent on the variables. Variables a, b, and n are not bound to each other. Hence, if we change the value of a, it doesn't change the value of b or n.

```
julia> r = [3.4, 5]
2-element Vector{Float64}:
3.4
5.0

julia> t = r
2-element Vector{Float64}:
3.4
5.0

julia> r[1] = 3
3

julia> t[1]
3.0

julia> s = copy(r)
2-element Vector{Float64}:
3.0
5.0

julia> r[2] = 7
7

julia> s[2]
5.0
```

You can see that the variable t is bound to variable r by the assignment operator. We changed the value of the first array element and it changed the value of both the variables t and r. While s is the copied value of the variable r and changing the second element of the variable r doesn't change the value of the copied variable s.

The address of the bound variable is linked to the original variable, hence changes in the original variable change the values of the bound variable. The address of the copy variable is altogether a separate address and is not linked to the original variable so s is not affected by the change in the original variable.

You can see that we are not defining any types with the variables. Julia is a dynamically typed language, the variables are associated with the type of value it stores. It is advised not to use the same variable for two different values although it won't be an error but performance might decrease. Julia is a compiled language, as we covered in the previous chapter. Julia attempts to discover all potential sorts of values that may be tied to a particular variable name during compilation. `julia> g = 7`

```
7


julia> typeof(g)

Int64


julia> h = 45.6

45.6


julia> typeof(h)

Float64
```

You can see we don't have to explicitly define the types of variables g or h, rather Julia determines the type `Int64` and `Float64` respectively on its own.

Constructing control flows

The control flow is the sequence in which statements in a script are processed by the computer. Unless the computer encounters (very common) structures that affect the control flow, such as conditionals and loops, code is run in sequence from the first line in the file to the final line. These common structures such as conditionals and loops are like little scripts inside the entire script. The flow is controlled within the structures for quite some time depending on the parameter that controls the flow sequence. Since the structures have their own control flow, the code is run in sequence from the first line in the structure to the final line as well. Julia has a number of control flow structures, such as:

1. Evaluation under conditions
2. Evaluation of short circuits
    a. Handling exceptions
    b. Loops (Repeated evaluation)
3. Expressions in compound form

Evaluation under conditions

Conditional evaluation is applied in cases where different outcomes should be undertaken based on the value of a criterion. This section demonstrates how to handle conditional expressions in Julia as well as common patterns to be aware of when dealing with Boolean conditional statements.

In *Figure 2.11*, we are trying to figure out breakfast for ourselves. We go through various options (criteria) and a complex web of yes and no answers attached to it. At each criterion, we stop and ask if we want a particular item for breakfast, then go on looking for some other item that will complement our previous breakfast choice.

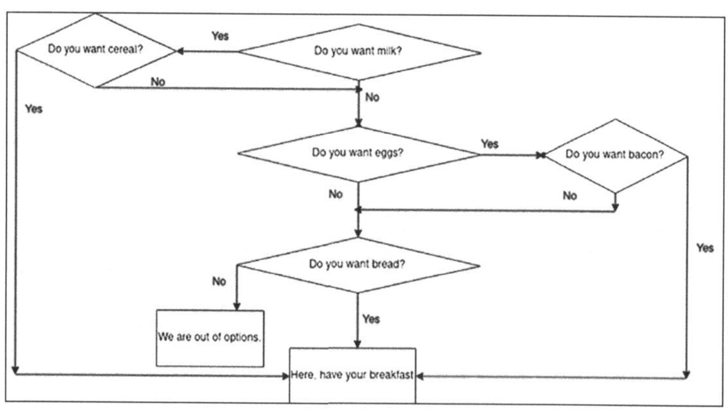

Figure 2.11: *A workflow of various breakfast ideas with some possible outcomes*

This complex web of various breakfast ideas includes the use of `if - elseif - elseif - ... - else - end`. The question is asking if the person wants milk, if yes then asks if the person wants some cereal and if no, it goes on providing other breakfast options. It goes on until you find your choice of breakfast or you are out of options in your house.

```
julia> milk = 0
0
julia> eggs = 1
1
julia> bacon = 1
1
julia> bread = 1
1
julia> if milk == 1
if cereal == 1
print("Here, have your breakfast!")
end
elseif eggs == 1
if bacon == 1
print("Here, have your breakfast!")
end
elseif bread == 1
print("Here, have your breakfast!")
else
print("We are out of options!")
end
Here, have your breakfast!
```

The code is the exact replica of our breakfast workflow in Julia. First, we need to define all the variables (milk, eggs, bacon, bread) and assign them values (0 or 1), like milk=0, eggs=1, bacon=1, and bread=1. Then we will start working our way through all the conditional statements checking each of the variables (0 - not available, 1 - available). == is used to check if the value of the variable is equal to a certain value. The if statement checks if the value of the variable is equal to a certain value, then if it is, it does a certain job or else continues checking further till out of options.

Let us understand the parts of the if - `elseif` - `else` - `end` statement. The if statement consists of the if keyword and a boolean value. If the boolean value is true, then it does the work otherwise it goes to the next keyword such as elseif or else. A boolean value is encountered and if it's true, then it does work otherwise it goes to the next keyword. milk == 1 is a conditional statement. It evaluates a logical statement. The value of every logical statement is a boolean value (true or false). We can use other logical expressions such as >, <, <=, >=, != (not equal to) and `isapprox()` function other than == in the conditional statements. elseif and else are also conditional statements.

Note: `isapprox()` function returns a boolean value. It is mostly used in floating-point integer evaluations to get a value close to the actual value. In the Julia REPL, type \approx and press the tab to get the approx (≈) character.

Tip In the sample code, I used a single tab to indent the code. You can use 4 spaces or 2 spaces. There is no hard and fast indentation rule in Julia as in Python. We generally use 2 spaces for better code readability. The Julia code usually looks for certain keywords like the end for completion of the statement or loop.

Evaluating short circuits

For evaluating logical expressions, we also use &&, ||, & (bitwise or) and | (bitwise or) operators. These operators are used along with <, >, ==, <=, >= and !=.

```
julia> 0.1 + 0.2 ≈ 0.3

true

julia> 0.1 + 0.2 ≈ 0.3 && false

false

julia> 0.1 + 0.2 == 0.3 && true

false
```

In general, && and || both perform short-circuit evaluation. This means the logical expressions connected by these operators evaluate the minimum possible number of logical expressions that are required to get the final value of the entire logical expression. Let us look at the code below to understand this better.

```
julia> true || print("Hello")

true

julia> false || print("Hello")

Hello

julia> true && print("Hello")
```

```
Hello
julia> false && print("Hello")
false
```

For ||, if the first expression is true, it doesn't evaluate the second or more expressions. Here, in the first line of code, before || we have true and the output shows true without even evaluating the rest of the expression. If the first statement or initial statements are false, then the statement connected by || goes on evaluating the rest of the expression as in the second line of code and it prints Hello.

For &&, if the first expression is false, it doesn't evaluate the second or more expressions. Here, in the fourth line of code, before && we have false and the output shows false without even evaluating the rest of the expression. If the first statement or initial statements are true, then the statement connected by && goes on evaluating the rest of the expression as in the third line of code and it prints Hello.

|| statement can be interpreted as a conditional statement.

```
julia> if !(true)
 print("Hello")
 end
```

&& statement can be interpreted as a conditional statement.

```
julia> if (true)
 print("Hello")
 end
Hello
```

We can interpret the ternary operations as an if-else-end statement in Julia.

```
julia> true ? print("Hi") : print("Hello")
Hi
julia> false ? print("Hi") : print("Hello")
Hello
```

Tip: Remember to add spaces before and after the operators other than ! operator. You can use the `print()` or `println()` function.

The preceding code can be interpreted as the following:

```
julia> if true
 print("Hi")
```

```
 else
 print("Hello")
 end
Hi
julia> if false
 print("Hi")
 else
 print("Hello")
 end
Hello
```

Handling exceptions

In the `if-else-end` statement, we get to assign tasks for both alternative choices. But sometimes, like in the breakfast ideas workflow (*Figure* 2.11), at the end we reached a point where we didn't have any options for breakfast, that is, *We are out of options*. What can we do if we encounter a similar issue with the code? We can term the breakfast dilemma option as an exception or error. We have a `try-catch-end` statement for handling such exceptions or errors. In such scenarios, it may be advisable to either end the program while issuing a diagnostic error notice, or, if the programmer has written code to handle such unusual conditions, let that code take the proper action. You can find more types of such exceptions and errors at https://docs.julialang.org/en/v1/manual/control-flow/#Built-in-Exceptions.

```
julia> try
 log(-54)
 catch e
 print("Can't be negative")
 end
Can't be negative
julia> x = try
log(-54)
 catch e
 print("Can't be negative")
 finally
 print("\n This will always be logged")
```

```
 end
Can't be negative
 This will always be logged
```

You can store the results of the **try-catch-end** block inside a variable. You can log the statement or else print out a placeholder value. The finally clause (if present) is always performed at the end of the **try-catch-finally-end** block.

```
julia> p = try
 log(-54)
 catch e
 throw(e)
 finally
 println("This will always be logged")
 end
This will always be logged
ERROR: DomainError with -54.0:
log will only return a complex result if called with a complex argument.
Try log(Complex(x)).
Stacktrace:
 [1] top-level scope
 @ REPL[38]:4

caused by: DomainError with -54.0:
log will only return a complex result if called with a complex argument.
Try log(Complex(x)).
```

Keywords like throw, rethrow, **catch_backtrace**, and so on are mostly used to get a general idea of the exception and the reason for the exception. Here, `throw(e)` shows the exception that occurred while handling the try block. You can generate exceptions on your own by using the `throw` keyword. You can get the rest of the `stacktrace` of the above code by replicating the code in your REPL.

Loops (Repeated evaluation)

As the name suggests, repeated evaluation occurs inside a loop. Julia supports two types of loops: `for-end` and `while-end`.

```
julia> for x in range(1, 1, 3)
  print("Help\n")
  end
  Help
  Help
  Help
```

You can see that in the for loop, we give certain conditions in the for loop. The `range()` function takes in the start point of the loop, step count of the loop, final point of the loop and length of the loop in the respective order. Here, the start point is 1 as the value of x gets started with 1. The final point is 3 as the value of x ends the loop when it surpasses 3. Step countimplies how many steps should the x jump, if it's 1, then the value of x should go 1-2-3 then drop the loop. If the step count is 2, then the value of x should go 1-3 then drop the loop. If the step count is 3, the value of x should go 1 then drop the loop. In the for-loop, you go through a set of values for the iterator, which is x in this case.

Note: An iterator goes through all the values step-wise.

```
julia> x = 1
julia> while x < 4
print("Help\n")
x += 1
end
Help
Help
Help
```

A while loop goes through all the values until a condition is satisfied. In this case, the condition to be met is that x should be less than 4. We initialize the variable x as 1. This loop also prints Help 3 times as the increment of the value of x happens inside the loop but since x is a global variable it gets incremented.

Tip: You can use shorthand notations for mathematical operations (+, -, *, /) such as +=, -=, *=,

/=. These are called unary operators. x += 1 means x = x + 1.

In Julia, the `break` keyword is used to exit the loop early. For example, if you have a for loop that is supposed to iterate over a collection of items, you can use `break` to exit the loop early if some condition is met. Here is an example:

```
for i in 1:10
        if i == 5
break
        end
        println(i)
end
1
2
3
4
```

In this code, the for loop will iterate over the numbers from 1 to 10, and print each number to the console. However, when i reaches 5, the if statement will evaluate to true and the break keyword will be executed, causing the loop to exit early and not print the remaining numbers. This will result in the following output.

The `break` keyword is often used in combination with the `continue` keyword, which allows you to skip the remaining code in the current iteration of the loop and move on to the next iteration. Together, these keywords allow you to control the flow of a loop and execute code only under certain conditions.

Expressions in compound form

It is better to execute numerous operations but group them together such that they seem to the outside world as one expression returning the value of the final expression inside it. Using two syntaxes, you can combine numerous expressions into one in Julia. Compound expressions in Julia are combinations of multiple expressions that are evaluated together as a single unit. They are commonly used to combine multiple operations into a single line of code or to create complex conditional statements.

Compound expressions are enclosed in parentheses and use the keywords **`begin`** and **`end`** to denote the start and end of the expression. The expressions within the compound expression are separated by semicolons, and the result of the last expression is returned as the result of the entire compound expression.

For example, the following compound expression combines two conditional statements and a mathematical operation:

```
result = (if x > y begin x - y end else begin y - x end);
x * result
```

In this case, the result of the first part of the compound expression will be used in the second part to calculate the final result. Compound expressions can help to make code more concise and easier to read.

Defining functions

In Julia, a function is a block of code that takes one or more inputs, performs some operations on those inputs, and then produces one or more outputs. Functions are a convenient way to encapsulate a piece of code that performs a specific task, and they can be used to organize and reuse code in a program.

To define a function in Julia, you use the function keyword, followed by the name of the function, a list of input arguments enclosed in parentheses, and the code that makes up the body of the function, enclosed in curly braces. Here is an example of a simple function that takes two numbers as input and returns their sum:

```
function add(x, y)
        return x + y
end
```

To call a function in Julia, you simply write the name of the function followed by the inputs that you want to pass to it, enclosed in parentheses. For example, you could call the add function defined above like this:

```
add(3, 4)
```

This would return the value 7.

Functions in Julia can also take default values for their arguments. This means that if you call the function without specifying a value for one of its arguments, it will use the default value instead. For example, you could define the add function like this:

```
function add(x, y = 0)
        return x + y
end
```

Now, if you call the add function with only one argument, it will use the default value of 0 for the y argument, and return the sum of the two numbers. For example:

```
add(3)
```

This would return the value 3.

Scope rules for variables

- The scope of the variable in Julia refers to the part of the code where the variable can be accessed and used. There are three types of variable scope in Julia: global, local, and anonymous.
- Global variables are defined outside of any function and can be accessed and used by any code in the program.
- Local variables are defined within a function and can only be accessed and used within that function.
- Anonymous variables are defined within an expression and can only be accessed and used within that expression.
- It is important to consider the scope of a variable when writing code in Julia to ensure that the correct variables are being used and to prevent unintended errors or conflicts.

Conclusion

In this chapter, we learnt to install and set up Julia in our system. We understood how to write and use various data values such as integer, floating point, boolean and string in Julia. We learnt about introducing and assigning values in variables as well as using variables in place of values that represent the values in programs. We learnt about control flows and functions in Julia along with handling errors and exceptions in Julia. We learnt about loops, broadcasting features, and various mathematical symbols in Julia.

In the next chapter, we will learn to extend capabilities of Julia by understanding the type systems, multiple dispatch and managing packages. Additionally, Julia macro writing and usage will be explained. These functionalities will help in scaling our Julia projects.

Questions

1. What are the various types of values that you can work on in Julia?
2. How will you add a package in Julia?
3. Can you handle an exception that occurred while using a `try-catch` block through an if `else-end` block? If yes, how?
4. What are the different ways to introduce a function?

CHAPTER 3

Features Assisting Scaling ML Projects

Introduction

In this chapter, we will be introducing several key concepts in the Julia programming language. We will begin by discussing functions, which are a fundamental building block of any programming language. In the last chapter, we learnt a basic way of introducing functions in Julia. In this chapter, we will learn and understand various other ways of writing and using functions in Julia. We will then move on to the topic of the type system, which is an important part of Julia's design that allows it to be both high-level and high-performance. Next, we will discuss multiple dispatch, which is a unique feature of Julia that allows functions to be dispatched to different implementations based on the types of their arguments. We will also cover how to manage packages and modules in Julia, which are essential for organizing and sharing code. Finally, we will briefly introduce macros, which are a powerful tool for extending the language and metaprogramming. By the end of this chapter, you should have a good understanding of these fundamental concepts in Julia, and be well on your way to becoming a proficient Julia programmer. Let's get started!

Structure

In this chapter, the following topics will be covered:

- Revisiting functions in Julia
- Type system in Julia
- Multiple dispatch in Julia

- Managing packages in Julia
- Using macros

Revisiting Functions in Julia

Functions are essential parts of any programming language, and Julia is no different. They allow us to write reusable pieces of code that can be called with different arguments to perform a specific task. In *Chapter 2, Getting started with Julia*, we learnt to define and call functions in Julia. In this chapter, we will understand the basic idea behind a function as well as how to use them to write modular and efficient code.

A general function in Julia consists of five parts.

1. The function-end keyword
2. The name of the function
3. The arguments used in the function
4. The body of the function
5. The return statement of the function

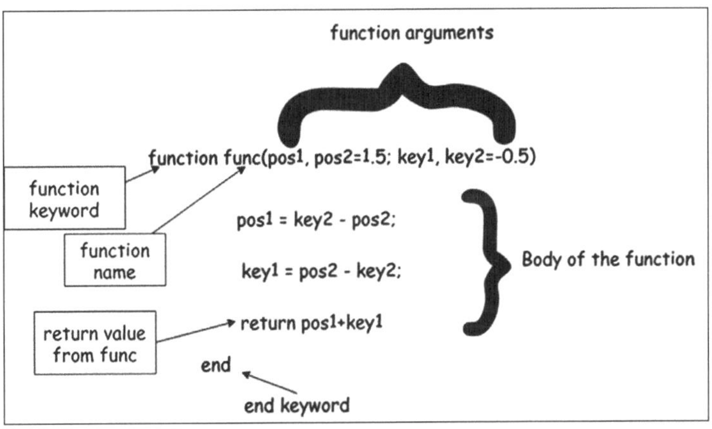

Figure 3.1: *Parts of a function*

The function-end keyword

Like any other language, Julia starts with the keyword function. In Julia, the function keyword is used to define a new function. For example, consider the following function definition:

```
julia> function saluer(name)
       println("Bonjour, $name")
end
```

This defines a function saluer that takes a single argument name and prints a greeting to the screen. To call the function, you would use its name followed by the arguments in parentheses:

```
julia> saluer("Julia")
```

This would print **`Bonjour, Julia`** on the screen.

Unlike other languages, Julia detects the end of a function by the **`end`** keyword. In Julia, the **`end`** keyword is used to mark the end of a block of code. It is often used to mark the end of a function definition. For example,

```
julia> function saluer(name)
       println("Bienvenue, $name")
end
```

Here, the **`end`** keyword marks the end of the saluer function definition. Every function definition in Julia must end with the end keyword.

The **`end`** keyword is also used to mark the end of other types of code blocks in Julia, such as loop constructs, conditional statements, and compound expressions.

The name of the function

In Julia, the name of a function is the identifier that is used to refer to the function. It is specified when the function is defined and is used to call the function. For example, consider the following function definition:

```
julia> function saluer(name)
       println("Bonne nuit, $name")
end
```

The name of this function is saluer. To call the function, you would use its name followed by the arguments in parentheses:

```
julia> saluer("Julia")
This would print "Bonne nuit, Julia" on the screen.
```

The name of the function can be any valid Julia identifier, as long as it is not already in use as a variable, function, or type name in the current scope. Function names are usually chosen to be descriptive of the function's purpose, to make it easier for other developers to understand what the function does.

Function naming rules in Julia

In Julia, there are a few rules that you should follow when naming functions:

- Function names must start with a letter or an underscore (_). They can also contain letters, digits, and underscores.
- Function names are case-sensitive. This means that foo and Foo are considered to be different names.
- Function names cannot be the same as any of the Julia built-in keywords, such as function, end, if, and so on.
- Function names should be descriptive and meaningful. It's a good idea to choose names that reflect the purpose of the function.
- It's also a good idea to follow the conventions of the Julia community when naming your functions, such as using `snake_case` for function names.

Some examples of valid function names in Julia are **`foo`**, **`_private`**, **`calculate_sum`**, and **`mean_and_variance`**.

```
julia> function add_two_numbers(x, y)
       return x + y
end
julia> function _private_function()
       # do something
end
julia> function compute_average(numbers)
       total = sum(numbers)
       return total/length(numbers)
end
```

On the other hand, the following names would not be allowed:

```
julia> function 123_invalid_name()
       # this is not allowed because it starts with a digit
end
julia> function function()
       # this is not allowed because function is a built-in keyword
end
```

The Arguments Used in the Function

In Julia, arguments are the values that are passed to a function when it is called. A function can have any number of arguments, and the arguments can be of any type. To define a function that takes arguments, you specify the names of the arguments in the function definition, separated by commas. For example,

```
julia> function add(x, y)
       return x + y
end
```

This defines a function add that takes two arguments, x and y. When calling the function, you pass the arguments in the same order as they are defined in the function definition: `julia> result = add(3, 4)`

This would call the add function with the arguments 3 and 4, and assign the result (7) to the variable result.

You can also define functions with multiple arguments, keyword arguments, and default values for arguments. For example,

```
julia> function saluer(name; greeting="Bonjour",
punctuation="!")
println("$greeting, $name$punctuation")
end
```

This defines a function saluer that takes a single positional argument: name and two keyword arguments: greeting and punctuation. The keyword arguments have default values, so you can call the function with just the name argument:

```
julia> saluer("Julia")
```

This will print **`Bonjour, Julia!`**. You can also specify the values of the keyword arguments by name:

```
julia> greet("Julia", greeting="Bonsoir", punctuation="!!")
```

This will print **`Bonsoir, Julia!!`**.

The Body of the Function

In Julia, the body of a function is the block of code that is executed when the function is called. The body of a function is typically defined between the function keyword and the end keyword and consists of one or more statements that perform some action or calculation. You can also define functions with more complex bodies, consisting of multiple statements and control structures such as if statements, for loops, and while loops.

The return Statement of the Function

In Julia, the return statement is used to specify the value that a function should return when it is finished executing. When the function is called, the result of the return statement will be the value that is returned to the caller. **`result = add(3, 4)`** would call the add function with the arguments 3 and 4, and assign the result `(7)` to the variable result.

The return statement is optional in Julia. If a function doesn't have a return statement, or the return statement is not reached, the function will return the special value nothing. This can be useful when you want a function to perform an action, but don't need to return a specific value.

```
julia> function saluer(name; greeting="Bonjour",
punctuation="!")
       println("$greeting, $name$punctuation")
end
julia> saluer("Julia")
```

This function does not have a return statement, so it will return nothing when it is called.

Positional and keyword arguments

Positional arguments in Julia are arguments that are passed to a function in a specific order, based on the position of the argument in the function definition. For example,

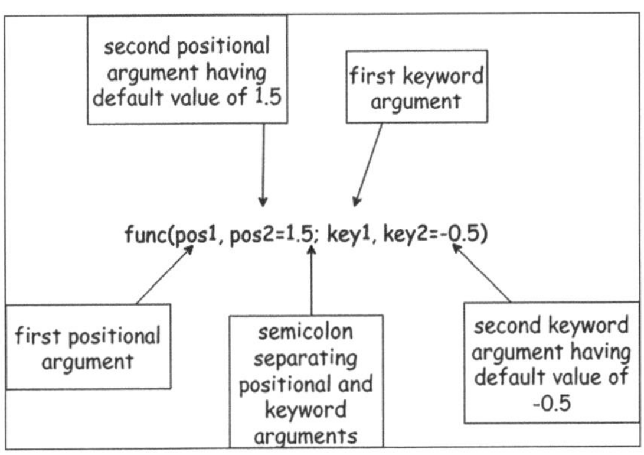

***Figure 3.2**: Positional and keyword arguments of a function*

```
julia> function greet(greeting, name)
       println("$greeting, $name")
end
julia> greet("Hello", "Julia")
```

Here, the greet function takes two arguments: greeting and name. When the function is called with the arguments **Hello** and **Julia**, the values are assigned to the greeting and name arguments in the order in which they are defined in the function definition.

Keyword arguments in Julia are arguments that are passed to a function by name, rather than by position. For example,

```
julia> function greet(; greeting="Hello", name)
       println("$greeting, $name")
end
julia> greet(name="Julia", greeting="Hola")
```

Here, the greet function takes two arguments: a keyword argument greeting with a default value of **Hello**, and a positional argument name. When the function is called with the arguments **name="Julia"** and **greeting="Hola"**, the values are assigned to the name and greeting arguments based on the names of the arguments, rather than their position.

Here is a pictorial representation of the difference between positional and keyword

```
arguments: Positional arguments:
function greet(greeting, name)
greet("Hello", "Julia")
-------------------
| greeting | name |
-------------------
| "Hello" | "Julia" |
-------------------
Keyword arguments:
function greet(; greeting="Hello", name)
greet(name="Julia", greeting="Hola")
-------------------
| greeting | name |
```

```
-------------------
| "Hola" | "Julia" |
-------------------
```

Passing arguments in Julia

The use of the `=` assignment to set the default values of the parameters demonstrates another essential aspect of Julia. If you send a value to a function, Julia binds the function parameter name to this value, in the same way, binding a variable to a value works. Adding! as a suffix to the function name **`(func!)`** is a stylistic practice that informs users that the function's parameters may change. Here is an example of a function named f! that alters the contents of an array by adding 1 to each element:

```
julia> function func!(arr)
       for i in 1:length(arr)
              arr[i] += 1
       end
end
```

Test the function

```
julia> arr = [1, 2, 3, 4]
julia> func!(arr)
julia> println(arr) # Output: [2, 3, 4, 5]
```

Here is another example of a function named func! that alters the contents of a dictionary by adding a key-value pair:

```
julia> function func!(dict)
dict["new key"] = "new value"
end
```

Test the function

```
julia> dict = {"key1" => "value1", "key2" => "value2"}
julia> func!(dict)
println(dict) # Output: Dict("key1"=>"value1", "key2"=>"value2", "new key"=>"new value")
```

Note that the `!` at the end of the function name is a convention that signals to users that the function may modify its arguments. It is not required for the function to actually modify its arguments, but it is good practice to use this convention to indicate to other users of the function that it may have side effects.

Short Syntax for Writing Functions in Julia

You can also use the short syntax for defining functions, which omits the function keyword and uses the = symbol to separate the function name and arguments from the function body. For example, you can define an add function that takes in x, and y as its arguments and returns the sum. `julia> add(x, y) = x + y`

When passing a function as an argument to another function, it is common to define a function that does not require a name. We just want to define such a function momentarily and then pass it to another function. In Julia, such unnamed functions are referred to as anonymous functions.

The syntax is quite similar to the brief syntax we studied before, except that the function name is skipped, and `=` is replaced with `->`.

The input to the sum function in this example is a function and a list. The function is defined as `julia> x -> x ^ 2`, which is a shorthand way of writing an anonymous function that takes an input x and returns x squared. The list is `[1, 2, 3]`.

The sum function applies the anonymous function to each element of the list and returns the sum of the results. In this case, the anonymous function is applied to the elements 1, 2, and 3 in turn, resulting in the values 1, 4, and 9. The sum of these values is 14, which is the output of the sum function. So the code `sum(x -> x ^ 2, [1, 2, 3])` calculates the sum of the squares of the elements in the `list [1, 2, 3]`, which is `14`.

Type System in Julia

The type system in Julia is a powerful tool that helps the language to be fast and efficient. It allows us to specify the types of variables and function arguments, which can help the compiler to generate more efficient code and also prevent common mistakes. We will learn about the different types in Julia and how to use them effectively.

The ability to define multiple methods for a single function is a powerful feature of Julia, and it is made possible by the language's strong type system. In Julia, types are used to represent the kind of data that a variable can hold, and they play a central role in determining which method of a function will be called.

In Julia, a function can have multiple methods, which are different implementations of the function that are selected based on the types of arguments passed to the function. This is known as multiple dispatch, and it is one of the key features of Julia.

For example, consider the following function definition:

```
julia> function f(x, y)
      println("default method")
end
julia> f(x::Int, y::Int) = println("method for integer arguments") julia>
f(x::Float64, y::Float64) = println("method for float arguments")
```

In this case, the function `f` has three methods: the default method, which is selected if none of the other methods match the types of the arguments, and two specialized methods that are selected if the arguments are integers or floating-point numbers, respectively.

To call a specific method, you can use the @which macro, like this:

```
julia> @which f(1, 2)
julia> @which f(1.0, 2.0)
```

This will print out the code for the specific method that will be called in each case. In the function definition above, the specialized methods for f are selected based on the types of the arguments x and y, which must be either integers or floating-point numbers. This allows the programmer to write efficient and specialized code for different types of data, and it also helps the Julia compiler to generate highly optimized code. Overall, the combination of multiple dispatch and a strong type system makes Julia a powerful and flexible programming language for a wide range of applications.

In Julia, every value has a type, which determines the set of operations that can be performed on that value. Julia has a rich set of built-in types, including Int, Float64, String, and Array, as well as a number of composite types such as Tuple and Dict. Julia also supports user-defined types, allowing you to create custom types that can be used in your code.

In Julia, types are organized into a hierarchy, with more general types at the top and more specific types at the bottom. This allows you to define methods for a function that apply to a range of related types.

For example, consider the following function definition:

```
julia> function f(x)
       println("default method")
end
julia> f(x::Number) = println("method for numbers")
julia> f(x::Integer) = println("method for integers")
julia> f(x::Real) = println("method for reals")
```

In this case, the function f has four methods: the default method, and three specialized methods that are selected based on the type of the argument `x`. The Number method will be selected if **x** is any kind of number, including integers and floating-point numbers. The Integer method will be selected if **x** is an integer. The Real method will be selected if **x** is a real number, which includes both integers and floating-point numbers.

This allows you to write methods that apply to a range of related types, while still allowing you to write specialized methods for more specific types if needed. It also allows the Julia compiler to generate highly efficient code by selecting the most specific method that matches the type of the arguments.

The type system in Julia is a system for classifying and organizing data types in the language. This is an important feature of Julia because it allows the compiler to optimize code for specific data types, leading to faster execution times and fewer runtime errors.

One of the key features of the type system in Julia is its support for parametric types, which allow you to define types that are parameterized by other types. This allows you to write generic code that can work with a variety of different types. For example, you can define a **`Vector{T}`** type that represents a vector of values of type T, allowing you to write code that works with vectors of any type.

Julia's type system includes support for parametric types, which are types that can take one or more parameters to specify more specific types. This allows you to define types that are parameterized by other types, and it is a powerful feature that enables a wide range of programming techniques. In Julia, parametric types are a way to define types that can be parameterized by other types. They are similar to generics in other programming languages, and they allow you to write flexible and reusable code that can work with a wide range of types.

For example, consider the Vector type in Julia, which is defined as

```
follows: julia> immutable Vector{T}
        data::Array{T}
end
```

In this definition, Vector is a parametric type that takes a single type parameter T, which specifies the type of the elements in the vector. This means that you can create a Vector of any type by specifying the type parameter when you create a new instance of the type:

```
julia> v1 = Vector{Int}([1, 2, 3])
julia> v2 = Vector{Float64}([1.0, 2.0, 3.0])
```

In this case, v1 is a Vector of integers and v2 is a Vector of floating-point numbers.

Parametric types are a powerful feature of Julia's type system that allows you to write generic and flexible code that can work with a wide range of types. They are often used in combination with multiple dispatch to define functions that can work with a variety of different types in a type-safe and efficient way.

For example, consider the following definition of a Vector type:

```
julia> struct Vector{T}
        data::Array{T}
end
```

Here, the Vector type is parameterized by the type T, which represents the type of the elements in the vector. This means that you can define a Vector of any type by specifying the type parameter when you create an instance of the type:

```
julia> v1 = Vector{Int}([1, 2, 3]) # a vector of integers
julia> v2 = Vector{Float64}([1.0, 2.0, 3.0])
# a vector of floating-point numbers
```

You can also define methods for the Vector type that are parameterized by the type of the elements. For example:

```
julia> function dot(v::Vector{T}, u::Vector{T}) where T
        # compute dot product of v and u
end
```

This method will work for any type of Vector as long as the element types are the same.

Parametric types are a powerful feature of Julia, and they are used in many built-in types and libraries. They allow you to write code that is generic and flexible, while still taking advantage of the strong type system and multiple dispatch features of Julia.

Hierarchy in Julia's Type System

In Julia, types can be organized into a hierarchy, with subtypes inheriting properties and behaviors from their supertypes. This is similar to the way that classes work in object-oriented languages like Python or Java.

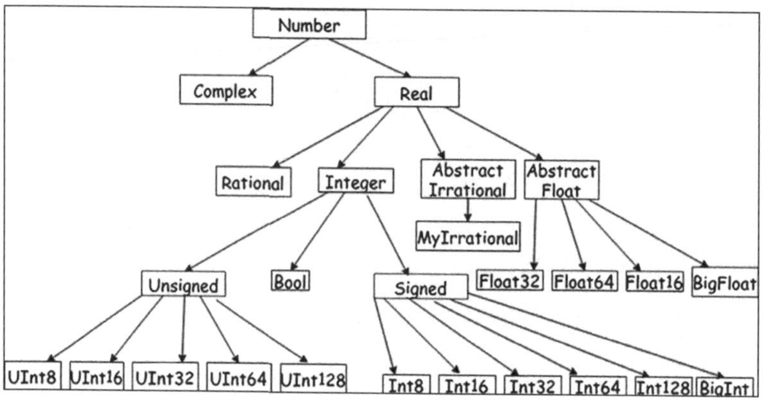

Figure 3.3: *Type hierarchy in Julia*

For example, consider the following type of hierarchy:

Any

|

AbstractString

|

|---- ASCIIString

|

|---- UTF8String

|

|---- UTF16String

|

|---- UTF32String

In this hierarchy, AbstractString is a supertype of all of the string types, and Any is the top-level supertype of all types in Julia. This means that a variable of type AbstractString can hold any kind of string, and a variable of type Any can hold any kind of value.

When defining methods for a function, you can use the type hierarchy to define methods that apply to a range of types. For example, you could define a method that applies to all types of strings by using the AbstractString type as the argument type:

```
f(s::AbstractString) = println("input is a string")
```

This method will be called for any input that is a subtype of AbstractString, including ASCIIString, UTF8String, UTF16String, and UTF32String.

Using the type hierarchy in this way allows you to write generic and flexible code that can handle a wide range of types, while still allowing you to define specialized methods for specific types when needed.

In Julia, types are arranged in a hierarchy, with a root type called Any at the top. All other types in Julia are subtypes of Any. This means that any value of any type in Julia can be stored in a variable of type Any. For Example:

```
julia> x = 1

1

julia> y = "hello"

"hello"

julia> z = [1, 2, 3]

[1, 2, 3]

julia> a: Any = x

1

julia> b: Any = y

"hello"

julia> c: Any = z

[1, 2, 3]
```

In Julia, it is also possible to define custom types, and these types will also be subtypes of Any. For example:

```
julia> struct MyType
```

```
        field::Int
end
julia> x = MyType(1)
MyType(1)
julia> y: Any = x
MyType(1)
```

It is also possible to define subtypes of existing types in Julia using the <: operator. For example:

```
julia> struct MySubType <: MyType
  field::Int
  extra_field::Int
  end
julia> x = MySubType(1, 2)
MySubType(1, 2)
julia> y: MyType = x
MySubType(1, 2)
julia> z: Any = x
MySubType(1, 2)
```

This type hierarchy allows for powerful type-based dispatch in Julia, where methods can be defined to apply to specific subtypes of a given type.

To find all the supertypes of a given type in Julia, you can use the supertypes function. This function takes a type as an argument and returns a tuple of all the supertypes of that type.

For example, to find all the supertypes of the **`Int64`** type, you can do the following:

```
julia> supertypes(Int64)
(Signed, Integer, Real, Number, Any)
```

This shows that the Int64 type is a subtype of the **`Signed, Integer, Real, Number`**, and **`Any`** abstract types.

```
julia> super(Int64)
(Signed, Integer, Real, Number, Any)
```

This returns the same result as supertypes because `Int64` directly inherits from all of its supertypes. However, if you use super on a type that inherits indirectly from some of its supertypes, you will see those supertypes in the result as well.

Note: **`supertypes()`** function only returns the supertypes that are directly inherited by the given type. To find all the supertypes of a type, including indirect supertypes, you can use the super function. This function returns a tuple of all the supertypes of a given type, including indirect supertypes, in the order that they are inherited.

You can also use the **`<:`** operator to check if a type is a subtype of another type. For example, to check if the Int64 type is a subtype of the Integer type, you can do the following:

```
julia> Int64 <: Integer
true
```

The supertype function only returns direct supertypes, not transitive supertypes. For example, if you want to find all the transitive supertypes of the Int64 type (i.e., all the supertypes of Int64, as well as the supertypes of those supertypes, and so on), you can use the **`transitive_supertype()`** function:

```
julia> transitive_supertype(Int64)
(Signed, Integer, Real, AbstractFloat, FloatingPoint, RealDomain,
Number, Any)
```

To find all supertypes of a type, including the immediate supertype and all of its supertypes, you can use a recursive function like the following:

```
julia> function all_supertypes(T)
       supertypes = []
       while true
       S = supertype(T)
       if S == Any
              return supertypes
       end
       push!(supertypes, S)
       T = S
       end
end
```

Here's an example of how you can use this function:

```
julia> all_supertypes(Int)
3-element Array{Any,1}:
 Signed
```

```
 Real
AbstractFloat
```

This function will return an array of all supertypes of the given type, with the most immediate supertype first and the ultimate supertype (Any) last.

In Julia, you can use the subtypes function to find the immediate subtypes of a given type. For example:

```
julia> subtypes(Real)
2-element Array{Union{DataType, UnionAll},1}:
 AbstractFloat
 Integer
```

To find all subtypes of a type, including the immediate subtypes and all of their subtypes, you can use a recursive function like the following:

```
julia> function all_subtypes(T)
      subtypes = []
      for S in subtypes(T)
      push!(subtypes, S)
      push!(subtypes, all_subtypes(S))
      end
      return subtypes
end
```

Here's an example of how you can use this function:

```
julia> all_subtypes(Real)
4-element Array{Any,1}:
 AbstractFloat
 Float16
 Float32
 Float64
 Integer
 BigInt
```

Note: This function will return an array of all subtypes of the given type, with the most immediate subtypes first and the ultimate subtypes last. This will also include all subtypes of the immediate subtypes, and so on, recursively.

You can also use the **`subtypes()`** function to find all subtypes of a particular type that have been defined in the current environment. For example:

```
julia> subtypes(Real)
2-element Array{Union{DataType, UnionAll},1}:
 AbstractFloat
 Integer
julia> subtypes(AbstractFloat)
3-element Array{Union{DataType, UnionAll},1}:
 Float16
 Float32
 Float64
```

This can be useful if you want to find all subtypes of a particular type that have been defined in your code, rather than all subtypes of a type in the entire Julia language.

`subtypes()` function returns a Vector of all subtypes of the given type, including abstract and concrete types. Here's an example of how you can use the **`subtypes(`**) function:

```
julia> subtypes(Number)
2-element Vector{Any}:
 Complex
 Real

julia> subtypes(Real)
4-element Vector{Any}:
 AbstractFloat
 AbstractIrrational
 Integer
 Rational
```

In Julia, you can use the Union type to represent the union of two or more types. The Union type is a generic type that takes a variable number of type arguments. For example, you can create a Union of two types T1 and T2 like this:

```
julia> Union{T1, T2}
```

You can then use this Union type to represent values that can be of either the T1 or T2 type. For example:

```
julia> x = Union{Int, String}(5)
5
julia> x = Union{Int, String}("hello")
"hello"
```

You can also use the Union type to define a function that takes arguments of either T1 or T2 type:

```
julia> function foo(x::Union{Int, String})
       if isa(x, Int)
              println("x is an Int: ", x)
       elseif isa(x, String)
              println("x is a String: ", x)
       else
              println("x is of an unexpected type")
       end
end
foo (generic function with 1 method)

julia> foo(5)
x is an Int: 5
julia> foo("hello")
x is a String: hello
```

Note: The Union type is not the same as the union function in Julia, which is used to compute the union of two sets.

When defining a function or method in Julia, it's generally a good idea to specify the types of arguments and return value as accurately as possible in the function signature. This helps to ensure that the function is called with the correct types of arguments and can help the compiler to generate more efficient code.

There are a few factors to consider when deciding what type restrictions to put in a method signature:

- **Usefulness**: The type restrictions should be useful in helping the function to perform its intended task. For example, if a function expects a matrix as an argument, it would be useful to restrict the type of argument to `AbstractMatrix`.
- **Precision:** The type restrictions should be as precise as possible. For example, if a function expects a matrix with floating point elements,

it would be more precise to restrict the type of the argument to **`AbstractMatrix{<:FloatingPoint}`** rather than just **`AbstractMatrix`.**

- **Performance:** The type restrictions should be chosen with performance in mind. For example, if a function expects a matrix with floating point elements, it would be more efficient to use **`AbstractMatrix{<:FloatingPoint}`** rather than **`AbstractMatrix`** because the former allows the compiler to generate more efficient code.
- **Flexibility**: The type restrictions should be flexible enough to allow the function to be used in a wide range of contexts. For example, if a function expects a matrix with floating point elements, it would be more flexible to use
    - **`AbstractMatrix{<:FloatingPoint}`** rather than **`Matrix{Float64}`** because the former allows the function to be used with any type of floating point matrix, not just Float64 matrices.

Ultimately, the choice of type restrictions will depend on the specific needs and constraints of the function you are defining. It's usually a good idea to start with the most general type restrictions that are still useful, and then make them more specific as needed.

In Julia, composite types are user-defined types that are composed of a set of fields, each of which has a name and a type. Composite types are similar to structs or classes in other programming languages. Here is an example of how you can define a composite type in Julia:

```
julia> struct Person
       name::String
       age::Int
end
```

This defines a type called Person that has two fields: name, which is a String, and age, which is an Int.

You can create an instance of a composite type by using the Person constructor and providing values for the fields:

```
jane = Person("Jane", 30)
```

You can access the fields of a composite type using dot notation:

```
println(jane.name) # prints "Jane"
println(jane.age) # prints 30
```

You can also define methods for a composite type. For example, you might define a greet method for the Person type like this:

```
function greet(p::Person)
      println("Hello, my name is $(p.name) and I am $(p.age) years
old.")
end
greet(jane) # prints "Hello, my name is Jane and I am 30 years old."
```

Composite types are a powerful feature of Julia that allows you to create custom data structures with associated behavior. You can learn more about composite types in the Julia documentation.

Various Data Types in Julia

Julia has two major categories of data types - concrete and abstract. A concrete data type is a specific implementation of a data type, while an abstract data type is a set of operations that can be performed on a data type, without specifying how those operations are implemented.

Concrete data types are typically defined using the struct or mutable struct keyword in Julia. There are many concrete types in Julia that implement the AbstractArray interface, including **`Array`**, **`SparseMatrixCSC`**, and StridedArray, each of which represents arrays in a different way. For example, the following code defines a concrete data type called **`Person`**:

```
struct Person
      name::String
      age::Int
end
```

This data type has two fields: name, which is a string, and age, which is an integer. To create an instance of this data type, you can use the following syntax:

```
jane = Person("Jane", 30)
You can then access the fields of the Person instance using dot
notation: jane.name # Returns "Jane"
jane.age # Returns 30
```

Abstract data types, on the other hand, are defined using the abstract keyword in Julia. An abstract data type is essentially a template for a data type, specifying the operations that can be performed on it, but not the details of how those operations are implemented.

For example, the following code defines an abstract data type called Stack:

```
abstract type Stack
        push!(stack::Stack, item)
        pop!(stack::Stack)
        top(stack::Stack)
end
```

This abstract data type defines three operations: **`push!,`** which adds an item to the stack; pop!, which removes the top item from the stack; and top, which returns the top item from the stack.

To implement an abstract data type, you can define a concrete data type that implements the operations specified in the abstract data type. For example, the following code defines a concrete data type called **`ArrayStack`** that implements the **`Stack`** abstract data type using an array:

```
struct ArrayStack <: Stack
        items::Array{Any,1}
        function push!(stack::ArrayStack, item)
push!(stack.items, item)
        end
        function pop!(stack::ArrayStack)
pop!(stack.items)
        end
        function top(stack::ArrayStack)
stack.items[end]
        end
end
```

You can then use the ArrayStack data type like any other concrete data type, but it will also have all the operations specified in the Stack abstract data type. For example, in Julia, the AbstractArray type is an abstract data type that represents a multi-dimensional array of values. It defines operations like **`size`**, **`getindex`**, and **`setindex!,`** which allow you to manipulate arrays in a generic way, regardless of the underlying representation of the array.

Julia also has a number of built-in abstract data types that are used to represent common data structures, such as lists, queues, and sets. These types define a set of operations that can be performed on the data structure, and different concrete types can be used to implement those operations in different ways. For example, the `AbstractSet` type represents a set of values, and concrete types like **`Set`** and **`Dict`** can be used to implement sets in different ways.

In addition to the built-in abstract data types, you can also define your own abstract data types in Julia. To do this, you can use the abstract keyword to define a type that represents a set of operations, and then define concrete types that implement those operations. For example, you might define an abstract type called Shape that represents a geometric shape, and then define concrete types like **`Circle`**, **`Rectangle`**, and **`Triangle`** that implement the operations defined by the Shape type.

An immutable value is one that cannot be changed after it has been created. For example, integers and floating-point numbers are immutable in Julia, as are strings and symbols. When you assign an immutable value to a variable, the variable becomes a reference to the value. You can change the value of the variable by assigning it a new value, but you cannot modify the value itself.

A mutable value, on the other hand, can be modified after it has been created. Arrays, dictionaries, and composite types are all mutable in Julia. When you assign a mutable value to a variable, the variable becomes a reference to the value, just as with immutable values. However, you can also modify the value itself by using functions or methods that change its state. In Julia, the type system is aware of mutability, which means that you can define types that are either mutable or immutable. This can be useful when you want to ensure that certain values are never modified, or when you want to allow values of a certain type to be modified in certain ways. To define an immutable type in Julia, you can use the immutable keyword when defining the type. Starting from Julia 0.7, immutable keyword has been replaced with **`struct`**. For example,

```
struct Point

        x::Float64

        y::Float64

end
```

This defines an immutable type called **`Point`**, which has two fields: x and y, both of which are Float64 values. You can create an instance of Point using the constructor and access its fields using dot notation, just as with any other composite type:

```
p = Point(1.0, 2.0)
println(p.x) # prints 1.0
println(p.y) # prints 2.0
```

However, you cannot modify the fields of an instance of Point after it has been created. If you try to do so, you will get an error. For example:

```
p.x = 3.0 # error: cannot assign to immutable field `x`
```

To define a mutable type in Julia, you can use the mutable struct syntax. For example,

```
mutable struct MutablePoint
        x::Float64
        y::Float64
end
```

This defines a mutable type called **`MutablePoint`** which has the same fields as the Point type. You can create an instance of **`MutablePoint`** using the constructor and access its fields using dot notation, just as with any other composite type. However, you can also modify the fields of an instance of **`MutablePoint`** after it has been created:

```
mp = MutablePoint(1.0, 2.0)
mp.x = 3.0
println(mp.x) # prints 3.0
```

In general, it is a good idea to use immutable types whenever possible in Julia, since they can be easier to work with and can lead to more predictable and reliable code. However, mutable types can be useful in certain situations, such as when you need to store and modify large amounts of data.

The type system in Julia is also closely tied to the multiple dispatch feature of the language. Multiple dispatch allows you to define multiple methods for a function, each specialized for a particular combination of argument types. This allows the function to behave differently depending on the types of its arguments, making it easier to write code that is expressive and efficient. Overall, the type system in Julia is a key feature of the language that allows you to write code that is optimized for specific data types and that can work with a variety of different types.

Multiple Dispatch in Julia

Multiple dispatch is a unique feature of Julia that allows us to define functions that can behave differently depending on the types of their arguments. This allows us to write code that is both flexible and efficient, as the correct implementation of a function can be selected at runtime based on the types of its arguments.

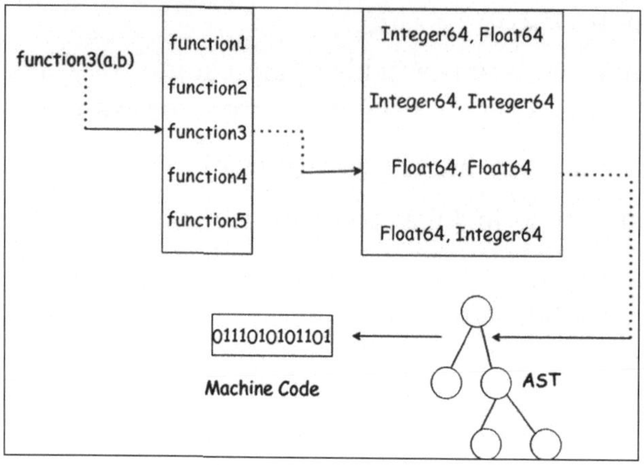

Figure 3.4: *Multiple Dispatch in Julia*

In Julia, the method ambiguity problem occurs when there are multiple methods defined for a function that could be selected to handle a particular set of arguments. This can occur when the methods have overlapping definitions in terms of the types of their arguments.

For example, consider the following function:

```
function foo(x::Int, y::Int)
        return "Int, Int"
end
function foo(x::Int, y::Float64)
        return "Int, Float64"
end
function foo(x::Float64, y::Int)
        return "Float64, Int"
end
function foo(x::Float64, y::Float64)
        return "Float64, Float64"
end
```

In this example, the foo function has four methods defined, each with a different combination of argument types. If we call foo with Int arguments, both the first and second methods could potentially be selected. Similarly, if we call foo with Float64 arguments, all four methods could potentially be selected.

When this happens, Julia will raise a **`MethodError`**, indicating that the method selection process was ambiguous and could not determine which method to execute.

To avoid the method ambiguity problem, it is important to carefully consider the types of arguments that a function will accept and to ensure that the methods are defined in a way that avoids overlap. For example, in the case of the foo function above, we could define the methods in a different order to avoid ambiguity:

```
function foo(x::Int, y::Int)
        return "Int, Int"
end
function foo(x::Float64, y::Float64)
        return "Float64, Float64"
end
function foo(x::Int, y::Float64)
        return "Int, Float64"
end
function foo(x::Float64, y::Int)
        return "Float64, Int"
end
```

With this definition, the method selection process will always be able to determine the most specific method to execute based on the types of arguments. This is called **multiple dispatch**.

In Julia, multiple dispatch is a feature that allows a function to behave differently based on the types of its arguments. This is different from traditional function overloading, which determines the behavior of a function based on the number or types of its arguments, but does not allow the function to behave differently depending on the combination of argument types. Multiple dispatch is achieved by defining multiple methods for a function, each of which is specialized for a particular combination of argument types. When a function is called with a set of arguments, Julia will select the most specific method that matches the argument types and execute it.

To use multiple dispatch in a function, you first define the function and its methods. Each method is defined by specifying the function name, the types of its arguments, and the body of the method. Here is an example of how multiple dispatch can be used in Julia:

```
julia> function add(x::Int, y::Int)
 return x + y
 end
add (generic function with 1 method)
julia> function add(x::Float64, y::Float64)
 return x + y
 end
add (generic function with 2 methods)
julia> add(1, 2)
3
julia> add(1.0, 2.0)
3.0
```

In this example, the add function has two methods defined: one for **Int** arguments and another for **Float64** arguments. When add is called with Int arguments, the first method is selected and executed, while the second method is selected and executed when add is called with **Float64** arguments. This allows the add function to behave differently depending on the types of its arguments.

Multiple dispatch is a useful feature because it allows a function to behave differently based on the types of its arguments. This allows you to write code that is more flexible and efficient, as it can adapt to a variety of different input types and situations.

One of the main benefits of multiple dispatch is that it allows you to write code that is more expressive and intuitive. With traditional function overloading, you might have to write separate functions for different combinations of argument types, leading to code that is more difficult to read and understand. With multiple dispatch, you can define a single function with multiple methods, each specialized for a particular combination of argument types, making it easier to understand how the function will behave in different situations.

Additionally, multiple dispatch can lead to more efficient code because the most specific method for a given set of argument types is selected at runtime, allowing the code to take advantage of type information that may not be available at compile time. This can lead to faster execution times and fewer runtime errors.

Overall, multiple dispatch is a powerful feature of Julia that allows you to write more expressive, intuitive, and efficient code.

Managing code structure in Julia

Managing packages and modules is an important aspect of working with Julia. In Julia, you can use modules to structure your code and keep related functions and variables together in a single file or a set of files. A module is a collection of Julia code that is defined in a separate file, and it can be used to organize your code into logical units. Modules allow us to organize our code into logical groups and prevent naming conflicts.

Modules are used to specify distinct variable namespaces. Each module specifies its own independent global scope. The default global scope in Julia is called the **Main module**. To create a module, you can use the module keyword followed by the name of the module and a block of code:

```
julia> module MyModule
export myfunc
function myfunc()
       # code for myfunc
       println("Aloha!")
end
end # defining MyModule
Main.MyModule
```

The export keyword specifies which functions, types, and constants defined in the module should be made available to users of the module. You can also use the using keyword to import all the exports from a module into your current namespace:

```
using MyModule
myfunc()
```

You can also selectively import specific functions, types, or constants from a module using the import keyword:

```
import MyModule.myfunc
myfunct()
```

Modules can also contain types and constants. For example,

```
module MyModule
export MyType, MY_CONSTANT
struct MyType
      # fields for MyType
      W
      b
end
const MY_CONSTANT = 3.14
end #defining a module
Main.MyModule
```

end keyword marks the end of the module in Julia. Usually, we comment on the code at the end keyword to show that the module ends at that time. If you are reproducing the code using a Julia REPL, then you can see that the output shows the namespace and the module name. In this case, the REPL prints out **Main.MyModule.** You can use the exported types and constants in the same way as exported functions.

In Julia, you can use the include function to include the contents of another file or module in the current module. This can be useful for breaking up large modules into smaller files or for including code from external libraries in your module. To use the include function, you simply pass the file or module that you want to include as an argument. For example,

```
module MyModule
include("foo.jl")
include("bar.jl")
end
```

This will include the contents of the **foo.jl** and **bar.jl** files in the MyModule module. You can also use the include function to include the contents of another module. For example,

```
module MyModule
include(OtherModule)
end
```

This will include the contents of the **OtherModule** module in the **MyModule** module. It is important to note that the include function does not import the definitions from the included file or module into the current namespace. Instead, it simply evaluates the code in the included file or module within the context of the current module. To make the definitions from an included file or module available to your code, you can use the using or import keywords.

Modules can also be nested, with inner modules being able to access the exports of their outer modules. This can be useful for organizing your code into logical hierarchies. Modules are a useful way to organize and reuse your code in Julia. They allow you to group related definitions together and provide a clear separation between different parts of your code.

In Julia, packages are collections of modules (that is, Julia code files) that provide additional functionality for your programs. Packages are collections of Julia code that can be easily shared and reused. When we register a module at the Julia general registry (https://github.com/JuliaRegistries/General), it becomes a package. This package is available to other users who want to use the functions, types, and constants from the package in their code.

We learnt to add a specific package to our current code by using Julia's package manager, Pkg. Once the package is added to the namespace, we can access the package at any time, even after you reload a new Julia session. Once a package is installed, you can use it in your code by using the **`using`** keyword followed by the name of the package. This will import the exported definitions from the package into the current namespace.

```
using ExamplePackage

# now you can use the definitions from the ExamplePackage package
```

You can also import specific definitions from a package using the import keyword. For example:

```
import ExamplePackage: foo

# now you can use the foo function from the ExamplePackage package
```

Packages in Julia are often distributed as compiled code, which means that they are pre compiled for a specific platform and can be loaded into Julia quickly. This makes packages an efficient way to include large amounts of code in your projects. In addition to reusable code, Julia packages can also include documentation, tests, and other resources. You can use the Pkg package manager to access these resources and manage the packages that you have installed. Overall, packages are a powerful tool for organizing and sharing code in Julia, and they are an important part of the Julia ecosystem.

Using Macros

Macros are a powerful feature that allows us to modify the behavior of the language itself and are often used to create domain-specific languages or to optimize performance-critical code. We will learn how to define and use macros in Julia, and how they can help us to write more expressive and efficient code.

In Julia, a macro is a piece of code that is executed at compile-time to generate other code. Macros allow you to generate code dynamically and can be used to implement powerful and flexible abstractions in Julia.

To define a macro in Julia, you can use the **@** symbol followed by the name of the macro and any arguments that the macro takes. For example:

```
macro mymacro(x)
        quote
# Code generated by the macro goes here
        end
end
```

The **quote** and **end** keywords define a block of code that is treated as a single expression and can be passed around and manipulated like any other value in Julia.

To use a macro, you can call it like a function, using the **@** symbol followed by the name of the macro and any arguments that it takes. For example:

```
@mymacro(42)
```

Inside the body of the macro, you can use the **esc** function to escape the code generated by the macro and the: operator to unquote symbols. For example:

```
macro mymacro(x)
        quote
y = $(esc(x)) + 1
z = :($(y))
        end
end
```

This macro takes a single argument x and generates code that adds 1 to x and creates a symbol with the name of the resulting value.

```
macro my_macro(x)
```

```
    return :($x + 1)
end
```

This macro defines a simple macro that takes an argument **x** and returns a new expression that increments **x** by 1.

To use a macro, you can call it like a function and pass it the arguments that you want to use as inputs. The macro will then generate the corresponding code and return the value. Otherwise, you can call the macro without the parenthesis with just a space in between the macro name and the argument used. For example:

```
julia> @my_macro(2)

3

julia> @my_macro 2

3
```

Macros are functions that accept a parsed reference of Julia code and return the transformed code. Macros work at the level of abstract syntax trees (https://en.wikipedia.org/wiki/Abstract_syntax_tree). Macros are performed after Julia code has been parsed but before it has been compiled. Macros are a powerful feature of Julia that allow you to generate code dynamically and create abstractions that are not possible with normal functions. They are often used to implement domain-specific languages, optimize performance, and simplify code by hiding complex details behind a simple interface.

We will discuss some of the most used macros in Julia like time, elapsed, assert and benchmark.

The time macro in Julia is a tool for measuring the performance of code. It can be used to measure the time it takes to execute a block of code or to measure the time it takes to execute a specific function or expression.

To use the time macro, you can use the **`@time`** or **`@elapsed`** macro. The **`@time`** macro will execute the code that follows it and print the wall-clock time, the CPU time, and the allocated memory used by the code. The **`@elapsed`** macro will only print the wall-clock time that the code took to run.

For example, you can use the @time macro to measure the time it takes to run a function like this:

```
@time my_function()
```

Or you can use the @elapsed macro to measure the time it takes to evaluate an expression like this:

```
@elapsed result = my_expression
```

The **`@time`** macro will print the wall clock time, the CPU time, and the allocated memory used by the code. You can also use the @elapsed macro, which will only print the wall-clock time that the code took to run.

```
@time begin
 # code to measure goes here
end
@elapsed begin
 # code to measure goes here
end
```

Both **`@time`** and **`@elapsed`** can be used to measure the performance of specific functions or expressions.

It's important to note that the time it takes to execute code can vary depending on a number of factors, such as the speed of the CPU, the workload of the system, and the presence of other running processes. As such, it is generally a good idea to take multiple measurements and calculate an average time when trying to determine the performance of code.

Here is an example of how you can use the @time macro in Julia to measure the time it takes to run a function:

```
# Define a function that takes some time to run
function slow_function()
 sleep(1) # pause for 1 second
end
# Measure the time it takes to run the function
@time slow_function()
```

The output of this code might look something like this:

```
0.000352 seconds (5 allocations: 176 bytes)
```

The **`@time`** macro will print the wall clock time, the CPU time, and the allocated memory used by the code. In this case, the function took about 0.000352 seconds to run, and it required 5 memory allocations that used a total of 176 bytes.

You can also use the **@elapsed** macro to measure the time it takes to run a function. For example:

```
# Define a function that takes some time to run
function slow_function()
 sleep(1) # pause for 1 second
end
# Measure the time it takes to run the function
@elapsed slow_function()
```

The output of this code might look something like this:

```
1.000625 seconds
```

The **@elapsed** macro will only print the wall-clock time that the code took to run. In this case, the function took about 1.000625 seconds to run.

The assert macro in Julia is used to check if a condition is true, and throw an error if it is not. It is commonly used as a way to validate the correctness of code and to catch and handle errors that might occur during execution.

To use the assert macro, you provide a condition as the first argument and an optional error message as the second argument. If the condition is true, then the assert macro does nothing and the code continues to execute. If the condition is false, then the assert macro throws an `AssertionError`, which can be caught and handled using a try/catch block. Here are some examples of how you can use the assert macro in Julia:

```
# Check that a variable has a certain value
x = 10
assert x == 10, "x should be 10"
# Check that a function returns a certain value
function test_function()
return 10
end
assert test_function() == 10, "test_function should return 10"
# Check that an expression evaluates to true
assert 1 + 1 == 2, "1 + 1 should equal 2"
# Check that a value is within a certain range
x = 10
```

```
assert x >= 0 && x <= 10, "x should be between 0 and 10"
```

If the condition being checked by the assert macro is true, then nothing will happen and the code will continue to execute. If the condition is false, then an AssertionError will be thrown and the code will stop executing.

You can also use the **@assert** macro to include the expression being checked in the error message if the condition is not met. For example:

```
# Check that a variable has a certain value
x = 10
@assert x == 10 "x should be 10, but it is $(x)"
```

This will include the value of x in the error message if the condition is not met, which can be helpful for debugging. The assert macro is often used in conjunction with a try/catch block to handle errors and prevent them from crashing the program. For example,

```
try
 # Code that might throw an error goes here
 x = y # y is not defined, so this will throw an error
 assert x == 10, "x should be 10"
catch e
 # Code to handle the error goes here
 println("An error occurred: $(e)")
end
```

In this example, the code in the try block will be executed, and if an error occurs it will be caught by the catch block, which will print an error message to the console.

The **macroexpand** function in Julia is used to expand the macro into its underlying code. Macros in Julia are used to write code that generates other code at compile time, which can be helpful for tasks such as code generation, code optimization, and metaprogramming.

To use the **macroexpand** function, you pass it a macro as an argument and it will return the expanded code as an Expr object. For example,

```
# Define a simple macro that adds 1 to a number
macro add_one(x)
 return :($x + 1)
end
```

```
# Expand the macro
expanded_code = macroexpand(:(@add_one 10))
# The expanded code is now an expression that can be evaluated
eval(expanded_code) # returns 11
```

In this example, the **add_one** macro takes a single argument x and returns an expression that adds 1 to x. When the macro is expanded using **macroexpand**, it returns the expanded code as an expression that can be evaluated using eval.

You can also use the **@macroexpand** macro, which will print the expanded code to the console instead of returning it as an Expr object.

```
# Define a simple macro that adds 1 to a number
macro add_one(x)
return :($x + 1)
end
# Expand the macro
@macroexpand @add_one 10
# Output: quote
# 10 + 1
# end
```

The **macroexpand** function can be helpful for debugging macros and understanding how they work. It can also be used to optimize code by expanding macros at compile time to avoid the overhead of macro expansion at runtime.

Conclusion

Julia is a powerful programming language that offers a variety of features for managing code structure and complexity. Functions are a key part of Julia's design, and the language provides a number of features for defining and calling functions, including optional and keyword arguments, anonymous functions, and currying. The Julia type system is also a key feature of the language, allowing you to define and work with composite types, immutable values, and mutable values. Julia's support for multiple dispatch allows you to define functions that behave differently depending on the types of their arguments, making it easier to write flexible and reusable code. Managing code structure in Julia is made easier by the use of modules and packages, which allow you to organize your code into logical units and share it with others. Julia's macro system allows you to extend the language with custom syntax and transform code at compile time, making it easier to write concise and expressive code. Overall, Julia's functions, type system, multiple dispatch, and support for code organization and macros make it a powerful and flexible language for a wide range of programming tasks.

In the next chapter, we will delve deeper into Julia's key features and data structures. We will learn about arrays, mapping values to keys, and tuples. We will also explore broadcasting and module subtyping in Julia. Finally, we will learn how to integrate Julia with Python and R and use these languages with Julia packages.

Questions

1. How do you define and call functions in Julia? What are the different types of arguments that you can use, and how do you handle optional and keyword arguments?
2. How does Julia's type system work, and how can you define and work with composite types, immutable values, and mutable values?
3. What is multiple dispatch, and how does it work in Julia? How can you use it to define functions that behave differently depending on the types of their arguments?
4. How can you organize your code in Julia using modules and packages? How do you import and use code from other modules and packages, and how can you define and use your own modules and packages?
5. What are macros in Julia, and how do they work? How can you use macros to extend the language with custom syntax and transform code at compile time?

CHAPTER 4

Data Structures in Julia

Introduction

Julia is a high-level, high-performance programming language for technical computing, with syntax that is familiar to users of other technical computing environments. Julia is particularly well-suited to data manipulation and numerical analysis and has a number of built-in data structures that make it easy to work with large amounts of data efficiently. One of the most basic and useful data structures in Julia is the array. An array is an ordered collection of values: all of which must be of the same type. Arrays can be one-dimensional (vectors) or multi-dimensional (matrices). Julia provides a number of functions for creating and manipulating arrays, including functions for indexing, slicing, and reshaping arrays. Another common data structure in Julia is the tuple. A tuple is an immutable sequence of values, similar to an array, but unlike an array, the values in a tuple can be of different types. Tuples are often used to store small amounts of related data and are particularly useful for returning multiple values from a function. Julia has a data structure called a dictionary, which is similar to an array, but instead of being indexed by a numerical position, the values in a dictionary are indexed by a key. This makes it easier to store and retrieve data by name, rather than by position. Dictionaries are often used to store data in a more structured way or to store data that is not easily represented as an array.

Structure

In this chapter, the following topics will be covered:

- Arrays in Julia
- Tuple data structure in Julia
- Mapping value to its keys
- Operations on arrays
- Example with module subtyping
- Integrating with Python and R

Arrays in Julia

Arrays are ordered collections of elements that can be of any type and are indexed using integers. They are similar to lists in other programming languages and are often used to store and manipulate large amounts of data efficiently. Arrays are ordered collections of elements of the same type. They are indexed starting at 1 and are very efficient for mathematical operations and indexing. In other programming languages, arrays start from 0. To create an array, we can use the [ ] syntax and separate the elements with a comma. For example,

```
julia> numbers = [1, 2, 3, 4, 5]
5-element Array{Int64,1}:
1
2
3
4
5
julia> names = ["Alice", "Bob", "Charlie", "Daisy"]
4-element Array{String,1}:
"Alice"
"Bob"
"Charlie"
"Daisy"
julia> mixed = [1, "Bob", 3.14, true]
4-element Array{Any,1}:
1
```

```
"Bob"
3.14
true
```

You can access the elements of an array using the indexing operator ([]). The indexing operator is used to fetch a specific item in the array. The indexing starts from 1 for the first element and goes up to n for the nth element, where n is the number of items in the array.

```
julia> numbers = [1, 2, 3, 4, 5]
5-element Array{Int64,1}:
1
2
3
4
5
julia> numbers[1] # returns 1 (the first element)
1
julia> numbers[3] # returns 3 (the third element)
3
julia> numbers[end] # returns 5 (the last element)
5
julia> numbers[end-1] # returns 4 (the second last element)
4
```

You can also use slicing to access a range of items in the array. The syntax for slicing is **`array_name[start:stop]`**, where start is the index of the first item and stop is the index of the item just after the last item.

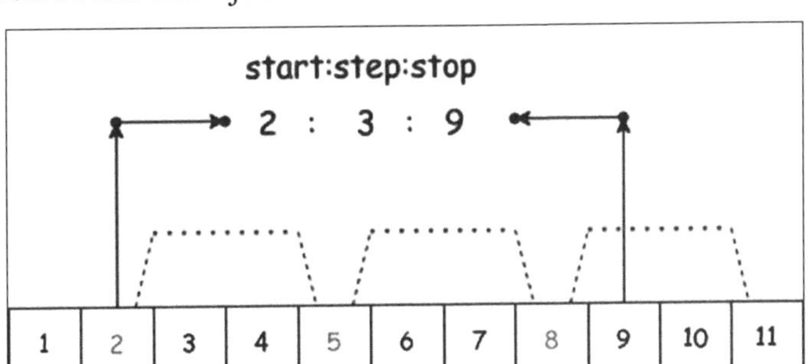

Figure 4.1: *The parameters of the collect function or array indexing - start, step, stop*

```
julia> numbers = [1, 2, 3, 4, 5] # Vector is a 1-dimensional Array, so
when we write Vector{Int} it is a shorthand to Array{Int, 1}. In new
Julia versions, Vector{Int} will show by default

5-element Array{Int64,1}:

1

2

3

4

5

julia> numbers[2:3] # returns [2, 3, 4] (items at index 2, 3, and 4)
3-element Array{Int64,1}:

2

3

julia> numbers[2:4] # returns [2, 3, 4, 5] (items from index 2 to the
end) 4-element Array{Int64,1}:

2

3

4

julia> numbers[1:3] # returns [1, 2, 3] (items from the start to index
3) 3-element Array{Int64,1}:

1

2

3

julia> numbers[1:2:end] # returns [1, 3, 5] (all items with a step of 2)
3-element Array{Int64,1}:

1

3

5
```

You can also modify the elements of an array by assigning new values to them using the indexing operator.

```
julia> numbers = [1, 2, 3, 4, 5]

5-element Array{Int64,1}:

1

2

3
```

```
4

5
```

In Julia, collect is a function that creates an array by collecting the results of an iterator. The iterator can be any object that produces a sequence of values, such as a range, a channel, or a generator function.

```
julia> collect(1:5) # creates an array of the values 1, 2, 3, 4, 5
5-element Array{Int64,1}:

1

2

3

4

5

julia> collect(1:2:9) # creates an array of the values 1, 3, 5, 7, 9
5-element Array{Int64,1}:

1

3

5

7

9

julia> collect("hello")

5-element Vector{Char}:

'h': ASCII/Unicode U+0068 (category Ll: Letter, lowercase)

'e': ASCII/Unicode U+0065 (category Ll: Letter, lowercase)

'l': ASCII/Unicode U+006C (category Ll: Letter, lowercase)

'l': ASCII/Unicode U+006C (category Ll: Letter, lowercase)

'o': ASCII/Unicode U+006F (category Ll: Letter, lowercase)
```

The collect function is often used in combination with other functions that generate sequences of values, such as map, filter, and reduce.

```
julia> collect(map(x -> 2x+1, 1:5)) # creates an array of the values 3,
5, 7, 9, 11 5-element Array{Int64,1}:

3

5

7

9
```

```
11

julia> using Primes

julia> collect(filter(isprime, 1:10)) # creates an array of the prime
numbers between 1 and 10

4-element Array{Int64,1}:

2

3

5

7

julia> collect(reduce(*, 1:5)) # creates an array with the result of the
cumulative product of 1, 2, 3, 4, 5

0-dimensional Array{Int64, 0}:

120
```

We will learn more about the map, reduce and filter functions later in this chapter.

You can also use the length function to get the number of elements in an array. For a one dimensional array, length returns the size of the array along the first dimension. For a multi-dimensional array, length returns the size of the array along the first dimension.

```
julia> a = [1, 2, 3, 4, 5]

5-element Array{Int64,1}:

1

2

3

4

5

julia> length(a)

5

julia> b = [1 2; 3 4]

2×2 Matrix{Int64}:

1 2

3 4

julia> length(b)

4
```

```
julia> c = [1 2 3; 4 5 6]
2×3 Array{Int64,2}:
1 2 3
4 5 6
julia> length(c)
6
```

In Julia, you can use the size function to get the dimensions of an array. The size function returns a tuple of integers that represent the size of the array along each dimension.

```
julia> a = [1, 2, 3, 4, 5]
5-element Array{Int64,1}:
1
2
3
4
5
julia> size(a)
(5,)
julia> b = [1 2; 3 4]
2×2 Array{Int64,2}:
1 2
3 4
julia> size(b)
(2, 2)
julia> c = [1 2 3; 4 5 6]
2×3 Array{Int64,2}:
1 2 3
4 5 6
julia> size(c)
(2, 3)
```

We learned that the **size()** function returns a tuple. But what is a tuple? Let us learn about tuples data structure in the next section.

Tuple Data Structure in Julia

Tuples are also ordered collections of elements, but unlike arrays, the elements of a tuple cannot be modified. Tuples are often used to store small amounts of data that are not meant to be modified, such as the coordinates of a point. Tuples are also ordered collections of elements, but they can contain elements of different types. They are indexed starting at 1 and are often used to return multiple values from a function. To create a tuple, we can use the `()` syntax and separate the elements with a comma. For example,

```
julia> t = (1, "hello", 2.0)
(1, "hello", 2.0)
julia> typeof(t)
Tuple{Int64, String, Float64}
```

In Julia, a tuple is a fixed-size collection of items of different types. Tuples are similar to arrays, but they are immutable, which means that you cannot modify the values of the items once the tuple has been created.

To create a tuple in Julia, you can use the (...) syntax

```
julia> t = (1, 2, 3)
(1, 2, 3)
julia> t = ("Alice", "Bob", "Charlie")
("Alice", "Bob", "Charlie")
julia> t = (1, "Bob", 3.14, true)
(1, "Bob", 3.14, true)
```

You can access the elements of a tuple using the indexing operator **`([]).`** The indexing operator is used to fetch a specific item in the tuple. The indexing starts from 1 for the first element and goes up to n for the nth element, where n is the number of items in the tuple.

```
julia> t = (1, 2, 3)
(1, 2, 3)
julia> t[1] # returns 1 (the first element)
1
julia> t[3] # returns 3 (the third element)
3
julia> t[end] # returns 3 (the last element)
```

```
3
julia> t[end-1] # returns 2 (the second last element)
2
```

You can also use slicing to access a range of items in the tuple. The syntax for slicing is **`tuple_name[start:step:stop]`,** where start is the index of the first item, stop is the index of the item just after the last item, and step is the gap between the first and the next item.

```
julia> t = (1, 2, 3, 4, 5)
(1, 2, 3, 4, 5)
julia> t[2:4] # returns (2, 3, 4) (items at index 2, 3, and 4)
(2, 3, 4)
julia> t[2:5] # returns (2, 3, 4, 5) (items from index 2 to the
end) (2, 3, 4, 5)
julia> t[:3] # returns (1, 2, 3) (items from the start to index 3) 3
julia> t[1:2:end] # returns (1, 3, 5) (all items with a step of 2)
(1, 3, 5)
```

The immutable property of tuples makes them useful in situations where you want to store a set of values that should not be modified, such as in function arguments or as keys in a dictionary.

Since tuples are immutable, you cannot use the indexing operator (`[]`) to assign new values to the items in a tuple. If you try to do so, Julia will raise an error.

```
julia> t = (1, 2, 3)
(1, 2, 3)
julia> t[1] = 4
ERROR: MethodError: no method matching setindex!(::Tuple{Int64, Int64,
Int64}, ::Int64, ::Int64)
Stacktrace:
[1] top-level scope
@ REPL[26]:1
julia> t[2] = 5
ERROR: MethodError: no method matching setindex!(::Tuple{Int64, Int64,
Int64}, ::Int64, ::Int64)
Stacktrace:
[1] top-level scope
```

```
@ REPL[27]:1
```

Since tuples are immutable, you cannot modify the values of the items once the tuple has been created. However, you can create a new tuple with the modified values.

```
julia> t = (1, 2, 3)

(1, 2, 3)

julia> t = (4, t[2], t[3]) # creates a new tuple with the first element
modified (4, 2, 3)

julia> t = (t[1], 5, t[3]) # creates a new tuple with the second element
modified (4, 5, 3)

julia> t = (t[1], t[2], 6) # creates a new tuple with the third element
modified (4, 5, 6)
```

In Julia, tuples and arrays are two distinct data types that serve different purposes.

Tuples are similar to tuples in Python in that they are immutable and can contain a variety of elements with different types. They are often used to group together a fixed number of items that have some logical relationship. For example, you might use a tuple to represent the coordinates of a point in three-dimensional space as (x, y, z).

Arrays, on the other hand, are used to store collections of values that are all of the same type. They are more efficient for certain operations than tuples because the elements of an array are stored contiguously in memory, which can make them faster to access. However, arrays are mutable, which means that you can change the values of the elements after the array is created.

So, the main benefit of using tuples instead of arrays in Julia is that they are immutable, which can be useful if you want to ensure that the values of the elements cannot be changed after the tuple is created. However, this comes at the cost of not being able to take advantage of the performance benefits of arrays for certain operations. Whether to use tuples or arrays will depend on the specific needs of your program.

In Julia, a **`NamedTuple`** is a subclass of a Tuple that allows you to access elements of the tuple using names rather than indices. This can make your code more readable and easier to understand because the names of the elements provide a natural way to describe what the elements represent.

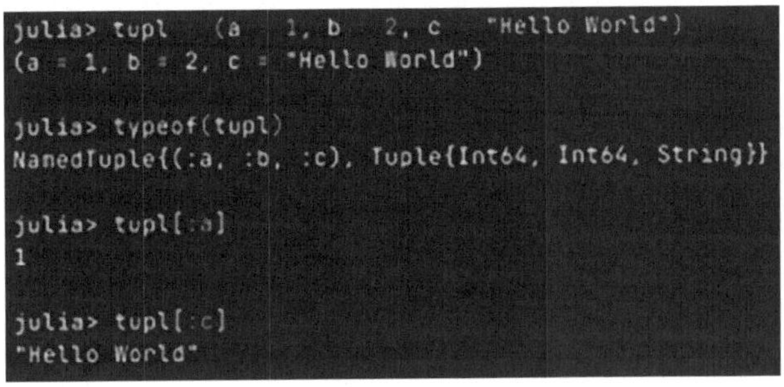

Figure 4.2:

Mapping Value to its Keys

Dictionaries are unordered collections of key-value pairs. The keys in a dictionary must be unique and are used to access the associated values. Dictionaries are often used to store data that needs to be quickly retrieved using a specific key. They are not ordered and are often used for efficient lookup and insertion of data. To create a dictionary, we can use the **`Dict()`** function and pass in pairs of keys and values. For example,

```
julia> d = Dict("a" => 1, "b" => 2, "c" => 3)
Dict{String,Int64} with 3 entries:
  "a" => 1
  "b" => 2
  "c" => 3
```

You can also create a dictionary using the **`Dict`** constructor and a list of key-value tuples.

```
julia> my_dict = Dict([("a", 1), ("b", 2), ("c", 3)])
Dict{String,Int64} with 3 entries:
"b" => 2
"a" => 1
"c" => 3
```

To access the value for a given key, you can use the get function or indexing syntax `julia> my_dict["a"]`

```
1
julia> get(my_dict, "a", 0)
1
```

You can also use the **setindex!** function to add or update a key-value pair in the dictionary

```
julia> my_dict["d"] = 4
4
julia> my_dict
Dict{String,Int64} with 4 entries:
  "b" => 2
  "a" => 1
  "c" => 3
  "d" => 4
```

In Julia, the type of a Dict object is parameterized by the types of keys and values it contains. For example, the type of a Dict that maps strings to integers is **Dict{String, Int64},** and the type of a Dict that maps symbols to floating-point numbers is **Dict{Symbol, Float64}.**

You can create a **Dict** with specific key and value types using the **Dict** constructor and the Pair type.

```
julia> my_dict = Dict{String, Int64}(Pair("a", 1), Pair("b", 2),
Pair("c", 3))
Dict{String,Int64} with 3 entries:
"b" => 2
"a" => 1
"c" => 3
```

You can also use the **keytype()** and **valuetype()** functions to get the key and value types of a **Dict** object.

```
julia> keytype(my_dict)
String
julia> valtype(my_dict)
Int64
```

Keep in mind that the keys in a Dict must be unique and are typically of a type that supports comparison (e.g. Int64, String, etc.), while the values can be of any type.

In Julia, the keys and values functions can be used to get the keys and values of a Dict object, respectively.

For example, given a dictionary **my_dict**

```
julia> my_dict = Dict("a" => 1, "b" => 2, "c" => 3)
Dict{String,Int64} with 3 entries:
  "b" => 2
  "a" => 1
  "c" => 3
```

You can use keys and values as follows:

```
julia> keys(my_dict)
Base.KeySet for a Dict{String,Int64} with 3 entries. Keys: "b" "a"
"c"

julia> values(my_dict)
Base.ValueIterator for a Dict{String,Int64} with 3 entries. Values: 2 1
3
```

The keys function returns a **KeySet** object, a collection of the keys in the dictionary. The values function returns a **ValueIterator** object, which is an iterator over the values in the dictionary.

You can convert the output of these functions to an array using the collect function:

```
julia> collect(keys(my_dict))
3-element Array{String,1}:
"b"
"a"
"c"
julia> collect(values(my_dict))
3-element Array{Int64,1}:
2
1
3
```

In Julia, the Dict type is implemented using a hash table, which is a data structure that allows for efficient insertion, deletion, and lookup of key-value pairs.

A hash table consists of an array of **buckets**, each of which can store a single key-value pair. When a key-value pair is added to the hash table, a **hash function** is used to map the key to a specific bucket in the array. The hash function ensures that keys are distributed evenly among the buckets so that most operations on the hash table have an average-case time complexity of **O(1)** (i.e. constant time).

When a key is looked up in the hash table, the hash function is used to find the appropriate bucket, and then the key is compared to the key in the bucket. If the keys match, the value is returned; if the keys do not match, the hash table must search for the key in the other buckets. In the worst case, the hash table must search all the buckets, resulting in a time complexity of **O(n)** (i.e. linear time). However, in practice, hash tables have a low worst-case time complexity due to the use of a good hash function and techniques such as **chaining** to handle collisions (i.e. when two keys are mapped to the same bucket).

In Julia, you can use a generator expression to create a dictionary from an iterable.

A generator expression is similar to a list comprehension, but it returns a generator object that produces the values one at a time, rather than creating a new list. This can be more efficient if you only need to iterate over the values once, or if the values take up a lot of memory.

Here's an example of how to create a dictionary using a generator expression:

```
julia> my_dict = Dict((i, i^2) for i in 1:5)

Dict{Int64,Int64} with 5 entries:

5 => 25

4 => 16

3 => 9

2 => 4

1 => 1
```

This creates a dictionary with keys 1, 2, 3, 4, and 5, and values 1, 4, 9, 16, and 25, respectively.

You can also use a generator expression to create a dictionary from an existing dictionary, by specifying a key-value pair for each element in the dictionary:

```
julia> my_dict = Dict((“a” => 1, “b” => 2, “c” => 3))

Dict{String,Int64} with 3 entries:

  “b” => 2

  “a” => 1

  “c” => 3

julia> new_dict = Dict((k, v + 1) for (k, v) in my_dict)
```

```
Dict{String,Int64} with 3 entries:
  "b" => 3
  "a" => 2
  "c" => 4
```

In Julia, the Dict type provides several functions for working with dictionaries. Here is a summary of some of the most commonly used functions:

- **`haskey(dict, key)`**: Returns true if dict has a key **`key`**, and false otherwise.
- **`get(dict, key, default)`**: Returns the value for key in dict, or default if key is not in dict.
- **`pop(dict, key, default)`**: Removes the key-value pair with key **`key`** from dict, and returns the value. If key is not in dict, returns default.
- **`delete!(dict, key)`**: Removes the key-value pair with key **`key`** from dict. Returns nothing.
- **`merge(dict1, dict2)`**: Returns a new dictionary that combines the key-value pairs from **`dict1`** and **`dict2`**. If a key is present in both dictionaries, the value from dict2 is used.
- **`merge!(dict1, dict2)`**: Updates dict1 with the key-value pairs from **`dict2`**. If a key is present in both dictionaries, the value from **`dict2`** is used. Returns nothing.
- **`mergeWith(f, dict1, dict2`**): Returns a new dictionary that combines the key-value pairs from **`dict1`** and **`dict2`**, using the function f to combine the values for keys that are present in both dictionaries.

Here's an example of how you can use some of these functions:

```
julia> my_dict = Dict("a" => 1, "b" => 2, "c" => 3)
Dict{String,Int64} with 3 entries:
  "b" => 2
  "a" => 1
  "c" => 3
julia> haskey(my_dict, "a")
true
julia> get(my_dict, "a", 0)
1
julia> pop!(my_dict, "a", 0)
1
```

```
julia> my_dict
Dict{String,Int64} with 2 entries:
  "b" => 2
  "c" => 3
julia> delete!(my_dict, "b")
julia> my_dict
Dict{String,Int64} with 1 entry:
  "c" => 3
julia> merge(my_dict, Dict("a" => 1, "d" =>
4))
Dict{String,Int64} with 3 entries:
  "d" => 4
  "a" => 1
  "c" => 3
julia> merge!(my_dict, Dict("a" => 1, "d" =>
4))
Dict{String,Int64} with 3 entries:
  "d" => 4
  "a" => 1
  "c" => 3
julia> mergewith(+, my_dict, Dict("a" => 1, "c" => 4))
Dict{String,Int64} with 3 entries:
  "d" => 4
  "a" => 2
  "c" => 7
```

Set Data Structure in Julia

In Julia, a Set is an unordered collection of unique elements. You can use a Set to store and manipulate data in a way that is similar to a Dict but without the key-value pairs.

Here's an example of how to create a Set in Julia:

```
julia> my_set = Set([1, 2, 3, 4, 4, 5])
Set([4, 5, 2, 3, 1])
```

This creates a **Set** with elements 1, 2, 3, 4, and 5. Note that the duplicate element 4 is only included once in the Set.

You can use the **union**, **intersect**, and **setdiff** functions to perform set operations on Set objects:

```
julia> set1 = Set([1, 2, 3])
Set([3, 2, 1])
julia> set2 = Set([3, 4, 5])
Set([5, 4, 3])
julia> union(set1, set2)
Set([5, 4, 3, 2, 1])
julia> intersect(set1, set2)
Set([3])
julia> setdiff(set1, set2)
Set([2, 1])
```

You can also use the push! and pop! functions to add and remove elements from a Set:

```
julia> push!(set1, 4)
Set([4, 3, 2, 1])
julia> pop!(set1)
4
julia> set1
Set([3, 2, 1])
```

Operations on Julia's Data Structures

Julia provides a number of built-in data structures that you can use to store and manipulate data. Here is a summary of some common operations that you can perform on Julia's data structures:

Arrays

- Indexing: You can access the elements of an array using indexing syntax. For example, **arr[i]** returns the **i**-th element of the array arr.
- Slicing: You can use slicing syntax to get a subarray of an array. For example, **arr[i:j]** returns a subarray of arr that starts at index i and ends at index j-1.

- Modification: You can modify the elements of an array using indexing syntax and assignment. For example, **`arr[i] = x`** sets the **`i`**-th element of arr to x.
- Concatenation: You can use the vcat function to concatenate two arrays vertically (i.e. stack them on top of each other), or the hcat function to concatenate them horizontally (i.e. join them side by side).
- Elementwise operations: You can use the .+, .-, .*, and ./ operators to perform elementwise operations on arrays. For example, **`arr1 .+ arr2`** adds the corresponding elements of **`arr1`** and **`arr2`** elementwise.

Tuples

- **Indexing:** You can access the elements of a tuple using indexing syntax. For example, **`tup[i]`** returns the **`i`**-th element of the tuple tup.
- **Modification**: Tuples are immutable, which means that you cannot modify their elements. However, you can create a new tuple with modified elements by
    - concatenating the original tuple with the modified elements.
- **Concatenation:** You can use the cat function to concatenate two tuples.

Dictionaries

- **Indexing**: You can access the value for a given key in a dictionary using indexing syntax. For example, **`dict[key]`** returns the value for key in dict.
- **Concatenation**: You can use the merge or merge! functions to combine two dictionaries.
- **Elementwise operations:** You can use the map function to apply a function to the values in a dictionary, or the **`mergewith`** function to combine the values of two dictionaries elementwise using a function.
- **Membership**: You can use the haskey function to check if a key is in a dictionary. For example, **`haskey(dict, key)`** returns true if key is in the dictionary **`dict`**, and false otherwise.
- **Addition and removal:** You can use the **`setindex!`** and delete! functions to add and remove key-value pairs from a dictionary. For example, **`dict[key] = value`** adds the key value pair

Sets

- **Membership**: You can use the in operator to check if an element is in a set. For example, x in the set returns true if x is in the set **`set`**, and false otherwise.

- **Addition and removal**: You can use the push! and pop! functions to add and remove elements from a set. For example, `push!(set, x)` adds x to the set `set`, and `pop!(set)` removes an arbitrary element from the set.
- **Set operations**: You can use the union, intersect, and setdiff functions to perform set operations. For example, `union(set1, set2)` returns a new set that contains the elements that are in either set1 or set2, and `intersect(set1, set2)` returns a new set that contains the elements that are in both set1 and set2.

Apart from these operations that are only specific to particular data structures, there are four common operations that we will learn in more detail.

Map

In Julia, the map function applies a function to each element of an iterable and returns a new iterable with the results. The type of the returned iterable depends on the type of the input iterable.

For example, given a function f and an array **arr**, you can use the map as follows:

```
julia> f(x) = x^2
f (generic function with 1 method)
julia> arr = [1, 2, 3, 4]
4-element Array{Int64,1}:
 1
 2
 3
 4
julia> map(f, arr)
4-element Array{Int64,1}:
 1
 4
 9
 16
```

This applies the function f to each element of arr and returns a new array with the results. You can use the map with other types of iterables as well, such as tuples:

```
julia> tup = (1, 2, 3, 4)
```

```
(1, 2, 3, 4)
julia> map(f, tup)
(1, 4, 9, 16)
```

Reduce

In Julia, the reduce function applies a function to the elements of an iterable, reducing the iterable to a single value. The type of the returned value depends on the type of input iterable and the function being applied.

For example, given a function **f** and an array **arr**, you can use reduce as follows:

```
julia> f(x, y) = x + y
f (generic function with 1 method)
julia> arr = [1, 2, 3, 4]
4-element Array{Int64,1}:
 1
 2
 3
 4
julia> reduce(f, arr)
10
```

This applies the function f to the elements of arr in a way that reduces the array to a single value. In this case, the function f adds the elements of arr together, so the final result is 10.

You can use reduce with other types of iterables as well, such as tuples and sets:

```
julia> tup = (1, 2, 3, 4)
(1, 2, 3, 4)
julia> reduce(f, tup)
10
julia> set = Set([1, 2, 3, 4])
Set([4, 3, 2, 1])
julia> reduce(f, set)
10
```

Filter

In Julia, the filter function applies a function to the elements of an iterable and returns a new iterable with only the elements for which the function returns true. The type of the returned iterable depends on the type of the input iterable.

For example, given a function f and an array arr, you can use the filter as follows:

```
julia> f(x) = x % 2 == 0
f (generic function with 1 method)
julia> arr = [1, 2, 3, 4, 5]
5-element Array{Int64,1}:
 1
 2
 3
 4
 5
julia> filter(f, arr)
2-element Array{Int64,1}:
 2
 4
```

This applies the function `f` to each element of `arr` and returns a new array with only the elements for which `f` returns true. In this case, `f` returns true for even numbers, so the returned array contains even elements of arr.

You can use a filter with other types of iterables as well, such as tuples and sets:

```
julia> tup = (1, 2, 3, 4, 5)
(1, 2, 3, 4, 5)
julia> filter(f, tup)
(2, 4)
julia> set = Set([1, 2, 3, 4, 5])
Set([5, 4, 3, 2, 1])
julia> filter(f, set)
Set{Int64} with 2 elements:
4
2
```

Broadcasting

In Julia, broadcasting is the process of applying a function to each element of an array or other iterable in a way that is similar to element-wise operations. You can use the . operator to broadcast a function over an array or other iterable.

For example, given a function **f** and array **arr**, you can use broadcasting as follows:

```
julia> f(x) = x^2
f (generic function with 1 method)
julia> arr = [1, 2, 3, 4]
4-element Array{Int64,1}:
 1
 2
 3
 4
julia> f.(arr)
4-element Array{Int64,1}:
 1
 4
 9
 16
```

This applies the function **f** to each element of **arr** and returns a new array with the results.

You can use broadcasting with other types of iterables as well, such as tuples, sets, and dictionaries:

```
julia> tup = (1, 2, 3, 4)
(1, 2, 3, 4)
julia> f.(tup)
(1, 4, 9, 16)
julia> set = Set([1, 2, 3, 4])
Set([4, 3, 2, 1])
julia> f.(set)
Set([16, 9, 4, 1])
```

Broadcasting over dictionaries and NamedTuples is reserved.

We can use various modules in Julia or other languages to write code in Julia. First, let us learn how to use various modules and sub-modules to write code in Julia.

Example of Module Subtyping

In Julia, module subtyping is a way to define a subtype relationship between two modules. This is similar to subtyping in object-oriented programming, where a subtype is a type that is derived from another type (the supertype) and is considered to be a more specific version of the supertype.

Module subtyping in Julia is implemented using the <: operator, which is used to specify that one module is a subtype of another. For example,

```
module A

end

module B <: A

end
```

Here, B is a subtype of A. This means that any function or method that expects an A can also accept a B.

Module subtyping is often used to create a hierarchy of types, where each module represents a more specific version of the type defined by its supertype. This can be useful for creating APIs or for organizing code in a logical and reusable way.

```
julia> module M

import InteractiveUtils: subtypes

export Foo, Bar, f

abstract type Super end

struct Foo <: Super end

struct Bar <: Super end

const FooConst = 1

const BarConst = 2

for T in subtypes(Super)

@eval f(::Type{$T}) = $(Symbol(nameof(T), "Const")) end

end # module

Main.M
```

```
julia> using .M; f(Foo)
1
julia> f(Bar)
2
```

In this example, the `M` module defines an abstract type called **`Super`**, and two concrete types **`Foo`** and **`Bar`** that are subtypes of **`Super`.** It also defines two constants **`FooConst`** and **`BarConst`,** and a function **`f`** that takes a type parameter **`T`** that is a subtype of **`Super`**.

Inside the module, the subtypes function is used to get a list of all subtypes of Super. Then, a loop iterates over this list and generates code to define the behavior of the `f` function for each subtype. The **`@eval`** macro is used to evaluate this code at runtime.

The code generated by the loop is equivalent to the following:

```
function f(::Type{Foo})
return FooConst
end
function f(::Type{Bar})
return BarConst
end
```

Therefore, when **`f(Foo)`** is called, it returns the value of **`FooConst`,** which is 1. Similarly, when **`f(Bar)`** is called, it returns the value of **`BarConst`,** which is 2.

We can use various modules to create a child/sub-module in Julia which contains the specific functionalities of the parent modules. We can use various modules/ packages from other languages to write code in Julia.

Integrating with Python

There are several ways to integrate Julia with packages from other languages:

- **RCall and PyCall**: These are Julia packages that allow you to call R and Python code from Julia, respectively. To use these packages, you will need to have R or Python installed on your system.
- **Cxx.jl:** This is a Julia package that allows you to call C++ code from Julia. To use this package, you will need to have a C++ compiler installed on your system.

- **FFI.jl:** This is a Julia package that allows you to call foreign functions (i.e., functions written in languages other than Julia) using Julia's foreign function interface (FFI). To use this package, you will need to have the development files (e.g., headers) for the foreign language installed on your system.
- **Using Julia as a bridge between languages:** Another option is to use Julia as a bridge between the languages you want to use. For example, you could use PyCall to call Python code from Julia, and then use RCall to call R code from Julia. This can be a useful way to integrate packages from multiple languages.

We will learn about integrating Python and R libraries in Julia. There are several ways to integrate Python and Julia. Here are a few options:

Use the **`PyCall`** package to call Python functions and use Python libraries directly from Julia. **`PyCall`** provides a simple, high-level interface for calling Python functions and using Python libraries from Julia.

```
julia> using PyCall

# Evaluate a Python expression and capture the result

julia> py"2 + 2"

4
```

PyCall is a package for Julia that allows you to call Python code from Julia. To use PyCall, you will first need to have Python installed on your system. There are a few reasons why you want to use PyCall to call Python functions from Julia:

- You may have an existing Python code that you want to use in a Julia project. PyCall allows you to use this code without the need to rewrite it in Julia.
- Some Python libraries have functionality that is not available in Julia. By using PyCall, you can access these libraries and use their functions from within Julia.
- You may find that some Python libraries are easier to use or more efficient than their Julia counterparts. In this case, PyCall allows you to take advantage of these libraries from within Julia.
- Some Python libraries have functionality that is not yet available in Julia. By using PyCall, you can use these libraries and their functions as a temporary workaround until the functionality is implemented in Julia.

```
julia> using PyCall

# Call a Python function

julia> @pyimport math
```

```
julia> println(math.sin(math.pi / 2))
1.0
# Use a Python library
julia> @pyimport numpy as np
julia> a = np.array([1, 2, 3])
julia> println(a .+ 1)
[2, 3, 4]
# Define the Python function
julia> @pyimport math
julia> function py_sin(x)
return math.sin(x)
end
# Call the Python function from Julia
julia> julia_sin(x) = py_sin(x)
julia> julia_sin(math.pi/2)
1.0
```

Use the PyPlot package to use the Matplotlib library for plotting from Julia. **PyPlot** is a Julia interface to Matplotlib, a popular plotting library for Python (see *Figure 4.2*).

```
julia> using PyPlot
julia> x = range(0, 2*pi, 100)
0.0:0.06346651825433926:6.283185307179586
julia> plot(x)
1-element Vector{PyObject}:
 PyObject <matplotlib.lines.Line2D object at 0x7f7ea90c2d00>
```

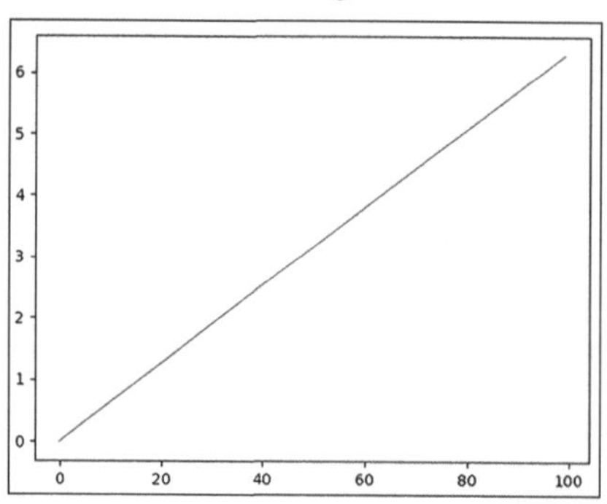

Figure 4.3: *Plotting the values of x on the scale*

Use the **Conda** package to create a Conda environment and run Python code within it from Julia. This can be useful if you need to use specific versions of Python libraries that are not available in the default Python installation.

```
julia> using Conda
julia> Conda.runconda(`create -y --name pyenv numpy`)
[ Info: Running `conda create -y --name pyenv numpy` in root
environment Collecting package metadata (current_repodata.json): done
Solving environment: done
julia> Conda.add("numpy")
[ Info: Running `conda install -y numpy` in root environment
Collecting package metadata (current_repodata.json): done
Solving environment: done
```

The activate and run various python commands in the conda environment. For more details refer to https://github.com/JuliaPy/Conda.jl. We mostly use the PyCall package as it is easy to use.

Integrating with R

RCall is a package for Julia that allows you to call the R code from Julia. To use RCall, you will first need to have R installed on your system. Here are a few reasons why you want to use RCall to call R functions from Julia:

- You may have an existing R code that you want to use in a Julia project. RCall allows you to use this code without the need to rewrite it in Julia.
- Some R libraries have functionality that is not available in Julia. By using RCall, you can access these libraries and use their functions from within Julia.
- You may find that some R libraries are easier to use or more efficient than their Julia counterparts. In this case, RCall allows you to take advantage of these libraries from within Julia.
- Some R libraries have functionality that is not yet available in Julia. By using RCall, you can use these libraries and their functions as a temporary workaround until the functionality is implemented in Julia.

Before installing its own copy of R, the RCall build script, triggered by **Pkg.add**, will check for an existing R installation in the following order:

1. The **R_HOME** environment variable, if set, is checked as the location of the R home directory.

2. The **R HOME** command is run, assuming R is in the PATH.
3. On Windows, the Windows registry is checked.
4. If no existing installation is found, the **r-base** package is installed.

It is important to set the **R_HOME** environment variable or run the R HOME command if R is installed in a non-standard location before adding the RCall package to avoid installation of another copy of R which may not be intended.

To specify the R installation to be used by RCall, set the **R_HOME** environment variable and run **Pkg.build("RCall").** Then, RCall will remember this location for future updates, so you don't have to set **R_HOME** permanently. Here is an example of how to set **R_HOME** to a specific installation of R:

```
ENV["R_HOME"] = "/usr/local/Cellar/r/3.6.1/lib/R"
ENV["PATH"] = "....directory of R executable..."
Pkg.build("RCall")
```

You can also set the **R_EXE** environment variable to the path of the R executable if it's not in your system's PATH.

```
ENV["R_EXE"] = "/usr/local/Cellar/r/3.6.1/bin/R"
```

Keep in mind that you will need to restart Julia after setting these environment variables to take effect.

```
julia> using RCall
# Evaluate an R expression and capture the result
julia> r"2 + 2"
4
```

Conclusion

Arrays, tuples, and named tuples are basic data structures in Julia that are used to store and manipulate collections of data. Arrays are indexable and mutable, tuples are immutable, and named tuples are a subclass of tuples that have named fields. Sets are collections of unique elements, and dictionaries are key-value pairs.

Module subtyping is a feature in Julia that allows users to define new subtypes of existing types, while still inheriting the behavior and properties of the parent type. This allows for more flexibility and modularity in code development.

Julia has strong integration with both Python and R, making it easy to use functions and packages from these languages within Julia. This allows Julia to tap into the vast ecosystems of both Python and R and makes it a powerful tool for data analysis and scientific computing. Overall, Julia offers a wide range of data structures and features that make it a useful language for a variety of applications.

In the next chapter, we will cover a variety of topics related to working with data in Julia. This will include getting and inspecting data, working with numerical data, working with textual data, working with temporal data, and handling data in general.

Questions

1. How do arrays, tuples, and named tuples differ in terms of their properties and uses in Julia?
2. How can sets be used to store and manipulate unique elements in Julia?
3. How do dictionaries allow users to store and retrieve data by key in Julia?
4. How does module subtyping work in Julia, and what are some use cases for it?
5. How can Julia be integrated with Python and R, and what are some benefits of this integration?
6. How can arrays, tuples, and dictionaries be used to store and manipulate data in Julia?
7. How do named tuples differ from regular tuples in Julia, and when might they be preferred?
8. How can sets be used to efficiently perform common set operations, such as union and intersection, in Julia?
9. What are some best practices for handling data in general in Julia, such as cleaning and preprocessing data?
10. How can module subtyping be used to create new subtypes of existing types in Julia, and what are some benefits of this approach?

Chapter 5
Working With Datasets In Julia

Introduction

In this chapter, we will cover the following topics: Getting and inspecting data, working with numerical data, working with textual data, working with temporal data, and handling data. We will start by discussing how to acquire and examine data, including methods for identifying and dealing with missing or inaccurate data. The quality and relevance of the data will determine the accuracy and credibility of the analysis and insights, having clean, relevant, and accurate data can help ensure that the results of the analysis are reliable, and combining data from multiple sources can provide a completer and more accurate picture of the situation and the ability to acquire data in real-time allows for faster decision making and improved efficiency. It is essential to inspect the data to identify any issues or patterns that may affect the accuracy and reliability of the analysis. Additionally, it helps to identify any data preprocessing as well as cleaning that may be necessary and any assumptions or hypotheses that can be made about the data. Next, we will explore techniques for working with numerical data, including data cleaning, transformation, and visualization. We will also cover working with textual data, such as text preprocessing, tokenization, and feature extraction. We will then move on to working with temporal data, including handling time series data and working with date and time formats. Finally, we will discuss general best practices for handling data, including data storage and management, and ethical considerations.

Structure

In this chapter, the following topics are covered:

- Getting and inspecting data
- Working with
    - numerical data
    - textual data
    - temporal data
- A data science problem

Getting and Inspecting Data in Julia

Studying the methods of getting and inspecting data is important to ensure that we have high quality data that is accurate and relevant, to prepare the data for analysis, to acquire and inspect data efficiently, to gain better insights, and make better decisions. Studying the methods of getting and inspecting data is important for several reasons:

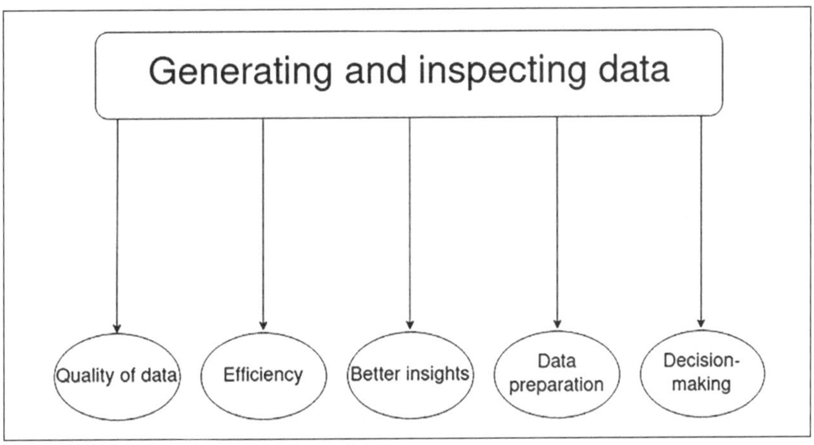

***Figure 5.1**: Generating and inspecting data*

- **Quality of data:** By studying the various methods of getting data, we can learn how to acquire high-quality data from trustworthy sources. This will ensure that the data used in our analysis is accurate and relevant, which in turn will improve the credibility and reliability of our analysis.
- **Data preparation:** Data inspection allows us to identify any issues or patterns in the data that may affect the accuracy and reliability of our analysis. Analyzing the different techniques of data inspection, we

will be able to identify and address these issues, such as cleaning and transforming the data, before we begin our analysis.

- **Efficiency:** Acquiring and inspecting data in an efficient manner is important for time sensitive tasks. By studying the different methods of getting and inspecting data, we can learn how to acquire and inspect data quickly and efficiently, which can be especially useful in real-time applications such as finance or healthcare.
- **Better insights:** We can learn how to integrate data from numerous sources by researching different approaches to getting and examining data. This can help us gain a more complete and accurate understanding of the situation at hand, and to identify patterns and trends that may not be apparent from a single data source.
- **Better decision-making:** The ability to acquire and inspect data effectively is crucial for any data-driven decision-making process. The ability to make informed decisions based on accurate, relevant, and trustworthy data can be gained by examining the techniques for obtaining and analyzing data.

Acquiring Data from Julia

Acquiring data is an essential aspect of data analysis because it forms the foundation of any data driven decision-making process. The quality and relevance of the data will determine the accuracy and credibility of the analysis and insights.

Having clean, relevant, and accurate data is essential to ensure that the results of the analysis are reliable. The data needs to be collected from trustworthy sources, and it should be cleaned, transformed, and formatted correctly to be ready for analysis.

Additionally, acquiring data from multiple sources can help to provide a completer and more accurate picture of the situation at hand. This can be especially useful when trying to understand complex systems or phenomena. For example, combining data from different sources such as surveys, social media, and sensor data can give a more comprehensive understanding of customer sentiment or environmental conditions.

Furthermore, the ability to acquire data in real-time allows for faster decision-making and improved efficiency. For example, in the field of finance, the ability to acquire stock prices in real time can help traders make more informed decisions. In healthcare, real-time monitoring of patient vital signs can help in early diagnosis and treatment.

There are several ways to get data in Julia. Some popular methods include:

- **Reading data from a file**: Reading data from a file in Julia is a common task in data analysis. Julia provides several built-in and external libraries that can be used to read data from a variety of file formats such as CSV, Excel, JSON, and more.
- Here are a few examples of how to read data from a file in Julia:
- **CSV files**: The most common file format for data is CSV (Comma Separated Values) format. The built-in Julia library **`CSV.jl`** can be used to read and write CSV files. The **`CSV.read()`** function is used to read a CSV file and returns a DataFrame object. Here is an example of how to read a CSV file:

```
using CSV
data = CSV.read("data.csv")
```

- **Excel files:** To read Excel files in Julia, we can use the package **`ExcelReaders.jl/Taro.jl/XLSX.jl`** which provides a simple and flexible way to read Excel files. Here is an example of how to read an Excel file using the package:

```
using ExcelReaders
data = readxl("data.xlsx", "Sheet1")
```

For example, **`readdlm("data.txt", ',')`** can be used to read a CSV file named **`data.txt`** and store it in a variable. Julia provides several built-in functions such as **`readdlm(), readcsv(), readtable(),`** etc. that can be used to read data from a file and store it in a variable.

- **JSON files:** The built-in Julia library **`JSON.jl`** can be used to read and write JSON files. The **`JSON.parse()`** function is used to parse a JSON file and returns a Dict object. Here is an example of how to read a JSON file:

```
using JSON
data = JSON.parsefile("data.json")
```

- Other file formats: Julia also provides built-in support for reading and writing other file formats such as HDF5, JLD, and more. Additionally, there are many external libraries available for reading specific file formats such as the package **`Feather.jl`** which provides support for reading feather files. **`Feather.jl`** is a package that is used for reading an older feather format, referred to as **`Feather v1`**. However, the current standard for feather format is **`Feather v2`**, which is based on the Apache Arrow format when it is written to disk. Therefore, if you need to read and write the current standard **`Feather v2`** format, you should use the package, **`Arrow.jl`** instead. **`Feather.jl`** only allows you to read feather v1 but not feather v2.

Columnar data, also known as columnar storage or columnar databases, is a method of organizing and storing data in a database or data storage system. In contrast to row-based storage, where data for each row is stored sequentially, columnar data storage stores data for each column together.

It is worth noting that when reading the data, you should ensure that the file path is correct, that the file exists and that it is accessible. Also, you may need to adjust the parameters of the functions to fit the specific format of the data you are reading.

- Scraping data from the web: Scraping data from the web is a process of extracting data from websites. In Julia, there are several libraries available for web scraping, such as **`HTTP.jl`, `WebIO.jl`, `Requests.jl`, `Gumbo.jl`** and **`Cascadia.jl`.** These libraries can be used to send HTTP requests, parse HTML and CSS, and extract data from web pages.

Here are a few examples of how to scrape data from the web in Julia:

- **`HTTP.jl`**: This library provides a low-level API for sending HTTP requests. It can be used to send GET, POST, PUT, and DELETE requests to the server and retrieve the response. Here is an example of how to use **`HTTP.jl`** to send a GET request and retrieve the HTML source code of a web page:

```
julia> r = HTTP.request("GET", "http://httpbin.org/ip")
HTTP.Messages.Response:
""""

HTTP/1.1 200 OK
Date: Wed, 23 Aug 2023 07:23:13 GMT
Content-Type: application/json
Content-Length: 32
Connection: keep-alive
Server: gunicorn/19.9.0
Access-Control-Allow-Origin: *
Access-Control-Allow-Credentials: true
{
"origin": "185.82.240.22"
}
""""

julia> println(r.status)
```

```
200
julia> println(String(r.body))
{
"origin": "1185.82.240.22"
}
```

- **Requests.jl**([DEPRECATED in favor of https://github.com/JuliaWeb/HTTP.jl]): This library provides a high-level API for sending HTTP requests. It simplifies the process of sending requests and handling responses. Here is an example of how to use Requests.jl to send a GET request and retrieve the HTML source code of a web page:

```
using Requests
response = get("https://example.com")
html_source = response.text
```

- **Gumbo.jl**(a Julia wrapper around Google's gumbo C library for parsing HTML) and Cascadia.jl(a CSS selector library in Julia): These libraries can be used to parse HTML and CSS and extract data from web pages. **Gumbo.jl** is a pure Julia implementation of the Gumbo HTML5 parser, while **Cascadia.jl** is a CSS selector library. Here is an example of how to use **Gumbo.jl** and **Cascadia.jl** to extract the text of all the links on a web page:

```
using Gumbo, Cascadia
html_source = """
<html>
<body>
<a href='https://example.com'>Example 1</a>
<a href='https://example.com'>Example 2</a>
</body>
</html>
"""
doc = parsehtml(html_source)
selector = CSSSelector("a")
links = selector.(doc)
link_texts = [link.text for link in links]
```

There are several libraries available for web scraping in Julia such as **HTTP.jl, Requests.jl, Gumbo.jl** and **Cascadia.jl.** These libraries can be used to send HTTP requests, parse HTML and CSS, and extract data from web pages. **HTTP.jl** is a low-level library for sending HTTP requests, **Requests.jl** is a high-level library that simplifies the process of sending requests and handling responses, **Gumbo.jl** is a pure Julia implementation of the Gumbo HTML5 parser, and **Cascadia.jl** is a CSS selector library.

Accessing Data from a Database

Accessing data from a database in Julia can be done using the JDBC package. JDBC (Java Database Connectivity) is a Java-based data access technology that enables Java programs to connect to a wide variety of relational databases and allows for executing SQL statements and managing database connections.

The JDBC package provides a Julia interface to the JDBC API, allowing Julia programs to connect to a database and execute SQL statements. To use the JDBC package, you must first install a JDBC driver for the database you want to connect to.

Here are a few examples of how to use the JDBC package to access data from a database in Julia:

- Connect to a database: To connect to a database, you need to provide the JDBC driver class, the database URL, and the username and password. Here is an example of how to connect to a MySQL database:

  ```
  using JDBC
  # Connect to the database
  driver = "com.mysql.jdbc.Driver"
  url = "jdbc:mysql://hostname:port/database"
  username = "username"
  password = "password"
  conn = JDBC.connect(driver, url, username, password)
  ```

- Execute a **SELECT** statement: To execute a **SELECT** statement, you can use the execute function, which returns a **ResultSet** object. Here is an example of how to execute a **SELECT** statement and retrieve the first column of the first row:

  ```
  using JDBC
  # Connect to the database
  driver = "com.mysql.jdbc.Driver"
  url = "jdbc:mysql://hostname:port/database"
  username = "username"
  password = "password"
  ```

```
conn = JDBC.connect(driver, url, username, password)
# Execute a SELECT statement
results = conn.execute("SELECT * FROM table")
# Retrieve the first column of the first row
row = results[1]
value = row[1]
```

- Execute an **INSERT** statement: To execute an **INSERT** statement, you can use the execute! function, which returns the number of rows affected by the statement. Here is an example of how to execute an INSERT statement:

```
using JDBC
# Connect to the database
driver = "com.mysql.jdbc.Driver"
url = "jdbc:mysql://hostname:port/database"
username = "username"
password = "password"
conn = JDBC.connect(driver, url, username, password)
# Execute an INSERT statement
nrows = conn.execute!("INSERT INTO table (column1, column2)
VALUES (1, 'value')")
```

Julia provides several libraries such as **ODBC.jl, JDBC.jl,** and **MySQL.jl** that can be used to access data from a database. These libraries can be used to establish a connection to a database, execute SQL queries and retrieve data. For example, using ODBC and **conn = ODBC.Connection("DSN=mydsn;UID=myusername;PWD=mypassword")** to establish a connection, then query **= ODBC.load(table, conn, mytable")** to retrieve the data from the table.

- **Generating synthetic data:** Generating synthetic data in Julia can be done using various libraries such as **Distributions.jl, Random.jl** and others. These libraries provide a wide range of probability distributions and random number generators that can be used to generate synthetic data.

Here are a few examples of how to use these libraries to generate synthetic data in Julia:

- Generating random numbers from a distribution: The **Distributions.jl** library provides a wide range of probability distributions, including Normal, Poisson, Binomial, etc. You can use the rand function to generate random numbers from a particular distribution. Here is an example of how to generate 10 random numbers from a normal distribution with mean 0 and standard deviation 1:

```
using Distributions

# Create a normal distribution

normal = Normal(0, 1)

# Generate random numbers

rand(normal, 10)
```

- Generating random samples from an array: The **`Random.jl`** library provides a rand function that can be used to generate random samples from an array. The following code exemplifies how to generate 10 random samples from an array of integers:

```
using Random

# Create an array of integers

array = [1, 2, 3, 4, 5]

# Generate random samples

rand(array, 10)
```

- **Generating synthetic data using `Random.jl`:** The **`Random.jl`** package provides a rand function that can be used to generate random numbers and arrays of a certain size and shape. Here is an example of how to generate a random 2×3 matrix of floating-point numbers between -1 and 1:

```
using Random

rand(-1:1, 2, 3)
```

- **Generating synthetic categorical data**: The **`CategoricalArrays.jl`** package provides a rand function that can be used to generate random categorical data. An example given here shows how to generate 10 random categorical data from a given set of categories:

```
using CategoricalArrays

# Create an array of categories

categories = [“A”, “B”, “C”]

# Generate random categorical data

rand(categories, 10)
```

Julia provides several libraries such as **`Distributions.jl`** and **`Random.jl`** that can be used to generate synthetic data for testing and experimentation. For example, using Distributions and data = rand(Normal(0, 1), 100) to generate 100 random samples from a normal distribution with a mean of 0 and a standard deviation of 1.

These are just examples, and the specific details of the implementation may vary depending on the data source and the specific use case. But overall, Julia provides a wide range of tools to easily access and import data from various sources.

Inspecting Data in Julia

Inspecting data is a significant aspect of data analysis because it allows you to understand the characteristics and properties of the data before you begin your analysis. It is essential to inspect the data to identify any issues or patterns that may affect the accuracy and reliability of the analysis.

Data inspection involves looking at the data in different ways to understand its characteristics, such as its size, structure, distribution, and missing values. This can be done by using various tools such as summary statistics, visualizations, and data profiling.

For example, summary statistics can provide information about the mean, median, and standard deviation of the data, which can indicate the distribution of the data and identify outliers. Visualizations such as histograms and scatter plots can help to identify patterns and trends in the data, while data profiling can reveal inconsistencies, errors, and missing values in the data.

Inspecting data also helps to identify any data preprocessing and cleaning that may be necessary. For example, if the data contains missing values, outliers, or errors, it may need to be cleaned or transformed to make it suitable for analysis.

Additionally, data inspection is also essential for identifying any assumptions or hypotheses that can be made about the data. For example, if the data shows a clear relationship between two variables, it may be appropriate to analyze the correlation between them.

`readlines` is a function that reads the contents of a file and returns it as an array of strings, one for each line in the file. For example,

```
using DataFrames

lines = readlines("myfile.txt")
```

It should be noted that readlines is not a function from **`DataFrames.jl`** package but from the Base Julia library.

DataFrames in Julia

In Julia, the CSV package provides a convenient way to load data from a CSV file into a DataFrame. The **CSV.read()** function is used to read a CSV file and return a DataFrame.

We use the **CSV.read()** function to load data from a CSV file into a DataFrame. The header parameter can be used to specify whether the first row of the CSV file contains column names. Another useful parameter is delim, to specify the delimiter used in the csv file, which by default is ','. You can also use the types parameter to specify the types of columns.

```
# Specify the types of columns
df = CSV.read("data.csv", header=true, delim=';',
types=[Int, Float64, String])
# You can also read directly from the file object.
open("data.csv") do file
 df = CSV.read(file, header=true)
end
```

Once the data is loaded into a DataFrame, you can use the standard DataFrame operations to manipulate and analyze the data.

In Julia, once you have loaded the data into a DataFrame, you can use several functions to inspect the contents of the DataFrame.

Here are a few examples:

- **size(df)** returns the dimensions of the DataFrame (i.e., the number of rows and columns)
- **nrow(df)** returns the number of rows in the DataFrame
- **ncol(df)** returns the number of columns in the DataFrame
- **names(df)** returns the names of the columns in the DataFrame
- **describe(df)** returns basic statistics of the DataFrame including mean, std, min, 25th percentile, median (50th percentile), 75th percentile, and max.

Here is an example:

```
using DataFrames
df = DataFrame(A = 1:3, B = ["a", "b", "c"])
size(df) # (3, 2)
```

```
nrow(df) # 3
ncol(df) # 2
names(df) # [:A, :B]
describe(df)
```

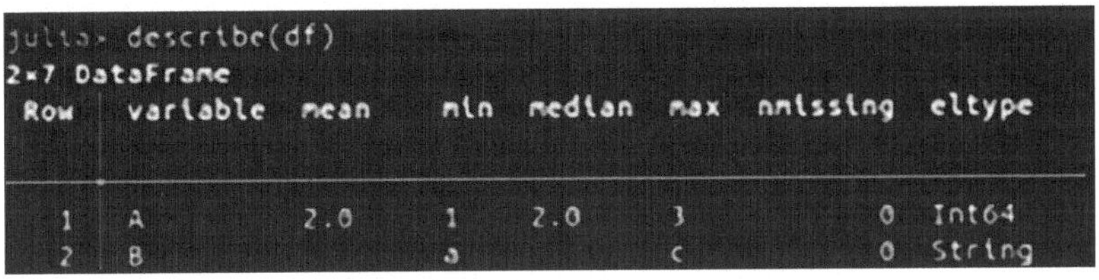
julia> describe(df)
2×7 DataFrame

Row	variable	mean	min	median	max	nmissing	eltype
1	A	2.0	1	2.0	3	0	Int64
2	B		a		c	0	String

Figure 5.2: *describe function in dataframes*

You can also use the **head()** and **tail()** functions to display the first or last n rows of the DataFrame respectively. For example,

```
first(df, 2) # display the first 2 rows of the DataFrame
```

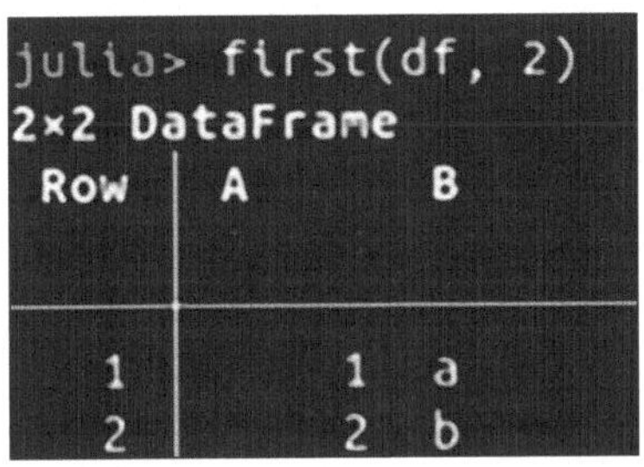
julia> first(df, 2)
2×2 DataFrame

Row	A	B
1	1	a
2	2	b

Figure 5.3: *first function in dataframes*

```
last(df, 1) # display the last row of the DataFrame
```

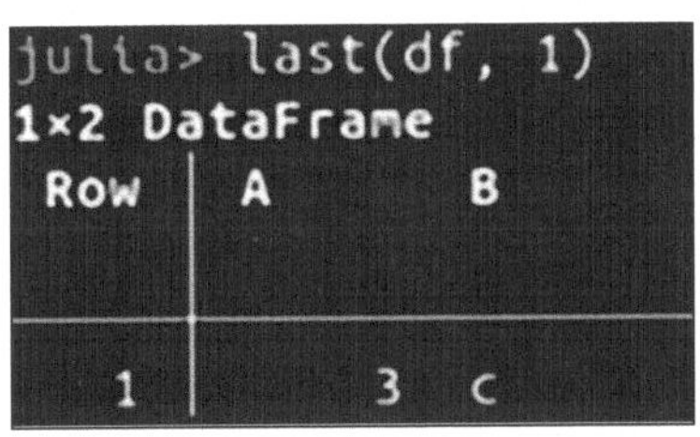
julia> last(df, 1)
1×2 DataFrame

Row	A	B
1	3	c

Figure 5.4: *last function in dataframes*

You can access individual rows, columns, and elements of the DataFrame using the [] operator. For example,

```
df[1, :] # access the first row of the DataFrame
df[:, "A"] # access the column with name "A" of the DataFrame
df[1, "A"] # access the element in the first row and first column of the
```

`DataFrame` You can also filter and select a subset of a DataFrame using the filter() and select() functions. `filter(row -> row.A > 1, df) # filter rows where A > 1`

```
select(df, :A) # select column A
```

Additionally, you can use the **`groupby()`** function to group the data and perform aggregate operations on the groups.

```
using Statistics

combine(groupby(df, :B), :A => mean)# group by column B and calculate the mean of  column A for each group
```

In the Julia programming language, the **`DataFrames.jl`** package provides a data structure for working with tabular data.

- **`names`** refers to the column names of a DataFrame. You can access the column names of a DataFrame by calling the **`names`** function on the DataFrame object. For example,

  ```
  using DataFrames

  df = DataFrame(a = 1:3, b = 4:6)

  names(df)

  # Output: ["a", "b"]
  ```

- **`show`** is a function that displays the first few rows of a DataFrame in the console. For example,

  ```
  using DataFrames

  df = DataFrame(a = 1:3, b = 4:6)

  show(df)

  # Output:

  # a b

  # 1 4

  # 2 5

  # 3 6
  ```

These are just a few examples of how you can inspect the contents of a DataFrame in Julia. The DataFrames package provides many other functions and methods that can be used to manipulate and analyze data in a DataFrame.

Saving text files

In the Julia programming language, you can save DataFrame to a CSV file using the **`CSV.jl`** package. The package provides a **`write`** function that can be used to write a DataFrame into a CSV file. The basic syntax for saving a DataFrame to a CSV file is as follows:

```
using CSV
CSV.write("filename.csv", df)
```

where **filename.csv** is the name of the file to be created, and **df** is the DataFrame that you want to save.

By default, the first row of the CSV file will contain the column names of the DataFrame. You can also specify the delimiter character to be used in the CSV file by passing an additional argument to the **write** function. For example, to use a tab character as a delimiter, you can add **delim='\t':**

```
using CSV
CSV.write("filename.csv", df, delim='\t')
```

You can also specify the option to write the header or not, by passing the option header = true/false to the write function. By default, it is set to true. For example,

```
using CSV
CSV.write("filename.csv", df, header = false)
```

You can also write a specific part of the DataFrame by passing the rows you want to write. For example,

```
using CSV
CSV.write("filename.csv", df[1:3,:])
```

The code will only write the first three rows of DataFrame in the file.

There are many more options that you can pass to the **write** function to customize the output, you can find more details in the package documentation.

hasproperty is a function in Julia that is used to check if an object has a certain property or field. For example, if you have a struct or object called **myobj** and you want to check if it has a field called **field1,** you would use the **hasproperty** function like this:

```
hasproperty(myobj, :field1)
```

This will return true if the field exists and false if it does not.

columnindex is a function in Julia used to extract the index of a column from a DataFrame. The function takes two arguments: the DataFrame and the column name. For example, if you have a DataFrame called **df** and you want to find the index of the column called **column1**, you would use the **columnindex** function like this:

```
columnindex(df, :column1)
```

This will return an integer representing the index of the specified column.

Packages for Text Analysis

The **TextAnalysis** package in Julia provides a range of tools for processing text data, including tokenization, stemming, and stopword removal. Here are a few code examples to illustrate how to use the **TextAnalysis** package:

```
using TextAnalysis
# Tokenize a string into words
text = "This is a sample text."
tokens = tokenize(text)
# Remove stop words from the tokens
stopwords = ["is", "a", "the"]
filtered_tokens = filter(t -> !(t in stopwords), tokens)
Output:
3-element Vector{String}:
 "this"
 "sample"
 "text"
```

In the preceding code, we use the tokenize function from the TextAnalysis package to tokenize the string text into words. The resulting tokens are then passed through the stem function to perform stemming on the tokens. Finally, the filter function is used to remove stop words from the tokens by filtering out any tokens that are present in the stopwords list.

This is just a small example of the functionality offered by the TextAnalysis package, which also includes functions for text normalization, word frequency analysis, and n-gram extraction. The package provides a convenient and flexible platform for processing text data in Julia. The Tokenize package in Julia provides tools for tokenizing text data, i.e., splitting text into smaller units such as words, sentences, or paragraphs.

Visualizing the DataFrame

In Julia, there are several ways to visualize data stored in columns of a DataFrame. One popular package for data visualization is **`Plots.jl`**, which provides a wide range of plot types and customization options. Some examples show here how to use **`Plots.jl`** for visualizing data in a DataFrame:

- **Line Plot:** To create a line plot of a column in a DataFrame, you can use the **`plot()`** function and pass in the DataFrame and the column name. For example, if you have a DataFrame called **`df`** and you want to create a line plot of the column **`column1`**, you would use the following code:

  ```
  using Plots
  plot(df.column1)
  ```

- **Scatter Plot:** To create a scatter plot of two columns in a DataFrame, you can use the **`scatter()`** function and pass in the DataFrame and the column names. For example, if you have a Data Frame called **`df`** and you want to create a scatter plot of the columns **`column1`** and **`column2`**, you would use the following code:

  ```
  using Plots
  scatter(df.column1, df.column2)
  ```

- **Histogram**: To create a histogram of a column in a DataFrame, you can use the **`histogram()`** function and pass in the DataFrame and the column name. For example, if you have a DataFrame called **`df`** and you want to create a histogram of the column **`column1`**, you would use the following code:

  ```
  using Plots
  histogram(df.column1)
  ```

- **Bar Plot:** To create a bar plot of a column in a DataFrame, you can use the **`bar()`** function and pass in the DataFrame and the column name. For example, if you have a DataFrame called df and you want to create a bar plot of the column **`column1`**, you would use the following code:

  ```
  using Plots
  bar(df.column1)
  ```

These are just a few examples of the types of plots that can be created with **`Plots.jl`**. The package offers many more options for customizing the appearance of the plots and representing data in different ways.

You can also try other popular packages such as **`Gadfly.jl`**, **`VegaLite.jl`** and **`PyPlot.jl`** to visualize data stored in columns of a data frame in Julia.

Working with Strings

In Julia, strings are sequences of characters and are represented by double quotes (""). They can be concatenated using the * operator and repeated using the ^ operator. For example,

```
a = "Hello"
b = " World"
c = a * b # "Hello World"
d = a ^ 3 # "HelloHelloHello"
```

You can access individual characters in a string using indexing, for example,

```
a = "Hello"
a[1] # 'H'
```

You can also access a range of characters using slicing, for example,

```
a = "Hello"
a[1:3] # "el"
```

There are many string functions available in Julia, some examples are:

- length(s) returns the length of a string
- uppercase(s) returns an uppercase version of a string
- lowercase(s) returns a lowercase version of a string
- split(s, delim) splits a string into an array of substrings using the specified delimiter
- replace(s, old, new) replaces all occurrences of a specified string with another string

You can also use string interpolation with the **$** sign to include the value of a variable in a string. For example,

```
name = "Julia"
"Hello, $name" # "Hello, Julia"
```

You can use the * operator to repeat a string and the ^ operator to repeat a string a specified number of times.

```
a = "Hello "
b = a^3 # "Hello Hello Hello "
```

You can use **findfirst()** and **findlast()** to find the first and last position of a substring inside a string, respectively.

```
a = "Hello World"
findfirst("W", a) #7:7
findlast("o", a) #8:8
```

There are many other string functions and operations available in Julia. here are a few more examples of string operations in Julia:

- **Concatenation**: You can concatenate two strings using the * operator. For example,

  ```
  string1 = "Hello"
  string2 = "world"
  result = string1 * " " * string2
  println(result)
  "Hello world"
  ```

- **Replacing a substring**: You can use the replace() function to replace a specific substring within a string. For example,

  ```
  string = "Hello world"
  new_string = replace(string, "world" => "Julia")
  println(new_string)
  "Hello Julia"
  ```

- **Extracting a substring**: You can use indexing to extract a specific substring from a string. For example,

  ```
  string = "Hello world"
  substring = string[7:11]
  println(substring)
  "world"
  ```

- **Converting to uppercase or lowercase**: You can use the **uppercase()** and **lowercase()** functions to convert a string to uppercase or lowercase respectively. For example,

  ```
  string = "Hello World"
  uppercase_string = uppercase(string)
  lowercase_string = lowercase(string)
  println(uppercase_string)
  println(lowercase_string)
  ```

```
"HELLO WORLD" "hello world"
```

- **Finding the length of a string**: You can use the **`length()`** function to find the number of characters in a string. For example,

```
string = "Hello world"
len = length(string)
println(len)
11
```

- **Counting the occurrences of a substring**: You can use the **`count()`** function to find the number of occurrences of a specific substring within a string. For example,

```
string = "Hello world, Hello universe"
count = count("Hello", string)
println(count)
```

Reading from a Text File

You can also use the open function to open a file and read its contents into a string. Here's an example:

```
file = open("path/to/file.txt")
file_contents = read(file, String)
close(file)
println(file_contents)
```

The open function takes the path of the file as its argument and returns a file object. The read function takes the file object and the type of data you want to read as its arguments, in this case, String. The close function is used to close the file after reading.

Another approach is to use the readlines function to read the contents of a file into an array of strings, where each element of the array represents a line in the file. Here's an example:

```
file_contents = readlines("path/to/file.txt")
for line in file_contents
 println(line)
end
```

The **`readlines`** function takes the path of the file as its argument and returns an array of strings.

Once you have the contents of the file in a string, you can perform various operations on it like substring, replacing, etc., using the string functions mentioned in the previous examples.

It's important to note that when reading large files, it is recommended to use the open function to avoid loading the entire file into memory at once.

Another example of reading a file incrementally by a certain number of bytes:

```
file = open("path/to/large_file.txt")
bytes_to_read = 4096
while !eof(file)
 buffer = read(file, bytes_to_read)
 println(buffer)
end
close(file)
```

In this example, the read function reads a certain number of bytes (in this case 4096) from the file. The while loop runs until the eof function indicates that the file has reached its end. The `println` function prints the buffer (the bytes read from the file).

It's important to keep in mind that, when reading a file incrementally, you need to close the file once you're done with it, to release any system resources that are being used by the file. The close function is used for that.

In addition, you can use the **`readbytes`** function to read the file in bytes if you want to process the file in binary format.

```
file = open("path/to/large_file.txt")
bytes_to_read = 4096
while !eof(file)
 buffer = readbytes!(file, bytes_to_read)
 println(String(buffer))
end
close(file)
```

Splitting Text String

In Julia, you can use the **`split()`** function to split a string into an array of substrings based on a specified delimiter. The delimiter can be a character or a regular expression.

For example, to split a string on the character "," you can use the following code:

```
julia> s = "a,b,c,d,e"
"a,b,c,d,e"
julia> split(s, ",")
5-element Array{SubString{String},1}:
"a"
"b"
"c"
"d"
"e"
```

You can also use regular expressions as delimiters. For example, to split a string on any non-alphanumeric character, the following code can be used:

```
julia> s = "Hello, World!"
"Hello, World!"
julia> split(r"[^\w]", s)
3-element Array{SubString{String},1}:
"Hello"
"World"
""
```

You can also provide a limit argument to the split function to limit the number of splits; also you can use the **strip()** function to remove any whitespaces from the resulting substrings.

```
julia> s = "a,b,c,d,e"
"a,b,c,d,e"
julia> split(s, ",", limit = 2)
2-element Array{SubString{String},1}:
"a"
"b,c,d,e"
julia> s = "a, b , c , d, e"
"a, b , c , d, e"
julia> map(strip, split(s, ","))
5-element Array{String,1}:
"a"
```

```
"b"
"c"
"d"
"e"
```

In addition to the **split()** function, Julia also has the **rssplit()** function, which splits a string using a specified character or regular expression, and returns an iterator over the resulting substrings.

Regular Expressions

Julia has a built-in Regex module that supports working with regular expressions.

You can create a regular expression by calling the **r"pattern"** string literal, or by calling the **Regex("pattern")** constructor. For example,

```
julia> r = r"\d+"
r"\d+"
julia> re = Regex("\\d+")
r"\d+"
```

You can use the **match()** function to check if a regular expression matches a string. For example,

```
julia> match(r"\d+", "123abc")
RegexMatch("123")
julia> match(r"\d+", "abc")
# Define a regular expression to match any string that starts with
"Julia" regex = r"^Julia"
# Check if the regular expression matches a string
match(regex, "Julia is a great programming language") # returns true
match(regex, "Python is also a great programming language") # returns
false
```

You can also use **eachmatch** to find all matches of a regular expression in a string and **eachmatch** will return an iterator over the matches.

```
# Define a regular expression to match any word that starts with "J"
regex = r"\bJ\w+"
# Find all matches
for match in eachmatch(regex, "Julia is a great programming language")
println(match.match)
```

```
end
```

You can use the **findall()** function to find all non-overlapping matches of a regular expression in a string and return them as an array of strings. For example,

```
julia> findall(r"\d+", "abc 123 def 456")
2-element Array{SubString{String},1}:
"123"
"456"
```

Julia's regular expressions support most of the common metacharacters and special sequences like., *, +, ?, {m,n}, |, ^, $, \d, \w, \s, etc. You can also use capture groups (()) to extract parts of the match and use them in the replacement string.

Temporal Data

Temporal data, also known as time-series data, refers to data points that are collected and recorded over a period of time at specific intervals. These data points are associated with timestamps or time indicators, which allow for the analysis and modeling of how a particular variable or set of variables changes over time. Temporal data is prevalent in various domains, including finance, weather forecasting, stock market analysis, healthcare, social sciences, and more.

Handling missing data is important in any data analysis task, including temporal data handling. Temporal data, or time series data, often have missing values due to various reasons such as sensors not working, data not being recorded, or data not being collected. Understanding the methods of handling missing data is important before analyzing temporal data because missing values can have a significant impact on the results of the analysis.

For example, if missing values are not handled properly, they can lead to incorrect results in time series analysis. If missing values are simply removed, it can result in loss of information, or if missing values are imputed with incorrect values, it can result in incorrect trend analysis.

Furthermore, it is essential to understand the nature of the missing data, as different methods of handling missing data are appropriate for different types of missing data. For instance, if the missing data is missing at random, imputing missing values is a suitable method, but if the missing data is not missing at random, removing missing values is a more convenient method.

Before learning how to handle temporal or time-series data, let us learn about missing data.

Handling missing Data

Handling missing data is a noteworthy task in data analysis. In Julia, the Missing type is used to represent the missing values in arrays. Some common ways to work with missing data in Julia are as follows:

- **Removing missing values**: The **`dropmissing()`** function from the DataFrames package can be used to remove rows with missing values.

  Removing missing values is the simplest way to handle missing data, but it can result in loss of information if the missing data is not missing at random. The **`dropmissing()`** function from the DataFrames package can be used to remove rows with missing values. It returns a new DataFrame with the missing values removed.

  ```
  using DataFrames
  df = DataFrame(A = [1, missing, 2, 3], B = [4, 5, missing, 7])
  df_without_na = dropmissing(df)
  ```

- **Imputing missing values:** Imputing missing values is a method of filling in the missing values with an estimate based on the available data. Mean imputation, median imputation, and regression imputation are some of the common methods for imputing missing values in Julia. The Impute package provides functions for imputing missing values.

  ```
  using Impute
  df = DataFrame(A = [1, missing, 2, 3.0], B = [4, 5,
  missing, 7.0])
  df_imputed = impute(df, Interpolate())
  ```

- **Using a sentinel value**: Another way to handle missing data is to use a sentinel value that represents missing data, such as -1 or NaN. The NA constant from the Missing module can be used to represent the missing data in Julia.

  ```
  using Missings
  A = [1, missings, 2, 3]
  fin = skipmissing(A)
  ```

- Dealing with missing data while computing statistics: The **`skipmissing`** function from the Statistics package can be used to ignore missing values while computing statistics such as mean, median, etc.

```
using Statistics
A = [1, missing, 2, 3]
mean(skipmissing(A))
```

- **Interpolation**: Interpolation is a method of estimating values between two known values. Interpolation can be used to fill in missing values in a time series. The Interpolations package in Julia provides functions for interpolating data.

```
using Interpolations
set = 1:6
sety = [i == 3 ? missing : i for i in set]
xf = [xi for (xi,a) in zip(set, sety) if !ismissing(a)]
Af = [a for a in sety if !ismissing(a)]
itp = interpolate((xf, ), Af, Gridded(Linear()))
```

It is important to consider the nature of the missing data and the purpose of the analysis before choosing an appropriate method for handling missing values.

The coalesce function in Julia is used to replace missing values (represented by NA) with a default value. It takes an array and a default value as arguments and returns a new array with the missing values replaced by the default value. The coalesce function is often used to fill in missing values in arrays, data frames, and other data structures in Julia.

Here's an example of using coalesce with missing values in Julia:

```
A = [1, missing, 2, 3]
B = coalesce.(A, 0)
```

In this example, the coalesce function replaces the missing value NA with the default value 0. The resulting array B is [1, 0, 2, 3].

Note that coalesce can also be used with arrays of different types, such as Float64 and Int64. In that case, the default value must be of a type that is compatible with both types.

Handling Temporal Data

Temporal data, also known as time series data, is a series of data points collected over time. It is a type of sequential data that has a time component, which means that each data point is associated with a specific time or date. Temporal data can be found in various fields such as finance, economics, weather forecasting, stock market analysis, and more.

Examples of temporal data include daily stock prices, monthly sales data, hourly temperature readings, and weekly rainfall measurements. Temporal data can be continuous, such as data collected every second, or discrete, such as data collected daily or monthly.

Temporal data analysis involves analyzing and modeling the underlying patterns and trends in the data over time. This requires specialized techniques and methods that take into account the time component of the data. The goal of temporal data analysis is to extract meaningful insights and make predictions about future trends and patterns in the data.

There are several packages in Julia that can be used to handle temporal data, including:

- **Dates**: This package provides an implementation of the Date type, which represents dates (years, months, and days) with an optional time of day. The package also provides functions for parsing dates and times, formatting dates and times, and performing arithmetic on dates and times.
- **TimeZones**: This package provides an implementation of the TimeZone type, which represents a time zone and its associated rules for converting between local time and coordinated universal time (UTC).
- **TimeSeries**: This package provides a TimeSeries type for representing time series data, which is a collection of values with associated timestamps. The package provides functions for aggregating, resampling, and transforming time series data.
- **DataFrames:** The DataFrames package provides a data structure for working with tabular data, which can include temporal data. The package provides functions for manipulating and aggregating data, as well as handling missing values.

The following example depicts how you can handle temporal data in Julia using the Dates and DataFrames packages:

```
using Dates, DataFrames
# Create a time series data frame
dates = [Date(2022,1,1), Date(2022,1,2), Date(2022,1,3), missing]
values = [1, 2, 3, missing]
df = DataFrame(date=dates, value=values)
# Handle missing values in the date column
df.date = coalesce.(df.date, Date(1900,1,1))
```

```
# Handle missing values in the value column
df.value = coalesce.(df.value, 0)
```

In this example, the coalesce function is used to replace missing values in the date and value columns with default values. The date column is filled with a default date 1900-01-01, and the value column is filled with a default value 0. The resulting data frame **df** contains no missing values.

Here are some additional methods that can be used to handle temporal data in Julia:

- **TimeZones:** The **TimeZones** package in Julia provides a **TimeZone** type, which represents a time zone and its associated rules for converting between local time and coordinated universal time (UTC). The package provides functions for parsing time zones, computing the offset between time zones, and converting between local time and UTC time.
- **TimeSeries**: The **TimeSeries** package provides a **TimeSeries** type for representing time series data, which is a collection of values with associated timestamps. The package provides functions for aggregating, resampling, and transforming time series data. The **TimeSeries** type is optimized for performance and can handle large time series data sets efficiently.
- **DataFrames:** The **DataFrames** package provides a data structure for working with tabular data, which can include temporal data. The package provides functions for manipulating and aggregating data, as well as handling missing values. The **DataFrames** package integrates well with other data analysis packages in Julia, such as Statistics and Plots, and provides a convenient way to work with time series data in a tabular format.

Here's an example of how you can handle temporal data:

```
using TimeZones, TimeSeries, DataFrames
# Define a time zone
tz = TimeZone("America/New_York")
# Create a time series
timestamps = [DateTime(2022,1,1,0,0,0),
 DateTime(2022,1,2,0,0,0),
 DateTime(2022,1,3,0,0,0)]
values = [1, 2, 3]
ts = TimeArray(timestamps, values)
# Convert the time series to a data frame
df = DataFrame(timestamp=timestamps, value=values)
```

In this example, the **`TimeZones`** package is used to define a time zone, and the **`TimeSeries`** package is used to create a time series data set. The **`DataFrames`** package is used to convert the time series data set to a data frame and aggregate the data.

A Data Science Problem

The Boston Housing problem is a classic machine learning problem that is commonly used for teaching the principles of regression analysis. The problem involves using a dataset of 13 features to predict the median value of owner-occupied homes in the suburbs of Boston in 1970s. The dataset contains 506 instances with each instance having 13 features or variables that are used to make predictions.

The dataset contains 14 columns or features that describe the homes and suburbs, including:

- **CRIM**: per capita crime rate by town
- **ZN**: proportion of residential land zoned for lots over 25,000 sq.ft.
- **INDUS**: proportion of non-retail business acres per town
- **CHAS**: Charles River dummy variable (1 if tract bounds river; 0 otherwise)
- **NOX:** nitric oxide concentration (parts per 10 million)
- **RM**: average number of rooms per dwelling
- **AGE**: proportion of owner-occupied units built prior to 1940
- **DIS**: weighted distances to five Boston employment centers
- **RAD**: index of accessibility to radial highways
- **TAX:** full-value property-tax rate per $10,000
- **PTRATIO:** pupil-teacher ratio by town
- B: 1000(Bk - 0.63)^2 where Bk is the proportion of blacks by town
- **LSTAT**: % lower status of the population
- **MEDV:** Median value of owner-occupied homes in $1000s. This is the target variable.

Each of these columns represents a different aspect of the town that can potentially affect the median value of owner-occupied homes in the suburb. The goal of this problem is to use these 13 features to predict the median value of owner-occupied homes in the suburbs of Boston.

```
using MLJ
using RDatasets
# Load the Boston Housing dataset
boston = dataset("MASS", "Boston")
# Split the data into training and test sets
train, test = partition(eachindex(boston), 0.7, shuffle=true, rng=42) #
Define the model
model = @load LinearRegressor pkg=MLJLinearModels
# Fit the model to the training data
MLJ.fit!(model, rows(boston, train))
# Make predictions on the test set
ŷ = MLJ.predict(model, rows(boston, test))
# Evaluate the model
    r² = r²(ŷ, boston.medv[test])
println("R²: $(r²)")
```

The code above is a solution to the Boston Housing problem using the Julia programming language and the MLJ and **RDatasets** packages. The code loads the Boston Housing dataset from the **RDatasets** library and splits it into training and test data sets, with 70% of the data used for training and 30% used for testing.

The code then defines the model, which is a linear regression model, and uses MLJ.fit! function to fit the model to the training data. This means that the model is trained on the training data and optimized to make accurate predictions.

After fitting the model, the code makes predictions on the test data set using the **MLJ.predict** function and calculates the R^2 value using the r^2 function to evaluate the accuracy of the model's predictions. The R^2 value measures the proportion of the variance in the target variable (in this case, the median value of owner-occupied homes in Boston) that is explained by the independent variables in the model.

Finally, the code prints out the R^2 value, which gives an indication of how well the model fits the data. A higher R^2 value indicates better fit and more accurate predictions.

Conclusion

Julia offers a rich set of tools for working with various types of data, including numerical, textual, and temporal data. DataFrames package is a powerful tool for reading and manipulating data in tabular format, and provides methods for handling missing values and summarizing data. The statistics package provides a comprehensive set of tools for working with numerical data, including methods for transforming and visualizing data. TextAnalysis and Tokenize packages offer a range of functions for processing text data, including tokenization and text processing. TimeZones and TimeSeries packages provide a convenient and easy-to-use interface for working with time zones and time series data and offer methods for aggregating, transforming, and visualizing temporal data. With these tools, Julia provides a comprehensive and efficient platform for data analysis and manipulation.

As Julia is a powerful tool for statistical data analysis, the next chapter offers a wide range of functionality to support various measures such as mean, median, mode, standard deviation, outlier detection, distance methods, counts and sampling, the relationship between features, and miscellaneous statistical functions like probability distributions and hypothesis testing. Additionally, it provides various methods to perform these tasks efficiently and accurately.

Questions

1. How can you load and inspect data from a CSV file in Julia?
2. What are the functions for summarizing and visualizing numerical data in Julia?
3. How can you handle missing values in numerical data in Julia?
4. How can you perform text preprocessing and analysis in Julia?
5. What are the best packages for working with text data in Julia?
6. How can you perform text classification and clustering in Julia?
7. How can you handle missing values in temporal data in Julia?
8. What are the best packages for working with time series data in Julia?
9. How can you perform time series analysis and forecasting in Julia?
10. How can you handle time zones and deal with temporal data in different formats in Julia?

11. How can you read a CSV file into a DataFrame in Julia?
12. What are the different ways to inspect the structure and summary statistics of a DataFrame in Julia?
13. How can you handle missing values in a DataFrame in Julia?
14. What are the different ways to manipulate and transform numerical data in Julia? 15. How can you create and visualize histograms and other plots in Julia?
16. How can you work with text data in Julia, including splitting strings and processing text data in a DataFrame?
17. How can you handle time zones and time series data in Julia using the TimeZones and TimeSeries packages?
18. What are the different ways to manipulate and aggregate temporal data in Julia, including resampling and grouping by time intervals?
19. How can you perform operations on time series data sets in Julia, such as computing the difference between two time-series data sets?
20. How can you visualize the time series data in Julia using the Plots package?

Chapter 6

Basics of Statistics

Julia is a high-level programming language that is widely used for data analysis and scientific computing. One of the areas where Julia excels is in statistical analysis, which is an essential component of data analysis.

In Julia, there are two main types of statistics: descriptive and inferential. Descriptive statistics involves summarizing and describing the main features of a dataset. These features include central tendency measures like mean, median, and mode, variability measures like standard deviation and variance, and distribution measures like histograms and density plots. Julia provides packages like **`StatsBase`** and **`DataFrames`** that have functions for carrying out these tasks.

The Statistics package in Julia provides a rich collection of functions for calculating various measures such as mean, median, mode, and standard deviation. These functions are essential for descriptive statistics. By using these functions, analysts can quickly and easily summarize and describe datasets, gain insights into the data, and communicate findings to others.

Inferential statistics, on the other hand, involves making predictions or inferences about a population based on a sample of data. Julia has packages like **`HypothesisTests`** and GLM that provide functions for carrying out hypothesis testing, regression analysis, and other inferential methods. These packages help analysts draw conclusions about populations, estimate population parameters, and quantify the uncertainty in their estimates.

Julia also provides more advanced statistical modeling packages like MCMC and Distributions. These packages enable analysts to build sophisticated models that can account for complex data structures and dependencies.

To get started with statistics in Julia, it's important to have a basic understanding of statistics and be familiar with programming in Julia. Analysts can leverage the available packages and functions to carry out basic and advanced statistical analysis. The available resources and community support make it easy for anyone to learn and master statistical analysis in Julia. These are just some of the basics of statistics in Julia, and there are many more concepts and packages available for further study.

Structure

In this chapter, the following topics will be covered

- Statistics in Julia
- Descriptive Statistics and its purpose
- Overview of the main descriptive statistics measures
- Outlier detection and treatment in data analysis
- Distance methods
- Counts and Sampling
- Relationship between various features in the dataset during data analysis
- Miscellaneous statistical functions that aid in data analysis
- Observational Estimation in data analysis

Statistics in Julia

Julia's Statistics module is a powerful tool for data analysis and modeling. One of its key features is its high level of performance, which allows it to handle large-scale data analysis tasks with ease. The Statistics module is built into the language, which means it is always available and requires no additional installation or setup.

The module is designed to be user-friendly and flexible, making it suitable for both simple and complex data analysis tasks. With its range of statistical functions and methods, the Statistics module can help analysts summarize and analyze their data quickly and accurately. Statistics module's capabilities also make it ideal for use in big data environments, where large datasets need to be processed efficiently.

In addition to the basic statistical measures like mean, median, mode, variance, and standard deviations, the Statistics module also provides a variety of other statistical methods such as correlation analysis, hypothesis testing, and regression analysis. The module supports both vectorized and parallel operations, which allows it to handle large datasets efficiently. Vectorized operations can be used to perform the same calculation on multiple data points simultaneously, while parallel operations can be used to distribute computation across multiple processors or computers.

Overall, Julia's Statistics module is a comprehensive and powerful tool for data analysis and modeling, with capabilities that can help analysts handle both simple and complex tasks with ease.

Descriptive Statistics and its purpose

Descriptive statistics is a vital branch of statistics that focuses on summarizing, presenting, and describing a set of observations. Its primary goal is to provide information about the main features of a dataset, such as the central tendency, variability, and distribution, using numerical and graphical methods. This branch of statistics is essential because it allows us to better understand the data and draw meaningful conclusions and inferences.

Descriptive statistics plays a significant role in the initial stages of data analysis. It is often the first step in analyzing a dataset, as it provides an overview of the data and helps identify patterns, outliers, trends, and relationships. These insights can provide a better understanding of the underlying phenomena being studied, allowing analysts to make more informed decisions.

Numerical methods, such as measures of central tendency (for example, mean, median, and mode), measures of variability (for example, standard deviation, and variance), and measures of shape (for example, skewness and kurtosis), are commonly used in descriptive statistics. Graphical methods, such as histograms, box plots, scatter plots, and density plots, are also used to visualize the data and identify trends.

Descriptive statistics is crucial for exploring the data and understanding its properties before applying more advanced statistical methods, such as inferential statistics. In summary, descriptive statistics is a fundamental branch of statistics that is essential for gaining insights into the data and providing a basis for more advanced statistical analysis.

Overview of the main descriptive statistics measures

StatsBase.jl is a Julia package that provides a suite of functions for descriptive statistics. Here's a brief overview of some of the main descriptive statistics measures that can be computed using **StatsBase.jl**:

- **Weighted sum and mean:**

The weighted sum and weighted mean are calculated by taking into account the importance or weight of each data point in the set. In **StatsBase.jl**, you can calculate the weighted sum using the `wsum()` function, and the weighted mean using the `wmean()` function.

```
using StatsBase
# Define the data set
data = [1, 2, 3, 4, 5]
weights = [1, 2, 3, 4, 5]
# Calculate the weighted sum and mean
wsum = sum(data .* weights)
wmean = mean(data, Weights(weights))
println("The weighted sum of the data is: ", wsum)
The weighted sum of the data is: 35
println("The weighted mean of the data is: ", wmean)
The weighted mean of the data is: 3.5
```

- **Mean:**

Mean, also known as average, is a measure of central tendency that represents the sum of all values in a dataset divided by the number of observations. It gives an idea of what the typical value in the dataset is. In **StatsBase.jl**, you can calculate the mean of a dataset by using the `mean()` function. Here's an example:

```
using StatsBase
data = [1, 2, 3, 4, 5]
mean_value = mean(data)
println("The mean of the dataset is: ", mean_value)
The mean of the dataset is: 3.0
```

- **Median:**

Median is the middle value of a dataset when it is sorted in ascending or descending order. It gives an idea of the center of the dataset and is useful when there are outliers in the dataset. In **StatsBase.jl**, you can calculate the median of a dataset by using the `median()` function. Here's an example:

```
using StatsBase
data = [1, 2, 3, 4, 5]
median_value = median(data)
```

```
println("The median of the dataset is: ", median_value)
The median of the dataset is: 3.0
```

- **Mode:**

Mode is the most frequently occurring value in a dataset. In **StatsBase.jl**, you can calculate the mode of a dataset by using the `mode()` function. Here's an example:

```
using StatsBase
data = [1, 2, 3, 4, 5, 5]
mode_value = mode(data)
# Calculate the modes
modes_values = modes(data)
println("The mode of the dataset is: ", mode_value)
The mode of the dataset is: 5
println("The modes of the data are: ", modes_values)
The modes of the data are: [5]
```

- **Range:**

Range is the difference between the maximum and minimum values in a dataset. It gives an idea of the spread of the dataset. In **StatsBase.jl**, you can calculate the range of a dataset by using the `range()` function. Here's an example:

```
using StatsBase
data = [1, 2, 3, 4, 5]
range_value = range(data)
println("The range of the dataset is: ", range_value)
The range of the dataset is: (1, 5)
```

- **Variance:**

Variance is a measure of the spread of a dataset, representing the average of the squared differences from the mean. It gives an idea of how spread out the values in the dataset are. In **StatsBase.jl**, you can calculate the variance of a dataset by using the `var()` function. Here's an example:

```
using StatsBase
data = [1, 2, 3, 4, 5]
variance_value = var(data)
println("The variance of the dataset is: ", variance_value)
The variance of the dataset is: 2.5
```

- **Standard Deviation:**

The standard deviation measures the spread or dispersion of a set of data. The standard deviation can be obtained by taking the square root of the variance. In **StatsBase.jl**, the standard deviation of a set of numbers can be calculated using the std function. This function takes an array of numbers as input and returns the standard deviation of the data.

```
using StatsBase
# Define the data set
data = [1, 2, 3, 4, 5]
# Calculate the standard deviation of the data
stddev = std(data)
println("The standard deviation of the data is: ", stddev)
The standard deviation of the data is: 1.5811388300841898
```

- **Covariance:**

Covariance is a statistical measure that describes the relationship between two variables. Specifically, it measures the degree to which two variables move together, either positively or negatively. A positive covariance indicates that the two variables tend to increase or decrease together, while a negative covariance indicates that one variable tends to increase as the other decreases. In other words, covariance measures the extent to which two variables are related to each other. It is calculated by taking the average of the product of the deviations of each variable from their respective means. Covariance can be used to assess the degree of association between variables and is often used in regression analysis and portfolio management.

The `cov` function in the Statistics package in Julia is a method that computes the covariance between two vectors x and y using a given covariance estimator *ce*. A covariance estimator "ce" is an object that implements the `CovarianceEstimator` interface, which provides methods for estimating (not exact computation) the covariance between two or more (multivariate-random vectors) sets of observations. This allows for flexible computation of the covariance (estimating the covariance), as different covariance estimators can be used depending on the properties of the data and the desired level of accuracy. For example, different estimators may use different techniques to handle missing values or to compute the covariance when the sample size is small. Here's an example of how you might use the `cov` method:

```
# Define two sets of observations
x = [1, 2, 3, 4, 5]
```

```
y = [1, 4, 9, 16, 25]
# Compute the covariance between x and y
c = cov(x, y)
println(c)
# Output:
# 15
```

- **Correlation:**

Correlation is a statistical measure that indicates the degree of association between two variables. It shows how two variables are related to each other and the direction of the relationship, whether it's positive or negative. A positive correlation means that as one variable increases, the other variable also tends to increase, while a negative correlation means that as one variable increases, the other variable tends to decrease. Correlation is measured using a correlation coefficient, which ranges from -1 to 1, with values of -1 indicating a perfect negative correlation, 1 indicating a perfect positive correlation, and 0 indicating no correlation between the variables. Correlation is a commonly used statistical tool in data analysis and is often used to assess the strength of a relationship between variables and to make predictions based on those relationships.

The cor function in the Statistics package in Julia computes the correlation between two vectors using a given covariance estimator *ce*, also known as the Pearson correlation matrix. A Pearson correlation matrix is a table that displays the Pearson correlation (linear relationship) coefficients between several pairs of variables. It is a way of summarizing the correlation between variables in a dataset, and is often used in data analysis and statistical modeling. The

Pearson correlation coefficient is a measure of the linear relationship between two variables, and ranges from -1 to +1. A value of +1 indicates a perfect positive linear relationship, 0 indicates no linear relationship, and -1 indicates a perfect negative linear relationship.

Here's an example of how you might use the `cor` method:

```
# Define a matrix of observations
X = [1 2 3; 4 5 6; 7 8 9]
# Compute the Pearson correlation matrix of X
c = cor(X)
println(c)
# Output:
```

```
# 3x3 Matrix{Float64}:
# 1.0 1.0 1.0
# 1.0 1.0 1.0
# 1.0 1.0 1.0
```

- **Entropy:**

The entropy(p, [b]) function in Julia computes the entropy of a collection of probabilities p. Entropy is a measure of the uncertainty or randomness of a system, and in the context of information theory, it represents the amount of information contained in a message or signal.

The p parameter is a collection of probabilities, where each element represents the probability of a particular outcome. The p parameter should be a vector or an array of non-negative values that sum to 1.

The b parameter is optional, and it is a real number that specifies the base of the logarithm used to compute the entropy. By default, b is set to e (Euler's number), which corresponds to using the natural logarithm. If you provide a value for b, the entropy will be scaled by `1/log(b)`. This scaling factor adjusts the units of the entropy measure, and it is useful in some contexts, such as in signal processing.

If the probability of an event is either 0 or 1, then the entropy of that event is 0 because there is either no uncertainty or no randomness in the outcome.

Here is an example usage of the entropy function in Julia:

```
julia> using StatsBase
julia> p = [0.1, 0.2, 0.3, 0.4];
julia> entropy(p)
1.2798542258336676
julia> entropy(p, 2) # entropy(p) / log2(2)
1.8464393446710157
julia> entropy([0.0, 0.5, 0.5])
0.6931471805599453
julia> entropy([1.0, 0.0, 0.0])
0.0
```

- **Quantiles:**

A quantile is a general term for a cut point that divides a set of data into equal-sized groups. For example, the median is a type of quantile that divides a dataset into two equal-sized groups. The term "quantile" is often used in reference to the median (a 2-quantile), the quartiles (a 4- quantile), or the percentiles (a 100-quantile).

A quartile, on the other hand, is a specific type of quantile that divides a dataset into four equal sized groups. The three quartiles are the 25th percentile, the 50th percentile (which is the median), and the 75th percentile. The interquartile range (IQR) is the range between the first and third quartiles and contains the middle 50% of the data.

Quantiles and quartiles are both measures of the distribution of a dataset, but they differ in the number of segments into which the data is divided.

In **StatsBase.jl**, the quartiles can be calculated using the quantile function. This function takes as input an array of numbers and a set of quartile values in the range of 0 to 1, (i.e. 0.0, 0.25, 0.75, 1.0), and returns the corresponding quartile values for the data.

```
using StatsBase
# Define the data set
julia> data = [1, 2, 3, 4, 5]
# Calculate the quartiles of the data
julia> q1, q3 = quantile(data, [0.25, 0.75])
julia> println("The first quartile (Q1) of the data is: ", q1)
The first quartile (Q1) of the data is: 2.0
julia> println("The third quartile (Q3) of the data is: ", q3)
The third quartile (Q3) of the data is: 4.0
```

- **Summary Statistics:**

You can calculate summary statistics for a set of data, such as the mean, median, mode, variance, standard deviation, and range, in one call using the describe or `summarystats` function from StatsBase.jl.

```
using StatsBase
# Define the data set
julia> data = [1, 2, 3, 4, 5]
# Calculate the summary statistics
julia> summary_stats = describe(data)
Summary Stats:
Length: 5
Missing Count: 0
```

```
Mean: 3.000000
Minimum: 1.000000
1st Quartile: 2.000000
Median: 3.000000
3rd Quartile: 4.000000
Maximum: 5.000000
Type: Int64
```

Note that these are just a few of the descriptive statistics measures available in **StatsBase.jl**. It's also worth mentioning that some of the functions mentioned above can accept additional parameters, such as the type of mean or type of quantile calculation, to allow for more specific calculations.

Outlier detection and treatment in data analysis

An outlier is an observation that is significantly different from other observations in a dataset. It is an extreme value that is much larger or smaller than the other values in the dataset. Outliers can be caused by various factors, such as measurement errors, data entry errors, or genuinely unusual events.

Detecting and handling outliers is an important step in data analysis, as they can have a significant impact on statistical measures and modeling results. Outliers can distort the estimates of central tendency, such as the mean and median, and can also affect measures of variability, such as the standard deviation. Therefore, it is important to identify and investigate outliers to determine if they are valid data points or if they should be removed from the dataset.

There are several techniques for identifying and treating outliers, including z-scores and the interquartile range.

- **Z-scores:**

A Z-score, also known as a standard score, is a statistical measurement that represents the number of standard deviations a data point is from the mean of a distribution. Data points with a z-score greater than a certain threshold (usually 2 or –2) are considered outliers. To calculate the z-score of a data point in Julia using **StatsBase.jl**, you can use the `zscore()` function.

```
using StatsBase
# Define the data set
julia> data = [1, 2, 3, 4, 5, 10]
6-element Vector{Int64}:
  1
  2
  3
  4
  5
 10
# Calculate the z-scores of the data set
julia> zscores = zscore(data)
julia> println("The z-scores of the data set are: ", zscores)
The z-scores of the data set are: [-0.993145909629702,
-0.6795208855361119, - 0.36589586144252184, -0.052270837348931766,
0.26135418674465827, 1.8294793072126085]
```

- **Interquartile Range (IQR):**

The interquartile range (IQR) is a measure of variability that indicates how spread out the middle 50% of a dataset is. It is calculated as the difference between the 75th percentile (Q3) and the 25th percentile (Q1) of the data. To identify outliers, a common rule of thumb is to consider any data point that falls below Q1 - 1.5IQR *or above* Q3 + 1.5IQR as an outlier. This means that data points outside this range are unusually far from the median and may be considered extreme values or errors in the data. The IQR method is a robust method for detecting outliers since it is less sensitive to extreme values compared to other methods such as using the standard deviation. To calculate the IQR of a data set in Julia using **StatsBase.jl**, you can use the `iqr()` function.

```
using StatsBase
# Define the data set
julia> data = [1, 2, 3, 4, 5, 10]
# Calculate the IQR of the data set
julia> iqr_value = iqr(data)
julia> println("The IQR of the data set is: ", iqr_value)
The IQR of the data set is: 2.5
```

Distance methods in StatsBase.jl

Evaluating distances or deviations between points in statistics is important because it helps understand how different the data points are from each other or from a central measure such as the mean. By measuring the distances, you can determine the spread or dispersion of the data. The information gained from these measurements can help in identifying outliers, detecting patterns and relationships in the data, and making predictions based on the data.

For example, in a normal distribution, the majority of the data will be close to the mean, with relatively few points deviating significantly from it. If the deviations from the mean are large, it could indicate a skewed or non-normal distribution.

Additionally, evaluating distances between points can be useful in cluster analysis, where the goal is to group similar points together. By measuring the distances between points, you can determine which points are closest to each other and group them accordingly.

- **`L1dist`**: The **`L1dist()`** function in **StatsBase.jl** returns the L1 distance between two arrays. L1 distance, also known as Manhattan distance or taxicab distance, is the sum of the absolute differences of the coordinates between two points , as if the distance had to be traveled along the edges of a square grid rather than in a straight line.

```
julia> using StatsBase
# Define two arrays
julia> array1 = [1, 2, 3]
julia> array2 = [2, 3, 4]
# Calculate the L1 distance between the two arrays
julia> L1_distance = L1dist(array1, array2)
julia> println("The L1 distance between the two arrays is: ", L1_dis-
tance) The L1 distance between the two arrays is: 3.0
```

- **`L2dist`**: The `L2dist` function in **StatsBase.jl** returns the L2 distance between two arrays. L2 distance, also known as Euclidean distance, is the square root of the sum of the squared differences between the coordinates of two points. It represents the length of the straight line connecting two points in a Euclidean space.

```
julia> using StatsBase
julia> # Define two arrays
 array1 = [1, 2, 3]
3-element Vector{Int64}:
```

```
julia> array2 = [2, 3, 4]
3-element Vector{Int64}:
julia> # Calculate the L2 distance between the two arrays
 julia> L2_distance = L2dist(array1, array2)
1.7320508075688772
julia> println("The L2 distance between the two arrays is: ", L2_dis-
tance) The L2 distance between the two arrays is: 1.7320508075688772
```

- **`sqL2dist`**: sqL2 is the sum of the squared differences between the coordinates. The `sqL2dist` function in **StatsBase.jl** returns the square of the L2 distance between two arrays.

```
# Define two arrays
julia> array1 = [1, 2, 3]
julia> array2 = [2, 3, 4]
# Calculate the square of the L2 distance between the two arrays sq_L2_
distance = sqL2dist(array1, array2)
julia> println("The square of the L2 distance between the two arrays is:
", sq_L2_distance) The square of the L2 distance between the two arrays
is: 2.0
```

- **`Linfdist`**: **`Linf`** is the maximum absolute difference between the coordinates. The **`Linfdist`** function in **StatsBase.jl** returns the L-infinity distance between two arrays. L-infinity distance is also known as the Chebyshev distance.

```
# Define two arrays
julia> array1 = [1, 2, 3]
julia> array2 = [2, 3, 4]
# Calculate the L-infinity distance between the two arrays
julia> L_inf_distance = Linfdist(array1, array2)
julia> println("The L-infinity distance between the two arrays is: ",
L_inf_distance)
The L-infinity distance between the two arrays is: 1.0
```

- **`msd`**: The **`msd`** function in **StatsBase.jl** returns the mean squared deviation of two arrays. The mean squared deviation is the average of the squared deviations of the values in an array from another array.

```
# Define the data set
julia> x = [1, 2, 3, 4, 5, 10]
julia> y = [4, 7, 2, 5, 9, 3]
```

```
# Calculate the mean squared deviation of the data set
julia> mean_squared_deviation = msd(x, y)
julia> println("The mean squared deviation of the data set is: ",
mean_squared_deviation) The mean squared deviation of the data set is:
16.833333333333332
```

- `rmsd`: The `rmsd` function in **StatsBase.jl** returns the square root of the average of the squared differences between corresponding values in two sets. The root mean squared deviation is the square root of the mean squared deviation.

```
# Define the data set
julia> x = [1, 2, 3, 4, 5, 10]
julia> y = [4, 7, 2, 5, 9, 3]
# Calculate the root mean squared deviation of the data set
julia> root_mean_squared_deviation = rmsd(x, y)
julia> println("The root mean squared deviation of the data set is:
",root_mean_squared_deviation)
The root mean squared deviation of the data set is: 4.102844541697057
```

- **meanad**: **meanad** calculates the mean absolute deviation of an array, which is the average of the absolute difference between each value in both the arrays of exact same size.

```
# Define the data set
julia> x = [1, 2, 3, 4, 5, 10]
julia> y = [4, 7, 2, 5, 9, 3]
# Calculate the mean deviation of the data set
julia> mean_deviation = meanad(x, y)
julia> println("The mean deviation of the data set is: ", mean_devia-
tion) The mean deviation of the data set is: 3.5
```

- **maxad**: **maxad** calculates the maximum absolute deviation of an array, which is the largest absolute difference between each value in both the arrays of exact same size.

```
# Define the data set
julia> x = [1, 2, 3, 4, 5, 10]
julia> y = [4, 7, 2, 5, 9, 3]
# Calculate the max deviation of the data set
julia> max_deviation = maxad(x, y)
julia> println("The mean deviation of the data set is: ", max_deviation)
The max deviation of the data set is: 7
```

- `gkldiv`: `gkldiv` calculates the **Kullback-Leibler** divergence between two arrays. **Kullback-Leibler** divergence is a statistical metric that quantifies the dissimilarity between two probability distributions. The syntax for using gkldiv is as follows:

```
# Define the data set
julia> p = [0.1, 0.2, 0.3, 0.4, 0.5, 1.0]
julia> q = [0.4, 0.7, 0.2, 0.5, 0.9, 0.3]
# Calculate the root mean squared deviation of the data set
julia> kullback_leibler_deviation = gkldiv(p, q)
julia> println("The kullback-leibler deviation of the data set is: ",
kullback_leibler_deviation)
The kullback-leibler deviation of the data set is: 1.0532795539705795
where p and q are the two input arrays representing the two probability
distributions.
```

Sampling and counting methods

Sampling and counting methods are two fundamental techniques used in data analysis to gain insights into a large dataset.

Sampling involves selecting a smaller, representative subset of the data for analysis instead of using the entire dataset. This helps reduce computational time and cost, and also allows for more efficient analysis and interpretation of the data. Sampling also helps avoid overfitting, where a model fits too closely to the data, making it difficult to generalize results to a new dataset.

Counting methods are used to determine the frequency of occurrence of specific values or events in a dataset. This provides insights into the distribution of data, such as the mode, median, and range, which are useful in understanding the central tendency and variability of the data. Counting methods also enable analysts to identify patterns and trends in the data and make inferences about the population based on the sample data.

Both sampling and counting methods are essential for data analysis and provide a solid foundation for further statistical analysis and modeling.

Counting methods

- `counteq`: The `counteq()` function in **StatsBase.jl** returns the count of elements that are in a specific index in both arrays of exact same size.

```
# Define the data set
julia> x = [1, 2, 3, 4, 5, 10]
julia> y = [4, 7, 3, 5, 9, 3]
# Count the number of elements equal to 3 in the data set
julia> count = counteq(x, y)
julia> println("The number of elements equal to 3 in the data set is: ", count) The number of elements equal to 3 in the data set is: 1
```

- **countne**: The **countne()** function in **StatsBase.jl** returns the count of elements that are not equal to a specific value at a specific index in both arrays of exact same size.

```
# Define the data set
julia> x = [1, 2, 3, 4, 5, 10]
julia> y = [4, 7, 3, 5, 9, 3]
# Count the number of elements not equal to 3 in the data set
julia> count = countne(x, y)
julia> println("The number of elements not equal to 3 in the data set is: ", count) The number of elements not equal to 3 in the data set is: 5
```

- **counts**: The counts() function takes an input x and returns a vector of length *length(levels)* that shows the number of times each value in x occurs. If a range of values (levels) or an integer k is provided, only the values within that range will be considered. If a weights vector *w* is provided, the proportions of weights will be calculated instead of the raw counts.

```
julia> x = [1, 2, 2, 3, 3, 3, 4, 4, 4, 4]
julia> counts(x) # returns [1, 2, 3, 4]
4-element Vector{Int64}:
1
2
3
4
julia> w = [1, 1, 2, 2, 2, 1, 2, 1, 1, 2]
julia> counts(x, w) #addcounts!(zeros(eltype(w), length(levels)), x, levels, w) 4×2 Matrix{Int64}:
1 0
1 1
1 2
```

```
2 2
```

- **`proportions`**: **`proportions()`** function calculates the proportion of values in the range of levels that occur in the input x. If a weights vector wv is provided, the proportion of weights will be calculated instead of the raw counts.

```
julia> x = [1, 2, 2, 3, 3, 3, 4, 4, 4, 4]
julia> proportions(x, 3) # returns [0.1, 0.2, 0.3]
3-element Vector{Float64}:
0.1
0.2
0.30000000000000004
```

- **`addcounts!`**: **`addcounts!()`** method adds the number of occurrences in x of each value in levels, to an existing array r. In case a weight vector (wv) is provided, the summation of the weights will be used instead of the unprocessed counts. **`addcounts!()`** method can also be used to add counts to a count map based on the input x. If a weighting vector wv is specified, the sum of weights will be used instead of the raw counts.

```
julia> r = [0,0,0,0,0];
julia> x = [1,2,3,2,1];
julia> levels = 1:5; #levels = [1,2,3,4,5]
julia> addcounts!(r, x, levels)
5-element Vector{Int64}:
2
2
1
0
0
julia> dict = Dict{Int64,Int64}();
julia> x = [1,2,3,2,1];
julia> addcounts!(dict, x)
Dict{Int64, Int64} with 3 entries:
 2 => 2
 3 => 1
 1 => 2
```

- **`countmap`**: **`countmap()`** function returns a dictionary mapping each unique value in array x to its number of occurrences. In case a weight vector (wv) is provided, the summation of the weights will be used instead of the unprocessed counts. The method can use either radix sort or a dictionary-based method to sort the input vector, depending on the type of data.

```
julia> x = [1,2,3,2,1];
julia> countmap(x)
Dict{Int64, Int64} with 3 entries:
 2 => 2
 3 => 1
 1 => 2
```

- **proportionmap:** `proportionmap()` function returns a dictionary mapping each unique value in array x to its proportion in x. If a weights vector wv is provided, the proportion of weights will be computed instead of the raw counts.

```
julia> x = [1,2,3,2,1];
julia> proportionmap(x)
Dict{Int64, Float64} with 3 entries:
 2 => 0.4
 3 => 0.2
 1 => 0.4
```

Sampling methods

The *sample()* function in Julia's **StatsBase** library is used to select a random sample from an array *a*. The sample can be either a single element, a random array of specified size (or dimensions). The sample can also be weighted based on the weights given in *wv*. The function can be used with or without a random number generator *rng*. There are 4 different forms of the sample function, each with a different purpose. *The* **`sample!()`** function is used to draw a random sample from an array *a* and store it in *x*. It has the same arguments as the sample function. The output array *a* must not share memory with *x* or *wv* to ensure the results are correct.

```
julia> a = [1, 2, 3, 4, 5];
julia> StatsBase.sample(a)
5
julia> StatsBase.sample(a, 2)
2-element Vector{Int64}:
5
```

```
4
julia> x = zeros(Int64, 2);
julia> StatsBase.sample!(a, x)
2-element Vector{Int64}:
5
1
```

Relationship between various features in the dataset during data analysis

Generalized variance, correlation, and covariance are important measures in statistical data analysis because they help to quantify the relationship between two or more variables.

- **Variance** measures the amount of variation or dispersion in a set of data. By understanding the variance, we can determine whether a set of data is spread out or concentrated.
- **Correlation** quantifies both the magnitude and direction of the linear association between two variables. It helps us to determine if a change in one variable is associated with a change in another variable and the extent to which this occurs.
- **Covariance** measures the joint variability of two random variables. It indicates how two variables are related to each other, but does not provide information about the direction of the relationship.

These measures are important in statistical data analysis because they provide a basis for making inferences and predictions about the relationship between variables, and they can be used to test hypotheses and make decisions (data transformations) based on data.

Generalized variance and total variance are measures of the spread of a set of data. By computing the determinant of the covariance matrix of X, the `genvar()` function from **StatsBase** library determines the generalized sample variance of matrix X. By summing the diagonal elements of the covariance matrix of X, the `totalvar()` function determines the total sample variance of X.

```
julia> X = [1 2; 3 4]
2×2 Matrix{Int64}:
1 2
3 4
```

```
julia> println("Generalized Variance: ", genvar(X))
Generalized Variance: 0.0
julia> println("Total Variance: ", totalvar(X))
Total Variance: 4.0
```

Assuming X is a matrix of numeric data, the **genvar()** function accepts it as input and returns its generalized sample variance. When X is a vector or a one-column matrix, the function computes the same result as the sample variance. If X is a matrix, the function returns the determinant of the covariance matrix of X.

Assuming X is a matrix of numeric data, the **totalvar()** function takes it as input and returns its total sample variance. When X is a vector or a one-column matrix, the function computes the sample variance. However, when X is a matrix, the function calculates the sum of the diagonal elements of its covariance matrix.

- **Partial correlation:** is a statistical measure that describes the linear relationship between two variables while controlling for the effects of one or more other variables (Z). It is used to evaluate the relationship between two variables while controlling the influence of other variables. The **partialcor()** function in the **StatsBase** library calculates the partial correlation between the vectors *x* and *y* given Z.

```
julia> x = [1, 2, 3, 4]
4-element Vector{Int64}:
1
2
3
4
julia> y = [2, 4, 6, 8]
4-element Vector{Int64}:
2
4
6
8
julia> Z = [3, 6, 9, 12]
4-element Vector{Int64}:
 3
 6
 9
```

```
12
julia> println("Partial Correlation: ", partialcor(x, y, Z))
Partial Correlation: NaN
```

In these examples, *x*, *y*, and Z are arrays of numerical data. In the **partialcor()** function, *x* and *y* are the two variables whose relationship is being evaluated, and Z is the set of control variables. The function returns the partial correlation between *x* and *y* after controlling for the effects of Z.

Autocorrelation and autocovariance are two related concepts in statistics that describe the degree of linear association between values of a time series.

Autocorrelation measures the linear relationship between a variable and its lagged values over time. A positive autocorrelation indicates that values tend to be similar to their lagged values, while a negative autocorrelation indicates that values tend to be dissimilar to their lagged values. Autocovariance, on the other hand, is a measure of the linear relationship between two lagged values of a variable, without normalizing for the scale of the variable. Like autocorrelation, autocovariance can be positive or negative, indicating a tendency for values to be similar or dissimilar to their lagged values.

autocov() and **autocor()** functions in **StatsBase** compute the autocovariance and autocorrelation, respectively, of a vector or matrix *x*. The **autocov()** function calculates the unnormalized autocovariance, while the **autocor()** function calculates the normalized autocorrelation. The **autocov()** and **autocor()** functions can optionally accept the lags argument to specify the lag values for calculating autocovariance or autocorrelation. Additionally, the demean argument can be used to determine whether the mean of x should be subtracted before computing the values. On the other hand, the **autocov!()** and **autocor!()** functions are analogous to **autocov()** and **autocor()**, but the results are stored in the provided matrix or vector, r.

```
julia> # Example data
 x = [1,2,3,4,5]
5-element Vector{Int64}:
1
2
3
4
5
julia> # Compute autocovariance
```

```
lags = [0,1,2]
3-element Vector{Int64}:
0
1
2
julia> acov = autocov(x, lags)
3-element Vector{Float64}:
 2.0
 0.8
-0.2
julia> # Compute autocorrelation
acor = autocor(x, lags)
3-element Vector{Float64}:
 1.0
 0.4
-0.1
julia> # Compute autocovariance in-place
r = zeros(length(lags))
3-element Vector{Float64}:
0.0
0.0
0.0
julia> autocov!(r, x, lags)
3-element Vector{Float64}:
 2.0
 0.8
-0.2
julia> # Compute autocorrelation in-place
acor_inplace = zeros(length(lags)) 3-element Vector{Float64}:
0.0
0.0
0.0
```

```
julia> autocor!(acor_inplace, x, lags)
3-element Vector{Float64}:
 1.0
 0.4
-0.1
```

In this example, *x* is a vector of numbers. The **autocov()** and **autocor()** functions are used to compute the autocovariance and autocorrelation of *x* at the specified lags. The **autocov!()** and **autocor!()** functions do the same computation, but store the results in-place in the specified *r* and `acor_inplace` arrays, respectively. Note that the output of the autocovariance functions is not normalized, while the autocorrelation functions normalize the output so that the lag 0 autocorrelation is 1.

Cross-correlation measures the degree of linear similarity between two variables as a function of the time lag between them. Specifically, cross-correlation measures the correlation between two variables, x and y, as a function of the lag, k, between them. A positive cross-correlation indicates that the two variables tend to be similar, while a negative cross-correlation indicates that they tend to be dissimilar. Cross-correlation is often used in signal processing and image recognition to compare two signals or images.

Cross-covariance, on the other hand, is a measure of the linear relationship between two variables over time, without normalizing the scale of the variables. It is the covariance between two variables, x and y, as a function of the lag, k, between them. Like cross-correlation, cross-covariance can be positive or negative, indicating a tendency for the two variables to be similar or dissimilar. Cross-covariance is often used in econometrics and finance to measure the relationship between two financial assets.

The **StatsBase.crosscor** function computes the cross correlation between two real-valued vectors or matrices, x and y. It has the same optional argument lags and boolean argument demean as the **crosscov** function.

Here's an example usage of these functions:

```
julia> using StatsBase
julia> x = [1, 2, 3, 4, 5]
5-element Vector{Int64}:
1
2
```

```
3
4
5
julia> y = [2, 3, 4, 5, 6]
5-element Vector{Int64}:
2
3
4
5
6
julia> lags = [-2, -1, 0, 1, 2]
5-element Vector{Int64}:
-2
-1
 0
 1
 2
julia> # Compute cross covariance
 ccf = StatsBase.crosscov(x, y, lags)
5-element Vector{Float64}:
-0.2
 0.8
 2.0
 0.8
-0.2
julia> # Compute cross correlation
 cc = StatsBase.crosscor(x, y, lags)
5-element Vector{Float64}:
-0.1
 0.4
 1.0
 0.4
-0.1
```

```
julia> # Compute cross covariance and store result in pre-allocated
vector
r = similar(lags)
5-element Vector{Int64}:
140643155552448
140643370844656
140643370850096
140643370849904
 0

julia> x = [1, 2, 3, 4, 5]
5-element Vector{Int64}:
1
2
3
4
5
julia> y = [5, 4, 3, 2, 1]
5-element Vector{Int64}:
5
4
3
2
1
julia> lags = [-2, -1, 0, 1, 2]
5-element Vector{Int64}:
-2
-1
 0
 1
 2
julia> crosscor(x, y, lags)
5-element Vector{Float64}:
```

```
 0.1
-0.4
-1.0
-0.4
 0.1
```

Miscellaneous statistical functions that aid in data analysis

The **StatsBase** module in Julia is a library for basic statistical analysis. It contains several functions for working with vectors and matrices. Here are a few of the functions, with code examples:

- **`rle(v): StatsBase.rle()`** is a function, which returns the run-length encoding of a given vector as a tuple. The run-length encoding is a way of representing a sequence where repeated elements are replaced with a single element and the count of occurrences of that element.

```
julia> rle([1,1,1,2,2,3,3,3,3,2,2,2])
([1, 2, 3, 2], [3, 2, 4, 3])
```

The above example inputs a vector [1,1,1,2,2,3,3,3,3,2,2,2] and returns the run-length encoding of it as a tuple. The first element of the tuple is [1, 2, 3, 2] which contains the unique elements in the original vector and the second element of the tuple is [3, 2, 4, 3] which is the count of occurrences of each unique element.

- **`inverse_rle(vals, lens)`:** *StatsBase.inverse_rle()* is a function which takes a run-length encoding and returns the original vector. The input to this function are two vectors: *vals* which is the array of unique elements of the original vector and *lens* which is the count of occurrences of each unique element.

```
julia> vals = [1, 2, 3, 2]
4-element Vector{Int64}:
1
2
3
2
julia> lens = [3, 2, 4, 3]
4-element Vector{Int64}:
3
```

```
2
4
3
julia> inverse_rle(vals, lens)
12-element Vector{Int64}:
```

- **`levelsmap(a)`: `StatsBase.levelsmap()`** is a function which returns a dictionary that maps each of the unique values in a given vector *a* to a number between 1 and the total number of unique values.

```
julia> levelsmap([1, 2, 2, 3, 3, 3, 4])
Dict{Int64, Int64} with 4 entries:
 4 => 4
 2 => 2
 3 => 3
 1 => 1
```

- **`indexmap(a)`: `StatsBase.indexmap()`** is a function which returns a dictionary that maps each unique value in a given vector *a* to the index of its first occurrence in the vector.

```
julia> indexmap([1, 2, 2, 3, 3, 3, 4])
Dict{Int64, Int64} with 4 entries:
 4 => 7
 2 => 2
 3 => 4
 1 => 1
```

- **`indicatormat(x, k::Integer; sparse=false)`: `StatsBase.indicatormat()`** is a function which constructs a boolean matrix from a given vector *x*. The function returns a matrix *I* of size *k* * *length(x)* such that *I[x[i], i]* = *true* and all other elements are set to *false*. The input to the function *x* is the vector to be converted to a boolean matrix, *k* is the number of unique values in the vector *x*. The function also has an optional argument "sparse", which when set to "true", returns a sparse matrix instead of a dense matrix. If the "c" argument is not provided, it defaults to a sorted unique version of *x*.

```
julia> indicatormat([1, 2, 2], 2)
2×3 Matrix{Bool}:
1 0 0
0 1 1
```

In this example, the vector [1, 2, 2] is passed as the input *x* and the number of unique values *k* is set to 2. The resulting boolean matrix *I* is 2x3 in size, with *I*[1, 1] set to true, *I*[2, 2] and *I*[2, 3] set to *true*, and all other elements set to *false*.

- **midpoints(v)**: **StatsBase.midpoints()** is a function that calculates the midpoints (pairwise mean of consecutive elements) of a vector *v*.

```
julia> v = [1, 2, 3, 4, 5]
5-element Vector{Int64}:
1
2
3
4
5
julia> midpoints(v)
4-element Vector{Float64}:
1.5
2.5
3.5
4.5
```

The **pairwise()** function and its in-place version **pairwise!()** are functions in the **StatsAPI** library in Julia programming language. They are used to apply a given function *f* to all possible pairs of elements in two inputs *x* and *y*. If y is not provided, *x* is crossed with itself to return a square matrix.

The result of applying *f* is stored in a matrix, where the rows correspond to entries in *x* and columns correspond to entries in *y*. In the case of **pairwise!()**, the result is stored in an existing matrix *dest*, and the function returns *dest*.

```
julia> x = [1 3 7
 2 5 6
 3 8 4
 4 6 2];
julia> pairwise(cor, eachcol(x))
3×3 Matrix{Float64}:
 1.0 0.744208 -0.989778
 0.744208 1.0 -0.68605
-0.989778 -0.68605 1.0
```

```
julia> y = [1 3 missing
 2 5 6
 3 missing 2
 4 6 2];
julia> pairwise(cor, eachcol(y), skipmissing=:pairwise)
3×3 Matrix{Float64}:
 1.0 0.928571 -0.866025
 0.928571 1.0 -1.0
-0.866025 -1.0 1.0
julia> dest = zeros(3, 3);
julia> pairwise!(cor, dest, eachcol(x));
julia> dest
3×3 Matrix{Float64}:
 1.0 0.744208 -0.989778
 0.744208 1.0 -0.68605
-0.989778 -0.68605 1.0
julia> pairwise!(cor, dest, eachcol(y), skipmissing=:pairwise);
julia> dest
3×3 Matrix{Float64}:
 1.0 0.928571 -0.866025
 0.928571 1.0 -1.0
-0.866025 -1.0 1.0
```

Observational estimation in data analysis

Observational estimation is a statistical method used in data analysis that involves the collection and analysis of data from observations that are made in the real world. This method involves observing a particular phenomenon or event and collecting data on various variables associated with it. The data can be either quantitative or qualitative and may be collected through surveys, interviews, or other methods of observation.

Observational estimation is particularly useful in situations where it is not possible or ethical to conduct a randomized controlled trial, as in the case of medical studies where it may not be feasible to conduct a trial with a placebo group. Instead, observational studies can be used to compare the effects of different treatments on a group of patients or to compare the effects of exposure to certain environmental factors on a population.

In observational estimation, statistical techniques are used to estimate the relationship between different variables and to determine whether there is a cause-and-effect relationship between them. One of the key challenges in observational estimation is to control for potential confounding variables, which are factors that may influence the relationship between the variables being studied. For example, in a study looking at the effect of a particular drug on a medical condition, other factors such as age, gender, and underlying health conditions may need to be controlled to accurately estimate the effect of the drug.

The **`StatsBase.Histogram`** is a type in Julia that represents data that has been tabulated into bins along the real line or over a real space in higher dimensions. You can fit a histogram to your data using the fit method, which can be called as follows:

```
fit(Histogram, data, [weight], [edges]; closed=:left, nbins)
```

The arguments are:

- **data:** either a vector (for a one-dimensional histogram) or a tuple of vectors of equal length (for an n-dimensional histogram).
- **weight (optional):** an **`AbstractWeights`** object of the same length as the data vectors, indicating the weight each observation contributes to the bin. If not provided, each observation has weight 1.
- **edges (optional):** a vector or a tuple of vectors that give the edges of the bins along each dimension. If not provided, the edges will be determined from the data.

The keyword arguments are:

- **closed:** if set to *:left* (default), the bin intervals are left-closed [a,b); if set to *:right*, intervals are right-closed (a,b].
- **nbins (optional):** when the edges argument is not specified, this value corresponds to the approximate number of bins to be utilized along each dimension. It can be expressed as a single integer or a tuple of integers.

You can also merge histograms using **`Base.merge!()`** and **`Base.merge()`**. These functions allow you to update a target histogram by merging it with one or more other histograms, or construct a new histogram by merging histograms. All histograms must have the same binning, shape of weights, and properties (*closed* and *isdensity*).

```
julia> using StatsBase

julia> # Univariate
 h = fit(Histogram, rand(100))
Histogram{Int64, 1, Tuple{StepRangeLen{Float64, Base.TwicePrecision
{Float64},  Base.TwicePrecision{Float64}, Int64}}}
edges:
 0.0:0.2:1.0
weights: [18, 15, 25, 21, 21]
closed: left
isdensity: false

julia> h = fit(Histogram, rand(100), 0:0.1:1.0)
Histogram{Int64, 1, Tuple{StepRangeLen{Float64, Base.TwicePrecision
{Float64},  Base.TwicePrecision{Float64}, Int64}}}
edges:
 0.0:0.1:1.0
weights: [8, 8, 11, 4, 8, 14, 13, 18, 8, 8]
closed: left
isdensity: false

julia> h = fit(Histogram, rand(100), nbins=10)
Histogram{Int64, 1, Tuple{StepRangeLen{Float64, Base.TwicePrecision
{Float64},  Base.TwicePrecision{Float64}, Int64}}}
edges:
 0.0:0.1:1.0
weights: [9, 7, 11, 8, 9, 12, 13, 7, 11, 13]
closed: left
isdensity: false

julia> h = fit(Histogram, rand(100), weights(rand(100)), 0:0.1:1.0)
Histogram{Float64, 1, Tuple{StepRangeLen{Float64, Base.TwicePrecision
{Float64},  Base.TwicePrecision{Float64}, Int64}}}
edges:
 0.0:0.1:1.0
weights: [9.03362694785457, 6.5630746683585155, 6.708583302844759,
1.8780191525470449, 5.176468819705679, 4.690381340041942,
2.4322472127857426,  7.8143366878106555, 3.857428925388602,
8.321820464999115]
```

```
closed: left
isdensity: false
julia> h = fit(Histogram, [20], 0:20:100)
Histogram{Int64, 1, Tuple{StepRange{Int64, Int64}}}
edges:
 0:20:100
weights: [0, 1, 0, 0, 0]
closed: left
isdensity: false
julia> h = fit(Histogram, [20], 0:20:100, closed=:right)
Histogram{Int64, 1, Tuple{StepRange{Int64, Int64}}}
edges:
 0:20:100
weights: [1, 0, 0, 0, 0]
closed: right
isdensity: false
julia> # Multivariate
 h = fit(Histogram, (rand(100),rand(100)))
Histogram{Int64, 2, Tuple{StepRangeLen{Float64, Base.TwicePrecision
{Float64},  Base.TwicePrecision{Float64}, Int64}, StepRangeLen{Float64,
Base.TwicePrecision{Float64}, Base.TwicePrecision{Float64}, Int64}}}
edges:
 0.0:0.2:1.0
 0.0:0.2:1.0
weights: [4 6 … 4 3; 1 3 … 3 4; … ; 4 3 … 6 5; 6 4 … 3 4]
closed: left
isdensity: false
julia> h = fit(Histogram, (rand(100),rand(100)),nbins=10)
Histogram{Int64, 2, Tuple{StepRangeLen{Float64, Base.TwicePrecision
{Float64},  Base.TwicePrecision{Float64}, Int64}, StepRangeLen{Float64,
Base.TwicePrecision{Float64}, Base.TwicePrecision{Float64}, Int64}}}
edges:
 0.0:0.1:1.0
 0.0:0.1:1.0
```

```
weights: [0 2 … 2 0; 1 0 … 0 0; … ; 2 0 … 0 1; 2 0 … 0 0]
closed: left
isdensity: false
```

Conclusion

The study of statistics in Julia provides a comprehensive understanding of the various aspects of data analysis. The purpose of descriptive statistics is to summarize and describe the characteristics of a dataset in a meaningful way. The measures discussed include central tendency, dispersion, and distribution shape. Outlier detection and treatment is a crucial step in ensuring the accuracy of the results. Distance methods provide a way to determine the similarity or difference between two or more observations. Counts and sampling play a vital role in determining the size and representativeness of the sample. The relationship between various features in a dataset can be evaluated using correlation and covariance. Miscellaneous statistical functions such as hypothesis testing, probability distributions, and regression analysis further aid in data analysis. Finally, empirical estimation provides a way to make predictions or generalizations about a population based on a sample. Julia has a comprehensive set of functions to perform these tasks. In conclusion, Julia provides a comprehensive set of tools for statistical data analysis, and it is a great tool for researchers and data scientists to use. All these topics covered in the study of statistics in Julia are essential for a complete and thorough data analysis.

In Julia, there are many functions that support the analysis of different types of distributions, including univariate distributions, censored distributions, multivariate distributions, matrix variate distributions, and even correlation and maximum likelihood estimation. We will learn about the various distributions in next chapters and learn to use the respective functions in the data analysis process in the next chapter.

Questions

1. What is the purpose of descriptive statistics in Julia and why is it important in data analysis?
2. Can you provide an overview of the main descriptive statistics measures in Julia and their uses?
3. How does one detect and treat outliers in data analysis using Julia?

4. Can you explain the concept of distance methods and their role in data analysis in Julia?
5. What is the relationship between counts and sampling in data analysis using Julia?
6. Can you discuss how the relationship between various features in a dataset is evaluated during data analysis in Julia?
7. What are the miscellaneous statistical functions available in Julia that aid in data analysis?
8. Can you explain the concept of observational estimation and its importance in data analysis in Julia?

CHAPTER 7
Probability Data Distributions

The field of statistics encompasses a wide range of techniques and tools for analyzing data. One important aspect of statistical analysis is the study of probability distributions, which provides a mathematical framework for understanding the behavior of random variables. In this chapter, we will explore some common functions in distributions and their implementation in Julia.

We will begin by discussing univariate distributions, which describe the behavior of a single random variable. We will then delve into censored distributions, which arise when some observations are truncated or otherwise incomplete. Moving on, we will explore multivariate distributions, which describe the joint behavior of multiple random variables. We will also look at matrix-variate distributions, which are used to model multivariate data that have a matrix structure.

Overall, this chapter provides a comprehensive overview of some important concepts in probability distributions and their implementation in Julia, highlighting the language's flexibility and efficiency for statistical analysis.

Structure

In this chapter, the following topics will be covered:

- Introduction to probability
- Introduction to probability package in Julia
- Introducing the distributions' package
- Common functions in distributions
- Univariate probability distributions
- Censored probability distributions

- Truncated probability distributions
- Multivariate probability distributions
- Matrix-variate probability distributions
- Mixture models in distributions
- Mixture models and convolutions in Distributions.jl
- Fitting a probability distribution

Introduction to probability

Probability is a branch of mathematics that deals with the study of random events or processes and the likelihood of their occurrence. It is concerned with the analysis and quantification of uncertainty and risk in various areas of study, including finance, statistics, physics, engineering, and more.

At its core, probability involves the assignment of numerical values to events or outcomes to quantify their likelihood or chance of occurrence. These numerical values, called probabilities, range from 0 to 1, with 0 indicating an impossible event and 1 indicating a certain event. Probabilities between 0 and 1 indicate varying degrees of likelihood, with values closer to 0 indicating lower probability and values closer to 1 indicating higher probability.

Probabilities can be calculated using a variety of techniques, including counting methods, empirical observation, and mathematical modeling. Probability theory provides a framework for understanding and analyzing the behavior of random events and processes and has numerous applications in fields, such as finance, risk management, data analysis, and scientific research.

In practice, probability is used to make informed decisions based on incomplete or uncertain information. For example, in finance, the probability is used to determine the risk and return associated with investment decisions. In healthcare, probability is used to assess the likelihood of disease outbreaks and the effectiveness of treatments. In engineering, probability is used to design and test products and systems for reliability and safety.

Conditional probability, Joint probability, and Bayes' theorem are essential concepts in probability theory and have numerous applications in various fields.

Conditional Probability: Conditional probability is the probability of an event happening, given that another event has already occurred. In other words, it is the probability of one event happening, given that we know another event has occurred. It is denoted as P(A|B), which means the probability of A given B. The formula for conditional probability is:

```
P(A|B) = P(A ∩ B) / P(B)
```

Where P(A ∩ B) represents the probability of the intersection of events A and B.

Joint Probability: Joint probability is the probability of two or more events occurring simultaneously. It is denoted as P(A ∩ B), which means the probability of A and B occurring at the same time. The formula for joint probability is:

```
P(A ∩ B) = P(A|B) x P(B) = P(B|A) x P(A)
```

Where P(A|B) and P(B|A) are conditional probabilities.

Bayes' Theorem: Bayes' theorem is a fundamental concept in probability theory that provides a way to revise or update the probability of an event happening based on new information. It allows us to calculate the conditional probability of an event, given some observed evidence. The formula for Bayes' theorem is:

```
P(A|B) = P(B|A) x P(A) / P(B)
```

Where P(A) and P(B) are the probabilities of events A and B, respectively. P(B|A) is the conditional probability of B given A, and P(A|B) is the conditional probability of A given B.

Bayes' theorem has many applications in fields such as machine learning, data science, medical diagnosis, and more. For example, in machine learning, it is used to calculate the probability of a hypothesis given some observed data, which is a fundamental step in Bayesian inference. In medical diagnosis, Bayes' theorem is used to calculate the probability of a disease given some observed symptoms.

Introducing probability package in Julia

Probability refers to the measure of the likelihood or chance of an event occurring. It is a numerical value between 0 and 1, where 0 indicates that the event is impossible and 1 indicates that the event is certain. Probability can be used to describe the likelihood of outcomes of a single event or multiple events.

On the other hand, a probability distribution is a function that describes the likelihood of different outcomes in a random process. It assigns probabilities to different outcomes or events and can be used to calculate the probability of an event occurring. Probability distributions can be discrete or continuous, depending on the type of random variable they describe.

For example, flipping a fair coin has a probability of 0.5 of getting heads or tails.

This is an example of probability. However, if we flip the coin multiple times and count the number of heads, we can describe the probability distribution of the number of heads. In this case, the probability distribution would be a binomial distribution, which describes the likelihood of getting a certain number of successes in a fixed number of trials.

The Distributions.jl package is a Julia package for working with probability distributions. It is part of Julia's extensive ecosystem of packages for scientific computing and data analysis. It provides a comprehensive set of tools for working with both common and uncommon probability distributions, including functions for probability density functions (PDFs), cumulative distribution functions (CDFs), quantile functions, and random number generation.

The package provides an extensive list of univariate probability distributions, including both continuous and discrete distributions, such as the normal distribution, the binomial distribution, the Poisson distribution, the gamma distribution, the t-distribution, the beta distribution, and many more. Each distribution is represented as a Julia type, with methods for all the standard distribution functions.

One of the key features of the Distributions.jl package is its ability to handle parameterized distributions. In many cases, probability distributions are parameterized by one or more parameters, such as the mean and standard deviation for the normal distribution. The Distributions.jl package provides a convenient way to create and manipulate parameterized distributions and includes functions for fitting distributions to data using maximum likelihood estimation.

In addition to the probability distribution functions, the Distributions.jl package provides a range of statistical functions and methods for working with probability distributions. For example, it provides functions for calculating moments, quantiles, and entropy of a distribution. It also provides methods for generating random numbers from a distribution, computing the probability density function, cumulative distribution function, and survival function.

In addition to working with probability distributions, the Distributions.jl package also provides tools for working with multivariate distributions, including the multivariate normal distribution and the Wishart distribution. These tools make it easy to perform calculations involving multiple random variables.

The Distributions.jl package is easy to use and integrates well with other packages in the Julia ecosystem, such as the StatsBase.jl package for statistical analysis, and the Plots.jl package for data visualization. It also provides support for automatic differentiation using the ForwardDiff.jl package, making it easy to perform gradient-based optimization on probability distributions.

The Distributions.jl package is a powerful and flexible tool for working with probability distributions in Julia and is well-suited for both simulation and statistical analysis. It also provides a wide range of functionality and integration with other Julia packages.

Introducing the Distributions.jl package

To start using the package, you need to install it through the Julia package system by running:

```
Pkg.add("Distributions")
```

Once installed, you can easily create and work with various probability distributions. For example, to create a standard normal distribution, you can use the Normal function with no arguments.

The first step is to set up the environment and set the seed. The standard-normal distribution object is created, and samples are obtained using rand. Object `d` represents a probability distribution, and we can query its properties, such as the mean. We can also draw samples from d with rand. You can also query various properties of a distribution such as its mean and obtain probability density, cumulative distribution, and quantile functions (*Figure 7.1*).

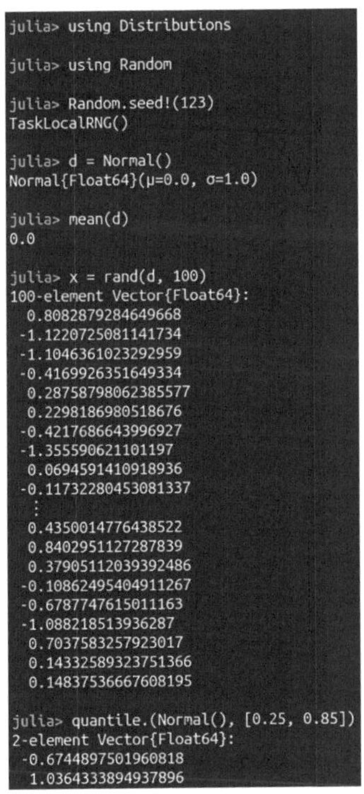
```
julia> using Distributions

julia> using Random

julia> Random.seed!(123)
TaskLocalRNG()

julia> d = Normal()
Normal{Float64}(μ=0.0, σ=1.0)

julia> mean(d)
0.0

julia> x = rand(d, 100)
100-element Vector{Float64}:
  0.8082879284649668
 -1.1220725081141734
 -1.1046361023292959
 -0.4169926351649334
  0.28758798062385577
  0.2298186980518676
 -0.4217686643996927
 -1.355590621101197
  0.0694591410918936
 -0.11732280453081337
  ⋮
  0.4350014776438522
  0.8402951127287839
  0.37905112039392486
 -0.10862495404911267
 -0.6787747615011163
 -1.088218513936287
  0.7037583257923017
  0.14332589323751366
  0.14837536667608195

julia> quantile.(Normal(), [0.25, 0.85])
2-element Vector{Float64}:
 -0.6744897501960818
  1.0364333894937896
```

Figure 7.1: *Using a Normal() distribution along with statistical functions*

Common functions in distributions

Distributions.jl provides a variety of common interfacing functions to create, manipulate, and operate on probability distributions. These interfacing functions are used to work with and manipulate probability distributions in a flexible and modular way. They allow users to calculate the statistical properties of distributions, evaluate the probability density and cumulative distribution functions, and draw random samples from distributions.

Type hierarchy

The Distributions.jl package in Julia provides a hierarchy of types that allows for generating samples from various types of probability distributions. This hierarchy is organized around the abstract type Sampleable, which subsumes any type of object from which one can draw samples, including both samplers and distributions.

The Sampleable type has two type parameters that define the kind of samples that can be drawn therefrom. These parameters are F<:VariateForm, which specifies the form of the samples (e.g., univariate or multivariate), and S<:ValueSupport, which specifies whether the samples take countably or uncountably many values (i.e., discrete or continuous).

The VariateForm parameter has subtypes that define the form of the samples. There are three types: Univariate, Multivariate, and Matrixvariate. The ValueSupport parameter has two subtypes: Discrete and Continuous.

For example, a discrete univariate distribution can be defined as Distribution{Univariate, Discrete}, while a continuous multivariate distribution can be defined as Distribution{Multivariate, Continuous}. These types are subtypes of the Distribution abstract type, which is a subtype of Sampleable.

```
                         Sampleable
                  /                    \
               /                          \
            /                                \
      VariateForm<:F                    ValueSupport<:S
     /      |      \                         /   \
    /       |       \                       /     \
Univariate Multivariate Matrixvariate   Discrete   Continuous
```

```
      |
  Distribution
      |
UnivariateDistribution<:S
      |
ContinuousDistribution<:F
```

The basic functionalities that a sampleable object provides are to retrieve information about the samples it generates and to draw samples. For example, the rand method can be used to draw samples from a sampleable object. The type of the samples returned by rand is determined by the `eltype()` method, which returns the default element type of a sample.

In addition to the basic functionalities, distributions typically come with additional methods to compute properties, such as the probability density function (PDF), cumulative distribution function (CDF), and quantiles.

To simplify the use of distributions in practice, the Distributions.jl package provides a series of type aliases, such as **`UnivariateDistribution{S<:ValueSupport}`** and **`ContinuousDistribution{F<:VariateForm}`**, which are more convenient to use than the full **`Distribution{F,S}`** type.

Here's an example code snippet (*Figure* 7.2) that demonstrates how to draw samples from a normal distribution:

```
julia> using Distributions

julia> # create a normal distribution with mean 0 and standard deviation 1
       normal = Normal(0, 1)
Normal{Float64}(μ=0.0, σ=1.0)

julia> # draw a single sample
       x = rand(normal)
0.028766636052271793

julia> # draw 10 samples
       xs = rand(normal, 10)
10-element Vector{Float64}:
 -0.7470397661634814
 -0.2900143051127036
  0.12412397060725551
  0.032114510283638494
  0.2322909372677087
 -1.2653140705580803
 -1.1759655690989972
 -0.1383989248694004
  0.14067210710997152
  1.4573699182901863

julia> # compute the PDF at x
       pdf_value = pdf(normal, x)
0.3987772483173623
```

Figure 7.2: *Using the Sampleable type for declaring Normal distribution and evaluating probability density function*

Parameter retrieval

We will learn about the methods available in the StatsAPI and Distributions packages for retrieving distribution parameters and related information. These methods are available for univariate distributions, which are distributions with a single random variable.

The params method is defined for all univariate distributions, and it returns a tuple of parameters that define the distribution. Given a distribution d of type D, the expression `D(params(d)...)` will create a new instance of the same distribution as d.

The scale, location, shape, rate, ncategories, and ntrials methods are defined for specific distributions, and they return the corresponding parameter value for that distribution. For example, the scale method is defined for the Gamma, InverseGamma, and Weibull distributions, while the ncategories method is defined for the Categorical distribution (*Figure* 7.3).

```
julia> # create a normal distribution with mean 0 and standard deviation 1
       d = Normal(0, 1)
Normal{Float64}(μ=0.0, σ=1.0)

julia> # retrieve the mean and standard deviation
       μ = mean(d)
0.0

julia> σ = std(d)
1.0

julia> # retrieve the parameters as a tuple
       params_tuple = params(d)
(0.0, 1.0)

julia> # create a new normal distribution from the parameters
       new_d = Normal(params_tuple...)
Normal{Float64}(μ=0.0, σ=1.0)

julia> # retrieve the scale parameter for the Gamma distribution
       gamma_d = Gamma(2, 3)
Gamma{Float64}(α=2.0, θ=3.0)

julia> scale_param = scale(gamma_d)
3.0

julia> # retrieve the number of categories for the Categorical distribution
       cat_d = Categorical([0.25, 0.5, 0.25])
Categorical{Float64, Vector{Float64}}(support=Base.OneTo(3), p=[0.25, 0.5, 0.25])

julia> num_categories = ncategories(cat_d)
3
```

***Figure 7.3**: Extracting all the parameters of the distribution*

For distributions where success and failure have a meaning, the succprob and failprob methods are defined for retrieving the probability of success and failure, respectively. These methods are defined for discrete univariate distributions, such as the Binomial and NegativeBinomial distributions (*Figure* 7.4).

```
julia> # retrieve the probability of success for the Binomial distribution
       binom_d = Binomial(10, 0.5)
Binomial{Float64}(n=10, p=0.5)

julia> p_success = succprob(binom_d)
0.5

julia> # retrieve the probability of failure for the NegativeBinomial distribution
       neg_binom_d = NegativeBinomial(5, 0.3)
NegativeBinomial{Float64}(r=5.0, p=0.3)

julia> p_failure = failprob(neg_binom_d)
0.7
```

Figure 7.4: *Checking the success and failing probability of the distribution*

Sampling

The `rand(rng::AbstractRNG, d::UnivariateDistribution)` method generates a scalar sample from the specified univariate distribution d. The method uses the random number generator rng to produce the random numbers. The default behavior is to use the quantile function of the distribution to generate the sample.

```
using Random, Distributions


# create a normal distribution with mean=0 and std=1
julia> d = Normal()


# create an array of zeros to store the samples
julia> samples = zeros(100)


# sample 100 values from the normal distribution and store them in the
samples array
julia> rng = MersenneTwister(1234)
julia> rand!(rng, d, samples)


julia> println("Sampled values: $samples")
```

Computation of statistics

There are various functions and methods for computing different statistics of probability distributions in the Julia programming language:

- **`Base.maximum`, `Base.minimum`, `Base.extrema`**: These functions return the maximum, minimum, and minimum and maximum values of the support of the distribution, respectively (*Figure* 7.5). For example:

```
julia> using Distributions

julia> d = Uniform(1, 5)
Uniform{Float64}(a=1.0, b=5.0)

julia> Base.maximum(d) # returns 5.0
5.0

julia> Base.minimum(d) # returns 1.0
1.0

julia> Base.extrema(d) # returns (1.0, 5.0)
(1.0, 5.0)
```

Figure 7.5: *Finding the maximum, minimum, and extremum values in a Uniform Distribution*

- **`Statistics.mean`, `Statistics.var`, `Statistics.std`, `Statistics.median`**: These functions compute the mean, variance, standard deviation, and median of a univariate distribution, respectively (*Figure* 7.6). For example:

```
julia> using Statistics

julia> using Distributions

julia> d = Normal(0, 1)
Normal{Float64}(μ=0.0, σ=1.0)

julia> Statistics.mean(d) # returns 0.0
0.0

julia> Statistics.var(d) # returns 1.0
1.0

julia> Statistics.std(d) # returns 1.0
1.0

julia> Statistics.median(d) # returns 0.0
0.0
```

Figure 7.6: *Finding the mean, variance, standard deviation, and median values of Normal Distribution*

- **`StatsBase.modes, StatsBase.mode`**: These functions compute the modes (local maxima) of a univariate distribution. `StatsBase.modes` returns all the modes, while `StatsBase.mode` returns only the first mode (*Figure* 7.7). For example:

```
julia> using StatsBase

julia> using Distributions

julia> d = Beta(2, 2)
Beta{Float64}(α=2.0, β=2.0)

julia> StatsBase.modes(d) # returns [0.5]
1-element Vector{Float64}:
 0.5

julia> StatsBase.mode(d) # returns 0.5
0.5
```

Figure 7.7: *Evaluating mode and modes of a Beta distribution*

- StatsBase.skewness, StatsBase.kurtosis: These functions compute the skewness and excess kurtosis of a univariate distribution, respectively (*Figure* 7.8). For example:

```
julia> d = Exponential(1)
Exponential{Float64}(θ=1.0)

julia> StatsBase.skewness(d) # returns 2.0
2.0

julia> StatsBase.kurtosis(d) # returns 6.0
6.0
```

Figure 7.8: *Evaluating skewness and kurtosis of exponential distribution*

- StatsBase.entropy: This function computes the entropy of a univariate distribution. The second version of the function allows you to specify a base for the logarithm.
- **`Distributions.mgf`**, **`Distributions.cgf`**, **`Distributions.cf`**: These functions evaluate the moment-generating function, cumulant-generating function, and characteristic function of a univariate distribution, respectively (*Figure* 7.9). For example:

```
julia> d = Normal(0, 1)
Normal{Float64}(μ=0.0, σ=1.0)

julia> StatsBase.entropy(d) # returns 1.4189385332046727
1.4189385332046727

julia> StatsBase.entropy(d, 2) # returns 0.9182958340544896
2.047095585180641

julia> Distributions.mgf(d, 0.5) # returns 1.133148453066826
1.1331484530668263

julia> Distributions.cgf(d, 0.5) # returns 0.17833751737402016
0.125

julia> Distributions.cf(d, 0.5) # returns 0.8775825618903728 + 0.479425538604
0.8824969025845955 + 0.0im
```

***Figure 7.9**: Evaluating entropy and moments of normal distribution*

Estimating probability

Probability evaluation is an important part of working with probability distributions. Here are some code samples that explain commonly used functions for probability evaluation:

`insupport()` is a method that checks whether a given scalar or array is within the support of a given univariate distribution. It returns true if the input is within the support and false otherwise. Distributions.pdf is a method that evaluates the probability density (mass) of a given univariate distribution at a given point x. It returns a scalar value that represents the probability density at the given point. Distributions.logpdf is a method that evaluates the logarithm of the probability density (mass) of a given univariate distribution at a given point x. It returns a scalar value that represents the logarithm of the probability density at the given point. Here is an example of using this method:

```
julia> d = Normal(0, 1) # Normal distribution with mean 0 and standard deviation 1
Normal{Float64}(μ=0.0, σ=1.0)

julia> insupport(d, 0)
true

julia> insupport(d, 10)
true

julia> x = [0, 1, 2, 3, 4]
5-element Vector{Int64}:
 0
 1
 2
 3
 4

julia> insupport(d, x)
5-element BitVector:
 1
 1
 1
 1
 1

julia> pdf(d, 0)
0.3989422804014327

julia> logpdf(d, 0)
-0.9189385332046728
```

***Figure 7.10**: Evaluating insupport, pdf, logpdf, of normal distribution*

These functions (*Figure* 7.10) are commonly used in probability calculations, and understanding their usage is important for working with probability distributions in Julia.

The Distributions.jl package provides various probability distributions and related functions for the Julia programming language. Among these functions, we have:

- **`cdf(d::UnivariateDistribution, x::Real)`**: This function computes the cumulative distribution function (CDF) of the given univariate probability distribution d at point x. The CDF is defined as the probability of observing a value less than or equal to x in the distribution. For example, if d is a standard normal distribution, cdf(d, 0.0) returns the probability of observing a value less than or equal to 0.0 in the distribution.
- **`logcdf(d::UnivariateDistribution, x::Real)`**: This function computes the natural logarithm of the CDF of the given univariate probability distribution d at the point x. This function can be more numerically stable than cdf for small probabilities (*Figure* 7.11).

```
julia> cdf_value = cdf(d, 0.5)
0.6914624612740131

julia> # compute the CDF at x=0.5
       cdf_value = cdf(d, 0.5)
0.6914624612740131

julia> # compute the natural logarithm of the CDF at x=0.5
       logcdf_value = logcdf(d, 0.5)
-0.36894641528865635
```

***Figure 7.11**: Evaluating cdf, logcdf of normal distribution*

- **`quantile(d::UnivariateDistribution, q::Real)`**: This function computes the inverse cumulative distribution function (also known as the quantile function) of the given univariate probability distribution d at the probability level q. The quantile function gives the value x such that **`cdf(d, x) = q`**.
- **`cquantile(d::UnivariateDistribution, q::Real)`**: This function computes the complementary quantile value of the given univariate probability distribution d at the probability level q. The complementary quantile is defined as quantile(d, 1-q).
- **`invlogcdf(d::UnivariateDistribution, lp::Real)`**: This function computes the inverse function of logcdf for the given univariate probability distribution d at the natural logarithm of the probability level lp (*Figure* 7.12).

```
julia> # compute the quantile at probability level q=0.95

       quantile_value = quantile(d, 0.95)
1.6448536269514717

julia> # compute the complementary quantile at probability level q=0.95

              cquantile_value = cquantile(d, 0.95)
-1.6448536269514717

julia> # compute the inverse function of logcdf at lp=ln(0.05)

              invlogcdf_value = invlogcdf(d, log(0.05))
-1.6448536269514722
```

***Figure 7.12**: Evaluating quantile, cquantile, inverse log cdf of normal distribution*

Dimension inspection

Length, size, and eltype are methods used in Julia to query the properties of a multivariate distribution and its samples.

- The `length(d::MultivariateDistribution) -> Int` method returns the sample dimension of the specified multivariate distribution d. The sample dimension is the number of dimensions in the distribution's support.
- The `size(d::MultivariateDistribution)` method returns a tuple representing the sample size of the specified multivariate distribution d. The sample size is a tuple with a single element, which is the sample dimension returned by length(d).
- The `eltype(::Type{Sampleable})` method returns the default element type of sample. This is the type of elements of the samples generated by the rand method. However, one can provide an array of different element types to store the samples using rand!.
- The reshape function can be used to reshape an array variate distributions to a different shape. It takes a distribution d and new dimensions as either an Int or Dims object and returns a new distribution object of the reshaped array variate. The default implementation returns a `ReshapedDistribution`, but for specific types of distributions and dimensions, more optimized distributions may be returned.
- The vec function reshapes the array variate to a 1D distribution with a length equal to the number of elements in the original array variate. The default implementation also returns a ReshapedDistribution, but like with reshape, more optimized distributions may be returned for specific types of distributions and dimensions.

Univariate probability distribution

Distributions.jl is a Julia package for working with probability distributions, including both univariate and multivariate distributions. In this response, we will focus on the univariate distributions available in Distributions.jl.

A univariate distribution is a probability distribution that describes the behavior of a single random variable. In Distributions.jl, there are many univariate distributions available, including the normal (Gaussian), t, chi-square, F, beta, gamma, Poisson, binomial, and many more.

Each univariate distribution in Distributions.jl is implemented as a type that defines its parameters and methods. For example, the normal distribution is implemented as Normal and takes two arguments: the mean and standard deviation. The following code defines a normal distribution with a mean of 0.0 and a standard deviation of 1.0:

```
julia> using Distributions

julia> normal = Normal(0.0, 1.0)
Normal{Float64}(μ=0.0, σ=1.0)
```

***Figure 7.13**: Normal univariate distribution*

Once a distribution is defined, it is possible to perform various operations with it, such as sampling from the distribution, evaluating the probability density function (PDF), and calculating moments. For example, the following code generates 1000 samples from the normal distribution defined above and calculates the sample mean and variance:

```
julia> samples = rand(normal, 1000)
julia> sample_mean = mean(samples)
julia> sample_var = var(samples)
```

```
julia> sample_mean = mean(samples)
0.029938484548656597

julia> sample_var = var(samples)
0.9662229656466321
```

***Figure 7.14**: Mean and variance of samples of normal distribution*

Distributions.jl also provides functions for computing the PDF and cumulative distribution function (CDF) of univariate distributions. For example, the following code computes the PDF of the normal distribution defined above at the point `x = 1.0`:

```
julia> x = 1.0
1.0

julia> pdf_value = pdf(normal, x)
0.24197072451914337
```

Figure 7.15: *Finding the pdf of univariate normal distribution*

Distributions.jl provides a comprehensive collection of univariate distributions that can be used for a wide range of statistical and probabilistic applications. Its easy-to-use interface and efficient implementation make it a powerful tool for working with probability distributions in Julia.

Censored probability distribution

Distributions.jl is a popular Julia package for probability distributions, and it includes a variety of different types of distributions that can be used for statistical analysis and simulation. One important feature of distributions is that they can be censored, meaning that the values are restricted to a certain range. The **Distributions.jl** package includes support for censored distributions through the Censored type.

The Censored type is used to represent censored distributions in Distributions.jl. It takes two arguments: the underlying distribution, which is the distribution that the censored distribution is based on, and a lower and/or upper bound, which specifies the range of the censored values. For example, if we wanted to represent a normal distribution with values between 0 and 10, we could create a Censored distribution using the following code:

```
julia> using Distributions

julia> d = Normal()
Normal{Float64}(μ=0.0, σ=1.0)

julia> c = censored(d, 0, 10)
Censored(Normal{Float64}(μ=0.0, σ=1.0); lower=0, upper=10)
```

Figure 7.16: *Censored Distribution on Normal probability distribution*

This would create a censored distribution based on a normal distribution with a mean of 0 and a standard deviation of 1 but with values between 0 and 10. Any values outside of this range are treated as missing data and are not included in calculations.

The censored type in Distributions.jl supports a variety of different distributions, including the normal, lognormal, exponential, and many others. In addition, it supports left-censoring, right-censoring, and interval-censoring, allowing for a wide range of different censored distributions to be represented.

Censored distributions are useful in a variety of statistical applications, particularly in survival analysis and censoring problems. For example, in a clinical trial, patients may drop out of the study before the end, which means that their outcomes are censored. By using a censored distribution to model the data, researchers can take into account the fact that some of the outcomes are unknown, which can improve the accuracy of the analysis.

Truncated probability distribution

In probability theory and statistics, a truncated distribution is a probability distribution derived from another distribution by restricting it to a subset of its original domain. That is, a truncated distribution is a distribution that is conditioned by the fact that its values are within a certain range. The Distributions.jl package in Julia provides several methods for working with truncated distributions.

The Distributions.jl package provides two types of truncated distributions, namely truncated distributions with finite bounds and truncated distributions with infinite bounds. The truncated distributions with finite bounds are denoted by Truncated{D}(a, b) where D is a distribution type and a and b are the lower and upper bounds, respectively. For example, to create a truncated normal distribution with lower bound -1 and upper bound 1, we can use the following code:

```
julia> using Distributions

julia> tn = Truncated(Normal(), -1, 1)
Truncated(Normal{Float64}(μ=0.0, σ=1.0); lower=-1.0, upper=1.0)
```

***Figure 7.17**: Truncated normal distribution with -1 as lower bound and 1 as upper bound*

Truncated distributions in **Distributions.jl** can be used to model situations where the data is known to lie within a certain range, or where data outside of a certain range is not meaningful. They can also be used for simulation studies or to perform inference on truncated data.

Difference between censored and truncated probability distributions

While both censored and truncated distributions are supported in the Distributions.jl package, there are some important differences between them.

Censored distributions restrict the observed values to a certain range, while truncated distributions restrict the possible values that the random variable can take. Specifically, a truncated distribution is a distribution that has been modified so that all values outside of a certain range are given a probability of zero. This means that the truncated distribution only takes on values within the range specified.

In contrast, a censored distribution does not restrict the possible values that the random variable can take, but instead restricts the range of observed values. Values outside of the specified range are not included in calculations and are treated as missing data.

To illustrate the difference between censored and truncated distributions, consider the following example. Suppose we have a normal distribution with a mean of 0 and a standard deviation of 1, and we want to create a distribution that is restricted to the range [-2,2]. If we use a truncated distribution, we would create a Normal distribution and then truncate it using the following code:

```
julia> d = Normal()
Normal{Float64}(μ=0.0, σ=1.0)

julia> t = Truncated(d, -2, 2)
Truncated(Normal{Float64}(μ=0.0, σ=1.0); lower=-2.0, upper=2.0)

julia> c = censored(d, -2, 2)
Censored(Normal{Float64}(μ=0.0, σ=1.0); lower=-2, upper=2)
```

Figure 7.18: *Truncated and censored normal distribution within the range [-2, 2]*

While both censored and truncated distributions are used to restrict the range of distribution, they differ in how they do so. A truncated distribution restricts the possible values that the random variable can take, while a censored distribution restricts the range of observed values. The choice of which type of distribution to use will depend on the specific problem being modeled and the assumptions being made about the data.

Multivariate probability distribution

Distributions.jl is a Julia package for working with probability distributions, including both univariate and multivariate distributions. In this response, we will focus on the multivariate distributions available in **Distributions.jl**.

A multivariate distribution is a probability distribution that describes the joint behavior of multiple random variables. In Distributions.jl, there are several multivariate distributions available, including the multivariate normal, multivariate t, multivariate F, multivariate beta, multivariate gamma, and multivariate Dirichlet distributions.

The multivariate normal distribution is perhaps the most well-known multivariate distribution and is defined by its mean vector and covariance matrix. The distribution is implemented in Distributions.jl as MvNormal, which takes a mean vector and covariance matrix as arguments. For example, the following code creates a multivariate normal distribution with a mean vector of [0.0, 0.0] and a covariance matrix of [1.0 0.5; 0.5 1.0]:

```
julia> using Distributions

julia> μ = [0.0, 0.0]
2-element Vector{Float64}:
 0.0
 0.0

julia> Σ = [1.0 0.5; 0.5 1.0]
2×2 Matrix{Float64}:
 1.0  0.5
 0.5  1.0

julia> mvnorm = MvNormal(μ, Σ)
FullNormal(
dim: 2
μ: [0.0, 0.0]
Σ: [1.0 0.5; 0.5 1.0]
)


julia> rand(mvnorm)
2-element Vector{Float64}:
 -0.4612008074355385
  1.228455561406077
```

Figure 7.19: *Multivariate normal distribution with two random variables, i.e., μ, Σ*

Other multivariate distributions in Distributions.jl have similar interfaces, taking appropriate arguments such as degrees of freedom for the multivariate t distribution and shape parameters for the multivariate beta distribution.

Once a multivariate distribution is defined, it is possible to perform various operations with it, such as sampling from the distribution, evaluating the probability density function (PDF), and calculating moments. For example, the following code generates 1000 samples from the multivariate normal distribution defined above and calculates the sample mean and covariance matrix:

```
julia> samples = rand(mvnorm, 1000)
2×1000 Matrix{Float64}:
 -0.514518  -1.63274   -0.0118623  -2.5185   0.644695  -1.28601    1.01538  …  1.28385   0.123216  -2.07341   -1.81636  1.37404  0.900283  1.1582
  0.20096   -0.979814   0.388234   -2.07491  0.523163  -0.352709  -0.796734    0.389393  -0.333713  -0.101391  -1.90651  0.47579  1.94761   1.41666

julia> sample_mean = mean(samples, dims=1)
1×1000 Matrix{Float64}:
 -0.156779  -1.30628  0.188186  -2.29671  0.583929  -0.819359  0.109322  …  0.836622  -0.105249  -1.0874  -1.86143  0.924917  1.42395  1.28743

julia> sample_cov = cov(samples)
1000×1000 Matrix{Float64}:
  0.255954   0.233578   0.14313    0.158691   -0.0434767   0.333878   -0.648263  …   0.705467  -0.0322485   -0.32134     0.37467     0.0924618
  0.233578   0.213157   0.130617   0.144817   -0.0396758   0.304689   -0.59159       0.643793  -0.0294293   -0.293248    0.341915    0.0843785
  0.14313    0.130617   0.0800387  0.0887402  -0.0243122   0.186705   -0.36251       0.394499  -0.0180335   -0.179694    0.209516    0.0517049
  0.158691   0.144817   0.0887402  0.0983877  -0.0269554   0.207003   -0.401921      0.437387  -0.019994    -0.19923     0.232294    0.057326
 -0.0434767 -0.0396758 -0.0243122 -0.0269554   0.007385   -0.0567129   0.110115     -0.119831   0.00547778   0.0545833  -0.0636419  -0.0157057
```

Figure 7.20: Getting samples of multivariate distribution and evaluating their mean and covariance

Distributions.jl also provides functions for computing the PDF and cumulative distribution function (CDF) of multivariate distributions. For example, the following code computes the PDF of the multivariate normal distribution defined above at the point (1.0, 1.0):

```
julia> x = [1.0, 1.0]
2-element Vector{Float64}:
 1.0
 1.0

julia> pdf_value = pdf(mvnorm, x)
0.09435389770895924
```

Figure 7.21: Finding the pdf of multivariate normal distribution

Distributions.jl provides a convenient and flexible framework for working with multivariate distributions in Julia.

Matrix-variate probability distribution

Matrix-variate distributions are a class of probability distributions that generalize the notion of scalar-valued probability distributions to matrices. They are useful for modeling multivariate data that is structured as a matrix, such as data from multiple sensors or measurements taken over time. The **Distributions.jl** package includes several matrix-variate distributions, which can be used for statistical analysis and simulation.

The most commonly used matrix-variate distributions in Distributions.jl are the matrix normal distribution and the Wishart distribution. The matrix normal distribution is a multivariate generalization of the normal distribution, in which both the rows and columns of the matrix are normally distributed. It is parameterized by a mean matrix, a row covariance matrix, and a column covariance matrix. The Wishart distribution is a generalization of the chi-squared distribution to matrices and is used to model the covariance matrix of a set of random variables.

The Distributions.jl package provides several other matrix-variate distributions as well, including the matrix t distribution, the matrix F distribution, and the inverse Wishart distribution. These distributions are used for modeling more complex multivariate structures, such as hierarchical models and mixed-effects models.

In addition to the standard probability distribution functions such as pdf, cdf, and quantile, Distributions.jl provides several functions that are specific to matrix-variate distributions. For example, the function:

```
rand(MatrixNormal(mean, rowcov, colcov))
```

```
julia> # Define the parameters for a matrix normal distribution
       meanVal = [1.0 2.0 3.0; 4.0 5.0 6.0]
2×3 Matrix{Float64}:
 1.0  2.0  3.0
 4.0  5.0  6.0

julia> rowcov = [2.0 0.5; 0.5 1.0]
2×2 Matrix{Float64}:
 2.0  0.5
 0.5  1.0

julia> colcov = [1.0 0.0 0.0; 0.0 1.0 0.0; 0.0 0.0 2.0]
3×3 Matrix{Float64}:
 1.0  0.0  0.0
 0.0  1.0  0.0
 0.0  0.0  2.0

julia> MatrixNormal(meanVal, rowcov, colcov)
MatrixNormal{Float64, Matrix{Float64}, PDMats.PDMat{Float64, Matrix{Float64}}, PDMats.PDMat{Float64, Matrix{Float64}}}(
M: [1.0 2.0 3.0; 4.0 5.0 6.0]
U: [2.0 0.5; 0.5 1.0]
V: [1.0 0.0 0.0; 0.0 1.0 0.0; 0.0 0.0 2.0]
)


julia> rand(MatrixNormal(meanVal, rowcov, colcov))
2×3 Matrix{Float64}:
 -2.40578  1.54093  6.77438
  1.99935  5.16854  7.1433
```

Figure 7.22: *Creating a random MatrixNormal probability distribution*

generates a random matrix that follows the matrix normal distribution with the specified mean, row covariance, and column covariance matrices.

The function:

```
loglikelihood(MatrixNormal(mean, rowcov, colcov), X)
```

```
julia> # Compute the log-likelihood of a set of observations under the matrix normal distribution
       obs = [2.0 3.0 4.0; 5.0 6.0 7.0]
2×3 Matrix{Float64}:
 2.0  3.0  4.0
 5.0  6.0  7.0

julia> loglik = loglikelihood(MatrixNormal(meanVal, rowcov, colcov), obs)
-8.474773490262544
```

Figure 7.23: *Creating loglikelihood of MatrixNormal Distribution*

returns the log-likelihood of a set of observations X under the specified matrix normal distribution.

Matrix-variate distributions can be used in a variety of statistical applications, including multivariate analysis, image processing, and signal processing. By using matrix-variate distributions to model multivariate data, researchers can take into account the complex dependencies and correlations that exist between different variables. The Distributions.jl package provides a convenient and efficient way to work with matrix-variate distributions, making it a valuable tool for probabilistic modeling and statistical analysis.

Mixture models in Distributions.jl

Mixture models are a class of probabilistic models that describe a population as a mixture of several subpopulations, each with its probability distribution. Mixture models are widely used in many areas of statistics and machine learning, including clustering, density estimation, and classification.

In **Distributions.jl**, mixture models are implemented as a combination of several probability distributions, where each component distribution represents one subpopulation. The overall distribution is defined as a weighted sum of the component distributions, where the weights represent the probabilities of each subpopulation.

Distributions.jl provides several mixture models, including the Gaussian mixture model (GMM), which is a mixture of multivariate normal distributions. The GMM is implemented as MixtureModel in Distributions.jl and takes as input a vector of component distributions and a vector of weights. For example, the following code defines a GMM with two components:

```
julia> using Distributions

julia> μ1 = [0.0, 0.0]
2-element Vector{Float64}:
 0.0
 0.0

julia> Σ1 = [1.0 0.5; 0.5 1.0]
2×2 Matrix{Float64}:
 1.0  0.5
 0.5  1.0

julia> μ2 = [1.0, 1.0]
2-element Vector{Float64}:
 1.0
 1.0

julia> Σ2 = [1.0 -0.5; -0.5 1.0]
2×2 Matrix{Float64}:
  1.0  -0.5
 -0.5   1.0

julia> gm = MixtureModel([MvNormal(μ1, Σ1), MvNormal(μ2, Σ2)], [0.6, 0.4])
MixtureModel{FullNormal}(K = 2)
components[1] (prior = 0.6000): FullNormal(
dim: 2
μ: [0.0, 0.0]
Σ: [1.0 0.5; 0.5 1.0]
)

components[2] (prior = 0.4000): FullNormal(
dim: 2
μ: [1.0, 1.0]
Σ: [1.0 -0.5; -0.5 1.0]
)
```

Figure 7.24: *Mixture model of two varying multivariate normal distributions*

In this example, the GMM has two components, with means μ1 and μ2, covariance matrices Σ1 and Σ2, and weights 0.6 and 0.4.

Once a mixture model is defined, it is possible to perform various operations with it, such as sampling from the distribution, evaluating the probability density function (PDF), and calculating moments. For example, the following code generates 1000 samples from the GMM defined above and calculates the sample mean and covariance matrix:

```
julia> samples = rand(gm, 1000)
2×1000 Matrix{Float64}:
 2.27152   0.46249   1.47382   -0.276737   0.514472  1.12344   -0.442114  …  -0.0216876  1.8951    0.010427  0.7263   -3.02587   0.119429  0.59138
 0.549966  1.21613  -0.328115   0.0862941  1.20154   0.169958  -0.339673     -0.24518    0.547555  2.82614   2.01041  -0.353985  0.124563  1.3307

julia> sample_mean = mean(samples, dims=1)
1×1000 Matrix{Float64}:
 1.41074  0.839312  0.572853  -0.0952214  0.858008  0.646699  -0.390893  …  -0.133434  1.22133  1.41829  1.36835  -1.68993  0.121996  0.961038

julia> sample_cov = cov(samples)
1000×1000 Matrix{Float64}:
  1.48188    -0.648719   1.55106   -0.312489   -0.591416   0.820737  …  -2.42371   -1.10533   -2.2999    -0.00441939   -0.636386
 -0.648719    0.283989  -0.679008   0.136798    0.258903  -0.359293      1.06102    0.483879   1.00682    0.00193467    0.27859
  1.55106    -0.679008   1.62348   -0.327079   -0.619029   0.859057     -2.53687   -1.15694   -2.40728   -0.00462573   -0.666099
 -0.312489    0.136798  -0.327079   0.0658957   0.124714  -0.173072      0.511096   0.233085   0.484989   0.000931933   0.134197
 -0.591416    0.258903  -0.619029   0.124714    0.236034  -0.327555      0.967299   0.441136   0.917888   0.00176377    0.253981
```

Figure 7.25: *Getting samples of mixture model distribution and evaluating their mean and covariance*

Distributions.jl also provides functions for computing the PDF and cumulative distribution function (CDF) of mixture models. For example, the following code computes the PDF of the GMM defined above at the point (1.0, 1.0):

```
julia> x = [1.0, 1.0]
2-element Vector{Float64}:
 1.0
 1.0

julia> pdf_value = pdf(gm, x)
0.13012285801494783
```

Figure 7.26: *Finding the pdf of the mixture model normal distribution*

Mixture models are a powerful and flexible class of probabilistic models that can be used to model complex data distributions. **Distributions.jl** provides a convenient and flexible framework for working with mixture models in Julia.

Mixture models and convolutions in Distributions.jl

Mixture models and convolutions are both used to construct complex probability distributions from simpler ones in Distributions.jl, but they differ in their underlying mathematical operations.

A mixture model is a weighted sum (prior distribution) of two or more probability distributions. The weights of each distribution represent the proportion of the mixture that each distribution contributes. For example, a mixture of two normal distributions can be created as follows:

```
julia> using Distributions

julia> # create two normal distributions
       d1 = Normal(0, 1)
Normal{Float64}(μ=0.0, σ=1.0)

julia> d2 = Normal(2, 1)
Normal{Float64}(μ=2.0, σ=1.0)

julia> # create a mixture of the two distributions
       mixture = MixtureModel([d1, d2], [0.5, 0.5])
MixtureModel{Normal{Float64}}(K = 2)
components[1] (prior = 0.5000): Normal{Float64}(μ=0.0, σ=1.0)
components[2] (prior = 0.5000): Normal{Float64}(μ=2.0, σ=1.0)
```

Figure 7.27: *Using two varying Normal distributions and adding them up in a mixture model*

In this example, a mixture is a probability distribution that is a weighted sum of the two normal distributions, d1 and d2. Each of the normal distributions contributes equally to the mixture, as indicated by the weights [0.5, 0.5].

On the other hand, convolution is a way of combining probability distributions to represent the distribution of the sum of random variables. For example, if we have two independent normal distributions with mean 0 and standard deviation 1, their sum will also be a normal distribution with mean 0 and standard deviation **sqrt(2)**. This can be computed using the convolution of the two normal distributions:

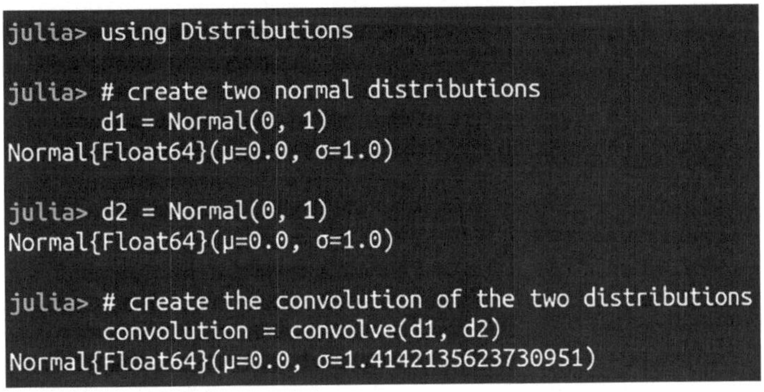

***Figure 7.28**: Adding up two varying normal distributions*

In this example, convolution is a probability distribution that represents the distribution of the sum of two independent normal distributions. The **convolve()** function is used to compute the convolution of the two distributions.

In summary, mixture models are used to combine distributions into a weighted sum (prior distribution), while convolutions are used to combine distributions to represent the distribution of the sum of random variables.

Fitting a probability distribution

In statistics, fitting a distribution to a dataset means finding the parameters of a probability distribution that best fit the observed data. The Julia programming language provides a package called Distributions, which offers a wide range of statistical distributions and methods for fitting them to data.

To fit a distribution, one can use the **fit** function, which takes a distribution type and a sample dataset as input and returns a fitted distribution. The most commonly used method for fitting a distribution is maximum likelihood estimation (MLE), which is the default method used by the **fit** function. Here is an example of fitting a normal distribution to a set of random numbers, that is, data:

```
# Generate a set of random numbers from a normal distribution

julia> data = randn(100)
```

```
julia> # Fit a normal distribution to the data using MLE
       normal_dist = fit(Normal, data)
Normal{Float64}(μ=-0.009678783997994947, σ=0.9170649986607784)

julia> # Print the estimated mean and standard deviation of the fitted distribution
       println("Estimated mean: $(mean(normal_dist)), estimated standard deviation: $(std(normal_dist))")
Estimated mean: -0.009678783997994947, estimated standard deviation: 0.9170649986607784
```

Figure 7.29: *Fitting a normal distribution to the data*

If the data is weighted, one can use the **fit_mle** function instead, which takes an additional input for the weights.

```
# Generate a set of random numbers from a normal distribution
julia> data = randn(100)
# Create a set of weights for the data
julia> weights = ones(100)
```

```
julia> # Fit a normal distribution to the weighted data using MLE
       normal_dist_weighted = fit_mle(Normal, data, weights)
Normal{Float64}(μ=0.0807655062010927, σ=0.9257232964968096)

julia> # Print the estimated mean and standard deviation of the fitted distribution
       println("Estimated mean: $(mean(normal_dist_weighted)), estimated standard deviation: $(std(normal_dist_weighted))")
Estimated mean: 0.0807655062010927, estimated standard deviation: 0.9257232964968096
```

Figure 7.30: *Fitting a normal weighted data matrix*

For some distributions, the estimation can be based on sufficient statistics computed from the dataset. In such cases, one can use the suffstats method to compute sufficient statistics and then use them to fit the distribution using **fit_mle**.

```
# Generate a set of random numbers from an exponential distribution
julia> data = rand(Exponential(2), 100)
```

```
julia> # Compute the sufficient statistics for the exponential distribution
       suff_stats = suffstats(Exponential, data)
Distributions.ExponentialStats(169.12748221243547, 100.0)

julia> # Fit the exponential distribution to the data using MLE and sufficient statistics
       exp_dist_suffstats = fit_mle(Exponential, suff_stats)
Exponential{Float64}(θ=1.6912748221243548)

julia> # Print the estimated rate of the fitted distribution
       println("Estimated rate: $(rate(exp_dist_suffstats))")
Estimated rate: 0.5912699621129184
```

Figure 7.31: *Sufficient statistics for the exponential distribution*

The Distributions.jl package provides a powerful set of tools for fitting statistical distributions to data, which can be useful in a wide range of applications.

Conclusion

In this chapter, we have provided an introduction to probability and its importance in various fields, such as statistics and machine learning. We have also introduced the probability package in Julia, which is a powerful tool for working with probability distributions.

One of the key packages in the Julia probability ecosystem is the Distributions.jl package, which provides a comprehensive collection of univariate and multivariate probability distributions, as well as various methods for working with them. We have covered the common functions available in Distributions.jl, including sampling, PDF and CDF evaluation, and moments calculation.

We have also discussed three important types of probability distributions - censored, truncated, and mixture models - and how they can be implemented in Distributions.jl. We have highlighted the importance of mixture models in modeling complex data distributions and how Distributions.jl provides a convenient framework for working with them.

Finally, we have briefly covered the topic of fitting a probability distribution to data, which is an important task in many statistical applications. We have shown how Distributions.jl provides various methods for fitting probability distributions to data, including maximum likelihood estimation and Bayesian methods.

In the next chapter, we will learn about DataFrames and handling data in Julia.

Questions

1. What is probability and why is it important in statistics and machine learning?
2. What is the probability package in Julia and how can it be used for probabilistic calculations?
3. How does the Distributions.jl package in Julia provide a comprehensive collection of univariate and multivariate probability distributions?
4. What are some common functions available in Distributions.jl for working with probability distributions?
5. What are univariate probability distributions and what are some examples available in Distributions.jl?

6. What are censored probability distributions and how can they be implemented in Distributions.jl?
7. What are truncated probability distributions and how can they be implemented in Distributions.jl?
8. What are multivariate probability distributions and how can they be implemented in Distributions.jl?
9. What are matrix-variate probability distributions and how can they be implemented in Distributions.jl?
10. What are mixture models and how can they be implemented in Distributions.jl for modeling complex data distributions?
11. How can mixture models and convolutions be used together in Distributions.jl?
12. What are some methods available in Distributions.jl for fitting a probability distribution to data, and how do they work?

CHAPTER 8

Framing Data in Julia

Framing data in Julia refers to the process of portraying data in a structured and organized way that is suitable for data analysis and manipulation. In Julia, data is typically framed as a table or a matrix, with each row representing an observation or data point and each column representing a variable or feature.

DataFrames.jl is a highly capable and efficient package that provides a range of features to handle tabular data. It allows users to create, modify, and investigate structured data in a way that is easy to understand and use. The package provides a similar interface to that of R's data.frame and Python's pandas library, which makes it easy for users to migrate from these languages to Julia. This familiar interface lets users perform a wide range of data manipulation tasks, including data cleaning, filtering, sorting, grouping, merging, and more. Users can apply the package to create DataFrames from various sources, such as CSV files, Excel spreadsheets, SQL databases, and more.

DataFrames.jl is designed to work with large datasets, making it an essential component of Julia's data analysis toolkit. It offers fast and memory-efficient operations, enabling users to work with big data in a timely manner. The package also provides several convenient functions for data import and export, which makes it easy for users to transfer data from other sources into Julia.

The package also provides a range of functions for cleaning and transforming data, such as imputing missing values, scaling and normalizing data, and encoding categorical variables. User can save time and effort by using these functions to make it easier for them to get their data ready for analysis, saving time and effort.

In addition to these features, **DataFrames.jl** provides a rich set of functions for data exploration and visualization. Users can summarize their data using various statistics and visualizations, such as histograms, scatterplots, and bar charts, to gain insights and explore relationships between variables.

Structure

In this chapter, the following topics will be covered:

- Introducing DataFrames.jl package
- Setting up the environment
- Constructing DataFrame objects
- Fetching, inspecting and manipulating data
- Major data manipulation frameworks in Julia
- Comparing with other data manipulation frameworks

Introducing DataFrames.jl package

DataFrames.jl is a powerful tool for working with tabular data in Julia, providing similar functionality and design to other popular data science tools like pandas in Python, and `data.frame`, `data.table` and `dplyr` in R. It is an essential component of the Julia data ecosystem, with tight integrations with a range of different libraries. This chapter aims to provide everything needed to get up and run with **DataFrames.jl**, and to showcase its functionality in conjunction with other popular packages like **GLM.jl, StatsModels.jl**, and **Plots.jl**. Additionally, users will find it effective to explore some of the other popular libraries in the Julia data ecosystem, like for **MLJ.jl** machine learning, **HypothesisTests.jl** for hypothesis testing, and **Plots.jl** for plotting.

Setting up the environment

Setting up the environment refers to the process of installing and configuring the necessary software and packages required to work with a particular programming language, package, or library. In this case, we are setting up the environment for working with the DataFrames.jl package, which is a package for working with tabular data in Julia.

To use the DataFrames.jl package in Julia, you first need to install it. This can be done using the Pkg module in Julia, which provides a package manager for Julia. To begin, you need to load the Pkg module by typing `using Pkg` in the Julia console.

Once the Pkg module is loaded, you can install the DataFrames.jl package by running `Pkg.add("DataFrames")` in the Julia console. This command will download and install the package and its dependencies, and make it available for use in your Julia environment.

Alternatively, you can use the package manager REPL mode to add the package by typing] in the Julia console. This will switch to the package manager REPL, and you can type `add DataFrames` to add the package.

After installing the DataFrames package, it is recommended to run its tests to ensure that everything is working as expected. You can do this by typing `Pkg.test("DataFrames")` in the Julia console. Note that running the tests may take more than 30 minutes, depending on your system's performance.

To check the version of DataFrames.jl that you have installed, you can use the status command in the package manager REPL mode. Type `]` in the Julia console to switch to the package manager REPL, and then type `status DataFrames` to see the version of the package.

Once you have installed and verified the package, you can load it into your Julia environment using the `using DataFrames` command. This will make the DataFrame type available, which is the most fundamental type provided by DataFrames.jl. In a DataFrame, each row represents an observation, and each column represents a feature. You can then use the various functions and operations provided by the DataFrames package to manipulate and analyze your data.

Constructing DataFrame objects

In Julia, constructors are functions that create an instance of a type. The DataFrame is a type provided by the DataFrames.jl package that represents tabular data.

Creating a new DataFrame instance with no data is done using an empty constructor. For example, `DataFrame()` creates an empty DataFrame with no rows or columns.

The most common way to create a DataFrame is by specifying the column names and data. This can be done using a keyword argument constructor (*Figure* 8.1). For example,

```
julia> DataFrame(A=20:30, B=40:50, fixed=1)
```

```
julia> DataFrame(A=20:30, B=40:50, fixed=1)
11×3 DataFrame
 Row │ A      B      fixed
     │ Int64  Int64  Int64
─────┼─────────────────────
   1 │    20     40      1
   2 │    21     41      1
   3 │    22     42      1
   4 │    23     43      1
   5 │    24     44      1
   6 │    25     45      1
   7 │    26     46      1
   8 │    27     47      1
   9 │    28     48      1
  10 │    29     49      1
  11 │    30     50      1
```

***Figure 8.1**: Creating a DataFrame with three columns named "A", "B", and "fixed" with their specified values.*

The "A" column contains the values 20, 21, ..., and 30. The "B" column contains the values 40, 41, 42, ..., and 50. The "fixed" column contains the scalar value 1, which gets broadcasted to all rows. Both columns A and B should be of the same dimensions.

If your column names contain spaces or are not valid Julia identifiers, you can use the => syntax to associate the names with their values as shown in the following example:

```
julia> DataFrame("age" => [45, 40, 15], "first name" => ["Rohan",
"Raghav", "Avyukta"])
```

```
julia> DataFrame("age" => [45, 40, 15], "first name" => ["Rohan", "Raghav", "Avyukta"])
3×2 DataFrame
 Row │ age    first name
     │ Int64  String
─────┼───────────────────
   1 │    45  Rohan
   2 │    40  Raghav
   3 │    15  Avyukta
```

***Figure 8.2**: Creating a DataFrame with two columns named "age" and "first name"*

DataFrames can also be created from dictionaries or NamedTuples. If the keys are strings or symbols, you can pass the dictionary or NamedTuple directly to the DataFrame constructor. For example,

```
julia> DataFrame(Dict(:age => [45, 40, 15], :first_name => ["Rohan",
"Raghav", "Avyukta"]))
```

```
julia> DataFrame(Dict(:age => [45, 40, 15], :first_name => ["Rohan", "Raghav", "Avyukta"]))
3×2 DataFrame
 Row │ age    first_name
     │ Int64  String
─────┼──────────────────
   1 │    45  Rohan
   2 │    40  Raghav
   3 │    15  Avyukta
```

Figure 8.3: *It creates the same DataFrame as the previous example*

If the column names are not provided, but the data is in a matrix or an array of NamedTuples, you can pass :auto as the second argument to automatically generate column names. For example,

```
julia> DataFrame([7 1; 9 4], :auto)
```

```
julia> DataFrame([7 1; 9 4], :auto)
2×2 DataFrame
 Row │ x1     x2
     │ Int64  Int64
─────┼──────────────
   1 │     7      1
   2 │     9      4
```

Figure 8.4: *Creating a DataFrame with two columns named "x1" and "x2"*

Finally, if you have a vector of column names, you can pass it as the second argument to the DataFrame constructor. For example,

```
julia> DataFrame([11 23 7 0; 85 50 65 21; 63 11 16 49], ["a", "b", "c",
"d"])
```

```
julia> DataFrame([11 23 7 0; 85 50 65 21; 63 11 16 49], ["a", "b", "c", "d"])
3×4 DataFrame
 Row │ a      b      c      d
     │ Int64  Int64  Int64  Int64
─────┼────────────────────────────
   1 │    11     23      7      0
   2 │    85     50     65     21
   3 │    63     11     16     49
```

Figure 8.5: *Creating a DataFrame with four columns named "a", "b", "c", and "d"*

Fetching, inspecting and manipulating data

In *Chapter 5, Working with datasets in Julia*, we learnt about fetching and inspecting data using various other methods, including CSV reader objects. We used the **CSV.jl** package to read and inspect our data. **DataFrames.jl** is a powerful package for working with tabular data in Julia, and it provides various functions and tools for fetching, unpacking, and inspecting data.

CSV is a Julia package that provides functionality for reading and writing tabular data from CSV and other delimited text files. The package is available for download from the Julia package manager and can be installed using the **`Pkg.add()`** command.

Once installed, the package must be imported into the session using the **`using`** command. This makes the package's functions available to use in your code. With Julia 1.9, one can skip **`Pkg.add`** for registered packages.

Here's an example of how to read a dataset from a CSV file:

```
julia> using CSV, DataFrames
julia> df = DataFrame(CSV.File("path/to/input.csv"))
```

This code imports the CSV and DataFrames packages and then reads a dataset from a CSV file located at "path/to/input.csv". The resulting dataset is stored in a DataFrame object called "df".

Similarly, you can write a DataFrame object to a CSV file using the following code:

```
julia> CSV.write("path/to/output.csv", df)
```

This code writes the contents of the DataFrame object **`df`** to a file located at **`path/to/output.cs3v`**.

You can also customize the behavior of the CSV functions by using keyword arguments. The available keyword arguments and their meanings can be found in the Julia documentation.

In some cases, the compilation latency of the **CSV.jl** package can be an issue. In such cases, the `DelimitedFiles` module from the Julia standard library can be used instead. Here's an example of how to read data from a CSV file using the DelimitedFiles module:

```
julia> using DelimitedFiles, DataFrames


julia> data, header = readdlm("path/to/input.csv", ',', header=true)
julia> df = DataFrame(data, vec(header))
```

This code imports the **`DelimitedFiles`** and DataFrames packages and reads the contents of a CSV file located at "path/to/input.csv". The resulting dataset is stored in a DataFrame object called "df".

It's worth noting that the read and write functions provided by **DelimitedFiles.jl** are more limited in functionality compared to **CSV.jl**, and cannot handle more advanced use cases such as handling missing or non-numeric data. Therefore, it's recommended to use CSV.jl in most cases.

Finally, if you need more information on the **CSV.jl** functions, you can use the "?" operator followed by the function name to access the documentation. For example, typing "?CSV.File" in the Julia REPL will display the documentation for the CSV.File function. Alternatively, you can check out the online CSV.jl documentation for more information.

To fetch data using **DataFrames.jl**, users can use the `CSV.read` function to read data from a CSV file. The package also provides support for various other file formats, including Excel spreadsheets and JSON files, using the appropriate functions.

Fetching data

CSV is a file format for tabular data, where each row is a record, and each column represents a variable or feature. To start, we need to make sure that we have the CSV.jl package installed in our Julia environment. We can do this by executing the following commands:

```
julia> using Pkg

julia> Pkg.add("CSV")
```

To read in a CSV file using Julia's **`CSV.jl`** package, first make sure it's installed. Then, you can use the **`CSV.read`** function to read the file. For example, if your data is stored in a file called "**iris.csv**" in the assets directory of the **DataFrames.jl** repository, you can obtain the path of the package file, navigate to the assets directory using the **`joinpath()`** function, and then use `CSV.read()` to read in the data.

```
julia> using CSV, DataFrames
# Obtain the path of the DataFrames.jl package file
julia> path_to_pkg = dirname(pathof(DataFrames))
# Navigate to the assets directory and the iris.csv file
julia> csv_file_path = joinpath(path_to_pkg, "..", "docs", "src",
"assets", "iris.csv")
```

```
# Read in the CSV file and store the resulting data in a DataFrame object
julia> df = CSV.read(csv_file_path, DataFrame)
```

Once the data is loaded, it's a good idea to create a copy using the copy function to avoid accidentally modifying the original data.

```
# Create a copy of the DataFrame object to avoid accidental modification
julia> df_copy = copy(df)
```

Note: Julia has different string types, including **String7** and **String15**, which have a fixed width that can make them faster and more efficient than the standard String type. You need to add **InlineStrings.jl** to your code base.

```
julia> # Define a fixed-width string
       str7 = String7("hello")
"hello  "
julia> str15 = String15("hello")
"hello          "
julia> # Print the length of each string
       println(length(str))   # 11
11
julia> println(length(str7))  # 7
7
julia> println(length(str15)) # 15
15
```

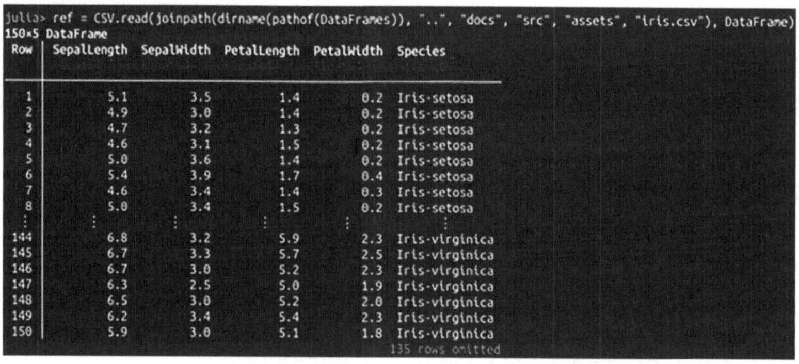

```
julia> ref = CSV.read(joinpath(dirname(pathof(DataFrames)), "..", "docs", "src", "assets", "iris.csv"), DataFrame)
150×5 DataFrame
 Row │ SepalLength  SepalWidth  PetalLength  PetalWidth  Species
─────┼──────────────────────────────────────────────────────────────
   1 │         5.1         3.5          1.4         0.2  Iris-setosa
   2 │         4.9         3.0          1.4         0.2  Iris-setosa
   3 │         4.7         3.2          1.3         0.2  Iris-setosa
   4 │         4.6         3.1          1.5         0.2  Iris-setosa
   5 │         5.0         3.6          1.4         0.2  Iris-setosa
   6 │         5.4         3.9          1.7         0.4  Iris-setosa
   7 │         4.6         3.4          1.4         0.3  Iris-setosa
   8 │         5.0         3.4          1.5         0.2  Iris-setosa
  ⋮  │      ⋮           ⋮            ⋮           ⋮            ⋮
 144 │         6.8         3.2          5.9         2.3  Iris-virginica
 145 │         6.7         3.3          5.7         2.5  Iris-virginica
 146 │         6.7         3.0          5.2         2.3  Iris-virginica
 147 │         6.3         2.5          5.0         1.9  Iris-virginica
 148 │         6.5         3.0          5.2         2.0  Iris-virginica
 149 │         6.2         3.4          5.4         2.3  Iris-virginica
 150 │         5.9         3.0          5.1         1.8  Iris-virginica
                                                    135 rows omitted
```

Figure 8.6: *Read and store the reference of the iris dataset.*

Keep in mind that your DataFrame object may be too wide or too tall to display in its entirety, causing it to be cropped in the output. To view the entire DataFrame, you need to change your environment variables such as,

```
# Set the option to show all columns and rows
julia> ENV["COLUMNS"] = 1000
julia> ENV["LINES"] = 1000
# Print the DataFrame
julia> println(df)
```

Inspecting data

Once the data has been fetched, **DataFrames.jl** provides several functions for unpacking and inspecting it. First, the size function is used to get the dimensions of the DataFrame. The size function returns a tuple containing the number of rows and columns in the DataFrame. For example, `size(df)` returns (150, 5), which means that the Iris DataFrame has 150 rows and 5 columns. We can also use the size function with the optional argument 1 or 2 to retrieve the number of rows or columns, respectively. For instance, `size(df, 1)` returns 150, which is the number of rows, and `size(df, 2)` returns 5, which is the number of columns.

```
julia> size(df)
(150, 5)

julia> size(df, 1)
150

julia> size(df, 2)
5
```

The `first()` and `last()` functions can be used to display the first and last few rows of the DataFrame.

```
julia> first(df)
DataFrameRow
 Row │ SepalLength  SepalWidth  PetalLength  PetalWidth  Species
     │ Float64      Float64     Float64      Float64     String15
─────┼──────────────────────────────────────────────────────────────
   1 │         5.1         3.5          1.4         0.2  Iris-setosa
```

```
julia> last(df)
DataFrameRow
 Row │ SepalLength  SepalWidth  PetalLength  PetalWidth  Species
     │ Float64      Float64     Float64      Float64     String15
─────┼──────────────────────────────────────────────────────────────
 150 │         5.9         3.0          5.1         1.8  Iris-virginica

julia> first(df, 3)
3×5 DataFrame
 Row │ SepalLength  SepalWidth  PetalLength  PetalWidth  Species
     │ Float64      Float64     Float64      Float64     String15
─────┼───────────────────────────────────────────────────────────
   1 │         5.1         3.5          1.4         0.2  Iris-setosa
   2 │         4.9         3.0          1.4         0.2  Iris-setosa
   3 │         4.7         3.2          1.3         0.2  Iris-setosa

julia> last(df, 4)
4×5 DataFrame
 Row │ SepalLength  SepalWidth  PetalLength  PetalWidth  Species
     │ Float64      Float64     Float64      Float64     String15
─────┼──────────────────────────────────────────────────────────────
   1 │         6.3         2.5          5.0         1.9  Iris-virginica
   2 │         6.5         3.0          5.2         2.0  Iris-virginica
   3 │         6.2         3.4          5.4         2.3  Iris-virginica
   4 │         5.9         3.0          5.1         1.8  Iris-virginica
```

We can also use the `nrow()` and `ncol()` functions to get the number of rows and columns in the DataFrame, respectively. For example, **`nrow(df)`** returns 150, which is the number of rows, and ncol(df) returns 5, which is the number of columns.

```
julia> nrow(df)
150
julia> ncol(df)
5
```

To get basic statistics of the data in the **DataFrame**, we can use the `describe()` function. The describe function displays the mean, minimum, median, maximum, number of missing values, and element type of each numerical column in the **DataFrame**. By default, the function skips the missing values when computing the summary statistics. We can customize the shown statistics by passing optional arguments to the describe function. For example, `describe(df, cols=1:3)` returns a **DataFrame** that only displays statistics for the first three columns.

```
julia> describe(df)
5×7 DataFrame
 Row │ variable     mean     min          median  max             nmissing  eltype
─────┼──────────────────────────────────────────────────────────────────────────────
   1 │ SepalLength  5.84333  4.3          5.8     7.9                    0  Float64
   2 │ SepalWidth   3.054    2.0          3.0     4.4                    0  Float64
   3 │ PetalLength  3.75867  1.0          4.35    6.9                    0  Float64
   4 │ PetalWidth   1.19867  0.1          1.3     2.5                    0  Float64
   5 │ Species               Iris-setosa          Iris-virginica         0  String15

julia> describe(df, cols=1:3)
3×7 DataFrame
 Row │ variable     mean     min      median   max      nmissing  eltype
─────┼─────────────────────────────────────────────────────────────────────
   1 │ SepalLength  5.84333      4.3  5.8          7.9         0  Float64
   2 │ SepalWidth   3.054        2.0  3.0          4.4         0  Float64
   3 │ PetalLength  3.75867      1.0  4.35         6.9         0  Float64
```

Figure 8.7: *describe() function is depicting the information about the iris dataset*

Lastly, we can adjust how the DataFrame is displayed by manually calling the show function. We can use the `allrows` and `allcols` optional arguments to show all rows and all columns of the DataFrame, respectively. For instance, `show(df, allcols=true)` prints all the columns of the DataFrame, even if they do not fit on the screen.

```
julia> show(df)
150×5 DataFrame
julia> show(df, allrows=true)
150×5 DataFrame
```

In Julia, a DataFrame can be very large and can take up a lot of memory. To make the DataFrame more memory efficient, one can create a view of it. Creating a view of a DataFrame is similar to creating a materialized selection, but a view is more memory efficient because it only stores pointers to the data in the original DataFrame.

In the code sample, the view function and @view macro can be used to create views of a DataFrame. The view function is used to create a view by specifying the DataFrame to be viewed and the row and column indices that will be included in the view. `@view` macro works in the same way, but it allows for more concise and readable code by using a slicing syntax.

The syntax for accessing elements in a view is the same as for accessing elements in a DataFrame. The only difference is that a view does not create a new object, but rather provides a view into the existing DataFrame.

```
julia> view(df, 1:2, 1:2)
2×2 SubDataFrame
 Row │ SepalLength  SepalWidth
     │ Float64      Float64
─────┼─────────────────────────
   1 │         5.1         3.5
   2 │         4.9         3.0

julia> @time df[1:2, 1:2]
  0.067101 seconds (1.10 k allocations: 52.766 KiB, 99.78% compilation time)
2×2 DataFrame
 Row │ SepalLength  SepalWidth
     │ Float64      Float64
─────┼─────────────────────────
   1 │         5.1         3.5
   2 │         4.9         3.0

julia> @time view(df, 1:2, 1:2)
  0.000014 seconds (1 allocation: 80 bytes)
2×2 SubDataFrame
 Row │ SepalLength  SepalWidth
     │ Float64      Float64
─────┼─────────────────────────
   1 │         5.1         3.5
   2 │         4.9         3.0
```

Figure 8.8*: Viewing only a certain part of the DataFrame*

A view is more memory efficient than creating a new **`DataFrame`** or array because it only stores pointers to the data in the original **`DataFrame`**. The benchmark comparison shows that creating a view is an order of magnitude faster and allocates much less memory than creating a new **`DataFrame`** or array.

Views can be useful when we want to manipulate a subset of a **`DataFrame`** without creating a copy. For example, we might want to multiply all the values in the **`PetalWidth`** column by 2:

```
julia> view1 = view(df, :, :PetalWidth)
150-element view(::Vector{Float64}, :) with eltype Float64:
 0.2
 0.2
…
julia> view1 .= 2 .* view1
150-element view(::Vector{Float64}, :) with eltype Float64:
 0.4
 0.4
…
```

Here, view1 is a view of the **PetalWidth** column of df. The second line multiplies every element of view1 by 2, which has the effect of modifying the original df **DataFrame**.

We can also append a row to the **DataFrame** using the `view()` function.

```
julia> new_row = [0.5, 6.4, 1.2, 5.4, "Iris-virginica"]
5-element Vector{Any}:
 0.5
 6.4
 1.2
 5.4
  "Iris-virginica"

julia> vcat(view1, new_row)
155-element Vector{Any}:
```

***Figure 8.9**: Appending the new row to the dataset using the view() function*

However, a view points to the same memory as its parent, so changing a view will change the parent, which can sometimes be undesirable. Additionally, some operations might be a bit slower as **DataFrames.jl** needs to perform a mapping of indices of a view to indices of the parent.

In this chapter, we will learn about a few other ways to fetch and inspect the data at hand using **DataFrames.jl**. Data frames can be indexed using a syntax that allows for a flexible selection of rows and columns. By understanding the available options for indexing, you can extract the relevant data for your analysis. A DataFrame can be indexed using the same syntax as matrices. The general syntax for indexing is `data_frame[selected_rows, selected_columns]`, where `selected_rows` and `selected_columns` are vectors or ranges of row or column indices to select. Unlike matrices, which allow the selection of either rows or columns, DataFrames always require both row and column selectors.

A colon : can be used as a wildcard to indicate that all rows or columns should be retained. For example, `df[1:5, [:SepalWidth, :PetalWidth]]` returns the first five rows of the "iris" DataFrame, with only the "**SepalWidth**" and "**PetalWidth**" columns included.

```
julia> df[1:5, [:SepalWidth, :PetalWidth]]
5×2 DataFrame
 Row │ SepalWidth  PetalWidth
     │ Float64     Float64
─────┼────────────────────────
   1 │        3.5         0.2
   2 │        3.0         0.2
   3 │        3.2         0.2
   4 │        3.1         0.2
   5 │        3.6         0.2
```

***Figure 8.10**: View only sepal and petal width*

Similarly, `df[1:5, :]` returns the first five rows of all columns in the "iris" **`DataFrame`**.

```
julia> df[1:5, :]
5×5 DataFrame
 Row │ SepalLength  SepalWidth  PetalLength  PetalWidth  Species
     │ Float64      Float64     Float64      Float64     String15
─────┼──────────────────────────────────────────────────────────────
   1 │         5.1         3.5          1.4         0.2  Iris-setosa
   2 │         4.9         3.0          1.4         0.2  Iris-setosa
   3 │         4.7         3.2          1.3         0.2  Iris-setosa
   4 │         4.6         3.1          1.5         0.2  Iris-setosa
   5 │         5.0         3.6          1.4         0.2  Iris-setosa
```

***Figure 8.11**: View all the columns of the dataset but only from first to fifth rows*

A vector of specific row indices can also be used to index the DataFrame, as in `df[[1, 6, 15], :]`, which returns only the first, sixth, and fifteenth rows of all columns.

```
julia> df[[1, 6, 15], :]
3×5 DataFrame
 Row │ SepalLength  SepalWidth  PetalLength  PetalWidth  Species
     │ Float64      Float64     Float64      Float64     String15
─────┼──────────────────────────────────────────────────────────────
   1 │         5.1         3.5          1.4         0.2  Iris-setosa
   2 │         5.4         3.9          1.7         0.4  Iris-setosa
   3 │         5.8         4.0          1.2         0.2  Iris-setosa
```

***Figure 8.12**: View all the columns of the dataset but only of 1st, 6th and 15th row*

To select specific columns, the `[:, selected_columns]` syntax can be used. For example, `df[:, [:SepalLength, :PetalLength]]` returns all rows of only the "SepalLength" and "PetalLength" columns.

```
julia> df[:, [:SepalLength, :PetalLength]]
150×2 DataFrame
 Row │ SepalLength  PetalLength
     │ Float64      Float64
─────┼──────────────────────────
   1 │         5.1          1.4
   2 │         4.9          1.4
   3 │         4.7          1.3
   4 │         4.6          1.5
  ⋮  │      ⋮            ⋮
 148 │         6.5          5.2
 149 │         6.2          5.4
 150 │         5.9          5.1
                143 rows omitted
```

***Figure 8.13**: view only sepal and petal length*

Note: The syntax used for column selection can affect the type of the returned object. `df[:, [:PetalLength]]` and `df[!, [:PetalLength]]` both return a DataFrame with a single column, but `df[:, :PetalLength]` and `df[!, :PetalLength]` return a vector of strings with only the "`PetalLength`" column data. The difference between the two syntaxes lies in the use of a single symbol `:PetalLength` versus a vector `[:PetalLength]`. When using the latter, a vector is required to be passed (not just any iterable), so `df[:, (:SepalLength, :PetalLength)]` is not allowed, but `df[:, [:SepalLength, :PetalLength]]` is valid.

To perform basic operations on a `DataFrame`, such as extracting columns, one can use different syntaxes. The simplest way to extract a column is to use the dot notation: `dataframe.column_name`. This notation allows us to directly access the column data without making a copy. Therefore, changes made to the extracted column will affect the original `DataFrame`. For example, `df.PetalWidth` returns a vector of the petal width of various flowers and changing the value of this vector will also affect the values stored in the iris `DataFrame`:

```
julia> df.PetalWidth
150-element Vector{Float64}:
julia> df."PetalWidth"
150-element Vector{Float64}:
```

However, sometimes it is desirable to make a copy of a column to avoid affecting the original DataFrame. In such cases, one can use the indexing notation to extract a column: `dataframe[:, column_name] or dataframe[!, column_name]`, where `column_name` is a string or a symbol representing the name of the column. `dataframe[:, column_name]` will return a copy of the column and modifying it will not affect the original DataFrame while `dataframe[!, column_name]` returns the original `DataFrame`.

```
julia> df[!, :PetalWidth]
julia> df[!, "PetalWidth"]
```

We can check that both expressions produce the same object and confirm the behavior described above using the `===` function:

```
julia> df.PetalWidth === df[!, :PetalWidth]
true
julia> df.PetalWidth === df[:, :PetalWidth]
false
```

To get a vector of all column names in the DataFrame, one can use the `names(dataframe)` function. The function returns a vector of strings representing the column names.

```
julia> names(df)
```

```
julia> names(ref)
5-element Vector{String}:
 "SepalLength"
 "SepalWidth"
 "PetalLength"
 "PetalWidth"
 "Species"
```

***Figure 8.14**: Names of the columns of the iris datasets*

One can also use this function to filter columns by their element type or other criteria. For example, `names(dataframe, AbstractString)` return a vector of column names with elements of type `AbstractString`.

```
julia> names(df, AbstractString)
1-element Vector{String}:
 "Species"
```

If one needs to work with column names as symbols, the `propertynames(dataframe)` function can be used instead. It returns a vector of symbols representing the column names.

```
julia> propertynames(df)
5-element Vector{Symbol}:
 :SepalLength
 :SepalWidth
 :PetalLength
 :PetalWidth
 :Species
```

To get the data type of each column, one can use the `eltype` function on an iterator generated by the `eachcol(dataframe)` function. The eachcol function returns an iterator over the columns of the DataFrame, and the `eltype` function returns the element type of a collection.

```
julia> eltype.(eachcol(df))
5-element Vector{DataType}:
 Float64
 Float64
 Float64
 Float64
 String15
```

Finally, the `empty(dataframe)` function returns an empty DataFrame with the same column names and types as the original `DataFrame`. However, it does not modify the original `DataFrame`. If one needs to empty the original `DataFrame`, the `empty!(dataframe)` function should be used instead.

```
julia> empty(ref)
0×5 DataFrame
 Row │ SepalLength  SepalWidth  PetalLength  PetalWidth  Species
     │ Float64      Float64     Float64      Float64     String15
─────┴────────────────────────────────────────────────────────────

julia> empty!(ref)
0×5 DataFrame
 Row │ SepalLength  SepalWidth  PetalLength  PetalWidth  Species
     │ Float64      Float64     Float64      Float64     String15
─────┴────────────────────────────────────────────────────────────
```

It is important to note that column names in **DataFrames.jl** can be either symbols or strings. While using symbols is slightly faster, using strings is simpler when non-standard characters are present in the column names or one wants to manipulate them. For non-standard symbols, one can use Symbol("asd fgh").

In Julia, one can perform broadcasting assignments using the .= operation. Broadcasting is a powerful feature that allows performing operations element-wise over an array. This is particularly useful when we want to apply a scalar or vector operation on a column or a slice of a DataFrame.

The standard syntax to perform broadcasting in Julia is to use '.'. For example, to assign a scalar value to a slice of a vector, we need to use the .= operation. This is because assigning a scalar value to multiple locations is not supported. For instance, the following code would fail in Julia:

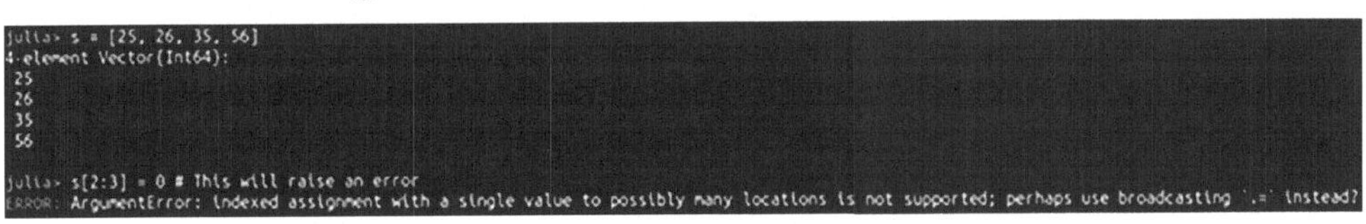

Figure 8.15: *A single value cannot be assigned to the multiple elements*

Instead, we need to write:

```
julia> s[2:3] .= 0
2-element view(::Vector{Int64}, 2:3) with eltype Int64:
```

```
 0
 0
```

This will assign 0 to the elements in the slice [2,3] of the vector s. The broadcasting syntax is fully supported in DataFrames.jl as well.

Here is an example using DataFrames.jl:

```
julia> df[3:8, :PetalLength] .= [8.5, 8.9, 7.8, 5.8, 9.6, 6.8] #
Broadcasting assignment
6-element view(::Vector{Float64}, 3:8) with eltype Float64:
 8.5
 8.9
 7.8
 5.8
 9.6
 6.8
```

This code will create a new column `:PetalLength` in the `DataFrame` df and assign the values in the vector [8.5, 8.9, 7.8, 5.8, 9.6, 6.8] to it.

Note: The ! operator in the broadcasting syntax performs an in-place operation while using : instead of, ! performs a replace operation. An in-place operation replaces the old values with new ones in the existing vector, while the replace operation allocates a fresh vector and replaces the old vector with it. The difference is important when the new values have a different type than the old ones. In the case of the replace operation, the new vector will have a new type.

For example, the following code will perform an in-place replacement of values stored in column number 3 by 4:

```
julia> df[:, 3] .= 4
150-element view(::Vector{Float64}, :) with eltype Float64:
```

The following code will replace the :PetalLength column with a new vector of type String:

```
julia> df[!, :PetalLength] .= “Economics”
150-element Vector{String}:
```

It is worth noting that using broadcasting on a row selector will not work in-place, and we need to use the ! operator instead for allocating a fresh vector.

Column selection is a fundamental operation when working with `DataFrames`. Julia provides a set of flexible and powerful column selection functions that allow us to select one or more columns from a `DataFrame` based on different criteria.

This response will explain four of the most useful column selectors for complex scenarios. The Not, Between, Cols, and All selectors are used to exclude columns, select a range of columns, select multiple columns, and select all columns, respectively. Additionally, we will see an example of using a regular expression to select columns based on their names.

The Not selector from the **InvertedIndices.jl** package allows us to specify the columns we want to exclude from the resulting `DataFrame`. We can put any other valid column selector inside Not. If we want to drop the `PetalLength` column from the iris `DataFrame`, we can use:

```
julia> df[:, Not(:PetalLength)]
150×4 DataFrame
 Row │ SepalLength  SepalWidth  PetalWidth  Species
     │ Float64      Float64     Float64     String15
─────┼─────────────────────────────────────────────
   1 │         5.1         3.5         0.4  Iris-setosa
   2 │         4.9         3.0         0.4  Iris-setosa
   3 │         4.7         3.2         0.4  Iris-setosa
   4 │         4.6         3.1         0.4  Iris-setosa
   5 │         5.0         3.6         0.4  Iris-setosa
```

Figure 8.16: *A part of the dataset can only be viewed and not some specific column or row of the dataset using Not()*

The Between selector allows us to specify a range of columns by passing the start and stop columns using any of the single-column selector syntaxes. For instance, to select columns starting from `:SepalLength` and ending at `:PetalWidth`, we can use:

```
julia> df[:, Cols("Species", Between("SepalWidth", "PetalWidth"))]
150×4 DataFrame
 Row │ Species      SepalWidth  PetalLength  PetalWidth
     │ String15     Float64     Float64      Float64
─────┼─────────────────────────────────────────────────
   1 │ Iris-setosa         3.5          1.4         0.2
   2 │ Iris-setosa         3.0          1.4         0.2
   3 │ Iris-setosa         3.2          1.3         0.2
   4 │ Iris-setosa         3.1          1.5         0.2
   5 │ Iris-setosa         3.6          1.4         0.2
```

Figure 8.17: *A part of the dataset can only be viewed and not some specific column or row of the dataset using Between()*

The `Cols(...)` selector picks a union of other selectors passed as its arguments. In the following example, the Cols selector is picking a union of Age and Between(`“SepalWidth”, “PetalWidth”`) selectors passed as its arguments:

```
julia> df[:, Cols("Species", Between("SepalWidth", "PetalWidth"))]
150×4 DataFrame
 Row │ Species      SepalWidth  PetalLength  PetalWidth
     │ String15     Float64     Float64      Float64
─────┼──────────────────────────────────────────────────
   1 │ Iris-setosa         3.5          1.4         0.2
   2 │ Iris-setosa         3.0          1.4         0.2
   3 │ Iris-setosa         3.2          1.3         0.2
   4 │ Iris-setosa         3.1          1.5         0.2
   5 │ Iris-setosa         3.6          1.4         0.2
```

Figure 8.18: *A part of the dataset can only be viewed and not some specific column of the dataset using Cols()*

Finally, the `All()` selector allows us to select all columns of a DataFrame, which is the same as passing. For example, to select all columns of the `df` DataFrame, we can use:

```
julia> df[:, All()]
150×5 DataFrame
 Row │ SepalLength  SepalWidth  PetalLength  PetalWidth  Species
     │ Float64      Float64     Float64      Float64     String15
─────┼──────────────────────────────────────────────────────────────
   1 │         5.1         3.5          1.4         0.2  Iris-setosa
   2 │         4.9         3.0          1.4         0.2  Iris-setosa
   3 │         4.7         3.2          1.3         0.2  Iris-setosa
   4 │         4.6         3.1          1.5         0.2  Iris-setosa
   5 │         5.0         3.6          1.4         0.2  Iris-setosa
```

Figure 8.19: *A part of the dataset can only be viewed and not some specific columns or rows of the dataset using All()*

Moreover, we can also use regular expressions to select columns whose names match them. For instance, we can select columns that have "S" in their names and use Not to drop row number 5 with the following command:

```
julia> df[Not(5), r"S"]
149×3 DataFrame
 Row │ SepalLength  SepalWidth  Species
     │ Float64      Float64     String15
─────┼───────────────────────────────────────
   1 │         5.1         3.5  Iris-setosa
   2 │         4.9         3.0  Iris-setosa
   3 │         4.7         3.2  Iris-setosa
   4 │         4.6         3.1  Iris-setosa
   5 │         5.4         3.9  Iris-setosa
```

Figure 8.20: *A part of the dataset can only be viewed and not some specific columns or rows of the dataset using regex*

These selectors are very useful when dealing with complex DataFrames. By combining these selectors in different ways, we can select a subset of columns that meet our criteria.

Manipulating data

We will learn about the usage of three functions from the **DataFrames.jl** package for transforming columns in a DataFrame.

- combine

The `combine()` function creates a new DataFrame by applying a transformation to one or more columns of the original `DataFrame`. The result is populated with columns that contain the transformed data, which can potentially combine the rows of the original `DataFrame`. Here's an example:

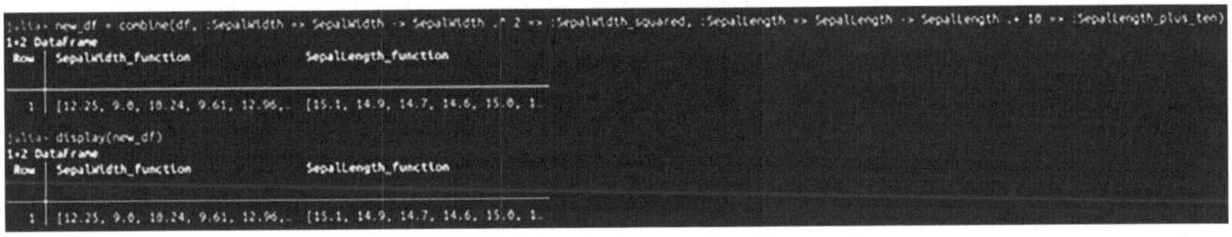

***Figure 8.21**: A new DataFrame can be created using the combine() function and the specified new columns or rows*

Here, we used combine to create a new DataFrame `new_df` that contains two new columns: `SepalWidth_squared` and `SepalLength_plus_ten`. The `SepalWidth_squared` column is the result of squaring the `SepalWidth` column from the original `DataFrame`, and the `SepalLength_plus_ten` column is the result of adding 10 to the `SepalLength` column from the original `DataFrame`.

- select

The `select!()` function creates a new `DataFrame` with the same number of rows as the original `DataFrame` but with the transformed data as new columns. Here's an example:

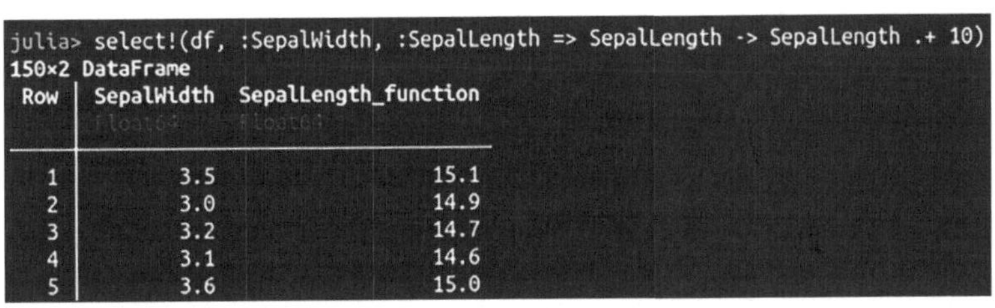

***Figure 8.22**: A new DataFrame can be created using the select() function and the specified new columns or rows*

Here, we used select! to modify the original `DataFrame df` by keeping the `SepalWidth` column and adding a new column `SepalLength_function`, which is the result of adding 10 to the `SepalLength` column.

- transform

The `transform()` function is similar to select but also keeps the columns from the original DataFrame that were not transformed and can potentially modify them. Here's an example:

```
julia> new_df = transform(df, :PetalLength => PetalLength -> PetalLength .+ 10)
150×6 DataFrame
 Row │ SepalLength  SepalWidth  PetalLength  PetalWidth  Species          PetalLength_function
─────┼──────────────────────────────────────────────────────────────────────────────────────────
   1 │         5.1         3.5          1.4         0.2  Iris-setosa                      11.4
   2 │         4.9         3.0          1.4         0.2  Iris-setosa                      11.4
   3 │         4.7         3.2          1.3         0.2  Iris-setosa                      11.3
   4 │         4.6         3.1          1.5         0.2  Iris-setosa                      11.5
   5 │         5.0         3.6          1.4         0.2  Iris-setosa                      11.4
```

Figure 8.23: *A new DataFrame can be created using the transform() function and the specified new columns or rows*

Here, we used transform to create a new `DataFrame new_df` that contains all the columns from the original `DataFrame` as well as a new column `PetalLength`, which is the result of adding 10 to the `PetalLength` column from the original `DataFrame`.

Major data manipulation frameworks in Julia

Data manipulation frameworks are software tools that provide convenient methods for working with tabular data, such as DataFrames, tables, or spreadsheets. In Julia, three such frameworks are available for manipulating DataFrames: **DataFramesMeta.jl, DataFrameMacros.jl,** and **Query.jl**. These frameworks enable users to write code for data manipulation in a way that is similar to dplyr in R or LINQ in C#.

We will understand the functionality of the three of these frameworks, **DataFramesMeta.jl**, **DataFrameMacros.jl** and **Query.jl**, and provide code samples to demonstrate how they work.

DataFramesMeta.jl

The **DataFramesMeta.jl package** provides a convenient macro-based interface to work with DataFrames. It provides a more convenient syntax for the transformation functions: transform, select, and combine via the macros @ transform, **`@select`**, **`@combine`**, and more. **DataFramesMeta.jl** also reexports the **`@chain`** macro from Chain.jl, allowing users to pipe the output of one transformation as an input to another, as with |> and %>% in R.

To use **DataFramesMeta.jl**, first, we need to install the package using the following command:

```
using DataFramesMeta
```

then press y followed by Enter.

Here are some examples of how to use the **DataFramesMeta.jl** package:

- Subset rows of the source `DataFrame` using a logical condition and select two columns, renaming one of them:

```
julia> @chain df begin
           @rsubset :SepalLength > 6.0
           @select(:name_of_species = :Species, :PetalWidth)
       end
61×2 DataFrame
 Row │ name_of_species  PetalWidth
     │ String15         Float64
─────┼─────────────────────────────
   1 │ Iris-versicolor         1.4
   2 │ Iris-versicolor         1.5
   3 │ Iris-versicolor         1.5
   4 │ Iris-versicolor         1.5
   5 │ Iris-versicolor         1.6
```

***Figure 8.24**: A subset of the DataFrame can be created and select some columns to be visible through a continuous chain function*

The preceding code selects only the rows where the sepal length column is greater than 6.0 and renames the Species column to `name_of_species`.

- Split the `DataFrame`, apply a function to each group, and then combine the results:

```
julia> @chain df begin
           @rsubset :PetalLength > 4.5
           @by(:Species, :min = minimum(:PetalLength), :max = maximum(:PetalLength))
           @select(:Species, :range = :max - :min)
       end
2×2 DataFrame
 Row │ Species          range
─────┼─────────────────────────
   1 │ Iris-versicolor      0.5
   2 │ Iris-virginica       2.1
```

***Figure 8.25**: Creating a subset of the DataFrame and selecting some columns to be visible through a continuous chain function*

The preceding code subsets the `DataFrame` to only select rows where the petal length column is greater than 4.5, groups the data by the Species column, and computes the range of the values for each group.

- Transform the `DataFrame` by creating a new column:

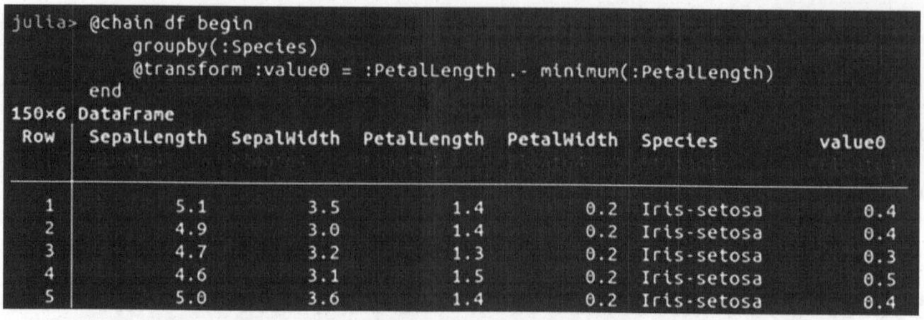

```
julia> @chain df begin
           groupby(:Species)
           @transform :value0 = :PetalLength .- minimum(:PetalLength)
       end
150×6 DataFrame
 Row │ SepalLength  SepalWidth  PetalLength  PetalWidth  Species      value0
─────┼───────────────────────────────────────────────────────────────────────
   1 │         5.1         3.5          1.4         0.2  Iris-setosa     0.4
   2 │         4.9         3.0          1.4         0.2  Iris-setosa     0.4
   3 │         4.7         3.2          1.3         0.2  Iris-setosa     0.3
   4 │         4.6         3.1          1.5         0.2  Iris-setosa     0.5
   5 │         5.0         3.6          1.4         0.2  Iris-setosa     0.4
```

Figure 8.26: *Creating a subset of the DataFrame and selecting some columns to be visible through a continuous chain function*

The preceding code groups the DataFrame by the Species column and then subtracts the minimum value of the petal length column from each value of petal length, creating a new column named value0.

DataFrameMacros.jl

DataFrameMacros.jl is an alternative to **DataFramesMeta.jl**, with a focus on convenient solutions for the transformation of multiple columns at once. It provides a similar functionality to **DataFramesMeta.jl** but is more flexible in how transformations can be applied.

To use **DataFrameMacros.jl**, first, we need to install the package using the following command:

```
using DataFramesMacros
```

then press y followed by Enter.

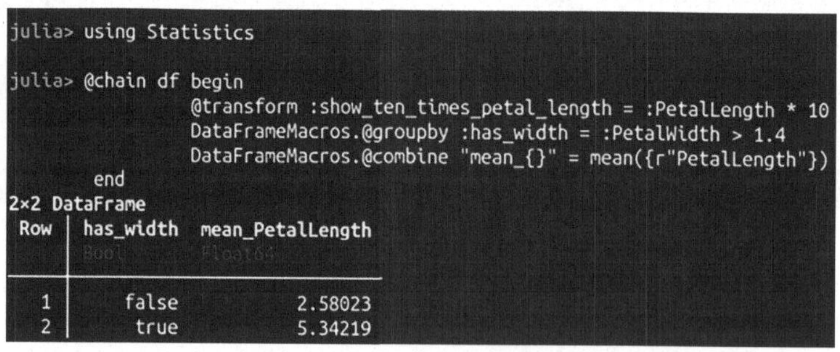

```
julia> using Statistics

julia> @chain df begin
                   @transform :show_ten_times_petal_length = :PetalLength * 10
                   DataFrameMacros.@groupby :has_width = :PetalWidth > 1.4
                   DataFrameMacros.@combine "mean_{}" = mean({r"PetalLength"})
              end
2×2 DataFrame
 Row │ has_width  mean_PetalLength
     │ Bool       Float64
─────┼─────────────────────────────
   1 │     false           2.58023
   2 │      true           5.34219
```

Figure 8.27: *Creating a subset of the DataFrame and selecting some columns to be visible through a continuous chain function*

Query.jl

Query.jl is a package that implements a LINQ-like interface for querying data. It allows for easy filtering, grouping, joining and aggregating of DataFrames. The following instructions are for version 1.0.5 of **Query.jl**.

First, install the Query.jl package:

```
using Query
```

then press y followed by Enter.

Query.jl uses the `@> macro` to chain together queries in a readable and flexible way. We present a few examples of its usage:

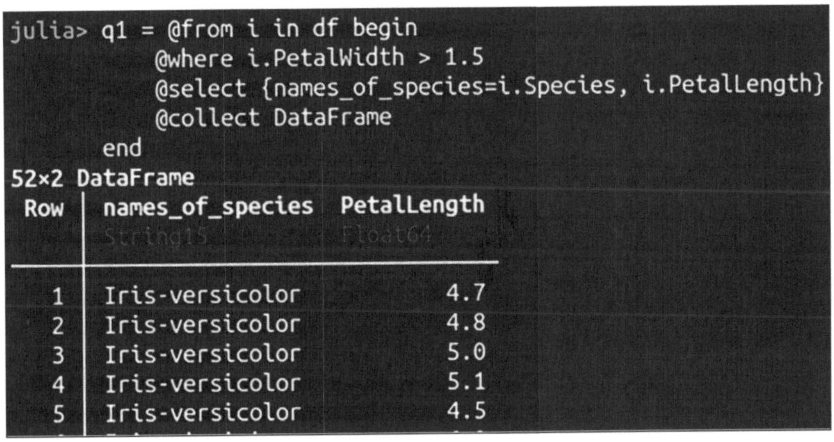

```
julia> q1 = @from i in df begin
           @where i.PetalWidth > 1.5
           @select {names_of_species=i.Species, i.PetalLength}
           @collect DataFrame
       end
52×2 DataFrame
 Row │ names_of_species  PetalLength
     │ String15          Float64
─────┼───────────────────────────────
   1 │ Iris-versicolor           4.7
   2 │ Iris-versicolor           4.8
   3 │ Iris-versicolor           5.0
   4 │ Iris-versicolor           5.1
   5 │ Iris-versicolor           4.5
```

***Figure 8.28**: Creating a subset of the DataFrame and selecting some columns to be visible through @from, @where, @select and @collect macros which is equivalent to SQL queries*

Query.jl provides the `@from` macro, which creates a query object that can be used to perform operations on the data. Queries can be filtered, sorted, aggregated, and joined.

In this example, the `@from` macro creates a query object with a reference to the input DataFrame. The query object is then used to filter the data with the @ where macro and select the desired columns with the `@select` macro. Finally, the `>` operator applies the query and converts the output to a DataFrame.

In addition to the examples shown here, **Query.jl** provides many more useful functions for data manipulation, such as join, order, and distinct. In summary, **DataFramesMeta.jl**, **DataFrameMacros.jl**, and **Query.jl** are three powerful frameworks for data manipulation in Julia. They provide convenient methods for filtering, selecting, transforming, and aggregating data in a way that is familiar to users of dplyr or LINQ. Each framework has its strengths and weaknesses, so it is worth exploring all three to find the best fit for your use case.

Comparing with other language frameworks

We will compare the Julia data manipulation framework **DataFrames.jl** with similar tools in other programming languages like Python, R, and Stata. We will use the example of creating a data set, and then we will compare various functions available in **DataFrames.jl** with their counterparts in the pandas package in Python.

Comparing with pandas - a Python framework

Both Pandas and **DataFrames.jl** are designed to manipulate tabular data, but they have some differences in terms of syntax, structure, and time taken for certain operations. Here are some key differences:

- **Language:** Pandas is a Python library, while **DataFrames.jl** is a package for the Julia language.
- **Syntax**: Both libraries have similar syntax for many operations, such as filtering and grouping data. However, there are some differences in syntax, especially for more complex operations. For example, in Pandas, you can use the `apply()` method to apply a function to each row or column of a `DataFrame`, while in DataFrames.jl, you would use the `transform()` function for the same purpose.
- **Data structures:** Both Pandas and **DataFrames.jl** use a DataFrame structure to represent tabular data. However, there are some differences in the details of the data structures. For example, **DataFrames.jl** allows for more flexible handling of missing data, while Pandas has more built-in support for time series data.
- **Time taken:** In general, Julia is faster than Python, which means that **DataFrames.jl** can be faster than Pandas for some operations. For example, sorting a `DataFrame` can be much faster in Julia, especially for larger datasets.

Overall, both Pandas and **DataFrames.jl** are powerful tools for working with tabular data, and the choice between the two will depend on factors such as the specific requirements of the task at hand and the programming language preferences of the user.

Comparing with dplyr - an R framework

dplyr is a data manipulation package in R, while **DataFrames.jl** is a data manipulation package in Julia. Both dplyr and **DataFrames.jl** provide similar functionality for working with DataFrames, but there are some differences in their syntax and structure.

- **Time taken**: **DataFrames.jl** is generally faster than dplyr. Julia is designed to be a faster language than R, and **DataFrames.jl** is optimized for performance.
- **Syntax**: The syntax of `dplyr` and **DataFrames.jl** is similar but not identical. In `dplyr`, you chain together multiple operations using the %>% operator. In **DataFrames.jl**, you typically use the |> operator to chain together multiple operations. For example, to filter rows in dplyr, you would use the `filter()` function, while in DataFrames.jl, you would use the `filter()` function and the |> operator.
- **Structure**: The structure of DataFrames in dplyr and DataFrames.jl is also similar but not identical. In dplyr, DataFrames are represented as tibble objects, which are similar to DataFrames in base R but with additional functionality. In DataFrames.jl, DataFrames are represented as DataFrame objects, which are similar to tibble objects in `dplyr`. However, DataFrame objects in DataFrames.jl are more flexible than tibble objects in `dplyr`.

Overall, `dplyr` and **DataFrames.jl** provide similar functionality for working with `DataFrames`, but there are some differences in their syntax and structure. The choice of which package to use depends on the project-specific needs as well as individual preferences and familiarity with the programming languages.

Conclusion

The **DataFrames.jl** package is a powerful tool for data manipulation in the Julia programming language. By setting up the environment and constructing `DataFrame` objects, users can easily fetch, inspect, and manipulate data. The package provides numerous functionalities for handling data, including filtering, merging, sorting, and aggregating data.

Moreover, **DataFrames.jl** is just one of the major data manipulation frameworks in Julia, which offers great performance and ease of use, compared to other popular data manipulation frameworks like Pandas and R. It also has features that make it stand out: its integration with the wider Julia ecosystem, support for parallel processing, and ability to cope with large datasets efficiently.

Overall, **DataFrames.jl** package provides a great option for users looking for a fast and flexible data manipulation tool, and its ease of use and performance make it a viable alternative to other popular data manipulation frameworks in other programming languages.

DataFrames.jl provides robust tools for working with missing and categorical data, including advanced imputation techniques. It also offers efficient functions for sorting, reshaping, joining, and performing split-apply-combine operations on data, making it a comprehensive data manipulation package for Julia users. We will learn about these in the next chapter.

Questions

- What is the **DataFrames.jl** package, and what are some of its key features?
- How do you set up the environment to use the **DataFrames.jl** package in Julia?
- What are DataFrame objects, and how are they constructed in the **DataFrames.jl** package?
- What are some of the techniques for fetching, inspecting, and manipulating data in the **DataFrames.jl** package?
- What are the major data manipulation frameworks available in Julia, and how does **DataFrames.jl** compare to them?
- How does **DataFrames.jl** compare to other popular data manipulation frameworks in other programming languages?
- How does **DataFrames.jl** compare to other popular data manipulation packages in terms of performance and memory usage?
- What are some advanced data manipulation techniques that can be performed using **DataFrames.jl**, such as imputation or merging datasets?
- How does **DataFrames.jl** handle missing data and what are some of the available methods for imputing missing values?
- What are the advantages of using **DataFrames.jl** for data manipulation, compared to using other programming languages such as Python or R?
- Can **DataFrames.jl** handle large datasets efficiently? What are some of the tools and techniques available for optimizing performance?
- How can **DataFrames.jl** be used in combination with other packages and libraries in the Julia ecosystem for advanced data analysis and modeling?
- Are there any limitations or drawbacks to using **DataFrames.jl** for data manipulation? How can these be addressed or mitigated?

- What are some of the functions available in **DataFrames.jl** for fetching and importing data from various sources, such as CSV or SQL databases?
- How can one use **DataFrames.jl** to perform exploratory data analysis and inspect the contents of a dataset, such as by summarizing or visualizing its key features?

Chapter 9

Working on Data in DataFrames

As data analysts and scientists, we often encounter extensive and complicated datasets that require preprocessing before meaningful insights can be obtained. In this chapter, we will cover crucial data manipulation techniques, including handling missing data, sorting data, reshaping data, dealing with categorical data, splitting data into subsets, and combining data from multiple sources.

Effectively cleaning and preprocessing data is critical to data analysis. Missing data is a common issue that can have a significant impact on the accuracy of our analysis results. We will explore various methods for handling missing data and discuss the best techniques to address this problem. Additionally, we will demonstrate how to sort data in ascending or descending order based on specific columns and how to reshape data into more convenient formats using functions such as pivot and melt.

Categorical data requires special handling, and we will learn how to encode categorical variables and handle their levels using the DataFrames.jl package. We will also discuss grouping data and applying functions to subsets of data using the split-apply-combine paradigm, which is an effective way to summarize data and generate insights.

Finally, we will delve into the topic of joining DataFrames, where we can combine data from multiple sources using common keys or columns. This technique is invaluable when integrating data from different datasets into a single DataFrame for further analysis. By the end of this chapter, you will have a solid foundation in essential data manipulation techniques and will be well-equipped to handle complex datasets using the DataFrames.jl package in Julia.

Overall, mastering these data manipulation techniques is crucial for working with complex datasets and deriving meaningful insights. The DataFrames.jl package provides a flexible and powerful platform for manipulating data, and these techniques can be applied to a wide range of datasets across various fields, including finance, healthcare, and social sciences.

Structure

In this chapter, the following topics will be covered:

- Missing data in DataFrames
- Sorting data in DataFrames
- Reshaping data in DataFrames
- Categorical data in DataFrames
- Joining data in DataFrames
- Split-apply-combine data in DataFrames

Missing data in DataFrames

Missing data is a common problem in datasets and can lead to biased or incomplete results if not handled appropriately. There are different approaches to handle missing data, such as deleting missing values, imputing missing values, or ignoring missing values.

Deleting missing values involves removing rows or columns with missing data, but it can lead to a loss of information, bias in the results, and decreased statistical power. This method is only recommended when the proportion of missing data is small and the missing data is randomly distributed.

Imputing missing values involves replacing missing values with estimated values based on statistical techniques. Single imputation methods include mean, median, and mode imputation, while multiple imputation creates multiple imputed datasets and provides more reliable estimates. However, single imputation methods can lead to biased results and underestimate the variance of the data.

Ignoring missing values is acceptable in some cases, but it can also lead to biased results, especially when the missing data is not random. The choice of method depends on the type of data, the proportion of missing values, and the characteristics of the dataset. Handling missing data is an essential step in data preprocessing and requires careful consideration and appropriate techniques.

Missing values in Julia

In Julia, missing values in data are represented using the object missing, which is the single instance of the type Missing. The Missing type lets users create vectors and DataFrame columns with missing values.

To create a vector with a missing value, we can use the following code:

```
julia> using DataFrames

julia> x = [1, 2, missing]

3-element Vector{Union{Missing, Int64}}:

1

2

missing
```

The element type of the returned vector is Union{Missing, Int64}. We can exclude missing values when performing operations by using skipmissing, which returns a memory-efficient iterator. For example:

```
julia> sum(skipmissing(x))

3
```

The coalesce function can be used to replace missing values with another value. For example:

```
julia> coalesce.(x, 0)

3-element Vector{Int64}:

 1

 2

 0
```

The **`dropmissing`** and **`dropmissing!`** functions can be used to remove the rows containing missing values from a **`DataFrame`** and either create a new **`DataFrame`** or mutate the original in place respectively. Here is an example:

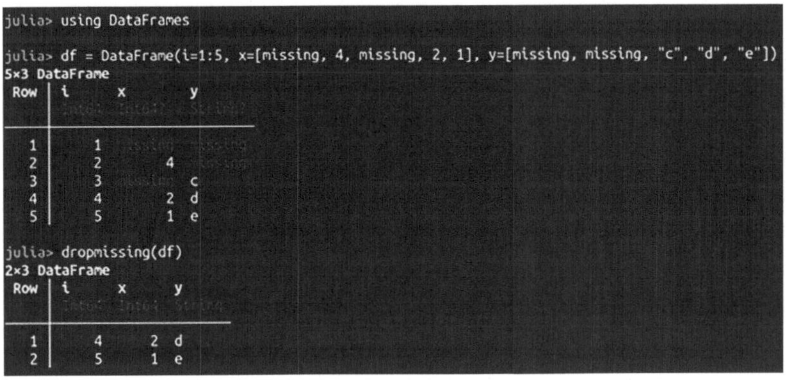

```
julia> using DataFrames

julia> df = DataFrame(i=1:5, x=[missing, 4, missing, 2, 1], y=[missing, missing, "c", "d", "e"])
5×3 DataFrame
 Row │ i      x        y
     │ Int64  Int64?   String?
─────┼─────────────────────────
   1 │     1  missing  missing
   2 │     2        4  missing
   3 │     3  missing  c
   4 │     4        2  d
   5 │     5        1  e

julia> dropmissing(df)
2×3 DataFrame
 Row │ i      x      y
     │ Int64  Int64  String
─────┼──────────────────────
   1 │     4      2  d
   2 │     5      1  e
```

Figure 9.1: *Create a DataFrame and use the dropmissing() function to remove all the missing values*

By default, the dropmissing and dropmissing! functions keep the `Union{T, Missing}` element type in columns selected for row removal. To remove the Missing part, if present, set the `disallowmissing` keyword argument to true.

Finally, it is possible to allow or disallow support of missing values in some columns of a DataFrame using the `allowmissing`, `allowmissing!`, `disallowmissing`, and `disallowmissing`! functions. For example:

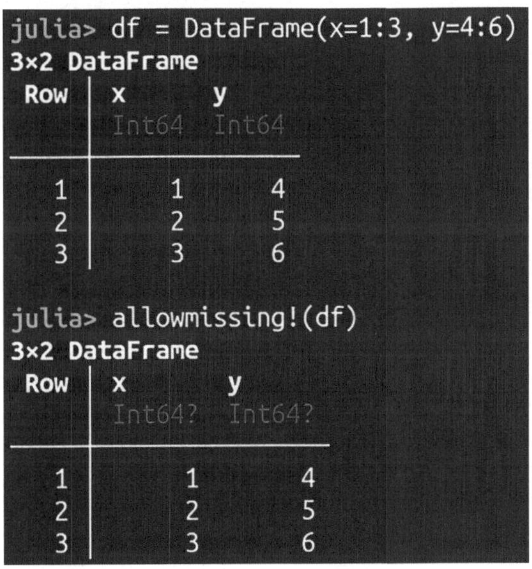

```
julia> df = DataFrame(x=1:3, y=4:6)
3×2 DataFrame
 Row │ x      y
     │ Int64  Int64
─────┼──────────────
   1 │     1      4
   2 │     2      5
   3 │     3      6

julia> allowmissing!(df)
3×2 DataFrame
 Row │ x       y
     │ Int64?  Int64?
─────┼────────────────
   1 │      1       4
   2 │      2       5
   3 │      3       6
```

Figure 9.2: *Create a DataFrame and allow missing values in the DataFrame*

Now df allows missing values in all its columns. We can take advantage of this fact and set some of the values in df to missing. Let's take the example `DataFrame` `df = DataFrame(x=1:3, y=4:6)` which has no missing values initially. To allow missing values in all columns, we use `allowmissing!(df)` which modifies the DataFrame in place. Now, we can set some values to missing, for example, `df[1, 1] = missing`.

The Julia language provides functions to allow or disallow missing values in a `DataFrame`. These functions are useful when dealing with data that may have missing values in some columns, but not in others. The `allowmissing`, `allowmissing!`, `disallowmissing`, and `disallowmissing!` functions can be used to allow or disallow missing values in a `DataFrame`.

To disallow missing values in some columns, we can use the `disallowmissing` function. If we want to disallow missing values in column `:y`, we can use `disallowmissing(df, :y)`. This creates a new `DataFrame` with the specified column(s) disallowed missing values. If we want to modify the original `DataFrame` in place, we use `disallowmissing!(df, :y)`.

```
julia> # Set a value to missing
       df[1, 1] = missing
missing

julia> # Disallow missing values in column y
       disallowmissing(df, :y)
3×2 DataFrame
 Row │ x        y
     │ Int64?   Int64
─────┼────────────────
   1 │ missing      4
   2 │       2      5
   3 │       3      6

julia> # Modify data frame in place to disallow missing values in column y
       disallowmissing!(df, :y)
3×2 DataFrame
 Row │ x        y
     │ Int64?   Int64
─────┼────────────────
   1 │ missing      4
   2 │       2      5
   3 │       3      6

julia> # Disallow missing values in all columns that do not contain them
       disallowmissing(df, error=false)
3×2 DataFrame
 Row │ x        y
     │ Int64?   Int64
─────┼────────────────
   1 │ missing      4
   2 │       2      5
   3 │       3      6
```

Figure 9.3: *Disallowing() function doesn't allow missing values in particular columns*

If we want to disallow missing values in all columns that do not contain them, we can use `disallowmissing(df, error=false)` which keeps the columns that have some missing values unchanged without having to list them explicitly.

```
julia> # Example usage of passmissing
       f(x, y) = x + y
f (generic function with 1 method)

julia> g = passmissing(f)
(::Missings.PassMissing{typeof(f)}) (generic function with 2 methods)

julia> g(1, 2)  # returns 3
3

julia> g(1, missing)  # returns missing
missing
```

Figure 9.4: *passmissing() function allows the missing values in the DataFrame*

The **Missings.jl** package provides additional convenience functions for working with missing values. passmissing is a higher-order function that takes a function as an argument and returns a new function that returns missing if any of its positional arguments are missing and applies the function otherwise. This is useful when working with functions that do not support missing values as arguments.

Here are some code samples to illustrate the usage of these functions:

```
julia> # Example usage of replace
       using Missings
 │ Package Missings not found, but a package named Missings is available from a registry.
 │ Install package?
 │              add Missings
 └ (y/n/o) [y]: y
   Updating registry at `~/.julia/registries/General.toml`
  Resolving package versions...
   Updating `~/.julia/environments/v1.8/Project.toml`
            + Missings v1.1.0
 No Changes to `~/.julia/environments/v1.8/Manifest.toml`

julia> x = [1, 2, missing]
3-element Vector{Union{Missing, Int64}}:
 1
 2
  missing
```

Figure 9.5: *Missing package installed with the missing value*

The replace function returns an iterator that replaces missing elements with another value. The nonmissingtype function returns the element type in `Union{T, Missing}`. The missings function constructs vectors and arrays supporting missing values, using the optional first argument to specify the element type.

```
julia> # Example usage of nonmissingtype
       eltype(x)  # returns Union{Missing, Int64}
Union{Missing, Int64}

julia> nonmissingtype(eltype(x))  # returns Int64
Int64

julia> # Example usage of missings
       missings(1)  # returns [missing]
1-element Vector{Missing}:
 missing

julia> missings(3)  # returns [missing, missing, missing]
3-element Vector{Missing}:
 missing
 missing
 missing

julia> missings(1, 3)  # returns a 1x3 matrix with all elements missing
1×3 Matrix{Missing}:
 missing  missing  missing

julia> missings(Int, 1, 3)  # returns a 1x3 matrix with all elements of type Union{Missing, Int64}
1×3 Matrix{Union{Missing, Int64}}:
 missing  missing  missing
```

Figure 9.6: *missing() function returning missing values row-wise*

Sorting data in DataFrames

Sorting data is an important operation in working with datasets, as it allows you to organize the data in a meaningful way, making it easier to analyze and visualize. In Julia, sorting data in a DataFrame or a Vector is straightforward using the `sort` and `sort!` functions from the Base library.

Sorting a Vector

To sort a vector, we can use the sort function. The sort function returns a sorted copy of the original vector, leaving the original vector unmodified. For example, suppose we have the following vector of numbers. To sort the vector in ascending order, we can call the sort function as follows:

```
julia> x = [3, 1, 4, 1, 5, 9, 2, 6, 5, 3]
10-element Vector{Int64}:
 3
 1
 4
 1
 5
 9
 2
 6
 5
 3

julia> sort(x)
10-element Vector{Int64}:
 1
 1
 2
 3
 3
 4
 5
 5
 6
 9
```

Figure 9.7: *The sort() function is used to sort all the numbers in ascending order*

To sort the vector in descending order, we can pass the `rev=true` (here rev means reverse) keyword argument to the sort function:

```
julia> sort(x, rev=true)
10-element Vector{Int64}:
 9
 6
 5
 5
 4
 3
 3
 2
 1
 1
```

***Figure 9.8**: The rev keyword is used to reverse the order, that is, sort in a descending order*

Sorting a DataFrame

Sorting is the process of arranging items in a particular order. In data analysis, sorting is a fundamental component to better understand the data. Basic sorting in Julia is a trivial task, which can be done using the **`sort!`** function. The sort! function sorts all columns of a DataFrame in place.

We're creating a `DataFrame` from **german.csv** which contains information about Germany. The following code reads the CSV file containing the data and stores it in the `german DataFrame`:

```
julia> using DataFrames, CSV

julia> german = CSV.read((joinpath(dirname(pathof(DataFrames)), "..", "docs", "src", "assets", "german.csv")), DataFrame)
1000×10 DataFrame
 Row │ id     Age    Sex     Job    Housing  Saving accounts  Checking account  Credit amount  Duration  Purpose
─────┼──────────────────────────────────────────────────────────────────────────────────────────────────────────────
   1 │     0     67  male        2  own      NA               little                     1169         6  radio/TV
   2 │     1     22  female      2  own      little           moderate                   5951        48  radio/TV
   3 │     2     49  male        1  own      little           NA                         2096        12  education
   4 │     3     45  male        2  free     little           little                     7882        42  furniture/equipment
   5 │     4     53  male        2  free     little           little                     4870        24  car
   6 │     5     35  male        1  free     NA               NA                         9055        36  education
   7 │     6     53  male        2  own      quite rich       NA                         2835        24  furniture/equipment
   8 │     7     35  male        3  rent     little           moderate                   6948        36  car
   9 │     8     61  male        1  own      rich             NA                         3059        12  radio/TV
  10 │     9     28  male        3  own      little           moderate                   5234        30  car
  11 │    10     25  female      2  rent     little           moderate                   1295        12  car
  12 │    11     24  female      2  rent     little           little                     4308        48  business
  13 │    12     22  female      2  own      little           moderate                   1567        12  radio/TV
  14 │    13     60  male        1  own      little           little                     1199        24  car
  15 │    14     28  female      2  rent     little           little                     1403        15  car
  ⋮  │   ⋮      ⋮      ⋮       ⋮      ⋮          ⋮                 ⋮                  ⋮            ⋮          ⋮
```

***Figure 9.9**: Introducing the german dataset*

To sort the `german DataFrame` in place, we can use the `sort!` function:

```
julia> sort!(german)
1000×10 DataFrame
 Row │ id     Age    Sex      Job    Housing  Saving accounts  Checking account  Credit amount  Duration  Purpose
─────┼─────────────────────────────────────────────────────────────────────────────────────────────────────────────
   1 │     0     67  male         2  own      NA               little                     1169         6  radio/TV
   2 │     1     22  female       2  own      little           moderate                   5951        48  radio/TV
   3 │     2     49  male         1  own      little           NA                         2096        12  education
   4 │     3     45  male         2  free     little           little                     7882        42  furniture/equipment
   5 │     4     53  male         2  free     little           little                     4870        24  car
   6 │     5     35  male         1  free     NA               NA                         9055        36  education
   7 │     6     53  male         2  own      quite rich       NA                         2835        24  furniture/equipment
   8 │     7     35  male         3  rent     little           moderate                   6948        36  car
   9 │     8     61  male         1  own      rich             NA                         3059        12  radio/TV
  10 │     9     28  male         3  own      little           moderate                   5234        30  car
```

Figure 9.10: *Sorting the german dataset in ascending order in place*

This sorts the `DataFrame` lexicographically with respect to the first column. Since, in the `german` dataset, the first column is ids, and it is already in ascending order, you can see no change in the `DataFrame`.

Alternatively, we can create a new DataFrame with sorted vectors using the `sort` function. This function returns a new DataFrame with sorted columns, leaving the original `DataFrame` unmodified.

```
julia> german_sorted = sort(german)
1000×10 DataFrame
 Row │ id     Age    Sex      Job    Housing  Saving accounts  Checking account  Credit amount  Duration  Purpose
─────┼─────────────────────────────────────────────────────────────────────────────────────────────────────────────
   1 │     0     67  male         2  own      NA               little                     1169         6  radio/TV
   2 │     1     22  female       2  own      little           moderate                   5951        48  radio/TV
   3 │     2     49  male         1  own      little           NA                         2096        12  education
   4 │     3     45  male         2  free     little           little                     7882        42  furniture/equipment
   5 │     4     53  male         2  free     little           little                     4870        24  car
   6 │     5     35  male         1  free     NA               NA                         9055        36  education
   7 │     6     53  male         2  own      quite rich       NA                         2835        24  furniture/equipment
   8 │     7     35  male         3  rent     little           moderate                   6948        36  car
   9 │     8     61  male         1  own      rich             NA                         3059        12  radio/TV
  10 │     9     28  male         3  own      little           moderate                   5234        30  car
```

Figure 9.11: *Sorting the german dataset in ascending order with respect to the id column*

We can also sort a DataFrame based on specific columns. The `sort!` function accepts a by keyword argument to specify the columns to use for sorting. The by argument takes a tuple of column names or numbers, and the sorting is done based on the order of the columns in the tuple. For example, to sort the German `DataFrame` by the Age column, we can use the following code:

```
sort!(::OrderedCollections.OrderedDict; byvalue, args...)
```

In Julia, using a colon (`:`) in front of a symbol is a shorthand for creating a Symbol, which is a type of object used to represent identifiers in Julia. A symbol is often used to refer to a name or label without evaluating it. On the other hand, using double quotes (" ") creates a string. Here, `:Age` is a symbol representing the identifier "`Age`", and "`credit amount`" is a string representing the label "`credit amount`". In many contexts, especially in data analysis or machine learning libraries, you might encounter a syntax like this when specifying column names or features.

```
julia> sort!(german, :Age)
1000×10 DataFrame
 Row │ id    Age    Sex      Job    Housing  Saving accounts  Checking account  Credit amount  Duration  Purpose
─────┼────────────────────────────────────────────────────────────────────────────────────────────────────────────────
   1 │  391     19  female     1  rent     rich             moderate                    983        12  furniture/equipment
   2 │  633     19  female     2  rent     little           NA                         1980         9  furniture/equipment
   3 │   93     20  male       2  rent     NA               rich                       3617        24  furniture/equipment
   4 │  155     20  female     2  rent     little           little                     1282        12  furniture/equipment
   5 │  167     20  female     2  own      rich             moderate                   1577        11  furniture/equipment
   6 │  188     20  male       2  own      moderate         little                      674        12  radio/TV
   7 │  296     20  female     2  rent     NA               NA                         4675        12  car
   8 │  410     20  female     2  own      little           moderate                   1967        24  radio/TV
   9 │  420     20  female     2  rent     rich             NA                         3186        15  car
  10 │  428     20  male       2  own      little           NA                         1313         9  furniture/equipment
```

Figure 9.12: *Sorting the german dataset in place in ascending order with respect to the age column*

This code sorts the German DataFrame based on the **`Age`** column in ascending order.

To sort a DataFrame in descending order, we can use the rev function to reverse the order of the sorting. For example, to sort the German DataFrame based on the **`Age`** column in descending order, we can use the following code:

```
julia> sort!(german, :Age, rev = true)
1000×10 DataFrame
 Row │ id    Age    Sex      Job    Housing  Saving accounts  Checking account  Credit amount  Duration  Purpose
─────┼────────────────────────────────────────────────────────────────────────────────────────────────────────────────
   1 │  330     75  male       3  free     little           little                     6615        24  car
   2 │  536     75  female     3  own      NA               little                     1374         6  car
   3 │  186     74  female     3  free     little           moderate                   5129         9  car
   4 │  430     74  male       1  own      little           NA                         3448         5  business
   5 │  606     74  male       3  own      little           NA                         4526        24  business
   6 │  756     74  male       0  own      little           rich                       1299         6  car
   7 │  163     70  male       3  free     little           moderate                   7308        10  car
   8 │  187     68  male       0  free     little           moderate                   1175        16  car
   9 │  846     68  male       2  rent     NA               NA                         6761        18  car
  10 │  917     68  male       3  own      little           little                    14896         6  car
```

Figure 9.13: *Sorting the german dataset in place in descending order with respect to the age column*

This code sorts the **`german DataFrame`** based on the `Age` column in descending order.

```
julia> sort!(german, [:Age, "Credit amount"], rev = true)
1000×10 DataFrame
 Row │ id    Age    Sex      Job    Housing  Saving accounts  Checking account  Credit amount  Duration  Purpose
─────┼────────────────────────────────────────────────────────────────────────────────────────────────────────────────
   1 │  330     75  male       3  free     little           little                     6615        24  car
   2 │  536     75  female     3  own      NA               little                     1374         6  car
   3 │  186     74  female     3  free     little           moderate                   5129         9  car
   4 │  606     74  male       3  own      little           NA                         4526        24  business
   5 │  430     74  male       1  own      little           NA                         3448         5  business
   6 │  756     74  male       0  own      little           rich                       1299         6  car
   7 │  163     70  male       3  free     little           moderate                   7308        10  car
   8 │  917     68  male       3  own      little           little                    14896         6  car
   9 │  846     68  male       2  rent     NA               NA                         6761        18  car
  10 │  187     68  male       0  free     little           moderate                   1175        16  car
```

Figure 9.14: *Sorting the German dataset in place in descending order with respect to the age and credit amount*

You can pass rev as an array of boolean values as well. Check the difference between the two images.

```
julia> sort!(german, [:Age, "Credit amount"], rev = [true, false])
1000×10 DataFrame
 Row │ id    Age  Sex     Job  Housing  Saving accounts  Checking account  Credit amount  Duration  Purpose
─────┼──────────────────────────────────────────────────────────────────────────────────────────────────────
   1 │  536   75  female    3  own      NA               little                     1374         6  car
   2 │  330   75  male      3  free     little           little                     6615        24  car
   3 │  756   74  male      0  own      little           rich                       1299         6  car
   4 │  430   74  male      1  own      little           NA                         3448         5  business
   5 │  606   74  male      3  own      little           NA                         4526        24  business
   6 │  186   74  female    3  free     little           moderate                   5129         9  car
   7 │  163   70  male      3  free     little           moderate                   7308        10  car
   8 │  187   68  male      0  free     little           moderate                   1175        16  car
   9 │  846   68  male      2  rent     NA               NA                         6761        18  car
  10 │  917   68  male      3  own      little           little                    14896         6  car
```

Figure 9.15: *Sorting the german dataset in place in descending order with respect to the age and ascending order with respect to the credit amount*

We can use keywords such as order, by and **`Cols`**, **`All`**, **`Not`**, **`Between`**, and so on, for sorting **`DataFrame`**:

```
julia> sort!(german, [order(:Housing, by=length), order(:Job, rev=true)])
1000×10 DataFrame
 Row │ id    Age  Sex     Job  Housing  Saving accounts  Checking account  Credit amount  Duration  Purpose
─────┼──────────────────────────────────────────────────────────────────────────────────────────────────────
   1 │  536   75  female    3  own      NA               little                     1374         6  car
   2 │  606   74  male      3  own      little           NA                         4526        24  business
   3 │  917   68  male      3  own      little           little                    14896         6  car
   4 │  554   67  female    3  own      little           moderate                   1199         9  education
   5 │  213   66  male      3  own      little           rich                       1908        30  business
   6 │  784   60  male      3  own      NA               moderate                   6468        20  car
   7 │  448   55  female    3  own      NA               rich                       1424        12  furniture/equipment
   8 │  190   54  male      3  own      rich             NA                         4591        24  business
   9 │  175   53  female    3  own      NA               NA                         7485        30  car
  10 │   56   52  male      3  own      NA               moderate                   6468        12  radio/TV
```

Figure 9.16: *Sorting the german dataset in place by length of the values of the Housing column and descending order with respect to job*

In summary, sorting is a crucial part of data analysis. Julia provides a variety of functions to sort DataFrames based on specific columns in ascending or descending order. The `sort!` function can sort all columns of a DataFrame in place, while the sort function returns a new DataFrame with sorted columns, leaving the original DataFrame unmodified.

Reshaping data in DataFrames

Reshaping data in a DataFrame refers to the process of transforming the structure of the DataFrame to make it easier to analyze and visualize. There are several ways to reshape data in DataFrames, including pivoting, stacking, and melting.

- Pivoting: Pivoting is the process of transforming a DataFrame from a long format to a wide format. In a long format DataFrame, each row represents a unique observation, and each column represents a variable. In a wide format DataFrame, each row represents a unique variable, and each column represents an observation. To pivot a DataFrame, we use the `pivot()` method and specify the index, columns, and values we want to use.

- Stacking: Stacking is the process of transforming a DataFrame from a wide format to a long format. To stack a DataFrame, we use the `stack()` method.
- Melting: Melting is the process of transforming a DataFrame from a wide format to a long format by unpivoting it. It is similar to stacking, but it allows us to specify which columns we want to use as the identifiers and which columns we want to melt. To melt a DataFrame, we use the `melt()` method and specify the `id_vars`, `value_vars`, `var_name`, and `value_name` parameters.

Reshaping data in DataFrames can be useful for several reasons. For example, it can help us to better understand the relationships between variables, compare different observations or groups, and perform various types of analysis and visualization.

Reshaping data in Julia

The `stack()` function in Julia's DataFrames package is used to convert a wide-format `DataFrame` into a long-format `DataFrame`. This means that the function can be used to transform a DataFrame where columns represent multiple variables to a DataFrame where those variables are stacked in a single column. The **`stack()`** function takes two arguments, the first being the DataFrame to be transformed, and the second is an optional argument that specifies the columns that are to be stacked. You can look into https://csv.juliadata.org/stable/reading.html#CSV.read to better understand ".." passed as a parameter.

Here is some code that demonstrates the use of the `stack()` function in Julia:

```
julia> using DataFrames, CSV
# Load the german dataset
julia> german = CSV.read(joinpath(dirname(pathof(DataFrames)),
                        "..", "docs", "src", "assets", "german.csv"),
                DataFrame)
# Print the first few rows of the original german DataFrame
julia> @show german[1:5, :]
```

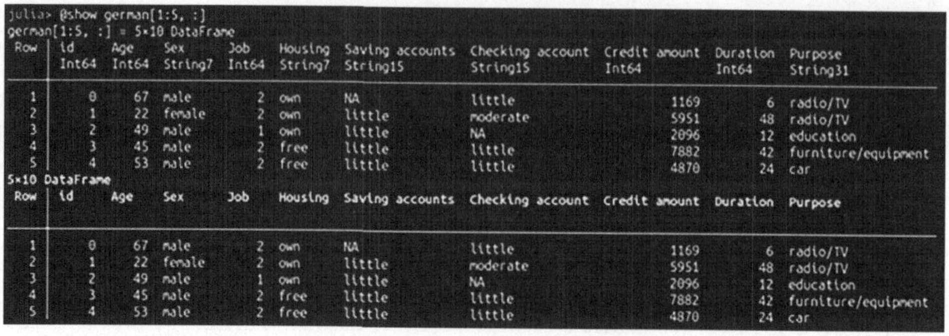

```
julia> @show german[1:5, :]
german[1:5, :] = 5×10 DataFrame
 Row │ id     Age    Sex      Job    Housing  Saving accounts  Checking account  Credit amount  Duration  Purpose
     │ Int64  Int64  String7  Int64  String7  String15         String15          Int64          Int64     String31
─────┼──────────────────────────────────────────────────────────────────────────────────────────────────────────────
   1 │     0     67  male         2  own      NA               little                     1169         6  radio/TV
   2 │     1     22  female       2  own      little           moderate                   5951        48  radio/TV
   3 │     2     49  male         1  own      little           NA                         2096        12  education
   4 │     3     45  male         2  free     little           little                     7882        42  furniture/equipment
   5 │     4     53  male         2  free     little           little                     4870        24  car
5×10 DataFrame
 Row │ id     Age    Sex      Job    Housing  Saving accounts  Checking account  Credit amount  Duration  Purpose
─────┼──────────────────────────────────────────────────────────────────────────────────────────────────────────────
   1 │     0     67  male         2  own      NA               little                     1169         6  radio/TV
   2 │     1     22  female       2  own      little           moderate                   5951        48  radio/TV
   3 │     2     49  male         1  own      little           NA                         2096        12  education
   4 │     3     45  male         2  free     little           little                     7882        42  furniture/equipment
   5 │     4     53  male         2  free     little           little                     4870        24  car
```

Figure 9.17: *Viewing the german dataset from the 1st row to the 5th row*

```
# Convert the german DataFrame from wide format to long format
julia> long_german = stack(german, 1:4)
```

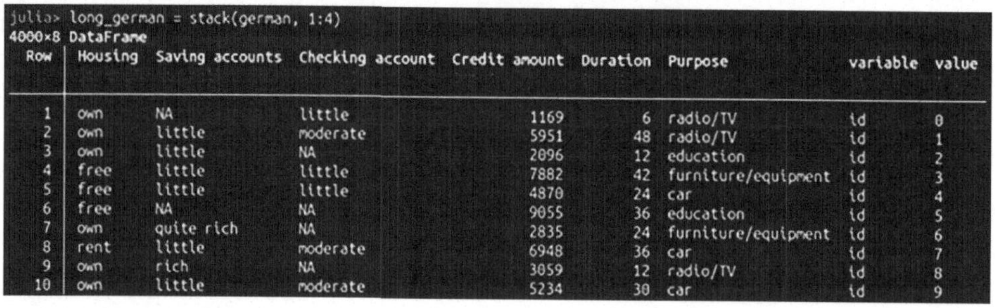

```
julia> long_german = stack(german, 1:4)
4000×8 DataFrame
 Row │ Housing  Saving accounts  Checking account  Credit amount  Duration  Purpose              variable  value
─────┼───────────────────────────────────────────────────────────────────────────────────────────────────────────
   1 │ own      NA               little                     1169         6  radio/TV             id        0
   2 │ own      little           moderate                   5951        48  radio/TV             id        1
   3 │ own      little           NA                         2096        12  education            id        2
   4 │ free     little           little                     7882        42  furniture/equipment  id        3
   5 │ free     little           little                     4870        24  car                  id        4
   6 │ free     NA               NA                         9055        36  education            id        5
   7 │ own      quite rich       NA                         2835        24  furniture/equipment  id        6
   8 │ rent     little           moderate                   6948        36  car                  id        7
   9 │ own      rich             NA                         3059        12  radio/TV             id        8
  10 │ own      little           moderate                   5234        30  car                  id        9
```

Figure 9.18: *Viewing the german dataset without the first four columns*

```
# Print the first few rows of the long_german DataFrame
julia> @show long_german[1:5, :]
```

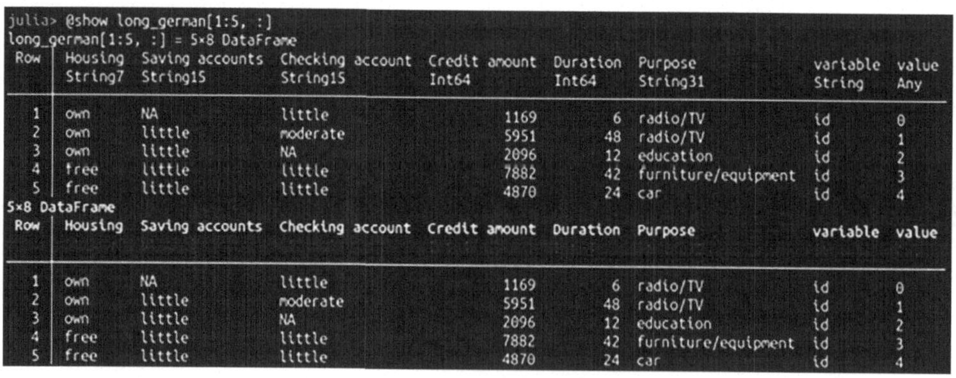

```
julia> @show long_german[1:5, :]
long_german[1:5, :] = 5×8 DataFrame
 Row │ Housing  Saving accounts  Checking account  Credit amount  Duration  Purpose              variable  value
     │ String7  String15         String15          Int64          Int64     String31             String    Any
─────┼───────────────────────────────────────────────────────────────────────────────────────────────────────────
   1 │ own      NA               little                     1169         6  radio/TV             id        0
   2 │ own      little           moderate                   5951        48  radio/TV             id        1
   3 │ own      little           NA                         2096        12  education            id        2
   4 │ free     little           little                     7882        42  furniture/equipment  id        3
   5 │ free     little           little                     4870        24  car                  id        4
5×8 DataFrame
 Row │ Housing  Saving accounts  Checking account  Credit amount  Duration  Purpose              variable  value
─────┼───────────────────────────────────────────────────────────────────────────────────────────────────────────
   1 │ own      NA               little                     1169         6  radio/TV             id        0
   2 │ own      little           moderate                   5951        48  radio/TV             id        1
   3 │ own      little           NA                         2096        12  education            id        2
   4 │ free     little           little                     7882        42  furniture/equipment  id        3
   5 │ free     little           little                     4870        24  car                  id        4
```

Figure 9.19: *Viewing the german dataset from the 1st row to the 5th row*

In this example, the `CSV.read()` function is used to load the german dataset from a CSV file. The `stack()` function is then used to transform the DataFrame from a wide format to a long format. The 1:4 argument specifies that the first four columns of the DataFrame should be stacked. The resulting DataFrame, `long_german`, has eight columns: Housing, `Saving accounts`, `Checking account`, `Credit amount`, `Duration`, `Purpose`, `variable`, and `value`. The `Housing`, `Saving accounts`, `Checking account`, `Credit amount`, `Duration`, and `Purpose` columns contain the values that were originally in the respective columns of the wide format DataFrame. The variable column contains the names of the columns that were stacked, which in this case are id, Age, Sex, and Job. The value column contains the values that were originally in the columns that were stacked.

The stack function is a useful tool for converting data from a wide format to a long format. It is easy to use and can be applied to a variety of datasets with multiple columns representing the same variable.

unstack is a function that converts a long-format `DataFrame` into a wide-format `DataFrame`. The long-format `DataFrame` has a column for each variable, and each row contains values for these variables. In contrast, the wide-format `DataFrame` has a column for each variable, and each row represents a single observation. The unstack function is used to convert a long-format `DataFrame` into a wide-format `DataFrame` by pivoting the data based on specified columns.

```
julia> german.id = 1:size(german, 1)
1:1000

julia> long_german = stack(german, Not([:Housing, :id]))
8000×4 DataFrame
  Row │ id     Housing  variable  value
      │ Int64  String7  String    Any
──────┼──────────────────────────────────────
    1 │     1  own      Age       67
    2 │     2  own      Age       22
    3 │     3  own      Age       49
    4 │     4  free     Age       45
  ⋮   │   ⋮       ⋮        ⋮          ⋮
 7998 │   998  own      Purpose   radio/TV
 7999 │   999  free     Purpose   radio/TV
 8000 │  1000  own      Purpose   car
                            7993 rows omitted

julia> unstack(long_german, :id, :variable, :value)
1000×9 DataFrame
  Row │ id     Age  Sex     Job  Saving accounts  Checking ⋯
      │ Int64  Any  Any     Any  Any              Any      ⋯
──────┼─────────────────────────────────────────────────────
    1 │     1  67   male    2    NA               little   ⋯
    2 │     2  22   female  2    little           moderate
    3 │     3  49   male    1    little           NA
    4 │     4  45   male    2    little           little
  ⋮   │   ⋮    ⋮     ⋮      ⋮         ⋮               ⋮    ⋱
  998 │   998  38   male    2    little           NA       ⋯
  999 │   999  23   male    2    little           little
 1000 │  1000  27   male    2    moderate         moderate
                          4 columns and 993 rows omitted
```

***Figure 9.20**: Viewing the german dataset after unstacking the columns*

In the given code sample, the unstack function is applied to a long-format `DataFrame` **`long_german`**. The function is called with three arguments, which specify the columns that will be used for id variables, column variable names, and column values, respectively. The first argument is :id, which specifies that the id column should be used as the id variable. The second argument is :variable, which specifies that the variable column should be used as the column variable names. The third argument is `:value`, which specifies that the value column should be used as the column values.

The resulting **`DataFrame`** will have the id column as the first column and columns for each unique value in the variable column. If a cell does not have a value for a particular combination of id and variable, the cell will contain a missing value.

```
julia> unstack(long_german, :variable, :value)
1000×10 DataFrame
 Row │ id     Housing  Age  Sex     Job  Saving accounts  ⋯
     │ Int64  String7  Any  Any     Any  Any              ⋯
─────┼─────────────────────────────────────────────────────
   1 │     1  own      67   male    2    NA               ⋯
   2 │     2  own      22   female  2    little
   3 │     3  own      49   male    1    little
   4 │     4  free     45   male    2    little
  ⋮  │   ⋮       ⋮      ⋮     ⋮      ⋮          ⋮         ⋱
 998 │   998  own      38   male    2    little           ⋯
 999 │   999  free     23   male    2    little
1000 │  1000  own      27   male    2    moderate
                                 4 columns and 993 rows omitted

julia> unstack(long_german)
1000×10 DataFrame
 Row │ id     Housing  Age  Sex     Job  Saving accounts  ⋯
     │ Int64  String7  Any  Any     Any  Any              ⋯
─────┼─────────────────────────────────────────────────────
   1 │     1  own      67   male    2    NA               ⋯
   2 │     2  own      22   female  2    little
   3 │     3  own      49   male    1    little
   4 │     4  free     45   male    2    little
  ⋮  │   ⋮       ⋮      ⋮     ⋮      ⋮          ⋮         ⋱
 998 │   998  own      38   male    2    little           ⋯
 999 │   999  free     23   male    2    little
1000 │  1000  own      27   male    2    moderate
                                 4 columns and 993 rows omitted
```

***Figure 9.21**: Viewing the german dataset after unstacking columns without mentioning id, value, or variable*

If the remaining columns are unique, we can skip the id variable, it will produce the same results. This will pivot the `long_german DataFrame` so that each unique value in the variable column becomes a row, and the values in the id and other remaining columns become the column names. The resulting DataFrame will have a row for each unique value in the variable column and columns for each unique value in the id and other remaining columns.

The stack function in Julia is used to stack columns of a DataFrame on top of each other, creating a new DataFrame with a single column of values and a column of "keys" indicating which original column each value came from. By default, the resulting DataFrame is a copy of the original data, meaning that it takes up additional memory. However, passing view=true to stack returns a DataFrame whose columns are views into the original wide DataFrame. This means that the new DataFrame takes up less memory since it does not create a copy of the original data.

Categorical data in DataFrames

In data analysis, we often encounter DataFrames with columns that contain only a small number of unique values. Instead of representing each unique value as a string in a vector, we can use a more memory-efficient and computationally efficient representation by replacing the strings with indices into a small pool of levels.

Julia provides two types of arrays for level pooling: PooledVector from **PooledArrays.jl** and CategoricalVector from **CategoricalArrays.jl**.

PooledVector is designed solely for data compression purposes, while CategoricalVector provides full support for working with categorical variables, both with unordered (nominal variables) and ordered categories (ordinal variables). CategoricalVector only allows `AbstractString`, `AbstractChar`, or Number element types, optionally in a union with Missing.

In **CategoricalArrays.jl**, we can create a `CategoricalVector` using the categorical function. We can pass in a vector of values, and it will create a `CategoricalVector` with the same values, but the values will be encoded as indices into a pool of levels. The resulting `CategoricalVector` will have lower memory usage and higher performance than a plain vector of strings.

Here is an example of creating a **`CategoricalVector`**:

```
julia> using CategoricalArrays
 │ Package CategoricalArrays not found, but a package named CategoricalArrays is available from a registry.
 │ Install package?
 │            add CategoricalArrays
 └ (y/n/o) [y]: y
   Resolving package versions...
   Installed CategoricalArrays ─ v0.10.7
    Updating `~/.julia/environments/v1.8/Project.toml`
             + CategoricalArrays v0.10.7
    Updating `~/.julia/environments/v1.8/Manifest.toml`
             + CategoricalArrays v0.10.7
Precompiling project...
  1 dependency successfully precompiled in 1 seconds. 54 already precompiled.

julia> v = ["Group A", "Group A", "Group A", "Group B", "Group B", "Group B"]
6-element Vector{String}:
 "Group A"
 "Group A"
 "Group A"
 "Group B"
 "Group B"
 "Group B"

julia> cv = categorical(v)
6-element CategoricalArray{String,1,UInt32}:
 "Group A"
 "Group A"
 "Group A"
 "Group B"
 "Group B"
 "Group B"
```

Figure 9.22: *categorizing data with Categorical Arrays*

We can see that cv is a **CategoricalArray** with the same values as v but with a more efficient encoding.

We can use the levels function to retrieve the pool of levels.

```
julia> levels(cv)
2-element Vector{String}:
 "Group A"
 "Group B"
```

***Figure 9.23**: The levels() function returns unique values in the categorical array*

This returns an array of the unique values in cv.

Overall, using `CategoricalVectors` instead of plain vectors of strings can lead to significant memory savings and performance improvements, especially when dealing with large datasets.

A `CategoricalVector` in Julia is a type of array that allows for efficient storage and manipulation of data that takes on a small number of levels. `CategoricalVectors` can also support missing values.

In the code sample provided, we create a `CategoricalVector` cv from a regular vector that includes some missing values. We can determine the allowed levels in cv using the levels function. In this case, there are two levels: "**`Group A`**" and "**`Group B`**". We can change the order of appearance of the levels using the levels! function. We can also compress the **`CategoricalVector`** to use less memory by calling the compress function.

```
julia> # create a regular vector with some missing values
       v = ["Group A", missing, "Group A", "Group B", "Group B", missing]
6-element Vector{Union{Missing, String}}:
 "Group A"
 missing
 "Group A"
 "Group B"
 "Group B"
 missing

julia> # create a CategoricalVector from v
       cv = categorical(v)
6-element CategoricalArray{Union{Missing, String},1,UInt32}:
 "Group A"
 missing
 "Group A"
 "Group B"
 "Group B"
 missing

julia> # determine the allowed levels in cv
       levels(cv)  # returns ["Group A", "Group B"]
2-element Vector{String}:
 "Group A"
 "Group B"

julia> # change the order of appearance of the levels in cv
       levels!(cv, ["Group B", "Group A"])
6-element CategoricalArray{Union{Missing, String},1,UInt32}:
 "Group A"
 missing
 "Group A"
 "Group B"
 "Group B"
 missing
```

***Figure 9.24**: The levels() function returns unique values in the categorical array*

Additionally, we can create an ordered **CategoricalVector** by setting the ordered keyword argument to true in the categorical function. An ordered **CategoricalVector** allows for comparisons between levels using the < operator. We can check if a **CategoricalVector** is ordered using the isordered function and change between ordered and unordered using the **ordered!** function.

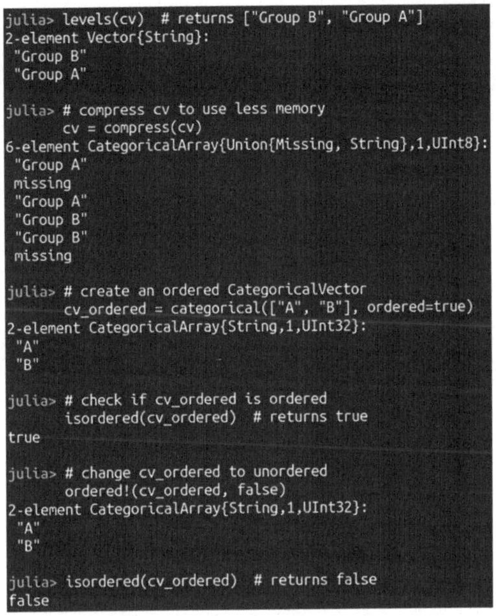

***Figure 9.25**: The ordered() function maintains the order of the categorical arrays*

Joining data in DataFrames

When working with data, it is often necessary to combine multiple data sets to get a more complete picture. This can be done using joins, which combine rows from different data sets based on a common key. In Julia, **DataFrames.jl** provides several functions for performing different types of joins:

- innerjoin: returns rows for values of the key that exist in all DataFrames.
- leftjoin: returns rows for values of the key that exist in the first DataFrame, whether or not that value exists in the second DataFrame.
- rightjoin: returns rows for values of the key that exist in the second DataFrame, whether or not that value exists in the first DataFrame.
- outerjoin: returns rows for values of the key that exist in any of the DataFrames.
- semijoin: like an inner join, but the output is restricted to columns from the first DataFrame.

- antijoin: returns rows for values of the key that exist in the first DataFrame but not the second DataFrame. As with semijoin, the output is restricted to columns from the first DataFrame.
- crossjoin: returns the cartesian product of rows from all DataFrames.

Here are some examples of using these functions with two data sets:

```
julia> house = DataFrame(Year=[2002, 1970], Name=["Jay", "Ray"])
2×2 DataFrame
 Row │ Year   Name
     │ Int64  String
─────┼───────────────
   1 │  2002  Jay
   2 │  1970  Ray

julia> occupation = DataFrame(Name=["Jay", "Ray"], Job=["Lawyer", "Doctor"])
2×2 DataFrame
 Row │ Name    Job
     │ String  String
─────┼────────────────
   1 │ Jay     Lawyer
   2 │ Ray     Doctor
```

Figure 9.26: *creates two DataFrames named house and occupation*

```
julia> # inner join
       innerjoin(house, occupation, on = :Name)
2×3 DataFrame
 Row │ Year   Name    Job
     │ Int64  String  String
─────┼───────────────────────
   1 │  2002  Jay     Lawyer
   2 │  1970  Ray     Doctor

julia> # left join
       leftjoin(house, occupation, on = :Name)
2×3 DataFrame
 Row │ Year   Name    Job
     │ Int64  String  String?
─────┼────────────────────────
   1 │  2002  Jay     Lawyer
   2 │  1970  Ray     Doctor

julia> # right join
       rightjoin(house, occupation, on = :Name)
2×3 DataFrame
 Row │ Year    Name    Job
     │ Int64?  String  String
─────┼────────────────────────
   1 │   2002  Jay     Lawyer
   2 │   1970  Ray     Doctor

julia> # outer join
       outerjoin(house, occupation, on = :Name)
2×3 DataFrame
 Row │ Year    Name    Job
     │ Int64?  String  String?
─────┼─────────────────────────
   1 │   2002  Jay     Lawyer
   2 │   1970  Ray     Doctor
```

Figure 9.27: *inner, outer, left and right join on the mentioned DataFrames*

```
julia> # semi join
       semijoin(house, occupation, on = :Name)
2×2 DataFrame
 Row │ Year   Name
     │ Int64  String
─────┼───────────────
   1 │  2002  Jay
   2 │  1970  Ray

julia> # anti join
       antijoin(house, occupation, on = :Name)
0×2 DataFrame
 Row │ Year   Name
     │ Int64  String
─────┴───────────────

julia> # cross join
       crossjoin(house, occupation, makeunique=true)
4×4 DataFrame
 Row │ Year   Name    Name_1  Job
     │ Int64  String  String  String
─────┼───────────────────────────────
   1 │  2002  Jay     Jay     Lawyer
   2 │  2002  Jay     Ray     Doctor
   3 │  1970  Ray     Jay     Lawyer
   4 │  1970  Ray     Ray     Doctor
```

***Figure 9.28**: semi, anti and crossjoin on the mentioned DataFrames*

In these examples, house and occupation are defined as DataFrames, each with a Name column. The on parameter is used to specify the key column for the join. Cross joins are the only kind of join that does not use an on key `:`.

When joining two DataFrames, it's common to use a key column to match up rows from each table. However, sometimes the key column may have different names in the left and right tables, which can make it difficult to join them.

To solve this problem, you can pass pairs of left and right key column names to the on argument. This syntax uses a special arrow (=>) to associate each left key column name with the corresponding right key column name.

```
julia> occupation = DataFrame(Occupant=["Jay", "Ray"], Job=["Lawyer", "Doctor"])
2×2 DataFrame
 Row │ Occupant  Job
     │ String    String
─────┼──────────────────
   1 │ Jay       Lawyer
   2 │ Ray       Doctor

julia> # inner join
       innerjoin(house, occupation, on = :Name => :Occupant)
2×3 DataFrame
 Row │ Year   Name    Job
     │ Int64  String  String
─────┼───────────────────────
   1 │  2002  Jay     Lawyer
   2 │  1970  Ray     Doctor
```

***Figure 9.29**: inner join varieties with separate column names but similar column values*

However, when there are duplicate keys in the DataFrames, the join operation can result in multiple rows being created. To avoid this, you can set the validate argument to true when performing the join. This will check that the columns passed as the on argument define unique keys in each input DataFrame.

```
julia> joineddf = innerjoin(house, occupation, on = :Name =>
 :Occupant, validate=(true, true))
2×3 DataFrame
 Row │ Year   Name    Job
     │ Int64  String  String
─────┼───────────────────────
   1 │  2002  Jay     Lawyer
   2 │  1970  Ray     Doctor
```

***Figure 9.30**: inner join varieties with separate column names but similar column values and keeping single key rather than multiple duplicate keys*

Finally, if you want to keep track of the source **DataFrame** for each row in the resulting **DataFrame**, you can use the source argument. This adds a column to the resulting **DataFrame** indicating whether the given row appeared only in the left, the right or both DataFrames.

When joining two DataFrames, it is often useful to keep track of the source of each column. To do this, you can pass the renamecols keyword argument to the join function.

The first example shows how to add a suffix to the column names to indicate their source. The suffix is added using a pair of left => right pairs, where the left side is the suffix for columns from the left table and the right side is the suffix for columns from the right table.

```
julia> innerjoin(house, occupation, on=:Name, renamecols = "
_lived" => "_worked")
2×3 DataFrame
 Row │ Year_lived  Name    Job_worked
     │ Int64       String  String
─────┼────────────────────────────────
   1 │       2002  Jay     Lawyer
   2 │       1970  Ray     Doctor
```

***Figure 9.31**: inner join varieties with separate column names with newer renamed column names*

This changes the first column name to lowercase and the last column name to uppercase.

```
julia> innerjoin(house, occupation, on=:Name, renamecols = l
owercase => uppercase)
2×3 DataFrame
 Row │ year   Name    JOB
     │ Int64  String  String
─────┼───────────────────────
   1 │  2002  Jay     Lawyer
   2 │  1970  Ray     Doctor
```

***Figure 9.32**: inner join varieties with separate column names with newer renamed column names*

When joining two DataFrames, if there are duplicate values for the joining columns in one or both DataFrames, then the join operation may produce unexpected results. Specifically, when using `innerjoin`, `outerjoin`, `leftjoin` or `rightjoin`, all possible combinations of matching rows will be produced.

To avoid such unexpected results, the validate keyword argument can be used. This argument takes a two-element tuple or pair of Boolean values, where each element corresponds to one of the input DataFrames. If set to true, it checks whether the joining columns in each DataFrame contain unique keys (that is, no duplicates). If duplicates are found, an error is raised and the join operation is not performed. As the joining columns in both input DataFrames contain duplicates, an error is raised as it produces 4 rows instead of 2 due to duplicates in City/London and Job/Lawyer.

```
julia> innerjoin(a, b, on=[(:City => :Location), (:Job => :W
ork)])
5×2 DataFrame
 Row │ City      Job
     │ String    String
─────┼──────────────────
   1 │ London    Lawyer
   2 │ London    Lawyer
   3 │ New York  Doctor
   4 │ London    Lawyer
   5 │ London    Lawyer
```

***Figure 9.33**: inner join varieties with separate column names with newer renamed column names*

We use the validate argument in an innerjoin operation. In this example, the **`on`** argument is set to join two pairs of columns, and validate is set to **`(true, true)`**.

```
julia> innerjoin(a, b, on=[(:City => :Location), (:Job => :W
ork)], validate=(true, true))
2×2 DataFrame
 Row │ City      Job
     │ String    String
─────┼──────────────────
   1 │ London    Lawyer
   2 │ New York  Doctor
```

Figure 9.34: *inner join varieties with separate column names with newer renamed column name values and keeping single key rather than multiple duplicate keys*

The source keyword argument can be used to add a column to the resulting DataFrame indicating the source of each row (whether it appears only on the left, only on the right, or in both input DataFrames).

```
julia> a = DataFrame(ID=[20, 40], Name=["John", "Jane"])
julia> b = DataFrame(ID=[20, 60], Job=["Lawyer", "Doctor"])
julia> outerjoin(a, b, on=:ID, validate=(true, true), source=:source)
```

The code produces a DataFrame with 3 rows, indicating that the row with ID=20 appears in both input DataFrames and the rows with ID=40 and ID=60 appear only in the left and right input DataFrames, respectively.

```
julia> outerjoin(a, b, on=:ID, validate=(true, true), source
=:source)
3×4 DataFrame
 Row │ ID     Name     Job      source
     │ Int64  String?  String?  String
─────┼───────────────────────────────────
   1 │    20  John     Lawyer   both
   2 │    40  Jane     missing  left_only
   3 │    60  missing  Doctor   right_only
```

Figure 9.35: *inner join varieties with separate column names with newer renamed column name values and keeping single key rather than multiple duplicate keys with a defined source*

When joining two DataFrames based on a common key, it is important to handle missing values in a proper way. By default, if the key column in one or both of the DataFrames contains missing values, you will get an error. However, you can choose to treat missing values as equal or drop the corresponding rows.

Let's see how this works with some code examples. Suppose we have two DataFrames with a common key column, but one of them contains missing values:

```
julia> df1 = DataFrame(id=[1, missing, 3], a=1:3)
julia> df2 = DataFrame(id=[1, 2, missing], b=1:3)
```

If we try to perform an inner join on the key column, we get an error because of the missing values

```
julia> innerjoin(df1, df2, on=:id)
ERROR: ArgumentError: missing values in key columns are not
allowed when matchmissing == :error
```

Figure 9.36: *can't do an inner join on unavailable columns*

To treat missing values as equal and include them in the join, we can pass the `matchmissing=:equal` keyword argument. Note that the row with the missing id value in the second DataFrame is included in the result.

Alternatively, if we want to drop all rows with missing values in the key column, we can pass the `matchmissing=:notequal` keyword argument. In this case, only the row with id=1 in both DataFrames is included in the result. The row with missing id value in the second DataFrame is dropped.

```
julia> innerjoin(df1, df2, on=:id, matchmissing=:equal)
2×3 DataFrame
 Row │ id       a      b
     │ Int64?   Int64  Int64
─────┼───────────────────────
   1 │       1      1      1
   2 │ missing      2      3

julia> innerjoin(df1, df2, on=:id, matchmissing=:notequal)
1×3 DataFrame
 Row │ id      a      b
     │ Int64?  Int64  Int64
─────┼──────────────────────
   1 │      1      1      1
```

Figure 9.37: *inner join on missing data*

When performing a join operation on two DataFrames, the order of the resulting rows is not always guaranteed. However, you can control the order of the rows in the resulting **DataFrame** by specifying the order parameter.

```
julia> df_left = DataFrame(id=[1, 2, 4, 5], left=1:4)
julia> df_right = DataFrame(id=[2, 1, 3, 6, 7], right=1:5)
```

To control the order of the rows in the resulting DataFrame, you can specify the order parameter. By default, order is set to :unsorted, which means that the order of rows in the resulting **DataFrame** is undefined. To keep the order of the rows in the left **DataFrame**, pass `order=:left`.

```
julia> # To keep the order of the rows in the left DataFrame
, pass `order=:left`
       outerjoin(df_left, df_right, on=:id, order=:left)
7×3 DataFrame
 Row │ id     left     right
     │ Int64  Int64?   Int64?
─────┼─────────────────────────
   1 │     1        1        2
   2 │     2        2        1
   3 │     4        3  missing
   4 │     5        4  missing
   5 │     3  missing        3
   6 │     6  missing        4
   7 │     7  missing        5
```

***Figure 9.38(a)**: outer join on missing data (left)*

This will produce a resulting DataFrame with rows in the same order as the left DataFrame. Note that in this case, keys `missing` from the left table are put after the keys present in it. Similarly, you can keep the order of the rows in the right DataFrame by passing **`order=:right`**.

```
julia> # To keep the order of the rows in the right DataFram
e, pass `order=:right`
       outerjoin(df_left, df_right, on=:id, order=:right)
7×3 DataFrame
 Row │ id     left     right
     │ Int64  Int64?   Int64?
─────┼─────────────────────────
   1 │     2        2        1
   2 │     1        1        2
   3 │     3  missing        3
   4 │     6  missing        4
   5 │     7  missing        5
   6 │     4        3  missing
   7 │     5        4  missing
```

***Figure 9.38(b)**: outer join on missing data (right)*

This will produce a resulting DataFrame with rows in the same order as the right DataFrame. Note that keys not present in the right table are put at the end of the resulting DataFrame.

Split-apply-combine data in DataFrames

The Split-Apply-Combine (SAC) strategy is a framework for data analysis tasks that involve splitting a dataset into groups, applying some functions to each group, and then combining the results. The SAC strategy is used in the **DataFrames.jl** package through the groupby function, which creates a GroupedDataFrame object from a DataFrame and a set of columns to group by. Operations can be applied to each group using functions such as combine, select, and transform. These functions take a specification of one or more functions to apply to each subset of the DataFrame, which can be in the form of standard column selectors, `cols => function` pairs, `col => target_cols` pairs, column-independent operations, vectors or matrices containing transformations, or a function that will be called with a SubDataFrame or the **`DataFrame`** itself. The output is a new DataFrame with the results of the specified computations.

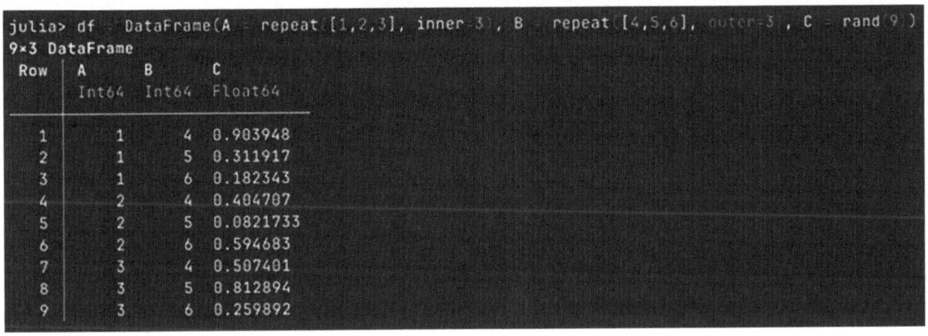

***Figure 9.39**: Creating a new dataframe by combining columns of another dataframe*

- Computing summary statistics by group using **`combine()`**

```
julia> using DataFrames,Random, Statistics

# create a dataframe

julia> df = DataFrame(A = repeat([1,2,3], inner=3), B = repeat([4,5,6],
outer=3), C = rand(9))

# group by column A and compute mean of column C for each group

julia> result = combine(groupby(df, :A), :C => mean)
```

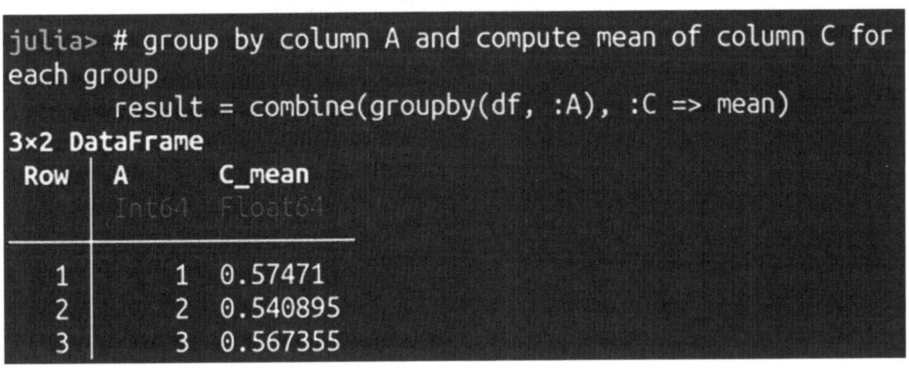

***Figure 9.40**: creating a new DataFrame by combining columns of another DataFrame using the combine() function*

- Creating new columns using `select()`

```
# create a dataframe

julia> df = DataFrame(A = repeat([1,2,3], inner=3), B = repeat([4,5,6],
outer=3), C = rand(9))

# group by column A and create new column D with mean of column C for
each group

julia> result = select(groupby(df, :A), :C => mean => :D)
```

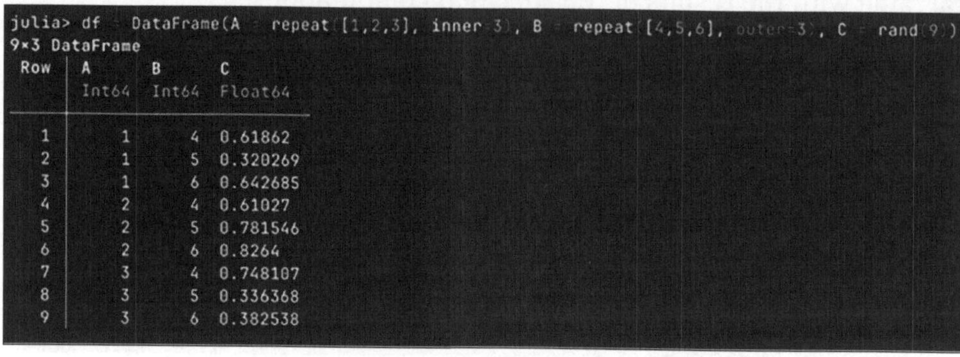

```
julia> df = DataFrame(A = repeat([1,2,3], inner=3), B = repeat([4,5,6], outer=3), C = rand(9))
9×3 DataFrame
 Row │ A      B      C
     │ Int64  Int64  Float64
─────┼─────────────────────────
   1 │     1      4  0.61862
   2 │     1      5  0.320269
   3 │     1      6  0.642685
   4 │     2      4  0.61027
   5 │     2      5  0.781546
   6 │     2      6  0.8264
   7 │     3      4  0.748107
   8 │     3      5  0.336368
   9 │     3      6  0.382538
```

Figure 9.41(a): *creating a new dataframe by combining columns of another dataframe using select() function*

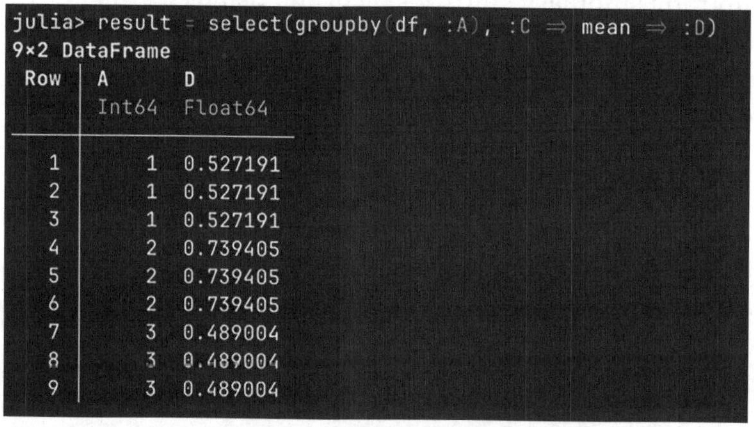

```
julia> result = select(groupby(df, :A), :C => mean => :D)
9×2 DataFrame
 Row │ A      D
     │ Int64  Float64
─────┼─────────────────
   1 │     1  0.527191
   2 │     1  0.527191
   3 │     1  0.527191
   4 │     2  0.739405
   5 │     2  0.739405
   6 │     2  0.739405
   7 │     3  0.489004
   8 │     3  0.489004
   9 │     3  0.489004
```

Figure 9.41(b): *Creating a new DataFrame by combining columns of another DataFrame using the select() function*

- Modifying existing columns using `transform()`

```
# create a dataframe

julia> df = DataFrame(A = repeat([1,2,3], inner=3), B = repeat([4,5,6],
outer=3), C = rand(9))

# group by column A and modify column C to be the difference between
column C and its mean within each group
```

```
julia> result = transform(groupby(df, :A), :C => (c -> c .- mean(c)) =>
:C)
```

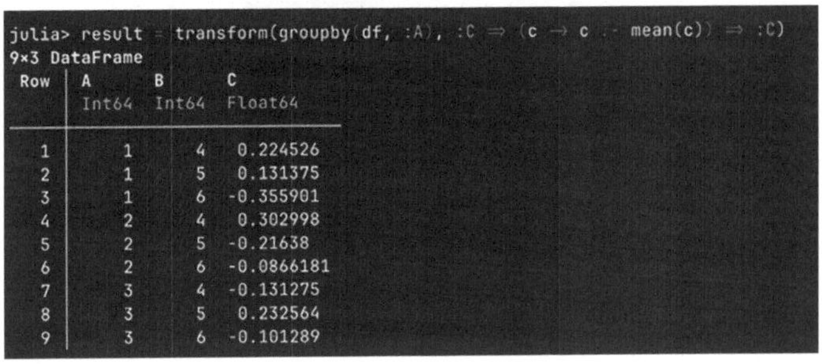

```
julia> result = transform(groupby(df, :A), :C => (c -> c .- mean(c)) => :C)
9×3 DataFrame
 Row │ A      B      C
     │ Int64  Int64  Float64
─────┼────────────────────────
   1 │     1      4   0.224526
   2 │     1      5   0.131375
   3 │     1      6  -0.355901
   4 │     2      4   0.302998
   5 │     2      5  -0.21638
   6 │     2      6  -0.0866181
   7 │     3      4  -0.131275
   8 │     3      5   0.232564
   9 │     3      6  -0.101289
```

Figure 9.42: *Creating a new DataFrame by combining columns of another DataFrame using the transform() and groupby() function*

The SQL WHERE clause is used to filter rows from a table based on certain conditions. In Julia, you can simulate this functionality using SubDataFrames.

A SubDataFrame is a view of a DataFrame that contains only a subset of the rows and/or columns. You can create a SubDataFrame using the indexing syntax: `df[row_selector, col_selector]`. The `row_selector` can be a vector of Boolean values or an integer index, while the `col_selector` can be a vector of column names or an integer index.

Once you have a SubDataFrame, you can perform operations on it just like a regular DataFrame. The only difference is that these operations may either create a new DataFrame or modify the original DataFrame in place, depending on whether you use the `transform` or `transform!` Function.

```
julia> df = DataFrame(a=1:5) # create a DataFrame

julia> sdf = @view df[2:3, :]

julia> transform(sdf, :a => ByRow(string))

julia> transform!(sdf, :a => ByRow(string)) # update the original
DataFrame in-place with the new column
```

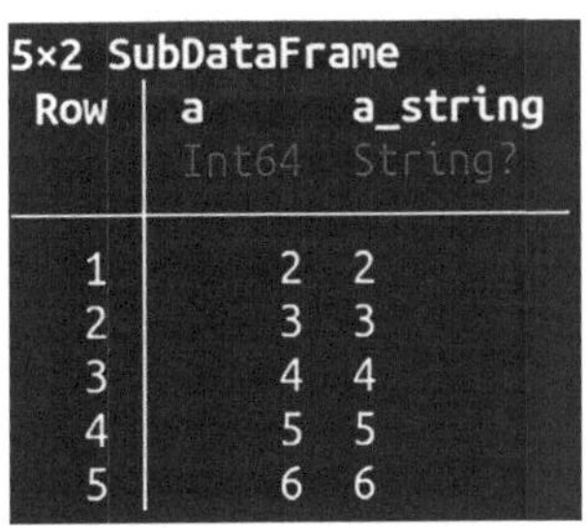

```
5×2 SubDataFrame
 Row │ a      a_string
     │ Int64  String?
─────┼─────────────────
   1 │     2  2
   2 │     3  3
   3 │     4  4
   4 │     5  5
   5 │     6  6
```

Figure 9.43: *Creating a new DataFrame by combining columns of another DataFrame using the transform function*

```
julia> df # the new column was added to the original DataFrame, with missing values in the filtered-out rows
```

7×2 DataFrame

Row	a Int64	a_string String?
1	1	missing
2	2	2
3	3	3
4	4	4
5	5	5
6	6	6
7	7	missing

Figure 9.44: *Creating a new DataFrame by combining columns of another DataFrame using the combine() function*

```
julia> select!(sdf, :a => -, renamecols=false) # subtract a constant from the "a" column in the SubDataFrame
```

5×1 SubDataFrame

Row	a Int64
1	-2
2	-3
3	-4
4	-5
5	-6

Figure 9.45: *Creating a new DataFrame by combining columns of another DataFrame using the select!() function*

```
julia> df # the "a" column in the original DataFrame was replaced with the modified column, reusing values in filtered-out rows
```

7×1 DataFrame

Row	a Int64
1	1
2	-2
3	-3
4	-4
5	-5
6	-6
7	7

Figure 9.46: *Creating a new DataFrame by combining columns of another DataFrame using the select!() function*

In the first example, we create a new column in the SubDataFrame sdf by applying the string function to each row of the column. We use the transform function, which creates a new DataFrame with the transformed column.

In the second example, we use the `transform!` function to modify a column of the original **`DataFrame df`** in place with the transformed column from sdf.

In the third example, we subtract a constant from a column of sdf using the **`select!`** function. We set renamecols=false to keep the original column name. We then use **`select!`** again to update a column of df with the modified column from sdf.

Note that in the third and fourth examples, the modified column in df reuses values from the original column in filtered-out rows. This is because the SubDataFrame is a view of the original DataFrame, and changes to the SubDataFrame affect the original DataFrame.

In Julia, the groupby function allows us to group rows of a DataFrame by one or more columns. By default, the order of groups produced by groupby is undefined. However, if we want to specify a group order, we can use the sort keyword argument.

```
julia> df = DataFrame(customer_id = ["a", "b", "b", "b", "c", "c"],
       transaction_id = [12, 15, 19, 17, 13, 11],
       volume = [2, 3, 1, 4, 5, 9])
```

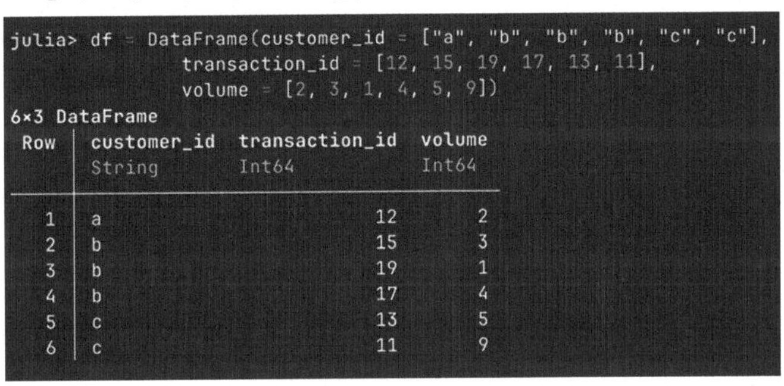

```
julia> df = DataFrame(customer_id = ["a", "b", "b", "b", "c", "c"],
                      transaction_id = [12, 15, 19, 17, 13, 11],
                      volume = [2, 3, 1, 4, 5, 9])
6×3 DataFrame
 Row │ customer_id  transaction_id  volume
     │ String       Int64           Int64
─────┼─────────────────────────────────────
   1 │ a                        12       2
   2 │ b                        15       3
   3 │ b                        19       1
   4 │ b                        17       4
   5 │ c                        13       5
   6 │ c                        11       9
```

Figure 9.47: *Output*

We can then group the rows by the volume column

```
julia> groupby(df, :volume)
```

By default, the order of groups is undefined. We can pass the sort keyword argument to specify the group order

```
julia> groupby(df, :volume, sort=true)
```

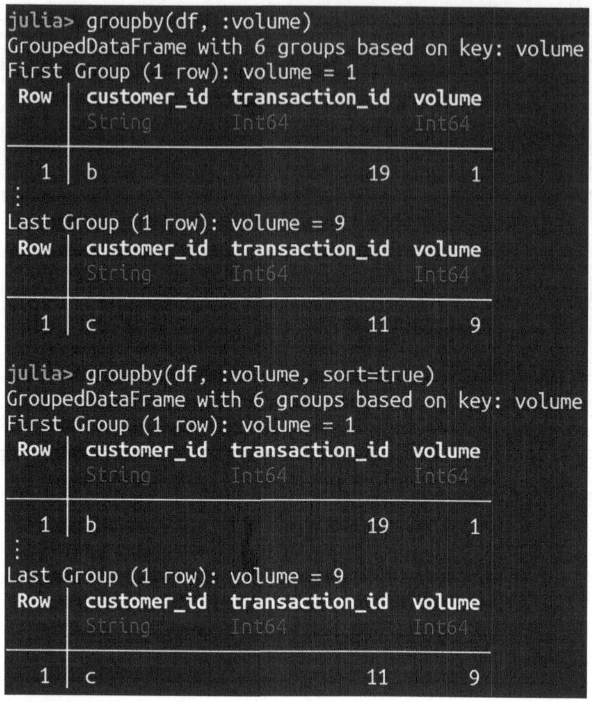

Figure 9.48: *creating a new DataFrame by combining columns of another DataFrame using the groupby() function*

Alternatively, we can use the order wrapper when passing a column name to a group by:

```
julia> groupby(df, [:customer_id, order(:volume, rev=true)])
```

We can also pass a named tuple as the sort keyword argument. The named tuple can contain one or more of the following fields:

- alg: the sorting algorithm (default is sort)
- lt: the comparison function (default is <)
- by: the transformation function (default is identity)
- rev: a boolean flag indicating whether to sort in reverse order (default is false)
- order: the order in which to sort the elements (default is sortperm, you can look into https://dataframes.juliadata.org/stable/lib/functions/#Base.sortperm to better understand sortperm)

For example, to sort the groups in reverse order of the volume column, we can pass the named tuple (rev=true,).

```
julia> groupby(df, :customer_id, sort=(rev=true,))
```

```
julia> groupby(df, [:customer_id, order(:volume, rev=true)])
GroupedDataFrame with 6 groups based on keys: customer_id, volume
First Group (1 row): customer_id = "a", volume = 2
 Row │ customer_id  transaction_id  volume
     │ String       Int64           Int64
─────┼─────────────────────────────────────
   1 │ a                        12       2
 ⋮
Last Group (1 row): customer_id = "c", volume = 5
 Row │ customer_id  transaction_id  volume
     │ String       Int64           Int64
─────┼─────────────────────────────────────
   1 │ c                        13       5

julia> groupby(df, :customer_id, sort=(rev=true,))
GroupedDataFrame with 3 groups based on key: customer_id
First Group (2 rows): customer_id = "c"
 Row │ customer_id  transaction_id  volume
     │ String       Int64           Int64
  ⋮  │      ⋮             ⋮            ⋮
                         2 rows omitted
 ⋮
Last Group (1 row): customer_id = "a"
 Row │ customer_id  transaction_id  volume
     │ String       Int64           Int64
─────┼─────────────────────────────────────
   1 │ a                        12       2
```

Figure 9.49: *creating a new DataFrame by combining columns of another DataFrame using the groupby() function*

Conclusion

The chapter covers important aspects of data analysis using DataFrames in Julia, including handling missing data, sorting data, reshaping data, working with categorical data, joining data, and split-apply-combine data analysis. The Missings.jl package is used for handling missing data while sorting is done using the sort and sort! functions. The melt and pivot functions are used for reshaping data, and the CategoricalArrays.jl package is used for working with categorical data. Joining DataFrames is done using the join function, while split-apply-combine data analysis is done using the groupby and combine functions. These techniques can help data analysts gain valuable insights from their data.

In the next chapter, we will learn about visualizing data. Julia has several powerful data visualization libraries such as Plots.jl that provide a wide range of options for creating interactive and high-quality plots and charts. These libraries allow for easy integration with Julia's data manipulation and analysis tools, making it an excellent choice for data visualization.

Questions

1. How do you detect and remove missing values in Julia DataFrames?
2. Can you sort a DataFrame by multiple columns in Julia?

3. How do you sort a DataFrame by a custom order specified by the user?
4. What are some common use cases for reshaping data in Julia DataFrames?
5. How do you handle missing data when reshaping data in Julia DataFrames?
6. How do you convert a column in a Julia DataFrame to a categorical data type?
7. How do you group and summarize data in a Julia DataFrame using categorical variables?
8. How do you handle missing values when joining DataFrames in Julia?
9. How do you split a Julia DataFrame into groups based on one or more columns?
10. What are some common aggregation functions used in the apply step of split-apply-combine in Julia DataFrames?

CHAPTER 10
Visualizing Data in Julia

Visualization is an essential aspect of data analysis and communication. In the realm of scientific computing, the ability to create rich, interactive visualizations of complex data sets is crucial. Julia, a high-performance programming language for numerical computing, provides a variety of tools for creating stunning visualizations.

We will introduce Plot.jl, a powerful and flexible plotting package that provides a wide variety of plot types and customization options. We will explore various plot types, including scatter plots, bar charts, and heat maps, and see how they can be used to represent different types of data. Finally, we will demonstrate how to create a recipe using Plot.jl, which allows us to quickly reproduce complex visualizations with just a few lines of code.

StatsPlots.jl is a popular data visualization package in the Julia programming language that provides a user-friendly and versatile interface for creating statistical plots. It builds on top of the widely used plotting library, Plots.jl, and incorporates many common statistical plot types such as scatter plots, histograms, box plots, and heatmaps. With StatsPlots.jl, users can easily customize their plots with different colors, themes, and annotations to effectively communicate their data insights. Additionally, StatsPlots.jl also supports statistical transformations, such as log scales and probability distributions, to enhance data visualization and analysis.

By the end of this chapter, you will have a solid understanding of the key features of Plots.jl and StatsPlots.jl and how they can be used to create high-quality visualizations in Julia.

Structure

In this chapter, the following topics will be covered:

- Introducing Plots.jl
- Installing Plots.jl
- Plots.jl package
- Attributes in plotting
- Scatter plots in Plots.jl
- Plotting backends
- Subplots in Plots.jl
- Recipes using Plots.jl
- Recipes using StatsPlots.jl
- Contour Plots
- Histograms in Plots.jl

Introducing Plot.jl

Data visualization has evolved significantly over the years, with plotting software making trade-offs between various features such as simplicity, speed, beauty, and static or dynamic interfaces. While some packages generate a display that remains unchanged, others make real-time updates.

Plots.jl is a visualization interface and toolset that sits above various backends, connecting commands with implementation. This package allows you to switch between backends such as GR, PythonPlot, PGFPlotsX, or Plotly, without having to alter your code or learn a new syntax. With its powerful, intuitive, concise, flexible, consistent, lightweight, and smart features, Plots.jl makes complex visualizations easy while maintaining modularity and separation of front-end code, algorithms, and backend graphics through the use of a preprocessing pipeline.

Plot.jl is a powerful and flexible plotting package for Julia, designed to create a wide variety of high-quality plots with minimal boilerplate code. It provides a simple, consistent interface for creating a wide range of plot types, including scatter plots, line plots, bar charts, histograms, heat maps, and more.

One of the key strengths of Plot.jl is its extensive support for customization. Users can customize almost every aspect of their plots, including the colors, line styles, marker types, fonts, and axis labels. The package also provides a range of layout options, making it easy to arrange multiple plots on a single page.

Plot.jl is built on top of the GR.jl graphics library, which provides a fast, high-quality rendering engine. This makes it possible to create interactive, high-resolution plots that can be used in scientific publications, presentations, or web applications.

Another notable feature of Plot.jl is its support for statistical plotting. It provides several functions for creating statistical plots, such as box plots, violin plots, and error bars, which can help users explore and analyze complex datasets.

In addition to its core functionality, Plot.jl is also highly extensible, with a large ecosystem of community-developed packages that provide additional functionality, such as advanced statistical plotting, 3D plotting, and animations.

Installing Plots.jl

Installing the Plots.jl package is a straightforward process. First, you need to have Julia installed on your system. Once you have installed Julia, you can launch the Julia REPL (read-eval-print loop) by typing "julia" on the terminal.

Next, you need to install the Plots package by typing the following command in the Julia REPL:

```
julia> using Pkg
julia> Pkg.add("Plots")
```

This command will download and install the Plots package and all its dependencies.

After the installation is complete, you can load the Plots package by typing the following command in the Julia REPL:

```
julia> using Plots
```

This command will load the Plots package and make all its functions available for use. You can now start creating beautiful and interactive visualizations using the Plots package in Julia.

We can customize the Plots package by choosing a specific backend or overriding default settings. A backend is a specific library or tool that Plots uses to create the visualizations. For example, some of the available backends are GR, PGFPlotsX, and PlotlyJS. To choose a backend, we can use a command like `gr()` or `plotly()`, followed by optional parameters such as size, legend, or ticks. These parameters can be used to customize the visual appearance of the plot. If you want to use a specific backend as the default, you can set an environment variable in your `~/.julia/config/startup.jl` file.

Plots.jl package

The Plots package provides a simple and flexible way to create plots in Julia. To create a plot, you can use the plot function, which takes various types of input arguments. For instance, you can pass in a single number to create an empty plot object with that many series, or a matrix to create a plot with multiple series. You can also pass in functions or data to create plots with custom series. To modify an existing plot, you can use the plot! function, which takes similar arguments as the plot. The plot object is not displayed automatically but can be shown by returning it to a REPL prompt or IJulia cell.

```
julia> # Create an empty plot object
       p = plot()
Warning: Ignoring XDG_SESSION_TYPE=wayland on Gnome. Use QT_QPA_
PLATFORM=wayland to run on Wayland anyway.
julia> # Add a scatter plot to the existing plot object
       x = rand(10)
10-element Vector{Float64}:
julia> y = rand(10)
10-element Vector{Float64}:
julia> plot!(p, x, y, seriestype=:scatter)
julia> # Add a line plot to the existing plot object
       z = sin.(x)
10-element Vector{Float64}:
julia> plot!(p, x, z, seriestype=:line)
julia> # Show the plot
       display(p)
```

This code outputs a graph as *Figure* 10.1.

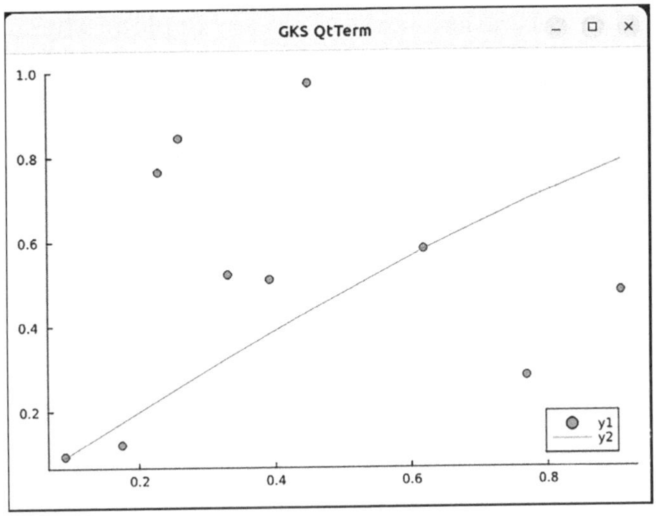

Figure 10.1: *Simple plot with random x and y values*

Keyword arguments can be used to customize the plot appearance, such as setting the color, marker, or fill color for the series, as well as setting the plot size, title, or legend. Many keyword arguments have aliases for convenience, and some special arguments can set multiple properties at once. Additionally, some arguments can accept multiple types of input, such as color names, color gradients, or vectors of colors or symbols. Understanding these keyword arguments is important for creating custom and visually appealing plots.

```
julia> plot(rand(10, 5)) #Plot 5 series with x-axis values 1:10
```

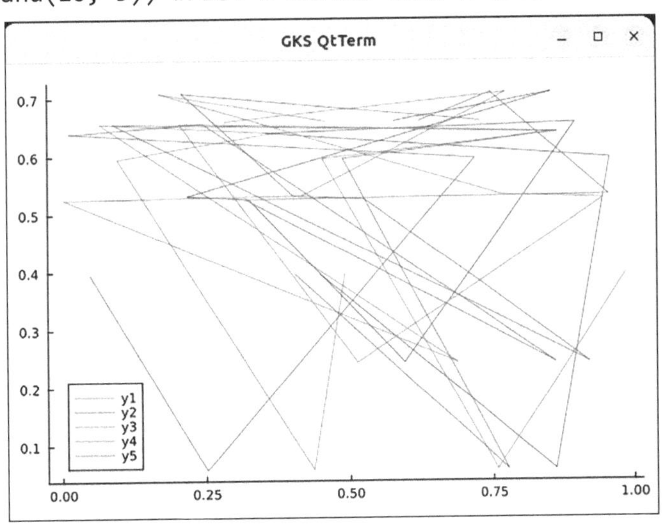

Figure 10.2: *Plot for 5 series with x-axis values ranging between 1 and 10*

We can also use keyword arguments to customize plots. These arguments can be used to change properties such as colors, markers, labels, legends, and more. Here is an example:

```
julia> using Plots
julia> # Plot a scatter plot with custom color and marker
julia> x = rand(10)
julia> y = rand(10)
julia> plot(x, y, color=:red, marker=:circle)
```

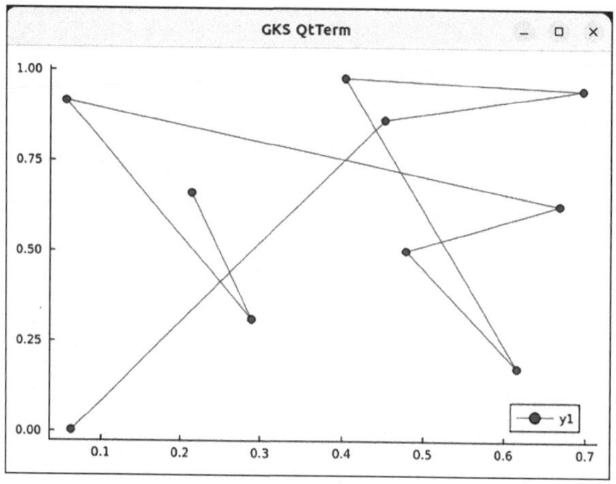

Figure 10.3: *A scatter plot with custom color and marker*

```
julia> # Plot a line plot with custom labels and legend
julia> z = sin.(x)
julia> plot(x, z, label="sin(x)", xlabel="x", ylabel="y")
```

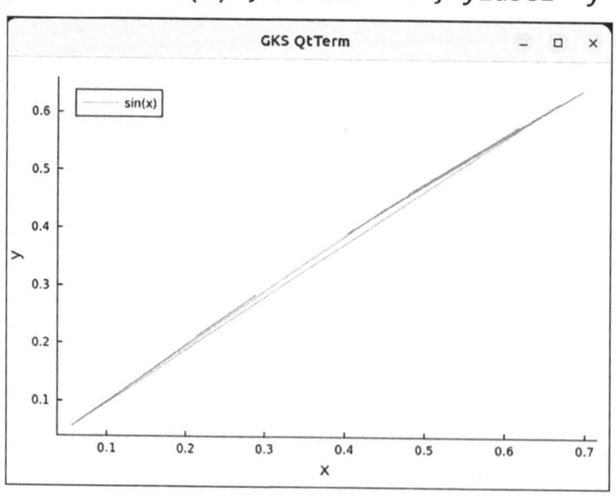

Figure 10.4: *A line plot with custom labels and legend*

Note that the color and marker arguments are examples of keyword arguments that accept symbols as input. Other keyword arguments may accept different types of input.

In Plots.jl, you can save your plots using the `savefig` command. By default, if the plot variable is not specified, the global `CURRENT_PLOT` is used automatically. The `savefig` command takes the filename and extension as its arguments, and it saves the current plot in the specified format. For example, to save the current plot as a PNG file, you can use the following code:

```
julia> savefig("myplot.png")
"/home/dnabanita7/myplot.png"
julia> png("myplot")
"myplot.png"
julia> savefig(p, "myplot.pdf")
```

You can also save a specific plot object p as a png file. In addition to `savefig`, there are other convenience functions such as `png()` that allow you to save your plots without specifying the extension.

Attributes in plotting

Plots.jl is a plotting package in Julia that allows for the easy customization of plots through the use of attributes. Attributes are modifiers to plots that can be applied using positional and keyword arguments, or through modifier functions. Positional arguments correspond to input data, while keyword arguments correspond to attributes.

For example, to change the line width of a plot, we can use the linewidth attribute (or its alias lw) as a keyword argument, like this:

```
julia> x = range(0, 10, length=100)
julia> y1 = sin.(x)
julia> y2 = cos.(x)
julia> plot(x, [y1 y2], title="Trigonometric functions", label=["sin(x)" "cos(x)"], linewidth=3)
```

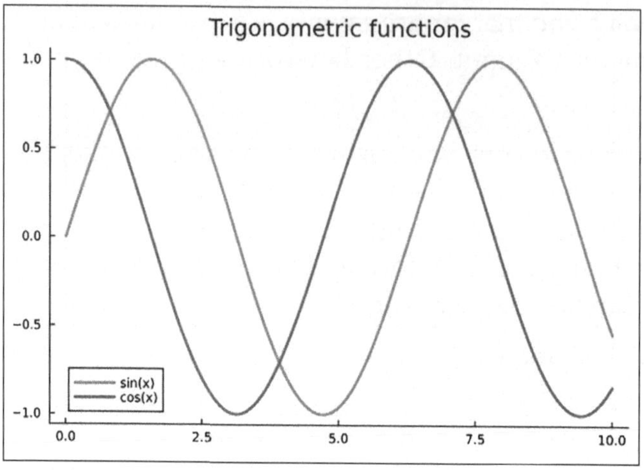

***Figure 10.5**: A plot with various attributes added*

Attributes can also be used to modify other aspects of a plot, such as axis labels, legend position, and line styles. For example, to add a label for the x-axis, we can use the xlabel attribute as a keyword argument or the `xlabel!` modifier function. Similarly, to change the legend position to be outside the plot and to have three columns, we can use the legend and `legendcolumns` attributes.

```
julia> xlabel!("x")
julia> plot!(legend=:outerbottom, legendcolumns=2)
```

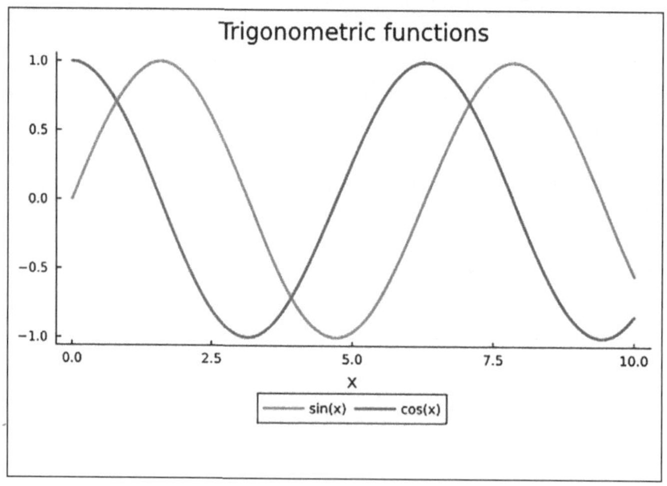

***Figure 10.6**: A plot with various attributes added with legend and labeled x-axis*

In addition, Plots.jl works with **LaTeXStrings.jl** to allow for LaTeX-formatted equation strings to be used in plots. To use **LaTeXStrings.jl**, simply install it with `Pkg.add("LaTeXStrings")` and prepend L to the LaTeX-formatted string.

```
(@v1.9) pkg> add LaTeXStrings
julia> using LaTeXStrings
julia> x = 10 .^ range(0, 4, length=100)
julia> y = @. 1/(1+x)
julia> plot(x, y, label=L”\frac{1}{1+x}”)
julia> plot!(xscale=:log10, yscale=:log10, minorgrid=true)
julia> title!(L”Log-log plot of $\frac{1}{1+x}$”)
julia> xlims!(1e+0, 1e+4)
julia> ylims!(1e-5, 1e+0)
julia> xlabel!(L”x”)
julia> ylabel!(L”y”)
```

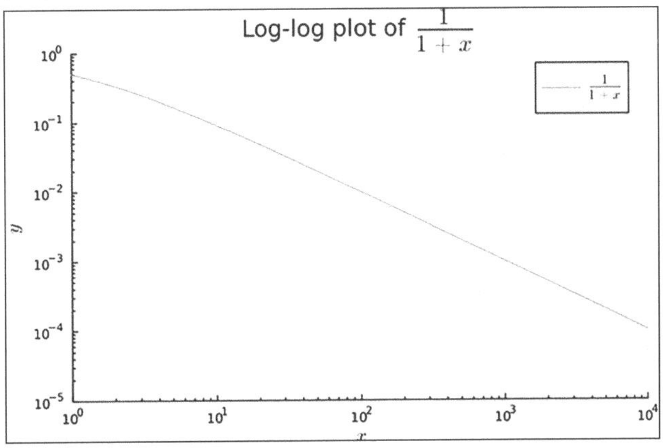

***Figure* 10.7**: *A plot with logarithmic graph*

Plots.jl allows for logarithmic scale plots to be created using the xscale and yscale attributes. These attributes can be set to :log10 to create a log-log plot, or `:identity` to keep the scale linear. Care should be taken to ensure that the data and limits are positive.

Scatter plots in Plots.jl

In Plots.jl, there are different options for plotting data, and line plots are the traditional way. However, there are other options called "series types," and one common type is a scatter plot that displays individual data points.

For example, we can define a sine function and create a vector called `y_noisy` that adds some randomness. To change from a line plot to a scatter plot, we can use the `seriestype` attribute, or use the shorthand function scatter!.

The series types available depend on the backend used. Additionally, other libraries can add new series types using recipes.

In the example code, the text provides common attributes used in scatter plots, such as line color (lc), line width (lw), marker color (mc), marker size (ms), and marker alpha (ma).

The final example code provided puts everything together and creates a scatter plot with a sine function and some noisy data points. The plot is customized with different colors, marker sizes, and a legend. The plot is also given a title, and the *x* and *y* axes are labeled to make it easier to interpret the data.

```
julia> using Plots

# Define a range of values for the x-axis

julia> x = range(0, 10, length=100)

# Define a sine function for the y-axis

julia> y = sin.(x)

# Add some noise to the sine function to create a "noisy" dataset

julia> y_noisy = @. sin(x) + 0.1*randn()

# Create a basic line plot of the sine function

julia> plot(x, y, label="sin(x)")

# Change the plot type to a scatter plot and add the noisy dataset

julia> scatter!(x, y_noisy, label="data")

# Customize the plot with different colors, marker sizes, and a legend

julia> plot!(

       legend=:bottomleft, # Position the legend in the bottom-left
corner

       title="Sine with noise", # Add a title to the plot

       xlabel="x", # Label the x-axis

       ylabel="y", # Label the y-axis

       lc=:black, lw=2, # Customize the line color and width of the sine
function

       mc=:red, ms=2, ma=0.5, # Customize the marker color, size, and
transparency of the noisy data

)
```

```
julia> plot!(
               legend = :bottomleft,
               title = "Sine with noise",
               xlabel = "x",
               ylabel = "y",
               lc = :black, lw = 2,
               mc = :red, ms = 2, ma = 0.5,
       )
```

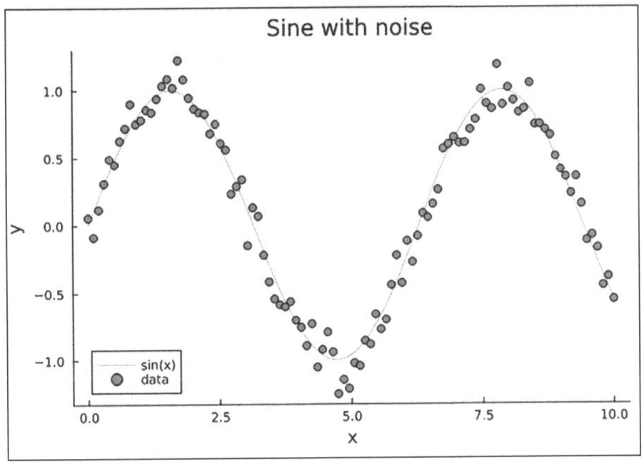

Figure 10.8: *A plot with sine graph with random data*

This code defines a range of x values and a corresponding sine function for the y values. It then adds some random noise to the sine function to create a new dataset, `y_noisy`.

The code first creates a basic line plot of the sine function using the plot function. It then changes the plot type to a scatter plot using the `seriestype` attribute with the value :scatter. The scatter! function can also be used to create the scatter plot directly.

Finally, the code customizes the plot using various attributes like legend, title, xlabel, ylabel, lc, lw, mc, ms, and ma. These attributes control the appearance of the plot, like the position and content of the legend, the color and width of the sine function line, and the color, size, and transparency of the noisy data points.

This code should produce a scatter plot with a sine function and some noisy data points, like the example provided in the original text.

Plotting backends

Plots.jl is a package that acts as an interface over multiple plotting libraries, which are called backends. The purpose of Plots.jl is to interpret your plot commands and generate the plot using one of the supported backends. This means you can use the same syntax across different plotting libraries, which is very convenient.

The default backend is GR, but you can easily switch to a different backend if you want. For example, if you want to use `Plotly`, you can install the package by running `Pkg.add("PlotlyJS")` in the REPL. Then, you can set the backend to `Plotly` by calling the `plotlyjs()` function. Similarly, you can switch back to GR by calling the gr() function.

Each backend has its features and limitations. For example, some backends like `Plotly` provide interactive plots, while others like GR are better at dealing with large datasets. Some backends can create 3D plots, while others are limited to 2D. Additionally, some backends like GR can save plots as vector graphics, while others like `Plotly` can only save plots as PNG images.

Here's an example of how to switch between backends and create plots using different backends:

```
julia> using Plots
# Set the backend to Plotly
julia> plotlyjs()
Plots.PlotlyJSBackend()
# Create a plot using Plotly
julia> x = range(0, 10, length=100)
julia> y = sin.(x)
julia> y_noisy = @. sin(x) + 0.1*randn()
julia> plot(x, y, label="sin(x)", lc=:black, lw=2)
[ Info: Listening on: 127.0.0.1:9171, thread id: 1
```

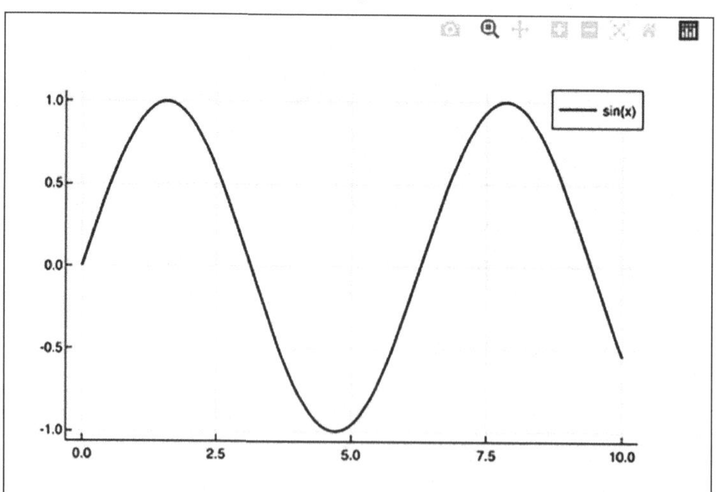

Figure 10.9: *A plot with sine graph*

```
julia> scatter!(x, y_noisy, label="data", mc=:red, ms=2, ma=0.5)
```

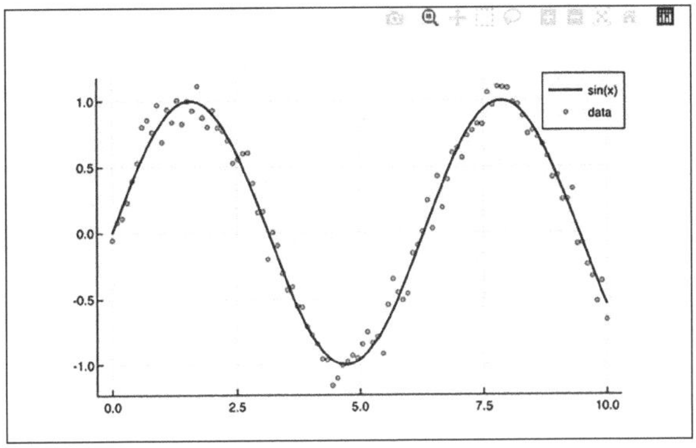

***Figure 10.10**: A plot with sine graph with random data*

```
julia> plot!(legend=:bottomleft)
julia> title!("Sine with noise, plotted with Plotly")
julia> xlabel!("x")
julia> ylabel!("y")
# Save the plot to a PNG file
julia> savefig("plotlyjs_tutorial.png")
"/home/dnabanita7/plotlyjs_tutorial.png"
```

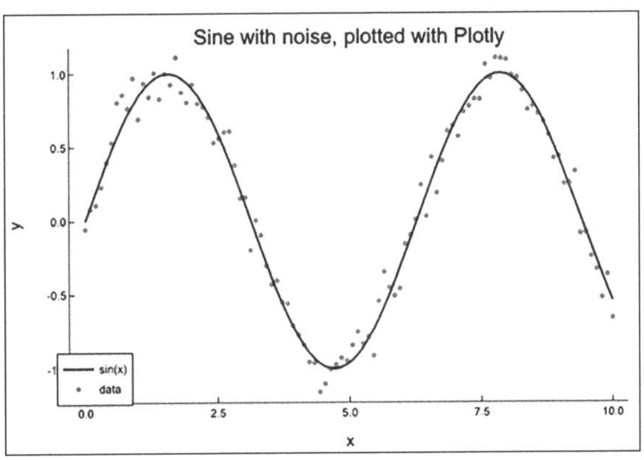

***Figure 10.11**: A plot with sine graph with random data which means some noise is added*

```
# Set the backend back to GR
julia> gr()
Plots.GRBackend()
# Create a plot using GR
julia> plot(x, y, label="sin(x)", lc=:black, lw=2)
```

```
julia> scatter!(x, y_noisy, label="data", mc=:red, ms=2, ma=0.5)
julia> plot!(legend=:bottomleft)
julia> title!("Sine with noise, plotted with GR")
julia> xlabel!("x")
julia> ylabel!("y")
```

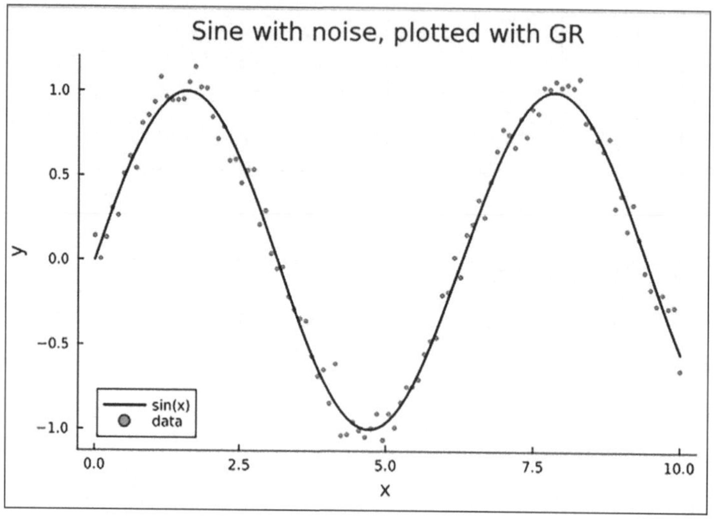

***Figure 10.12**: A plot with sine graph with random data with GR backend*

Subplots in Plots.jl

To combine multiple plots as subplots, we can use layouts. The layout command takes in a 2-tuple layout=(N, M) which builds an NxM grid of plots, and it will automatically split a series to be in each plot. For example, if we type layout=(3, 1) on a plot with three series, then we will get three rows of plots, each with one series in it.

Here's an example of how to use the layout command to plot three separate functions in three separate plots, each with only one series, and without a legend:

```
julia> x = range(0, 10, length=100)
julia> y1 = @. exp(-0.1x) * cos(4x)
julia> y2 = @. exp(-0.3x) * cos(4x)
julia> y3 = @. exp(-0.5x) * cos(4x)
julia> plot(x, [y1 y2 y3], layout=(3, 1), legend=false)
```

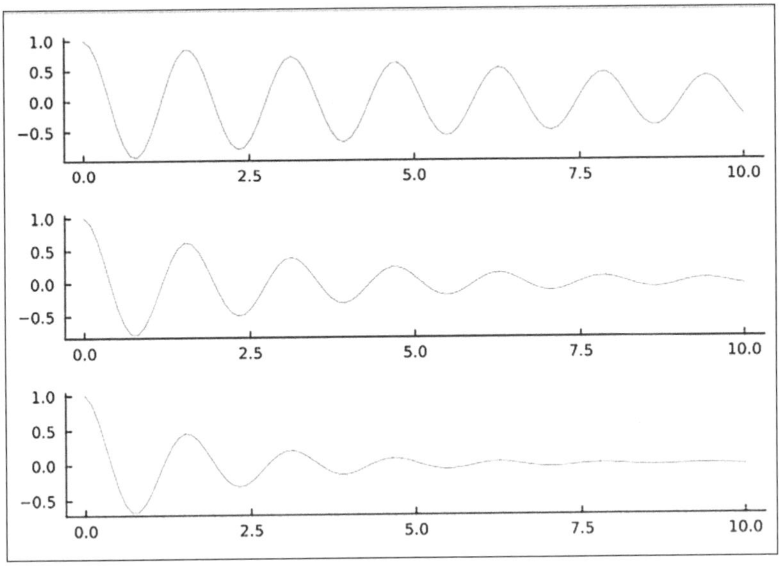

Figure 10.13: *Three subplots with exponential and cosine function*

We can also use layouts on plots of plot objects. For example, we can generate four separate plots and make a single plot that combines them into a 2×2 grid. Here's an example:

```
julia> x = range(0, 10, length=100)
julia> y1 = @. exp(-0.1x) * cos(4x)
julia> y2 = @. exp(-0.3x) * cos(4x)
julia> y3 = @. exp(-0.1x)
julia> y4 = @. exp(-0.3x)
julia> y = [y1 y2 y3 y4]
julia> p1 = plot(x, y)
julia> p2 = plot(x, y, title="Title 2", lw=3)
julia> p3 = scatter(x, y, ms=2, ma=0.5, xlabel="xlabel 3")
julia> p4 = scatter(x, y, title="Title 4", ms=2, ma=0.2)
julia> plot(p1, p2, p3, p4, layout=(2,2), legend=false)
```

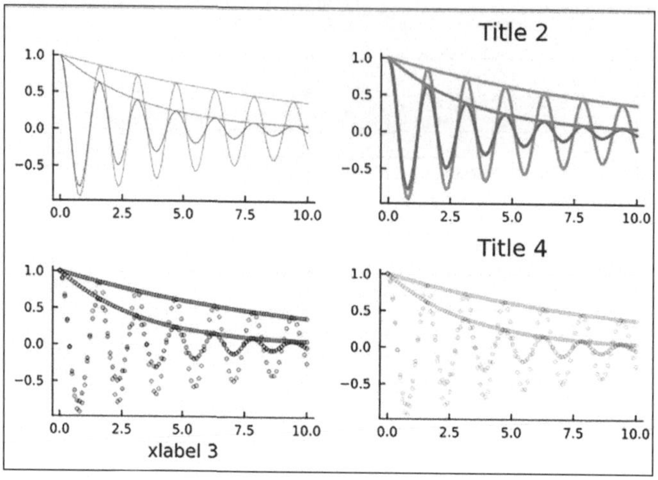

***Figure 10.14**: Multiple subplots of scattered data*

Recipes in Plots.jl

In Plots.jl, a recipe is a method for creating custom plot types or modifying existing plot types. Recipes allow users to extend the functionality of Plots.jl beyond the built-in series types, and they can be used to create custom plot types, modify plot attributes, or even create entirely new backends.

A recipe defines how to plot data with a specific type of plot and can be thought of as a set of instructions for creating a plot. A recipe specifies how to transform data to create the plot, what type of plot to create, and how to customize its appearance.

Recipes can be defined by users, and there are many examples of recipes available in the Plots.jl ecosystem. The Plots.jl documentation provides extensive guidance on how to create and use recipes to extend the capabilities of the package.

Using Statsplots.jl recipes

Plotting recipes in Julia's Plots.jl framework is an extension that adds new plot commands, default interpretations of Julia types as plotting data, new functions for generating plots, and new series types. Recipe libraries, such as PlotRecipes.jl and StatsPlots.jl, provide a collection of pre-made recipes that can be used to make advanced plots without having to write your recipes.

StatsPlots.jl is a recipe library that adds a type recipe for distributions and a plot recipe for marginal histograms, along with several new statistical plot series. It also provides a specialized macro, `@df`, that enables plotting directly from data tables.

Here are some examples of how to use StatsPlots.jl:

- **Using User Recipes**: The @df macro allows you to plot a `DataFrame` directly using column names. For instance, to plot a `DataFrame` with columns `a`, `b`, and `c` and use `a` as the x-axis and plot the series defined by columns `b` and `c`, you can use the following code:

```
(@v1.9) pkg> add StatsPlots
julia> using StatsPlots, DataFrames
julia> df = DataFrame(a=1:10, b=10*rand(10), c=10*rand(10))
10×3 DataFrame
 Row │ a      b       c
     │ Int64  Float64
─────┼──────────────────────────
   1 │      1  2.17912  9.95485
   2 │      2  5.54207  3.7425
   3 │      3  5.97152  1.39592
   4 │      4  1.92392  0.581316
   5 │      5  9.95078  2.85454
   6 │      6  1.19948  3.57068
   7 │      7  1.46569  0.900923
   8 │      8  8.10511  9.94493
   9 │      9  9.38279  5.05676
  10 │ 10  9.7275   8.22645
julia> @df df plot(:a, [:b :c])
```

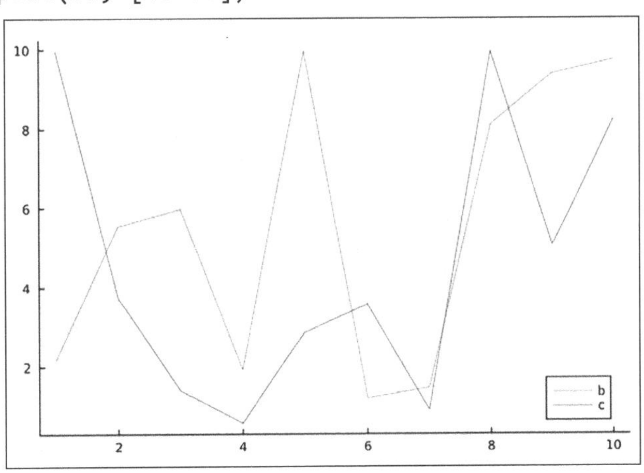

Figure 10.15: *Data plotted with Statsplots.jl*

- **Using Type Recipes**: **StatsPlots.jl** extends **Distributions.jl** by adding a type recipe for its distribution types, so they can be directly interpreted as plotting data. For example, to plot a normal distribution with a mean of 3 and a standard deviation of 5, you can use the following code:

```
(@v1.9) pkg> add Distributions
julia> using Distributions, StatsPlots
julia> plot(Normal(3, 5), lw=3)
```

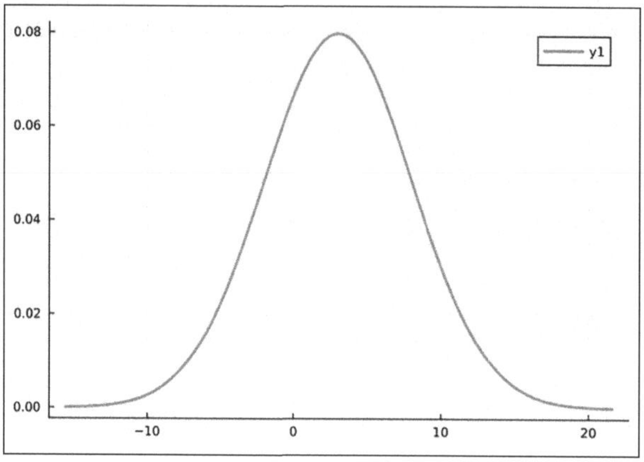

***Figure 10.16**: Normal distribution plotted with StatsPlots.jl*

- Using Plot Recipes: StatsPlots.jl adds the `marginalhist` multiplot via a plot recipe. For example, to plot a marginal histogram for the `PetalLength` and the `PetalWidth` columns of the iris dataset, you can use the following code:

```
julia> using RDatasets, StatsPlots
julia> iris = dataset("datasets", "iris")
julia> @df iris marginalhist(:PetalLength, :PetalWidth)
```

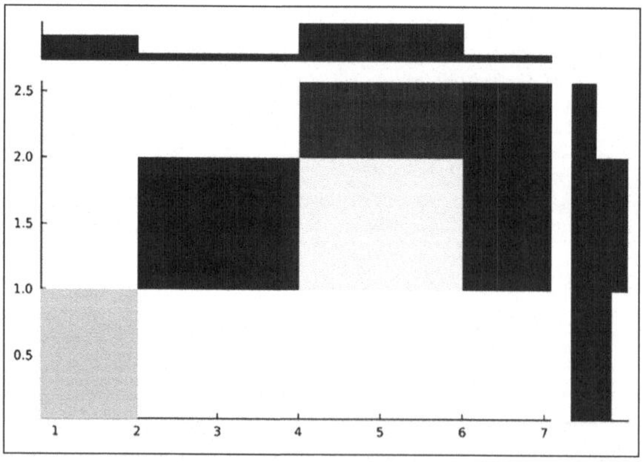

***Figure 10.17**: Iris dataset plotted with StatsPlots.jl*

- **Using Series Recipes**: StatsPlots.jl introduces new series recipes. For instance, to use the Violin plot on some random data and add a boxplot on top, you can use the following code:

```
julia> using StatsPlots

julia> y = rand(100, 4)

julia> violin(["Series 1" "Series 2" "Series 3" "Series 4"], y,
legend=false)

julia> boxplot!(["Series 1" "Series 2" "Series 3" "Series 4"], y,
legend=false)
```

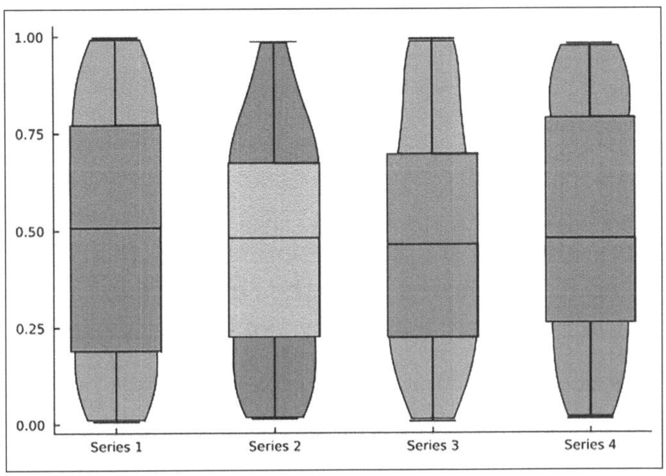

***Figure 10.18**: Violin and box plots plotted with StatsPlots.jl*

Contour plots

Contour plots are a way of visualizing a 3D surface on a 2D plane by using contour lines to represent the constant values of the surface. In Julia, we can create contour plots using the contour() function from the Plots.jl package.

Here is an example code that creates a simple contour plot:

```
julia> using Plots

julia> # Define a function to plot

julia> f(x, y) = x^2 + y^2

julia> # Generate x and y coordinates for the plot

julia> x = -5:0.1:5

julia> y = -5:0.1:5

julia> # Evaluate the function at each (x, y) point
```

```
julia> z = [f(xi, yj) for xi in x, yj in y]
julia> # Create the contour plot
julia> contour(x, y, z, levels=10)
```

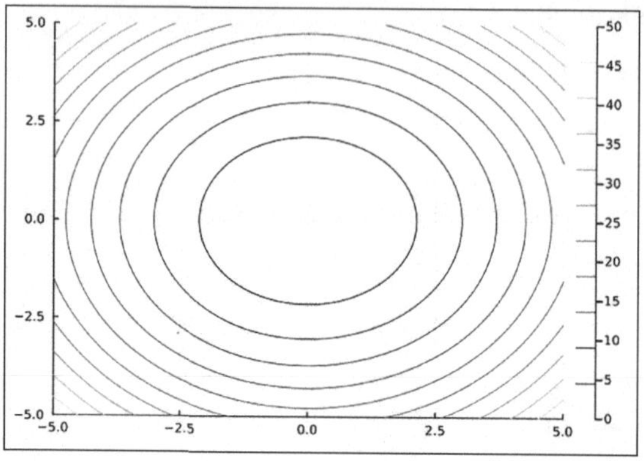

Figure 10.19: *3D contour plots using the Plots.jl package*

In this code, we first define a simple function `f(x, y)` that we want to plot. We then generate x and y coordinates using the `range()` function and evaluate the function at each point to create a 2D array z of function values.

Finally, we use the `contour()` function to create the plot by passing in the x, y, and z arrays as arguments. We also specify the number of contour levels we want to display using the levels argument.

We can also customize the appearance of the plot by passing in additional arguments to the `contour()` function. For example, we can add labels to the contour lines and change the color scheme:

```
julia> # Create the contour plot with customizations
julia> contour(x, y, z, levels=10, labels=true, color=:viridis)
```

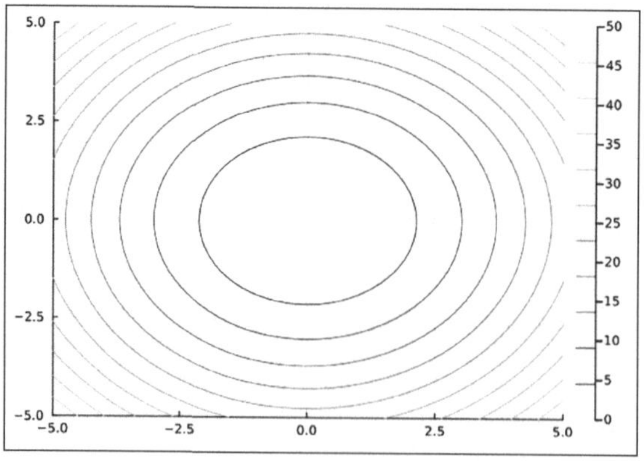

Figure 10.20: *3D contour plots using the Plots.jl package with various attributes*

In this code, we add the labels=true argument to display labels for each contour line and change the color scheme to `color=:viridis` using the color argument.

We can also create filled contour plots by using the `contourf()` function instead of `contour()`. Here is an example:

```
julia> # Create a filled contour plot
julia> contourf(x, y, z, levels=10, color=:plasma)
```

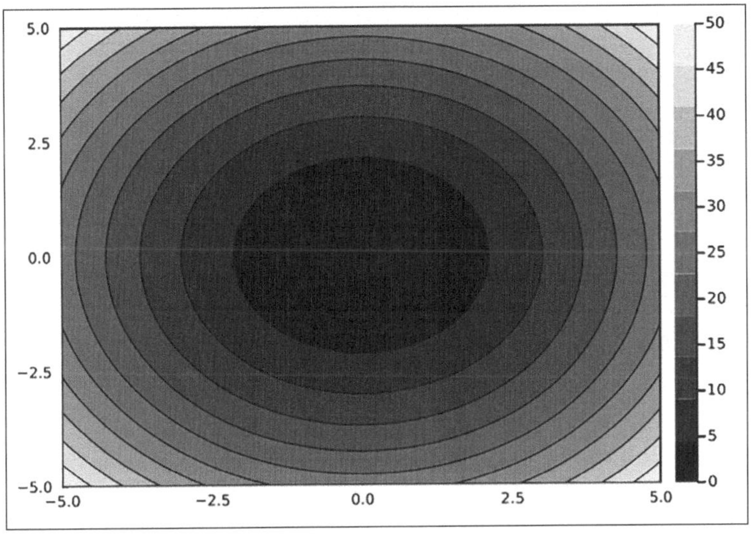

***Figure 10.21**: 3D filled Contour plots using the Plots.jl package with various attributes*

In this code, we use the `contourf()` function instead of `contour()` to create a filled contour plot. We also change the color scheme to color=:plasma using the color argument.

We can also create a contour plot with labeled contour lines by using the `clabels` keyword argument. The `clabels` argument takes a boolean value, indicating whether to add labels to the contour lines or not. Here's an example:

```
using Plots
# Define a function to plot
julia> f(x, y) = sin(x) * cos(y)
# Generate x and y coordinates for the plot
julia> x = range(-5, stop=5, length=100)
julia> y = range(-5, stop=5, length=100)
# Evaluate the function at each (x, y) point
julia> z = [f(xi, yj) for xi in x, yj in y]
```

```
# Create the contour plot
julia> contour(x, y, z, levels=10, clabels=true)
```

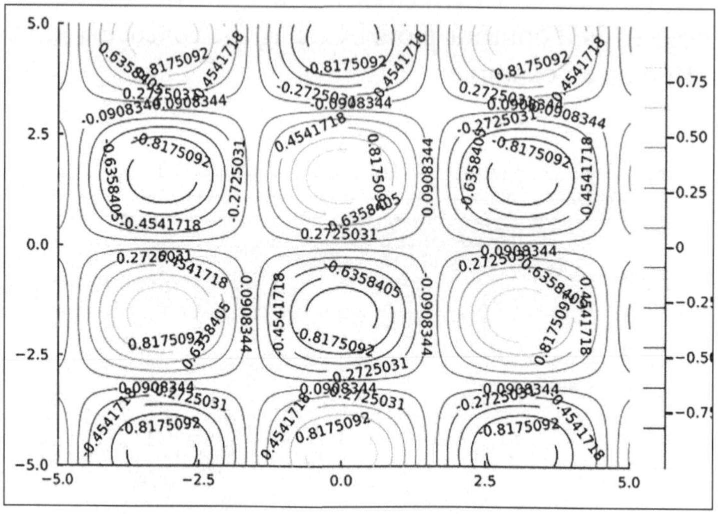

***Figure 10.22**: 3D Contour sub-plots using the Plots.jl package with various attributes*

In this example, we've defined a new function to plot, `f(x, y) = sin(x) * cos(y)`. We've also changed the x and y arrays to be generated using the `range()` function with a length argument instead of a step argument.

We've also added the `clabels=true` argument to the `contour()` function to add labels to the contour lines.

Finally, we can also customize the levels at which the contour lines are displayed by passing in an array of levels using the levels argument. Here's an example:

```
julia> using Plots
julia> # Define a function to plot
julia> f(x, y) = sin(x) * cos(y)
julia> # Generate x and y coordinates for the plot
julia> x = range(-5, stop=5, length=100)
julia> y = range(-5, stop=5, length=100)
julia> # Evaluate the function at each (x, y) point
julia> z = [f(xi, yj) for xi in x, yj in y]
julia> # Create the contour plot with custom levels
julia> contour(x, y, z, levels=[-0.8, -0.6, -0.4, -0.2, 0, 0.2, 0.4,
0.6, 0.8], clabels=true)
```

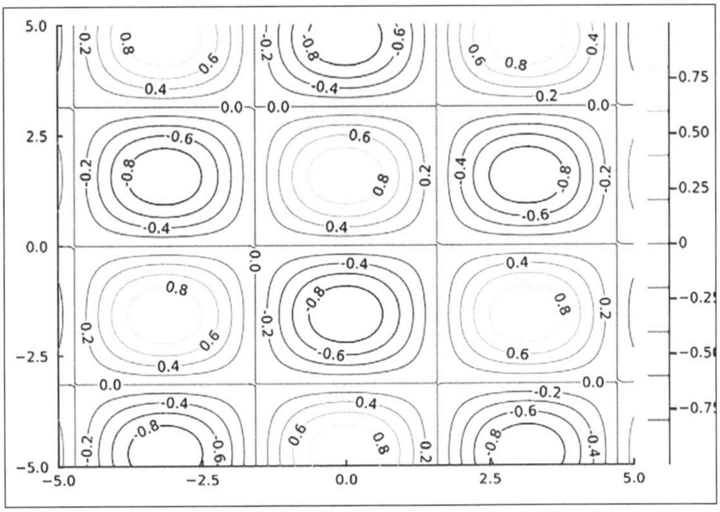

***Figure 10.23**: 3D Contour sub-plots using the Plots.jl package with various attributes*

In this example, we've specified a custom set of contour levels using the levels argument. The contour lines will be displayed only at these specified levels.

These are some examples of how to create and customize contour plots in Julia using the Plots.jl package.

Histograms in Plots.jl

Histograms are a way of visualizing the distribution of a dataset by showing the frequency or proportion of values that fall within each interval, or bin, of the dataset. In Julia, we can create histograms using the `histogram()` function from the Plots.jl package.

Here is an example code that creates a simple histogram:

```
julia> using Plots
julia> # Generate some random data
julia> data = randn(1000)
julia> # Create the histogram
julia> histogram(data)
```

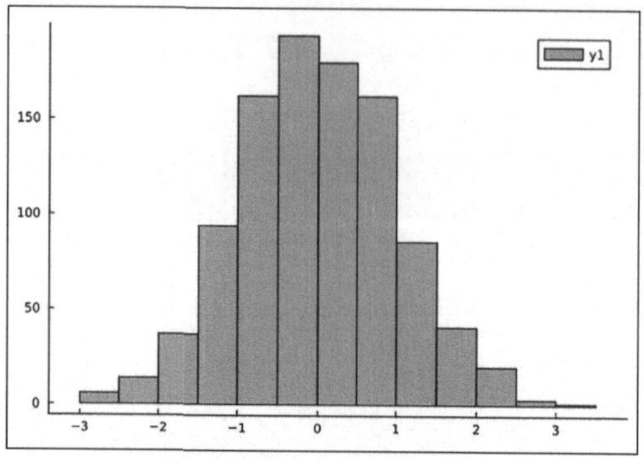

***Figure 10.24**: Histograms using the Plots.jl package*

In this code, we first generate a random dataset using the `randn()` function. We then pass this dataset to the `histogram()` function to create the plot.

By default, the `histogram()` function will use 10 equally spaced bins to display the distribution of the data. We can change the number of bins by passing in the `nbins` argument:

```
julia> # Create the histogram with 10 bins
julia> histogram(data, nbins=10)
```

In this code, we've specified that we want to use 10 bins to display the distribution of the data.

We can also customize the appearance of the histogram by passing in additional arguments to the `histogram()` function. For example, we can change the color of the bars and add a title to the plot:

```
julia> # Create the histogram with customizations
julia> histogram(data, nbins=10, color=:yellow, title="Random Data
Histogram")
```

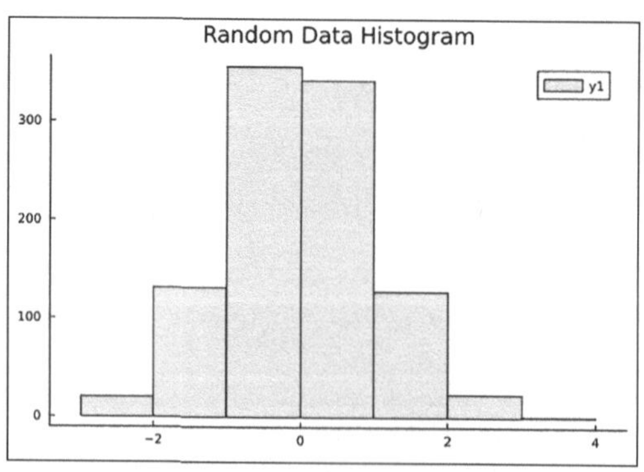

***Figure 10.25**: Histograms using the Plots.jl package with various attributes*

Finally, we can create a stacked histogram by passing in multiple datasets to the `histogram()` function:

```
julia> # Generate two random datasets
julia> data1 = randn(1000)
julia> data2 = randn(1000) .+ 2
julia> # Create a stacked histogram
julia> histogram(data1, data2, nbins=20, normalize=true, color="gray",
title="Stacked Histogram")
```

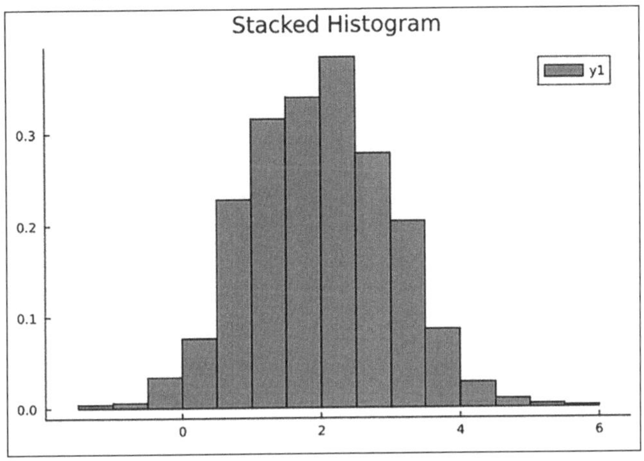

Figure 10.26: *Stacked histograms using the Plots.jl package with various attributes*

In this code, we've added the normalize=true argument to create a normalized histogram where the area of the bars sums to 1.

In this code, we've generated two random datasets, data1 and data2, and passed them both to the `histogram()` function. The resulting plot is a stacked histogram where the bars for each dataset are stacked on top of each other.

Weighted histograms

In a weighted histogram, each data point is associated with a weight, which determines its contribution to the histogram. The `histogram()` function in Julia can also be used to create weighted histograms.

Here is an example code snippet to create a weighted histogram of some random data:

```
julia> using Plots
# Generate some random data with weights
```

```
julia> data = [(randn(), rand()) for i=1:1000]
# Create a weighted histogram with 10 bins
julia> histogram(data, bins=10, weights=[d[2] for d in data])
```

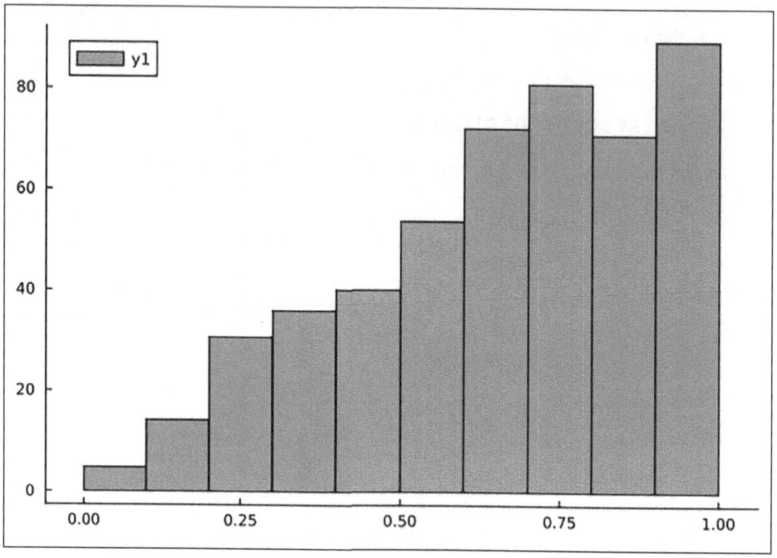

Figure 10.27: *Weighted histograms using the Plots.jl package with various attributes*

In the preceding code, we first load the Plots package. Then, we generate some random data with weights using a list comprehension. Finally, we create a weighted histogram of the data using the `histogram()` function and specifying the weights argument.

Here is another example that demonstrates some additional options:

```
julia> using Plots
julia> # Generate some random data with weights
julia> data = [(randn(), rand()) for i=1:1000]
julia> # Create a weighted histogram with 20 bins and a red color
julia> histogram(data, bins=20, weights=[d[2] for d in data],
color=:red)
julia> # Add a title and labels to the plot
julia> title!("Weighted Histogram of Random Data")
julia> xlabel!("Values")
julia> ylabel!("Weighted Frequency")
```

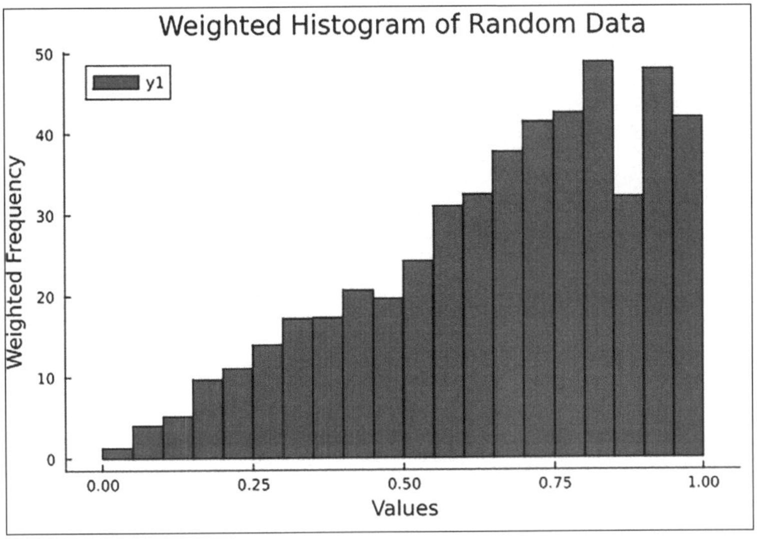

***Figure 10.28**: Weighted histograms of random data against weight frequency of data*

In this code, we create a weighted histogram with 20 bins and set the color to red. We also add a title and labels to the plot using the `title!()`, `xlabel!()`, and `ylabel!()` functions. Note that we have changed the y-axis label to reflect the fact that we are now plotting weighted frequencies.

In addition to standard and weighted histograms, the Plots package in Julia offers several other variations of histograms. Here are some examples of these variations, along with code samples:

Stacked histograms

A stacked histogram shows multiple histograms stacked on top of each other, with the heights of each bin representing the relative contributions of different groups. Here is an example code snippet:

```
julia> using Plots

julia> # Generate some random data for two groups

julia> data1 = randn(1000)

julia> data2 = randn(1000) .+ 2

julia> # Create a stacked histogram with 10 bins for each group

julia> histogram([data1, data2], bins=10, label=["Group 1" "Group 2"],
alpha=0.6)
```

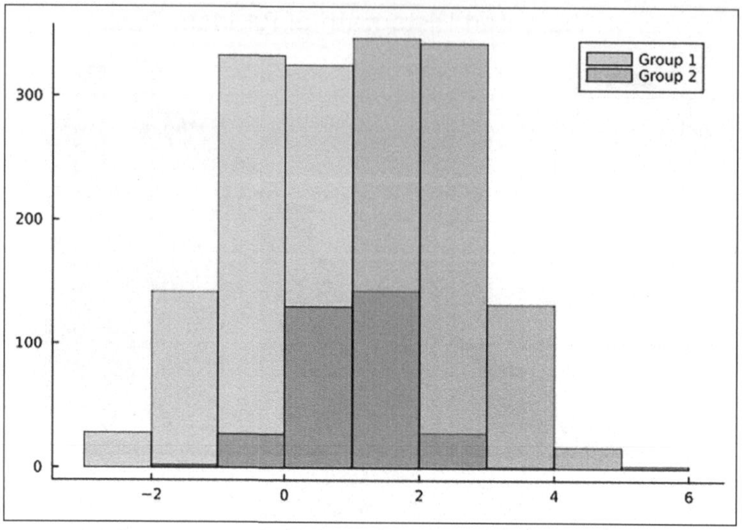

***Figure 10.29**: Stacked histograms with various color attributes*

In this code, we generate some random data for two groups and then create a stacked histogram of the data using the `histogram()` function with two arrays of data as input. We also specify the number of bins, add labels for each group, and set the transparency level using the alpha argument.

Overlaid histograms

An overlaid histogram shows multiple histograms overlaid on top of each other, with different colors representing different groups. Here is an example code snippet:

```
julia> using Plots

julia> # Generate some random data for two groups

julia> data1 = randn(1000)

julia> data2 = randn(1000) .+ 2

julia> # Create an overlaid histogram with 10 bins for each group

julia> histogram([data1, data2], bins=10, label=["Group 1" "Group 2"], alpha=0.6,
        normalize=true, xlim=(-4, 8), ylim=(0, 0.6), color=[:blue :red])
```

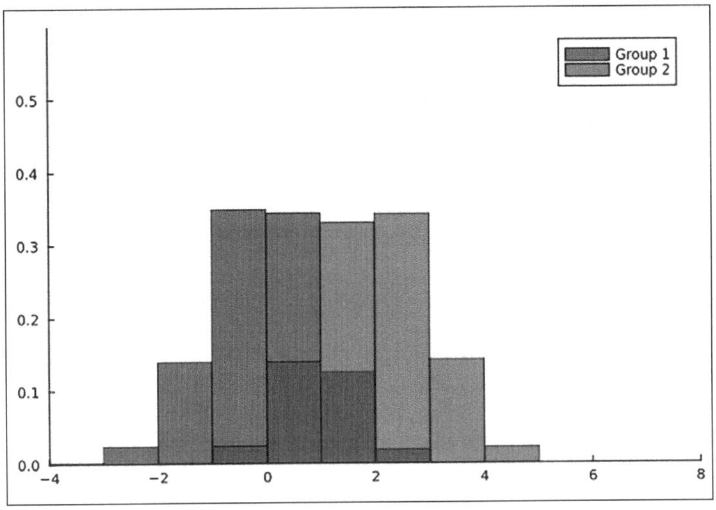

***Figure 10.30**: Stacked histograms overlaid on top of each other with various color attributes*

In this code, we generate some random data for the two groups and then create an overlaid histogram of the data using the `histogram()` function with two arrays of data as input. We also specify the number of bins, add labels for each group, set the transparency level, normalize the histograms, set the x- and y-axis limits, and set the colors using the color argument.

Cumulative histograms

A cumulative histogram shows the cumulative distribution function (CDF) of a dataset, which represents the probability that a randomly selected value from the dataset is less than or equal to a given value. Here is an example code snippet:

```
julia> using Plots
julia> # Generate some random data
julia> data = randn(1000)
julia> # Create a cumulative histogram with 20 bins
julia> histogram(data, bins=20, norm=:cdf, fillalpha=0.3, line=:step,
label="CDF")
```

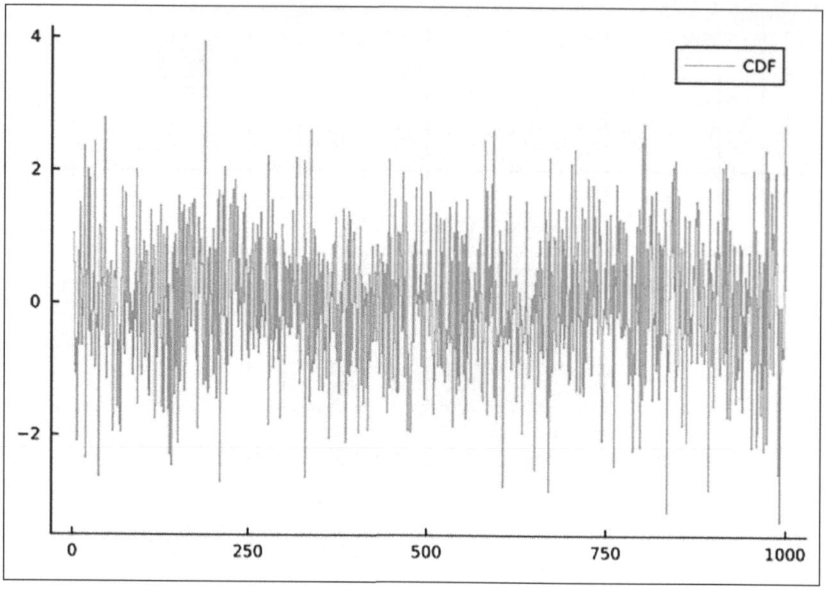

***Figure 10.31**: Cumulative histograms displaying the cumulative distribution function of data*

In this code, we generate some random data and then create a cumulative histogram of the data using the `histogram()` function with the norm argument set to :cdf. We also specify the number of bins, set the fill transparency level, use a step function to show the CDF and add a label.

2D histograms

2D histograms are a type of histogram that visualize the joint distribution of two variables. In Julia, 2D histograms can be created using the `histogram2d()` function from the Plots package. Here's an example code snippet to create a 2D histogram:

```
julia> using Plots
julia> # Generate some random 2D data
julia> data = randn(1000, 2)
julia> # Create a 2D histogram with 20 bins in each direction
julia> histogram2d(data[:,1], data[:,2], nbins=20, color=:heat)
```

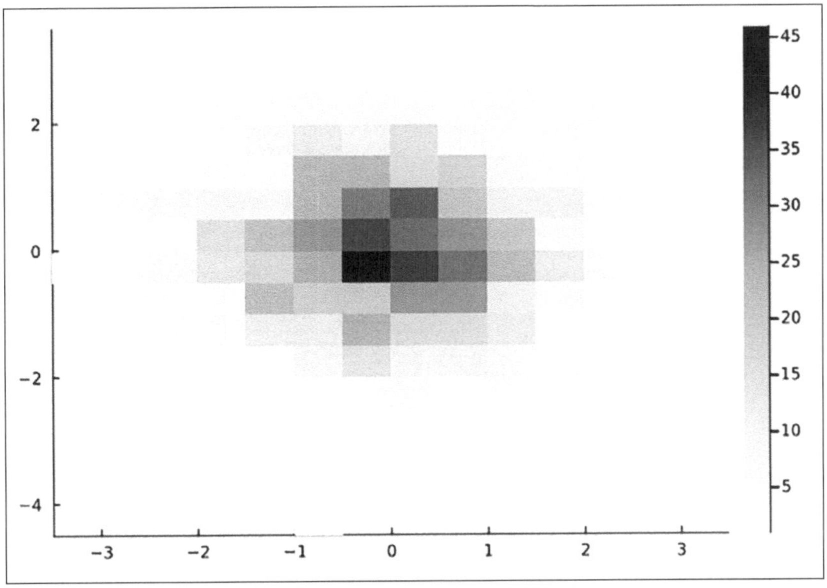

Figure 10.32: *2D histograms displaying the joint distribution of data*

In this code, we generate some random 2D data and then create a 2D histogram of the data using the `histogram2d()` function. We specify the x- and y-coordinates of the data, the number of bins in each direction, and the color scheme for the plot using the `nbins` and color arguments.

You can also create weighted 2D histograms by specifying the weights of each data point using the weights argument. For example, to create a weighted 2D histogram with the weight of each point proportional to its x-coordinate, you can do:

```
julia> using Plots
julia> # Generate some random 2D data
julia> data = randn(1000, 2)
julia> # Create weights proportional to the x-coordinate
julia> weights = data[:,1]
julia> # Create a weighted 2D histogram with 20 bins in each direction
julia> histogram2d(data[:,1], data[:,2], weights=weights, nbins=20,
color=:heat)
```

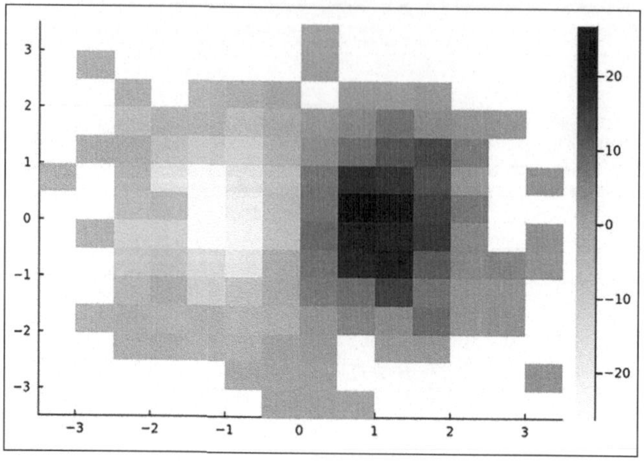

***Figure 10.33**: Weighted 2D histograms displaying the joint distribution of data*

In this code, we generate some random 2D data and then create weights proportional to the x-coordinate of each data point. We then create a weighted 2D histogram of the data using the `histogram2d()` function with the weights argument set to the weights we just created.

Conclusion

In this chapter, Plots.jl is a powerful and flexible data visualization package in the Julia programming language, offering a wide range of plotting functionalities to suit various needs. Installing and using Plots.jl is straightforward, and users can choose from different backends and attributes to customize their plots. Scatter plots and subplots are some commonly used plot types in Plots.jl, while StatsPlots.jl provides a convenient interface for creating statistical plots with added functionalities. Users can also create contour plots, histograms, and other types of plots using Plots.jl and StatsPlots.jl. With its user-friendly interface and extensive functionalities, Plots.jl is an essential tool for data visualization and analysis in Julia.

In the next chapter, we will learn about machine learning in Julia.

Questions

1. What is Plots.jl, and what are its main features?
2. How is Plots.jl different from other data visualization packages in Julia?
3. What are the benefits of using Plots.jl for data visualization and analysis?

4. How can I install Plots.jl on my local machine?
5. What are the dependencies required to install Plots.jl?
6. Can Plots.jl be installed on multiple operating systems?
7. What are the different plotting functionalities provided by Plots.jl?
8. How can I use Plots.jl to create different types of plots?
9. Can I customize the appearance of my plots using Plots.jl?
10. What are attributes in plotting, and how are they used in Plots.jl?
11. Can I use multiple attributes in a single plot using Plots.jl?
12. How can I change the default attributes in Plots.jl?
13. What is a scatter plot, and how can I create one using Plots.jl?
14. What are some commonly used attributes in scatter plots?
15. How can I customize the appearance of my scatter plot in Plots.jl?
16. What are plotting backends, and how do they work in Plots.jl?
17. How can I choose the appropriate backend for my plot in Plots.jl?
18. Can I switch between different backends while working on a plot in Plots.jl?
19. What are subplots, and how can I create them using Plots.jl?
20. How can I customize the layout and appearance of my subplots in Plots.jl?
21. Can I add different types of plots to a single subplot in Plots.jl?
22. What are recipes in Plots.jl, and how can I use them to create customized plots?
23. Can I create my own custom recipe in Plots.jl?
24. How can I share my custom recipe with other Plots.jl users?
25. What is StatsPlots.jl, and how is it related to Plots.jl?
26. How can I use StatsPlots.jl to create statistical plots?
27. What are some advanced features provided by StatsPlots.jl?

28. What are contour plots, and how can I create them using Plots.jl?
29. What are some commonly used attributes in contour plots?
30. How can I customize the appearance of my contour plot in Plots.jl?
31. What is a histogram, and how can I create one using Plots.jl?
32. What are some commonly used attributes in histograms?
33. How can I customize the appearance of my histogram in Plots.jl?

CHAPTER 11

Introducing Machine Learning in Julia

Introduction

Julia is a high-performance programming language that has been gaining popularity in the field of data science and machine learning due to its speed, ease of use, and versatility. With its powerful mathematical and statistical libraries and its ability to efficiently handle large datasets, Julia provides an excellent platform for performing machine learning tasks.

There are several libraries in Julia that support machine learning, each with its own unique set of features and capabilities. One of the most popular libraries is Flux.jl, which provides a high-level interface for building and training deep neural networks. Flux.jl offers a wide range of layers, loss functions, and optimization algorithms, making it a versatile and powerful tool for building complex models.

Another popular library for machine learning in Julia is MLJ.jl, which provides a unified interface for working with various machine learning algorithms, including classification, regression, clustering, and more. MLJ.jl also offers a range of tools for data preprocessing, feature selection, and model tuning, making it a comprehensive solution for machine learning tasks.

In addition to these libraries, several others provide specialized functionality for machine learning tasks. For example, **DecisionTree.jl** provides a fast and flexible implementation of decision trees, while **Clustering.jl** offers a range of clustering algorithms for unsupervised learning.

Overall, Julia provides a powerful and flexible platform for performing machine learning tasks, with a range of libraries and tools available for building, training, and deploying models. Whether you are a data scientist, machine learning researcher, or developer, Julia offers a rich set of tools and capabilities for tackling complex machine learning problems.

Structure

In this chapter, the following topics will be covered:

- The need for machine learning
- Introducing machine learning
- MLJ.jl - the machine learning library of Julia
- Specialties of MLJ.jl
- Handling data in MLJ.jl
- Generating data
- Models
- Revisiting weights
- Data preprocessing using transformers in MLJ

The need for machine learning

Imagine you are a sales manager for a large retail chain. Your company has stores across the country, and you are responsible for forecasting sales for each store to ensure that enough inventory is available to meet customer demand. However, forecasting sales accurately can be a challenging task, especially with so many stores and products to consider.

To improve your sales forecasting, you decide to try using machine learning. You gather historical sales data for each store, including information on product sales, pricing, promotions, and more. You also collect external data, such as weather and economic indicators, which may impact sales.

You begin by training a machine learning model on this data to predict sales for each store. You use a range of algorithms and techniques, including regression analysis, time series forecasting, and ensemble methods, to build a robust and accurate model.

As you continue to refine your model, you start to notice interesting patterns in the data. For example, you discover that sales for certain products are highly correlated with weather patterns, with sales increasing for certain items during hot weather or rainy days. You also find that promotions have a significant impact on sales, with certain types of promotions driving more sales than others.

With this new insight, you begin to adjust your sales and marketing strategies accordingly. You start to offer more targeted promotions based on weather patterns and customer preferences, and you optimize pricing strategies to maximize revenue. As a result, you are able to increase sales and profits for your company while improving customer satisfaction.

This story illustrates how machine learning can be used to improve sales forecasting and drive business success. By analyzing large and complex datasets, machine learning models can uncover valuable insights and patterns that can inform decision-making and drive better outcomes.

Introducing machine learning

Machine learning is a branch of artificial intelligence that focuses on the development of algorithms and statistical models that enable computers to learn from and make predictions or decisions based on data. In other words, machine learning is the process of teaching computers to learn from experience and improve their performance on a specific task.

Machine learning algorithms can be broadly classified into three types:

- supervised learning
- unsupervised learning
- reinforcement learning

Supervised learning involves training a model using labeled data, in which the input and output pairs are provided to the algorithm. Unsupervised learning, on the other hand, involves training a model on unlabeled data, with the algorithm tasked with identifying patterns and relationships within the data. Reinforcement learning involves training a model to make decisions based on feedback from its environment, with the goal of maximizing a reward function.

Machine learning has numerous applications across a wide range of fields, from natural language processing and computer vision to finance and healthcare. It is used to develop predictive models for tasks such as image classification, speech recognition, and fraud detection, as well as for decision-making systems such as autonomous vehicles and recommendation engines.

In recent years, machine learning has seen significant advancements, fueled by the availability of large amounts of data, powerful computing resources, and breakthroughs in algorithm development. With these tools and techniques, machine learning has the potential to revolutionize the way we approach complex problems and make decisions in a wide range of domains.

MLJ.jl - the machine learning library of Julia

MLJ (Machine Learning in Julia) is a comprehensive machine learning framework written in the Julia programming language. It offers a user-friendly interface for building, training, and evaluating machine learning models, as well as a wide range of algorithms and tools for data preprocessing and feature selection.

One of the key features of MLJ is its ability to handle different types of data, such as numerical, categorical, and text data, seamlessly and efficiently. This allows users to work with a variety of datasets and tasks, from regression and classification to clustering and dimensionality reduction.

MLJ also supports various model composition and ensembling techniques, allowing users to combine different models and algorithms to improve performance and generalize to new data. This includes techniques such as stacking, bagging, and boosting, as well as meta-learning and hyperparameter optimization.

Furthermore, MLJ provides a modular and extensible architecture, allowing users to add new algorithms, models, and data types as needed. It also integrates with other Julia packages, such as **DataFrames.jl**, **Flux.jl**, and **Knet.jl**, enabling seamless integration with other data science and machine learning tools.

Overall, MLJ is a powerful and flexible machine learning framework that offers a high-level and user-friendly interface, while also providing advanced capabilities and extensibility for expert users.

Specialties of MLJ.jl

MLJ.jl is a machine learning library that is built in the Julia programming language. It offers an extensive range of functionalities that make it suitable for solving various machine learning problems. Here are some of the key features of MLJ.jl:

- Unified Interface: MLJ.jl provides a unified interface for a wide range of machine learning models, making it easy to compare and experiment with multiple models.
- Customizable and Extensible: MLJ.jl is highly customizable and extensible, allowing users to create their own models, preprocessors, and pipelines by implementing a few simple functions.
- Data Preprocessing: MLJ.jl includes a comprehensive suite of data

preprocessing and feature engineering tools, enabling users to clean and prepare their data for modeling.

- Model Evaluation: MLJ.jl supports various model evaluation techniques, such as cross-validation, bootstrapping, and holdout validation, helping users to estimate the performance of their models.
- Hyperparameter Tuning: MLJ.jl includes a wide range of tools for hyperparameter tuning, such as grid search, random search, and Bayesian optimization, helping users to find the best hyperparameters for their models.

The key goals of MLJ.jl are:

- Ease of Use: MLJ.jl is designed to be easy to use and accessible to a wide range of users, from beginners to experienced data scientists.
- Flexibility: MLJ.jl is flexible and can be used for a variety of machine learning tasks, from classification and regression to clustering and anomaly detection.
- Performance: MLJ.jl is designed for high-performance computing, leveraging the power of Julia's just-in-time (JIT) compilation and parallelization capabilities.
- Interoperability: MLJ.jl can be easily integrated with other Julia libraries, such as DataFrames.jl, Flux.jl, and DifferentialEquations.jl, allowing users to leverage the power of multiple libraries and frameworks.
- Community: MLJ.jl has a large and active community of developers and users, who contribute to the development and improvement of the library.

Overall, MLJ.jl is a powerful and flexible machine learning library that offers a range of tools and functionalities for solving a variety of machine learning problems. Whether you are a beginner or an experienced data scientist, MLJ.jl can help you to build and evaluate effective machine learning models.

Handling data in MLJ.jl

In machine learning, the quality and quantity of data play a crucial role in the success of a model. Before building a model, you first need to gather, clean, and prepare the data that you'll use to train the model.

MLJ.jl provides a number of tools and methods to handle different types of data. MLJ.jl provides a unified interface for handling tabular data, which is data organized in a table format with rows and columns. This is the most common type of data used in machine learning, and it's usually stored in a CSV (Comma Separated Values) or TSV (Tab Separated Values) file format.

In addition to tabular data, MLJ.jl also supports handling other types of data, such as text, images, and time series. For example, to work with text data, MLJ.jl provides tools to preprocess and vectorize text data, which converts text data into a numerical format that can be used as input for machine learning models. Similarly, MLJ.jl provides methods for loading and preprocessing image data, which is important for image classification and object detection tasks.

Data containers and Scitypes

In order to use the MLJ package for machine learning tasks, it is important to understand the basic assumptions about the form of data expected by MLJ. MLJ uses data containers and scientific types to represent data.

Data containers are objects that contain data, such as tuples, vectors, matrices, and tables. Each data container has a scientific type parameterized by scitype, which describes the scientific interpretation of the elements it contains.

Scientific types are Julia types defined in the ScientificTypesBase.jl package, and are used to declare the permitted scientific type of the inputs and targets that can be bound to a machine in MLJ. The package **ScientificTypes.jl** implements the convention used in the MLJ universe for assigning a specific scientific type to each Julia object.

The basic "**`scalar`**" scientific types in MLJ are **`Continuous`**, **`Multiclass{N}`**, **`OrderedFactor{N}`**, **`Count`**, **`Textual`**, **`Missing`**, and **`Nothing`**. It is important to ensure that scalar data is interpreted correctly by using tools to coerce the data to have the appropriate scientific type. Here are some examples of using scientific types in MLJ:

- **`scitype(4.6)`** returns **`Continuous`**, indicating that 4.6 has a continuous scientific interpretation.
- **`scitype(42)`** returns **`Count`**, indicating that 42 has a count scientific interpretation.
- `x1 = coerce(["yes", "no", "yes", "maybe"], Multiclass)` coerces a vector of strings to have a Multiclass{3} scientific interpretation.
- `X = (x1=x1, x2=rand(4), x3=rand(4))` creates a "column table" containing three columns, each with a different scientific interpretation. **`scitype(X)`** returns `Table{Union{AbstractVector{Continuous}, AbstractVector{Multiclass{3}}}}`, indicating that the table contains columns with either a continuous or `Multiclass{3}` scientific interpretation.

By understanding data containers and scientific types in MLJ, users can ensure that their data is properly represented and interpreted for machine learning tasks.

Handling 2D data in MLJ

When we talk about two-dimensional data in machine learning, we are referring to data that is organized in rows and columns, like a spreadsheet. In MLJ (a machine learning library in Julia), this type of data is typically represented as a table. A table is a data container that can be accessed using the **`Tables.jl`** interface and is represented as a Table{K}, where K depends on the scientific types of the columns.

We can create a table from this matrix by calling **`MLJ.table(M)`**, where M is dimension. The resulting table will have the same number of rows and columns as the matrix, and the types of columns will be inferred from the values in the matrix. If we have a matrix (that is, an array of numbers) that we want to use as two-dimensional data in MLJ, we can wrap it as a table using the **`MLJ.table`** function.

To inspect the types of data in a table, we can use the schema function. For example, suppose we have a table X with three columns, the first column containing categorical values, and the second and third columns containing continuous values. We can use **`schema(X)`** to get a summary of the types:

```
julia> using Tables, MLJ

julia> X = table([1 4.0 "7"; 2 5.0 "8"; 3 6.0 "9"])
Tables.MatrixTable{Matrix{Any}} with 3 rows, 3 columns, and schema:
 :x1  Any
 :x2  Any
 :x3  Any

julia> schema(X)
┌───────┬────────────┬───────┐
│ names │ scitypes   │ types │
├───────┼────────────┼───────┤
│ x1    │ Count      │ Any   │
│ x2    │ Continuous │ Any   │
│ x3    │ Textual    │ Any   │
└───────┴────────────┴───────┘


julia> matrix = MLJ.matrix(X)
3×3 Matrix{Any}:
 1  4.0  "7"
 2  5.0  "8"
 3  6.0  "9"
```

***Figure 11.1**: Two-dimensional tabular and non-tabular data*

It is important to note that creating a table from a matrix using the **`MLJ.table`** function does not make a copy of the original matrix. Instead, the matrix is simply wrapped as a table, so changes made to the original matrix will also be reflected in the table. Conversely, if we want to convert a table back to a matrix, we can use the **`MLJ.matrix`** function.

To summarize, when using MLJ models with tables or matrices as input, it's important to make sure that the data is organized in the correct format. Each row should represent a different observation, and each column should represent a different feature of that observation. Additionally, the target data should be an **`AbstractVector`**, and if it has multiple values per observation, it can be represented as a table.

Machine Learning in Julia (MLJ) models typically assume tables as input, following the **`Tables.jl`** interface. However, it clarifies that any container adhering to the **`Tables.jl`** interface and containing compatible scientific types can be used as input. This flexibility means that users are not restricted to using only tables; they can employ various data structures or containers that meet the specified interface requirements and hold the appropriate data types. This design choice enhances the versatility of MLJ, allowing users to work with diverse data representations while still benefiting from the model's capabilities. Similarly, the target data should have a scientific type that is compatible with the model's **`target_scitype`**.

By organizing the data correctly and ensuring that it has the correct scientific type, it becomes easier to work with MLJ models and get accurate predictions from them.

When using MLJ models, it is important to know what types of data are acceptable as inputs and targets. You can inspect the admissible scientific types of a model's input and target without loading the code defining the model. This can be done using the info function in MLJ.

For example, if we want to inspect the admissible scientific types of the **`DecisionTreeClassifier`** model in the DecisionTree package, we can do:

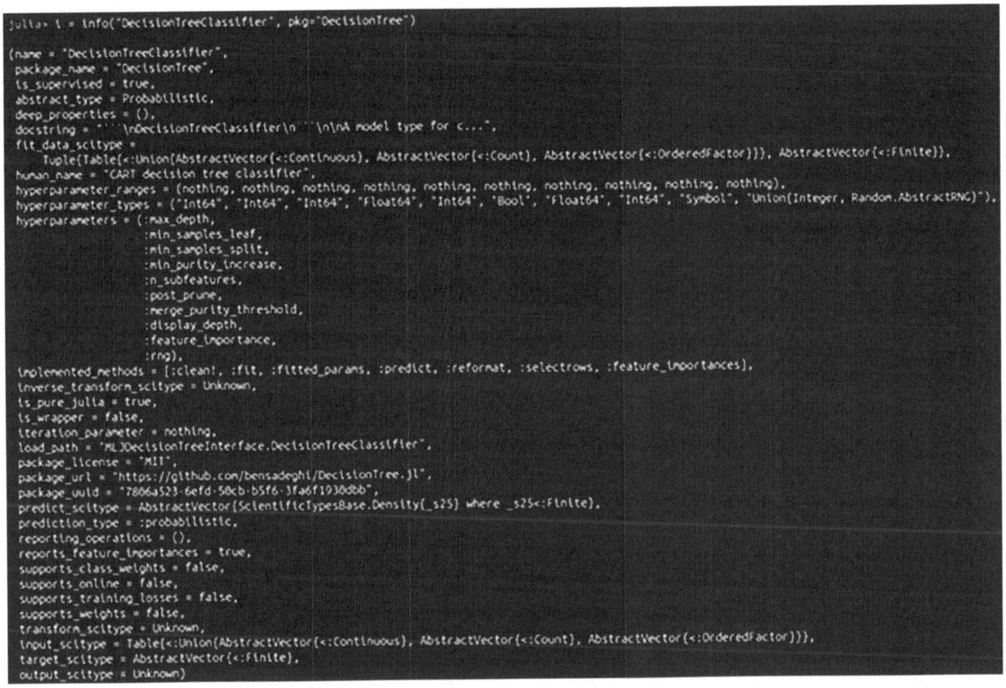

```
julia> i = info("DecisionTreeClassifier", pkg="DecisionTree")

(name = "DecisionTreeClassifier",
 package_name = "DecisionTree",
 is_supervised = true,
 abstract_type = Probabilistic,
 deep_properties = (),
 docstring = "```\nDecisionTreeClassifier\n```\n\nA model type for c...",
 fit_data_scitype =
     Tuple{Table{<:Union{AbstractVector{<:Continuous}, AbstractVector{<:Count}, AbstractVector{<:OrderedFactor}}}, AbstractVector{<:Finite}},
 human_name = "CART decision tree classifier",
 hyperparameter_ranges = (nothing, nothing, nothing, nothing, nothing, nothing, nothing, nothing, nothing, nothing),
 hyperparameter_types = ("Int64", "Int64", "Int64", "Float64", "Int64", "Bool", "Float64", "Int64", "Symbol", "Union{Integer, Random.AbstractRNG}"),
 hyperparameters = (:max_depth,
                    :min_samples_leaf,
                    :min_samples_split,
                    :min_purity_increase,
                    :n_subfeatures,
                    :post_prune,
                    :merge_purity_threshold,
                    :display_depth,
                    :feature_importance,
                    :rng),
 implemented_methods = [:clean!, :fit, :fitted_params, :predict, :reformat, :selectrows, :feature_importances],
 inverse_transform_scitype = Unknown,
 is_pure_julia = true,
 is_wrapper = false,
 iteration_parameter = nothing,
 load_path = "MLJDecisionTreeInterface.DecisionTreeClassifier",
 package_license = "MIT",
 package_url = "https://github.com/bensadeghi/DecisionTree.jl",
 package_uuid = "7806a523-6efd-50cb-b5f6-3fa6f1930dbb",
 predict_scitype = AbstractVector{ScientificTypesBase.Density{_s25} where _s25<:Finite},
 prediction_type = :probabilistic,
 reporting_operations = (),
 reports_feature_importances = true,
 supports_class_weights = false,
 supports_online = false,
 supports_training_losses = false,
 supports_weights = false,
 transform_scitype = Unknown,
 input_scitype = Table{<:Union{AbstractVector{<:Continuous}, AbstractVector{<:Count}, AbstractVector{<:OrderedFactor}}},
 target_scitype = AbstractVector{<:Finite},
 output_scitype = Unknown)
```

Figure 11.2: *Basic information about the Decision Tree classifier in the package*

This returns an object that contains a lot of information about the model. We can inspect the admissible scientific types for the model's input and target by accessing **`i.input_scitype`** and **`i.target_scitype`**, respectively.

For the **`DecisionTreeClassifier`**, we see that the input is acceptable as a Table with columns of type **`Continuous`**, **`Count`**, or **`OrderedFactor`**. The target is acceptable as a vector with element **`scitype <: Finite`**.

Knowing the admissible scientific types of a model's input and target is important because it ensures that we provide data that the model can process.

Scitypes of data

In machine learning, it is essential to understand the nature of the data and its type before modeling it. MLJ follows the convention described in **ScientificTypes.jl** to interpret the elements of container types. According to this convention, here are the key features:

- **`AbstractFloat`** is interpreted as Continuous.
- Integer is interpreted as Count.

- **CategoricalValue** is interpreted as Multiclass or **OrderedFactor**, depending on the value of **isordered(x)**.
- Strings and Chars are not interpreted as Multiclass or **OrderedFactor**; they have **scitypes** Textual and Unknown, respectively.
- Integers (including Bools) cannot represent categorical data, so use the preceding coerce operations to coerce to a Finite **scitype**.
- The scientific types of nothing and missing are Nothing and Missing, native types that we also regard as scientific.

You can use the coerce function to change the scientific type of an array or a table. Here's an example:

```
julia> using MLJ, CategoricalArrays, DataFrames

julia> X = DataFrame(name=["Siri", "Robo", "Alexa", "Cortana"],
                     height=[152, missing, 148, 163],
                     rating=[1, 5, 2, 1])
4×3 DataFrame
 Row │ name     height   rating
─────┼──────────────────────────
   1 │ Siri        152        1
   2 │ Robo                   5
   3 │ Alexa       148        2
   4 │ Cortana     163        1

julia> Xc = coerce(X, :name=>Multiclass, :height=>Continuous, :rating=>OrderedFactor)
┌ Info: Trying to coerce from `Union{Missing, Int64}` to `Continuous`.
└ Coerced to `Union{Missing,Continuous}` instead.
4×3 DataFrame
 Row │ name     height    rating
─────┼───────────────────────────
   1 │ Siri        152.0  1
   2 │ Robo                5
   3 │ Alexa       148.0  2
   4 │ Cortana     163.0  1

julia> schema(Xc).scitypes # (Multiclass, Continuous, OrderedFactor)
(Multiclass{4}, Union{Missing, Continuous}, OrderedFactor{3})
```

Figure 11.3: *Varying scitypes of tabular data in MLJ*

This code coerces a **DataFrame** X so that the name column is of type Multiclass, the height column is of type Continuous, and the rating column is of type **OrderedFactor**. The schema function is then used to retrieve the scitypes of the columns of the new DataFrame.

The function **scitype(X)** in **ScientificTypes.jl** returns the scientific type (interpretation) of X, as distinct from its machine type. For example, **scitype(3.14)** returns **Continuous**, **scitype([1, 2, missing])** returns **AbstractVector{Union{Missing, Count}}**, and **scitype((5, "beige"))** returns **Tuple{Count, Textual}**.

To convert a table X to a copy of X with element scientific types matching a new specification specs, you can use the coerce function. The specs argument can be either one or more **column_name=>Scitype** pairs, one or more **OldScitype=>NewScitype** pairs, or a dictionary of scientific types keyed on column names. For example, **coerce(X, :name=>Multiclass, :height=>Continuous, :rating=>OrderedFactor)** converts a DataFrame X to a new DataFrame Xc with column scientific types **Multiclass**, **Continuous**, and **OrderedFactor**.

Generating data

Generating Synthetic Data means creating fake data that looks similar to real data, but we know it's not real. We can use this fake data to test and try out our machine learning models, without worrying about hurting anyone's privacy or violating any laws.

MLJ has some functions called **make_blobs**, **make_circles**, **make_moons**, and **make_regression** that can help us create these mock data sets. For example, we can use **make_blobs** to create clusters of points (like bubbles) that we can use to test clustering algorithms.

make_blobs function can create a table of data with a certain number of rows and columns (features) and a corresponding vector of "target" labels that tell us which blob (cluster) each data point belongs to. We can adjust the properties of these blobs, like the number of clusters, their size and shape, and whether they are shuffled or not.

Here's an example code using **make_blobs** to create two clusters with different sizes:

```
julia> using MLJ, DataFrames
julia> X, y = make_blobs(100, 3; centers=2, cluster_std=[1.0, 3.0])
(Tables.MatrixTable{Matrix{Float64}} with 100 rows, 3 columns, and
schema:
 :x1  Float64
 :x2  Float64
 :x3  Float64, CategoricalValue{Int64, UInt32}[1, 1, 2, 1, 1, 2, 2, 2,
1, 1 … 2, 2, 1, 2, 2, 1, 1, 1, 2, 1])
julia> dfBlobs = DataFrame(X)
100×3 DataFrame
 Row │ x1          x2          x3
```

```
        │ Float64     Float64       Float64
────┼──────────────────────
   1 │  -1.99141   8.24332   -4.65529
   2 │  -4.04924   7.55333   -2.42757
        ⋮

julia> dfBlobs.y = y
100-element CategoricalArray{Int64,1,UInt32}:
 1

 ⋮


 1
julia> first(dfBlobs, 3)
3×4 DataFrame
 Row │ x1      x2      x3     y
       │ Float64        Cat…
────┼──────────────────────────
   1 │ -1.99141  8.24332  -4.65529  1
   2 │ -4.04924  7.55333  -2.42757  1
   3 │ -9.00246  3.44369   6.91574  2
```

This code generates a table with 100 rows and 3 columns (features) and two clusters of data points. The clusters have different sizes, with the second one being three times larger than the first one. We use the **DataFrames** package to create a **DataFrame** from the table of data, and add the target labels to it. Finally, we display the first three rows of the **DataFrame** to see what the data looks like.

We can also choose how many blobs we want, how spread out they are, and other things like that. After we make the pretend dataset, we can use it to test different types of computer programs and see how well they can understand the blobs and make predictions about them.

Regression data

Let's say you have some data, and you want to find a relationship between them. For example, you might have the height and weight of a bunch of people, and you want to know how height is related to weight.

Now, imagine that there is a relationship between height and weight that can be described by a straight line. The **make_regression** function can help you generate some data that follows this relationship, but with some added noise to make it more realistic.

Here's an example code:

```
julia> using MLJ, DataFrames

julia> X, y = make_regression(100, 5; noise=0.5, sparse=0.2,
outliers=0.1)

(Tables.MatrixTable{Matrix{Float64}} with 100 rows, 5 columns, and
schema:

 :x1  Float64

 :x2  Float64

 :x3  Float64

 :x4  Float64

 :x5  Float64, [-0.854598521465274,  … 2.287388237748642])

julia> dfRegression = DataFrame(X)

100×5 DataFrame

 Row │ x1            x2          x3           x4           x5

     │ Float64      Float64     Float64      Float64      Float64

─────┼──────────────────────────────────────────────────────────────

   1 │ -0.736704    -0.171908    0.0129722   0.400937     0.892407

                ⋮

 100 │ -0.660374     0.374358    0.253689   -2.3867   -1.94786

                                                   54 rows omitted

julia> dfRegression.y = y

100-element Vector{Float64}:

 -0.854598521465274

  ⋮

  2.287388237748642

julia> first(dfRegression, 3)

3×6 DataFrame

 Row │ x1            x2          x3           x4           x5
y

     │ Float64      Float64     Float64      Float64      Float64
```

```
Float64
─────┼──────────────────────────────────────────────────────────────
─
   1 │ -0.736704  -0.171908   0.0129722   0.400937  0.892407    -0.854599
   2 │ -0.463261   0.63076   -0.971391   -1.34927   0.252629
0.11885
   3 │ -1.50237   -1.338920.403449   -1.01186   0.0327883  -7.82129
```

In this example, we're generating 100 observations with five features (columns) and one continuous target variable (y). The noise parameter determines the amount of noise we add to the data, making it more difficult to see the true relationship between the features and the target. The sparse parameter determines the sparsity of the generating weight vector (that is, how many of the features are important). The outliers parameter determines the proportion of the response vector to make as outliers by adding a random quantity with high variance.

The output of the function is a tuple (X, y) where X is a table (or matrix) with the generated features, and y is a vector of the generated target values. We then convert the output into a `DataFrame` for easier manipulation and visualization.

Categorical data

Categorical data is a type of data that represents the characteristics or qualities of an object, person, or group. It consists of a limited number of values or categories that describe the attribute being measured. Examples of categorical data include gender, race, color, occupation, and education level.

Working with categorical data involves several steps to analyze, process, and model the data. Here are some key considerations when working with categorical data:

- **Data exploration**: Begin by examining the distribution of the categorical variables in your dataset. This can be done by creating frequency tables or visualizations, such as bar charts or pie charts.
- **Data cleaning**: Categorical data may contain missing values, inconsistent values, or typos. You may need to impute missing values or correct errors to ensure the data is accurate and complete.
- **Data encoding**: Categorical data needs to be transformed into a numerical form to be used in machine learning models.

Handling categorical data

We implement categorical variables in the MLJ machine learning library in Julia by using the `**CategoricalArrays.jl**` package to handle categorical values.

To create a categorical vector from raw labels, one can use the categorical function. The resulting v variable is of type **`CategoricalVector{Char, UInt32, Char, CategoricalValue{Char, UInt32}, Union{}}`** and represents a Multiclass vector with three levels.

When indexing a **`CategoricalVector`**, one gets a **`CategoricalValue`** instance instead of a raw label. The **`CategoricalValue`** knows the complete pool of levels from the vector from which it came.

To construct a **`UnivariateFinite`** distribution, which is the type of distribution returned by most probabilistic classifiers, one can use the **`UnivariateFinite`** constructor. The resulting d variable represents a distribution over the levels "no" and "yes" with probabilities 0.9 and 0.1, respectively. The pool argument is used to specify the set of levels that the distribution can take. To create a vector of **`UnivariateFinite`** distributions, one can use the **`UnivariateFiniteVector`** constructor.

```
julia> v = categorical(['A', 'B', 'A', 'A', 'C'])
5-element CategoricalArray{Char,1,UInt32}:
 'A'
 'B'
 'A'
 'A'
 'C'

julia> v = coerce(["yes", "no", "yes", "yes", "maybe"], Multiclass)
5-element CategoricalArray{String,1,UInt32}:
 "yes"
 "no"
 "yes"
 "yes"
 "maybe"

julia> d = UnivariateFinite(["no", "yes"], [0.9, 0.1], pool=v)
         UnivariateFinite{Multiclass{3}}

    no  ████████████████████ 0.9
   yes  ██ 0.1

julia> yes_probs = rand(5)
5-element Vector{Float64}:
 0.903286258421596
 0.4958288952816045
 0.4103332376289902
 0.9924666809751606
 0.6357305308038362

julia> probs = hcat(1 .- yes_probs, yes_probs)
5×2 Matrix{Float64}:
 0.0967137   0.903286
 0.504171    0.495829
 0.589667    0.410333
 0.00753332  0.992467
 0.364269    0.635731

julia> d_vec = UnivariateFinite(["no", "yes"], probs, pool=v)
5-element CategoricalDistributions.UnivariateFiniteVector{Multiclass{3}, String, UInt32, Float64}:
 UnivariateFinite{Multiclass{3}}(no=>0.0967, yes=>0.903)
 UnivariateFinite{Multiclass{3}}(no=>0.504, yes=>0.496)
 UnivariateFinite{Multiclass{3}}(no=>0.59, yes=>0.41)
 UnivariateFinite{Multiclass{3}}(no=>0.00753, yes=>0.992)
 UnivariateFinite{Multiclass{3}}(no=>0.364, yes=>0.636)
```

Figure 11.4: *Categorical values of varying mathematical and Boolean values*

The resulting **d_vec** variable is a vector of five **UnivariateFinite** distributions, each with levels "no" and "yes" and probabilities specified by the probs matrix.

Correct data scientific type for categorical data

In machine learning, it is important to ensure that your data is in the correct format for the algorithms you plan to use. MLJ uses scientific types to articulate the data requirements of models. There are three scientific types for discrete data: **Count**, **OrderedFactor**, and **Multiclass**.

Count data is used for data that represents a count or frequency of something. This type of data is generally unbounded, such as the number of phone calls or the population of a city. In MLJ, Count is represented as an **AbstractVector{Count}**.

OrderedFactor is used for data that has a natural ordering, such as the number of legs on an animal or the number of rooms in a house. This type of data is finite and can be coerced to an ordered set of integers. In MLJ, **OrderedFactor** is represented as an **AbstractVector{OrderedFactor}**.

Multiclass is used for unordered categorical data, such as the color of a car or the species of an animal. This type of data is also finite and can be coerced to a set of integers. In MLJ, Multiclass is represented as an `**AbstractVector{Multiclass}**`.

Binary data, which is data that can take only two values (for example, true/false, yes/no), can be represented as either **OrderedFactor{2}** if the data has a natural ordering or Multiclass{2} if the data is unordered. In MLJ, Binary data is represented as an `**AbstractVector{OrderedFactor}**` or `**AbstractVector{Multiclass}**`, depending on whether the data is ordered or unordered.

Changing the incorrect scitype of categorical data

First, we inspect the scientific type of data using the **scitype** function. To inspect all column scientific types in a table simultaneously, the schema function can be used.

Then, to coerce a single column, the coerce function is used. The machine type of the result is a `**CategoricalArray**`. To inspect the order of the levels, the levels function can be used. If needed, the `**levels!()**` function can be used to change the order of the levels.

Lastly, to coerce all remaining types simultaneously, the coerce function is used with the desired types specified for each column. In this example, the columns gender, **likes_soup**, height, and rating are coerced to `` `Multiclass` ``, `` `OrderedFactor` ``, `` `Continuous` ``, and `` `OrderedFactor` ``, respectively. In-place coercion can also be done using `` `coerce!()` ``.

Suppose you have a dataset that contains information about the passengers on the Titanic, and one of the columns is "`Embarked`" which contains the port of embarkation for each passenger (either "`S`", "`C`", or "`Q`"). However, upon inspecting the column with **`describe()`** function, you notice that it's being treated as a string, rather than a categorical variable.

```
julia> using DataFrames

julia> df = DataFrame(PassengerId = 1:5,
                      Embarked = ["S", "C", "S", "S", "Q"])
5×2 DataFrame
 Row │ PassengerId  Embarked
─────┼───────────────────────
   1 │           1  S
   2 │           2  C
   3 │           3  S
   4 │           4  S
   5 │           5  Q

julia> describe(df)
2×7 DataFrame
 Row │ variable     mean     min  median  max  nmissing  eltype
─────┼──────────────────────────────────────────────────────────
   1 │ PassengerId  3.0      1    3.0     5           0  Int64
   2 │ Embarked              C            S           0  String

julia> using CategoricalArrays

julia> df.Embarked = coerce(CategoricalArray(df.Embarked), OrderedFactor)
5-element CategoricalArray{String,1,UInt32}:
 "S"
 "C"
 "S"
 "S"
 "Q"

julia> describe(df)
2×7 DataFrame
 Row │ variable     mean     min  median  max  nmissing  eltype
─────┼──────────────────────────────────────────────────────────────────────────
   1 │ PassengerId  3.0      1    3.0     5           0  Int64
   2 │ Embarked              C            S           0  CategoricalValue{String, UInt32}
```

Figure 11.5: *Varying ways to see a dataframe object*

To properly represent this data as a categorical variable, you can use the **`CategoricalArrays`** package and the **`coerce()`** function. Now, the "**`Embarked`**" column is properly represented as a categorical variable.

Tracking all various categories

Imagine you have a toy box with different types of toys, such as balls, cars, and dolls. Let's say you want to pick only the red toys from the box. You don't want to lose track of the other types of toys in the box, so you separate the red toys while keeping the rest in the box.

In the same way, when we have data with different categories, such as different colors or types of toys, we want to keep track of all the categories, even if we only use some of them for a specific analysis. We do this by using a special type of code called "**`OrderedFactor`**" or "**`Multiclass`**", which allows us to track all the categories even when we only use some of them.

```
julia> cars = DataFrame(
           make = ["Toyota", "Honda", "Ford", "Toyota", "Honda"],
           model = ["Camry", "Accord", "Fusion", "Corolla", "Civic"],
           cylinders = [4, 4, 4, 4, 6]
       )
5×3 DataFrame
 Row │ make    model    cylinders
─────┼─────────────────────────────
   1 │ Toyota  Camry            4
   2 │ Honda   Accord           4
   3 │ Ford    Fusion           4
   4 │ Toyota  Corolla          4
   5 │ Honda   Civic            6

julia> using CategoricalArrays

julia> cars.cylinders = categorical(cars.cylinders)
5-element CategoricalArray{Int64,1,UInt32}:
 4
 4
 4
 4
 6

julia> levels(cars.cylinders)
2-element Vector{Int64}:
 4
 6

julia> row = cars[1, :]
DataFrameRow
 Row │ make    model   cylinders
─────┼────────────────────────────
   1 │ Toyota  Camry   4

julia> levels(row.cylinders)
2-element Vector{Int64}:
 4
 6
```

Figure 11.6: *Non-mathematical categorical values*

Suppose you have a dataset containing information about cars, including the make, model, and the number of cylinders in the engine. The number of cylinders is a categorical variable since it can only take a small number of discrete values (for example, 4, 6, or 8).

The cylinders column has been represented as integers, which is a common mistake when working with categorical data. To properly represent this variable, we can use the **`CategoricalArrays`** package. Now, we can inspect the levels of this variable. This returns an array of the possible values that the cylinders variable can take.

We can also access individual rows or subsets of the data, while preserving the information about the possible levels of the categorical variable. By properly representing categorical data in this way, we can ensure that our models are correctly handling the information and that we are not losing any important information about the variable.

Preparing data

Preparing data is a crucial step in any data analysis or machine learning project. It involves transforming raw data into a format that is suitable for analysis, modeling, and decision-making. Proper data preparation ensures that the data is accurate, consistent, complete, and in a structure that can be easily utilized by the algorithms or methods being applied.

Splitting data

There are two tools in MLJ for splitting data: partition and unpack.

partition is used for vertically splitting data (that is, splitting by observations), while unpack is used for horizontally splitting data (that is, breaking up a table based on feature names).

Using partition:

```
julia> using MLJBase

julia> # split multiple objects "synchronously"

      (Xtrain, Xtest), (ytrain, ytest) = partition((X, y), 0.8,
rng=123, multi=true)

(((x1 = [6.546574333729479,  … , 6.402576222222763])),
(CategoricalArrays.CategoricalValue{Int64, UInt32}[3, 1,  … , 3],
CategoricalArrays.CategoricalValue{Int64, UInt32}[1, …, 2]))
```

In the example, partition is used to split multiple objects **`"synchronously"`**, that is, X and y are split at the same indices, with 80% of the data in **`Xtrain`** and **`ytrain`**, and 20% of the data in **`Xtest`** and **`ytest`**.

Using unpack:

The unpack function is used to split the DataFrame into a dependent variable y and a set of independent variables X. The first argument to unpack is the DataFrame to split, and the second argument is a predicate that selects the dependent variable. In this case, **`==(:Species)`** selects the Species column, which contains the names of the different types of Iris flowers. The third argument is a predicate that selects all other columns by returning true for each column. In other words, **`colname -> true`** selects all columns in the DataFrame except for the Species column.

```
julia> using MLJ, RDatasets

julia> iris = dataset("datasets", "iris"); # a DataFrame

julia> y, X = unpack(iris, ==(:Species), colname -> true);

julia> first(X, 3) |> pretty
┌─────────────┬────────────┬─────────────┬────────────┐
│ SepalLength │ SepalWidth │ PetalLength │ PetalWidth │
│ Float64     │ Float64    │ Float64     │ Float64    │
│ Continuous  │ Continuous │ Continuous  │ Continuous │
├─────────────┼────────────┼─────────────┼────────────┤
│ 5.1         │ 3.5        │ 1.4         │ 0.2        │
│ 4.9         │ 3.0        │ 1.4         │ 0.2        │
│ 4.7         │ 3.2        │ 1.3         │ 0.2        │
└─────────────┴────────────┴─────────────┴────────────┘
```

***Figure 11.7**: Using `unpack` with datasets*

Finally, the pretty function is used to print the first three rows of the X DataFrame, which contains the measurements of the four attributes for each flower. The output shows the first three rows of the X DataFrame, which has four columns (**`SepalLength`**, **`SepalWidth`**, **`PetalLength`**, and **`PetalWidth`**) and three rows. The Continuous annotation for each column indicates that the data type is a continuous variable.

Note that partition has options like shuffle for shuffling the rows, rng for specifying the random number generator, and stratify for matching the stratification of a given vector. Similarly, unpack has options like **`wrap_singles`** for wrapping a single-column table as a vector, and **`coerce_options`** for specifying options for data type conversion.

Addressing the mismatched scitype of data-model

However, sometimes the function call fails because the input data has mixed scientific types. Specifically, height is a count variable, while time is continuous, mark is textual, and admitted is multiclass. Most supervised learning models require input features to be of a single continuous type. Therefore, we need to preprocess the data.

MLJ offers two tools to address data-model type mismatches, including:

- **Scientific type coercion**: This involves converting the data to the intended scientific interpretation. For example, if height is supposed to be continuous, mark is an ordered factor, and admitted is a binary multiclass, we can use the coerce function to convert the data to the intended scientific type.
- **Feature engineering**: This involves transforming the data by creating new features, selecting relevant features, or reducing the dimensionality of the data.

We will learn about searching and loading models in MLJ. Then we will revisit other transformation functions used for preparing data in MLJ.

Weights

In machine learning, weights can be used to assign more importance to certain samples or classes during model training and evaluation. In the MLJ (Machine Learning in Julia) framework, weights can be specified in both training and performance evaluation. The two types of weights are:

- **per observation weights**: weight vectors with the same length as the number of observations
- **class weights**: dictionaries that are keyed on the target classes (levels) used in classification problems

To specify weights in training, we need to bind the weights to the model along with the data when constructing a machine. To specify weights in performance evaluation, we need to provide the weights as the last argument when calling an MLJ measure (metric) that supports weights.

Models

In machine learning, a model is a mathematical representation of a real-world system or process. The model takes inputs, processes them using mathematical operations, and produces an output that can be used to make predictions or decisions.

In supervised learning, a model is trained on a labeled dataset, where the input data and the corresponding output or label are known. The model learns to map inputs to outputs by minimizing the difference between its predictions and the true outputs in the training data. Once the model is trained, it can be used to make predictions on new, unseen data.

In unsupervised learning, the model is trained on an unlabeled dataset, where only the input data is known. The goal is to find patterns or structure in the data without any prior knowledge of what the output should be.

Models in machine learning can take many forms, such as decision trees, neural networks, linear regression, support vector machines, and clustering algorithms, to name a few. The choice of model depends on the specific task and the characteristics of the data being used.

Supervised Learning Models:

- **Linear Regression**: Linear regression is a type of regression model used for predicting a continuous output variable based on one or more input features. It works by fitting a linear equation to the training data, which can then be used to make predictions on new data.
- **Logistic Regression**: Logistic regression is a type of classification model used for predicting a binary output variable (0 or 1) based on one or more input features. It works by fitting a logistic function to the training data, which can then be used to predict the probability of a given input belonging to the positive class.
- **Decision Trees**: Decision trees are a type of model used for both classification and regression tasks. They work by recursively partitioning the input space into smaller subsets based on the values of the input features, and making decisions based on these partitions.
- **Random Forests**: Random forests are an extension of decision trees that use an ensemble of decision trees to make predictions. They work by randomly sampling subsets of the input data and features, and building decision trees on each subset. The final prediction is then made by aggregating the predictions of all the individual decision trees.
- **Support Vector Machines (SVMs)**: SVMs are a type of model used for classification and regression tasks. They work by finding the hyperplane that best separates the input data into different classes or predicts the output variable in a regression problem.

Unsupervised Learning Models:

- **K-Means Clustering**: K-means clustering is a type of clustering algorithm used for partitioning a dataset into K distinct clusters based on their similarities. It works by iteratively updating the cluster centers until the clusters are well separated.
- **Principal Component Analysis (PCA)**: PCA is a type of dimensionality reduction technique used for finding the underlying structure in high-dimensional data. It works by identifying the principal components of the data that explain the maximum amount of variance.
- **Autoencoders**: Autoencoders are a type of neural network used for unsupervised learning. They work by learning to encode and decode input data, which can be used for tasks such as anomaly detection and image generation.
- **Gaussian Mixture Models (GMMs)**: GMMs are a type of probabilistic model used for clustering and density estimation tasks. They work by

modeling the input data as a mixture of Gaussian distributions, and using the maximum likelihood method to estimate the parameters of the model.

- **t-SNE**: t-SNE is a type of dimensionality reduction technique used for visualizing high-dimensional data in a low-dimensional space. It works by modeling the similarity between data points in the high-dimensional space and the low-dimensional space, and minimizing the difference between the two.

Model search

In machine learning, a model is a mathematical representation of a system or process that generates predictions or decisions based on input data.

In MLJ, a model registry is available to search models and their properties efficiently without loading all the packages containing model codes. This helps to find all models that can solve a specific machine learning task. The task is defined using the matching method and the search is executed with the models method.

To obtain information about a model, the `info()` command can be used. This returns a named tuple containing metadata, such as the name of the model, the package it is from, whether it is supervised or unsupervised, the input and output types it expects, the implemented methods, the hyperparameters and their ranges, and other properties such as whether it supports class weights, online learning, or training losses. You can find all the MLJ models at https://alan-turing-institute.github.io/MLJ.jl/dev/list_of_supported_models/#model_list. For example, the following code retrieves information about the DBSCAN model from the Clustering package. You need to specify the package name as the DBSCAN model is also in `MLJScikitLearnInterface`.

```
julia> info("DBSCAN", pkg="Clustering")
(name = "DBSCAN",
 package_name = "Clustering",
 is_supervised = false,
 abstract_type = Static,
 deep_properties = (),
 docstring = "```\nDBSCAN\n```\n\nA model type for constructing a DB...",
 fit_data_scitype = Tuple{},
 human_name =
     "DBSCAN clusterer (density-based spatial clustering of applications with noise)",
 hyperparameter_ranges = (nothing, nothing, nothing, nothing),
 hyperparameter_types = ("Real", "Int64", "Int64", "Int64"),
 hyperparameters = (:radius, :leafsize, :min_neighbors, :min_cluster_size),
 implemented_methods = [:clean!, :predict],
 inverse_transform_scitype = Table{<:AbstractVector{<:Continuous}},
 is_pure_julia = true,
 is_wrapper = false,
 iteration_parameter = nothing,
 load_path = "MLJClusteringInterface.DBSCAN",
 package_license = "MIT",
 package_url = "https://github.com/JuliaStats/Clustering.jl",
 package_uuid = "aaaa29a8-35af-508c-8bc3-b662a17a0fe5",
 predict_scitype = Unknown,
 prediction_type = :unknown,
 reporting_operations = (:predict,),
 reports_feature_importances = false,
 supports_class_weights = false,
 supports_online = false,
 supports_training_losses = false,
 supports_weights = false,
 transform_scitype = Unknown,
 input_scitype = Table{<:AbstractVector{<:Continuous}},
 target_scitype = Unknown,
 output_scitype = Unknown)
```

Figure 11.8: *Retrieves information about the DBSCAN model from the Clustering package*

The **doc()** function can be used to retrieve the model's documentation string without importing the code:

```
julia> doc("RandomForestClassifier", pkg="DecisionTree")
  RandomForestClassifier
  A model type for constructing a CART random forest classifier, based on
  DecisionTree.jl (https://github.com/bensadeghi/DecisionTree.jl), and
  implementing the MLJ model interface.
```

Model queries

This is used in the MLJ machine learning package to list and query available models.

Here is a brief explanation of the code:

- The **models()** function lists all available models in the MLJ package. It returns a vector of named tuples, where each tuple represents a machine learning model.

- The **localmodels()** function lists only the models for which the code is already loaded. It returns the same output format as **models()**.
- The named tuple returned by each function contains information about the model, such as its name, package name, abstract type, hyperparameters, and implemented methods.
- The **models()** function can be used to search for models containing specified strings or regular expressions in their docstring attribute.

Here's a sample code snippet showing how you can use these functions to query models:

```
julia> # List all available models
       all_models = models()
208-element Vector{NamedTuple{(:name, … , :output_scitype)}}:
(name = ABODDetector, package_name = OutlierDetectionNeighbors, ... )
 ⋮
(name = XGBoostRegressor, package_name = XGBoost, ... )
julia> # List only the models for which code is already loaded
       loaded_models = localmodels()
15-element Vector{NamedTuple{(:name, … , :output_scitype)}}:
 (name = ConstantClassifier, package_name = MLJModels, ... )
 ⋮
 (name = UnivariateTimeTypeToContinuous, package_name = MLJModels, ... )
```

This code first imports the MLJ package and then uses the **models()** and **localmodels()** functions to list all available models and the models for which code is already loaded, respectively.

Models matching

In the context of the MLJ (Machine Learning in Julia) package, the matching command is used to check whether a given model is compatible with input data and target variables of certain scientific types. Specifically, **matching(model, X, y)** returns true if the model is supervised and can accept inputs of type X and targets of type y, and **matching(model, X)** returns true if the model is unsupervised and can accept inputs of type X.

To search for all supervised probabilistic models that can handle input X and target y, one can define a testing function task that checks for model compatibility and probabilistic prediction, as follows:

```
task(model) = matching(model, X, y) && model.prediction_type ==
:probabilistic
```

This function returns true if the model can handle inputs of type X and targets of type y, and if it makes probabilistic predictions. Then, the search for such models can be executed using the models function:

```
models(task)
```

The models function lists all models in the MLJ registry that satisfy a given filter. By default, calling models() returns a list of all models in the registry, while calling **`models(filters..)`** returns a list of models that satisfy all given filters.

For example, to search for all models that are compatible with input X and target y, one can execute:

```
models(matching(X, y))
```

This returns a list of all supervised models that can handle inputs of type X and targets of type y.

Alternatively, one can use the models function with a do block and a customized filter to achieve the same result:

```
models() do model

        matching(model, X, y) &&

        model.prediction_type == :probabilistic

end
```

The **`localmodels`** function is similar to models, but it only lists models that are currently available to the user from a given module (by default, the Main module). The **`localmodels`** function can also take one or more filters to narrow down the list of models.

To load a specific model from the list returned by **`localmodels`**, one can use the **`load_path`** function, as in the following example:

```
ms = localmodels()

model = ms[1]

load_path(model)
```

Here, ms is a list of all models available in the current module, model is the first model in the list, and **`load_path(model)`** returns the path to the file defining the model.

Loading models

The process of loading a model in MLJ involves identifying the name of the model and the package that provides the MLJ interface for that model. Once these are identified, you can use the **`@load`** macro to load the model type into your current module, package, or function.

To use **`@load`**, you need to have the package providing the MLJ interface installed in your environment. You can determine the package by calling **`load_path(model_name, pkg="algorithm-providing package name")`**, where **`model_name`** is the name of the model you want to use, and pkg is the name of the package providing the algorithm for that model. This function returns the load path for the model type. If the MLJ interface package is not already installed in your environment, you can add it using **`Pkg.add("MLJAlgorithmInterface")`**.

Once you have the MLJ interface package installed, you can use **`@load`** to load the model type. For example, if you want to use the **`DecisionTreeClassifier`** model from the **DecisionTree.jl** package, you can call **`@load DecisionTreeClassifier pkg=DecisionTree`**. This will load the **`DecisionTreeClassifier`** model type into your current module, package, or function, and you can create an instance of the model using **`Tree()`**.

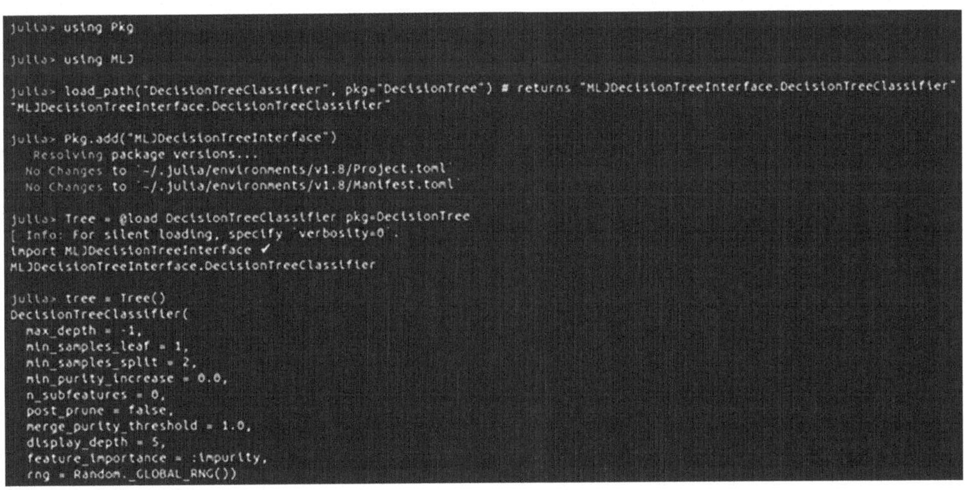

```
julia> using Pkg

julia> using MLJ

julia> load_path("DecisionTreeClassifier", pkg="DecisionTree") # returns "MLJDecisionTreeInterface.DecisionTreeClassifier"
"MLJDecisionTreeInterface.DecisionTreeClassifier"

julia> Pkg.add("MLJDecisionTreeInterface")
   Resolving package versions...
  No Changes to `~/.julia/environments/v1.8/Project.toml`
  No Changes to `~/.julia/environments/v1.8/Manifest.toml`

julia> Tree = @load DecisionTreeClassifier pkg=DecisionTree
[ Info: For silent loading, specify `verbosity=0`.
import MLJDecisionTreeInterface ✓
MLJDecisionTreeInterface.DecisionTreeClassifier

julia> tree = Tree()
DecisionTreeClassifier(
  max_depth = -1,
  min_samples_leaf = 1,
  min_samples_split = 2,
  min_purity_increase = 0.0,
  n_subfeatures = 0,
  post_prune = false,
  merge_purity_threshold = 1.0,
  display_depth = 5,
  feature_importance = :impurity,
  rng = Random._GLOBAL_RNG())
```

***Figure 11.9**: An example of loading the DecisionTreeClassifier model using @load*

Alternatively, you can use the **@iload** macro for interactive loading. This provides the user with options to install the required interface package and choose the relevant model-providing package in ambiguous cases.

Here's an example of loading the **DecisionTreeClassifier** model using **@iload**:

```
julia> @iload DecisionTreeClassifier
[ Info: For silent loading, specify `verbosity=0`.

Multiple packages provide DecisionTreeClassifier. Choose a package:

 > BetaML
   DecisionTree

import BetaML ✔
BetaML.Trees.DecisionTreeClassifier

julia> Tree = BetaML.Trees.DecisionTreeClassifier
BetaML.Trees.DecisionTreeClassifier

julia> tree = Tree()
DecisionTreeClassifier(
  max_depth = 0,
  min_gain = 0.0,
  min_records = 2,
  max_features = 0,
  splitting_criterion = BetaML.Utils.gini,
  rng = Random._GLOBAL_RNG())
```

Figure 11.10: *Basic information about Decision Tree Classifier*

Note that for models that are provided by only a single package, the pkg specification can be dropped.

Let us revisit the topic on weights. The MLJ package provides a way to specify weights during both model training and performance evaluation.

To specify weights during model training, you can bind the weights to the model along with the data when constructing a machine. For example, to specify weights for a **KNNRegressor** model:

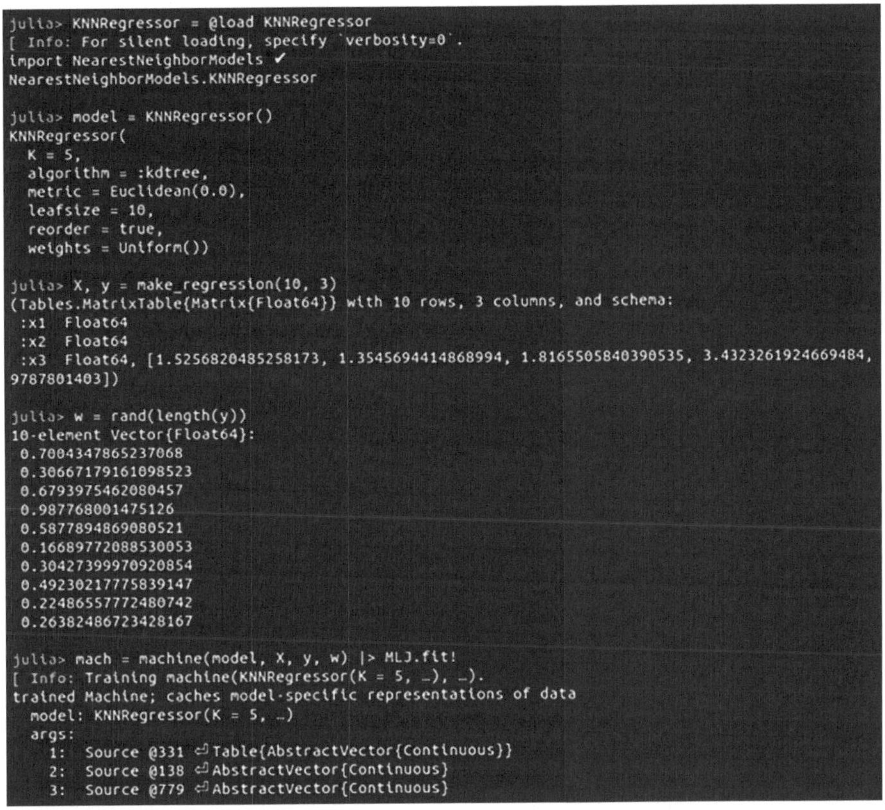

```
julia> KNNRegressor = @load KNNRegressor
[ Info: For silent loading, specify `verbosity=0`.
import NearestNeighborModels ✓
NearestNeighborModels.KNNRegressor

julia> model = KNNRegressor()
KNNRegressor(
  K = 5,
  algorithm = :kdtree,
  metric = Euclidean(0.0),
  leafsize = 10,
  reorder = true,
  weights = Uniform())

julia> X, y = make_regression(10, 3)
(Tables.MatrixTable{Matrix{Float64}} with 10 rows, 3 columns, and schema:
 :x1  Float64
 :x2  Float64
 :x3  Float64, [1.5256820485258173, 1.3545694414868994, 1.8165505840390535, 3.4323261924669484,
9787801403])

julia> w = rand(length(y))
10-element Vector{Float64}:
 0.7004347865237068
 0.30667179161098523
 0.6793975462080457
 0.987768001475126
 0.5877894869080521
 0.16689772088530053
 0.30427399970920854
 0.49230217775839147
 0.22486557772480742
 0.26382486723428167

julia> mach = machine(model, X, y, w) |> MLJ.fit!
[ Info: Training machine(KNNRegressor(K = 5, …), …).
trained Machine; caches model-specific representations of data
  model: KNNRegressor(K = 5, …)
  args:
    1:  Source @331 ⏎ Table{AbstractVector{Continuous}}
    2:  Source @138 ⏎ AbstractVector{Continuous}
    3:  Source @779 ⏎ AbstractVector{Continuous}
```

Figure 11.11: *KNN regressor model is used and fit (trained on) random dat.*

Note that the model needs to support per observation weights for this to work, which can be checked using **`supports_weights(model)`**.

Revisiting weights

To specify weights during performance evaluation, you can provide the weights as the last argument when calling an MLJ measure (metric) that supports weights. For example, to compute the macro F1 score with weights for a classification problem:

```
julia> _, y = @load_iris
((sepal_length = [5.1,  … , 5.9], sepal_width = [3.5,  …, 3.0], petal_
length = [1.4,  … , 5.1], petal_width = [0.2,  …  1.8]),
CategoricalArrays.CategoricalValue{String, UInt32}["setosa",  …
"virginica"])
julia> ŷ = shuffle(y)
150-element CategoricalArrays.CategoricalArray{String,1,UInt32}:
```

```
 "setosa"
 ⋮
 "virginica"
julia> w = Dict("versicolor" => 1, "setosa" => 2, "virginica"=> 3)
Dict{String, Int64} with 3 entries:
  "virginica"  => 3
  "versicolor" => 1
  "setosa"     => 2
julia> macro_f1score(ŷ, y, w)
0.66
```

You can use **supports_weights** and **supports_class_weights** on measures to check weight support. For example, to list all measures supporting per observation weights:

```
julia> measures() do m
       m.supports_weights
       end
34-element Vector{NamedTuple{(:name, :instances, :human_name, :target_
scitype, :supports_weights, :supports_class_weights, :prediction_type,
:orientation, :reports_each_observation, :aggregation, :is_feature_
dependent, :docstring, :distribution_type)}}:
 (name = BrierLoss, instances = [brier_loss], ...)
 ⋮
 (name = QuantileLoss, instances = [quantile_loss], ...)
```

Data preprocessing using transformers in MLJ

Let us revisit other data preprocessing techniques. We use Transformers in MLJ for loading and using various data preprocessing techniques. In MLJ, several unsupervised models are available out-of-the-box, including transformers that perform common transformations such as one-hot encoding. These models can be used to preprocess data before it is fed into a supervised model.

A transformer is considered "**static**" if it has no learned parameters. Such a transformer is essentially an ordinary function but can be realized as an MLJ static transformer by defining it as a subtype of **Static <: Unsupervised**. This can be useful, especially if the function depends on parameters that the user would like to manipulate (which become hyperparameters of the model). Here is an example of defining a static transformer:

```
using MLJ


struct MyTransformer <: Static{Tuple{}}
end


function MLJ.transform(::MyTransformer, X::DataFrame)
      # do some transformation on X here
      return transformed_X
end
```

You can learn more about built-in and static transformers in MLJModels.jl at https://alan-turing-institute.github.io/MLJ.jl/dev/transformers/#Built-in-transformers .

Conclusion

MLJ.jl is a powerful machine learning library in Julia that offers a variety of functionalities for building, training, and evaluating machine learning models. It offers a user-friendly and efficient API that enables users to work with a diverse range of models and datasets. MLJ.jl's support for data preprocessing through transformers, generation of synthetic data, and flexible model handling makes it a go-to tool for machine learning tasks in Julia. Additionally, its ability to handle supervised, unsupervised, and its integration with other Julia packages make it a valuable asset to the Julia community. Overall, MLJ.jl provides an efficient and flexible platform for machine learning, making it a valuable addition to the toolkit of any data scientist or machine learning practitioner.

In the next chapter, we will learn about model tuning, model performance, and modeling pipelines and various other transformers.

Questions

1. What is MLJ.jl, and what is its purpose?
2. How does MLJ.jl handle missing data?
3. What types of models are available in MLJ.jl?
4. Can MLJ.jl be used for both supervised and unsupervised learning tasks?
5. What is a transformer in MLJ.jl, and how is it used in data preprocessing?
6. Can users define their models in MLJ.jl?
7. What is cross-validation, and how is it used in MLJ.jl?
8. How does MLJ.jl handle imbalanced datasets?

CHAPTER 12

Data and Models

Introduction

MLJ.jl is a machine learning framework for Julia that provides a common interface for working with data and models. It provides a wide range of features for data preparation, model selection, tuning, evaluation, and composition. MLJ.jl supports a variety of data formats, including CSV, JSON, and HDF5. It also provides a number of tools for data preparation, such as imputation, normalization, and feature selection. MLJ.jl supports a wide range of machine learning models, including linear regression, logistic regression, decision trees, and neural networks. It also provides several tools for model selection, tuning, and evaluation.

MLJ.jl is an advanced framework for machine learning that offers a diverse set of capabilities to tackle a wide array of problems. Its user-friendly interface and rich feature set make it an indispensable resource for machine learning practitioners. Supporting various data formats like CSV, JSON, and HDF5, MLJ.jl facilitates seamless data integration. Additionally, it equips users with essential tools for data preprocessing, encompassing tasks such as imputation, normalization, and feature selection.

When it comes to model selection, MLJ.jl boasts extensive support for an extensive range of machine learning models, including linear regression, logistic regression, decision trees, and neural networks. It further provides an assortment of utilities to aid users in model evaluation, tuning, and selection. Before initiating the training process, it is vital to prepare the data meticulously. This typically involves data cleansing, outlier removal, and data transformation into a format compatible with the chosen model. MLJ.jl features a variety of tools that simplify the data preparation phase.

After preparing the data, the next step involves model selection. Given the multitude of models available, the optimal choice depends on the unique characteristics of the dataset. MLJ.jl furnishes several tools to facilitate the selection of the most suitable model for the problem at hand. Once a model is selected, the subsequent task entails parameter tuning, aiming to identify the parameter values that yield the best performance on the given dataset. MLJ.jl encompasses a range of tools designed to assist users in this crucial tuning process.

Following parameter tuning, evaluating the model's performance on a separate test set is crucial for assessing its generalization capabilities. This evaluation aids in determining how effectively the model will handle new, unseen data. MLJ.jl provides a comprehensive set of tools to facilitate performance evaluation. Moreover, MLJ.jl supports model composition, allowing users to combine multiple models into a composite model that surpasses the capabilities of the individual models. MLJ.jl incorporates numerous tools to simplify the process of model composition.

Structure

In this chapter, the following topics will be covered:

- Model interface in MLJ.jl
- The need for data frontend in MLJ
- Machines in MLJ
- Model composition
- Performance measures in MLJ
- What are iterative models?
- What are learning curves?

Model interface in MLJ.jl

A model is a container for the parameters of a machine learning algorithm. The parameters are the values that the algorithm learns from the data to make predictions. The model also stores the hyperparameters of the algorithm, which are the settings that control how the algorithm learns.

The name of the Julia type associated with a model indicates the associated algorithm. For example, the type `DecisionTreeClassifier` indicates the decision tree classifier algorithm. The outcome of training a learning algorithm is called a `fitresult`. A `fitresult` contains the information that the algorithm learned during training. For example, the coefficients and intercept of a linear regression model are stored in the fitresult. The ultimate supertype of all models in MLJ.jl is **`MLJModelInterface.Model`**. This type has two abstract subtypes: Supervised and Unsupervised.

Supervised models are used to predict a target variable from a set of features. For example, a supervised model could be used to predict the price of a house based on its features, such as its size, location, and number of bedrooms.

Unsupervised models are used to find patterns in data. For example, an unsupervised model could be used to find groups of customers who are similar to each other.

Supervised models can be further divided into two types: probabilistic and deterministic. Probabilistic models can predict the probability of a new observation belonging to a particular class. Deterministic models can only predict the class of a new observation. The division of model types is further realized through Trait declarations. Traits are a way of grouping together related types. For example, the Probabilistic trait is used to group together all of the probabilistic models in MLJ.jl.

Every concrete subtype of Model must have a fit method. The fit method is used to train the model on a set of data.

Every supervised model must have a predict method. The predict method is used to predict the target variable for a new observation.

Every unsupervised model must have a transform method. The transform method is used to transform the data into a new representation.

Methods such as fit, predict, and transform are called operations. Operations are dispatched on a model instance and a **`fitresult`** (plus other data).

Probabilistic supervised models optionally implement a **`predict_mode`** operation (in the case of classifiers) or a **`predict_mean`** and/or **`predict_median`** operations (in the case of regressors). These operations are used to predict the mode (most likely class) or the mean (expected value) of the target variable for a new observation.

Unsupervised models may implement an **`inverse_transform`** operation. This operation is used to transform the data back to its original representation.

Model representation

In MLJ.jl, models are represented by structs. To create a new model, you must first declare a struct for the model. The struct declaration must include the name of the model, the type of the model, and the hyperparameters of the model.

The following is an example of a struct declaration for a simple model:

```
struct MyModel <: MLJ.Deterministic
  lambda::Float64
end
```

The name of the model is **MyModel**. The type of the model is **MLJ.Deterministic**. The hyperparameter of the model is lambda.

Once you have declared a struct for the model, you can create a new instance of the model using the keyword constructor. The keyword constructor takes the hyperparameters of the model as arguments. The following is an example of how to create a new instance of the **MyModel** model:

```
my_model = MyModel(lambda=0.5)
```

The **my_model** variable now contains an instance of the **MyModel** model. The lambda hyperparameter of the model is set to 0.5.

The **clean!** method is a method that is used to clean the hyperparameters of the model. The **clean!** method can be used to check the hyperparameters for errors and to correct any errors that are found. The following is an example of the **clean!** method for the **MyModel** model:

```
function MyModel.clean!(model::MyModel)
  if model.lambda < 0
    warning = "Need lambda ≥ 0. Resetting lambda=0."
    model.lambda = 0
  end
end
```

The **clean!** method checks the lambda hyperparameter to make sure that it is greater than or equal to 0. If the lambda hyperparameter is less than 0, then **clean!()** method sets the lambda hyperparameter to 0.

The **@mlj_model** macro is a macro that can be used to simplify the process of declaring a model struct. The **@mlj_model** macro takes the name of the model, the type of the model, and the hyperparameters of the model as arguments. The following is an example of how to use the **@mlj_model** macro:

```
@mlj_model mutable struct MyModel <: MLJ.Deterministic
  lambda::Float64 = 0.5
end
```

The `@mlj_model` macro is equivalent to the following struct declaration:

```
struct MyModel <: MLJ.Deterministic
  lambda::Float64
end
function MyModel.clean!(model::MyModel)
  if model.lambda < 0
    warning = "Need lambda ≥ 0. Resetting lambda=0."
    model.lambda = 0
  end
end
```

Supervised model

Supervised models utilize features in training data to predict a target variable, which represents the value the model aims to predict. The training process involves learning the relationship between features and the target variable. There are many different types of supervised models, each with its own strengths and weaknesses. Some common types of supervised models include:

- **Linear regression models**: Linear regression models are used to make predictions for data that is linearly related. Linear regression models are simple to understand and implement. However, they are not always accurate for data that is not linearly related.
- **Logistic regression models**: Logistic regression models are used to make predictions for data that is binary. Logistic regression models are more complex than linear regression models, but they are more accurate for data that is binary.
- **Decision tree models**: Decision tree models are used to make predictions for data that is non-linear. Decision tree models are more complex than linear regression models or logistic regression models, but they can be very accurate for data that is non-linear.

Supervised models can be used to solve a variety of problems, including:

- Predicting the price of a stock
- Predicting the likelihood of a customer clicking an ad
- Predicting the likelihood of a patient developing a disease

Supervised models are a powerful tool that can be used to make predictions for a variety of problems. If you are working on a problem that involves making predictions, you should consider using a supervised model.

Here are some additional details about the supervised models in MLJ.jl:

- The MLJ.jl library provides a number of supervised models, including linear regression models, logistic regression models, and decision tree models.
- The MLJ.jl library also provides several tools for training and evaluating supervised models.
- The MLJ.jl library is open source and can be downloaded from the MLJ.jl website.

User-defined models in MLJ

To implement a new supervised model in MLJ, you need to follow three steps:

1. Define a mutable struct to store hyperparameters. This struct is the model, and it should be a subtype of either Probabilistic or Deterministic, depending on whether probabilistic or ordinary point predictions are intended.
2. Define a fit method, dispatched on the model, which returns learned parameters (**fitresult**). The fit method is used to learn the model's parameters on the training data.
3. Define a predict method, dispatched on the model and the **fitresult**, to return predictions on new patterns. The predict method uses the learned parameters to make predictions on new data.

```
julia> import MLJBase
julia> using LinearAlgebra
julia> mutable struct MyRegressor <: MLJBase.Deterministic
    lambda::Float64
end
MyRegressor(; lambda=0.1) = MyRegressor(lambda)
# fit returns coefficients minimizing a penalized rms loss function:
julia> function MLJBase.fit(model::MyRegressor, verbosity, X, y)
    x = MLJBase.matrix(X)                    # convert table to matrix
    fitresult = (x'x + model.lambda*I)\(x'y)  # the coefficients
    cache=nothing
    report=nothing
    return fitresult, cache, report
```

```
end
# predict uses coefficients to make a new prediction:
julia> MLJBase.predict(::MyRegressor, fitresult, Xnew) = MLJBase.
matrix(Xnew) * fitresult
```

This code sample provides an implementation of a simple deterministic regressor, specifically a ridge regressor with no intercept, using the Julia programming language and the **`MLJBase`** package.

Deterministic regressor

In MLJ.jl, a deterministic regressor is a model that can be used to predict a target variable from a set of features, and that always returns the same predicted value for a given set of features. This means that a deterministic regressor does not provide any information about the uncertainty in the predictions.

Deterministic regressors are often used in machine learning applications where it is important to be able to make accurate predictions. For example, deterministic regressors can be used to predict the price of a stock, the demand for a product, or the likelihood of a customer clicking an ad.

There are many different types of deterministic regressors, and the choice of which regressor to use depends on the specific machine learning problem that is being solved. Some common types of deterministic regressors include:

- Linear regression models
- Ridge regression models
- Lasso regression models
- Support vector machines (SVMs)
- Decision trees
- Random forests

MLJ.jl provides a number of deterministic regressors, and it also provides a number of tools for working with deterministic regressors. For example, MLJ.jl provides functions for calculating the mean squared error, the root mean squared error, and the R-squared of deterministic regressors, and it also provides functions for visualizing the predictions of deterministic regressors.

First, a mutable struct called **`MyRegressor`** is defined, which implements the **`MLJBase.Deterministic`** abstract type. This struct takes one parameter, lambda, which is a scalar value representing the regularization strength. The **`MyRegressor`** struct is also initialized with a constructor that takes a named parameter lambda with a default value of 0.1.

The fit function is then defined, which takes as input the **MyRegressor** model, a verbosity flag, a matrix of input features X, and a vector of output values y. The function first converts the input data from a table to a matrix using the **MLJBase.matrix** function. It then computes the coefficients using ridge regression, which minimizes a penalized root-mean-square (RMS) loss function. The resulting coefficients are returned along with cache and report variables, which are set to nothing.

Finally, the predict function is defined, which takes as input the **MyRegressor** model, the coefficients obtained from the fit function, and a new matrix of input features, **Xnew**. The function multiplies the input matrix **Xnew** by the coefficients to make a prediction.

```
julia> X, y = @load_boston;
julia> model = MyRegressor(lambda=1.0)
julia> regressor = machine(model, X, y)
julia> evaluate!(regressor, resampling=CV(), measure=rms, verbosity=0)
```

Once this code is loaded, the **MyRegressor** can be used to train and evaluate a model using the Boston housing dataset. A new instance of the **MyRegressor** model is created with a regularization strength of 1.0, and a machine object is created using the model, input features X, and output values y. The evaluate! function is then used to train and evaluate the model using cross-validation with root-mean-square (RMS) error as the performance metric. The resulting performance evaluation object shows the RMS error for each fold of the cross-validation.

Probabilistic regressor

In MLJ.jl, a probabilistic classifier is a model that can be used to predict a target variable from a set of features, and that also provides a probability distribution for the predicted value. This means that a probabilistic classifier cannot only tell you what the most likely class label is for a new pattern, but it can also tell you how likely it is that the new pattern belongs to each class.

Probabilistic classifiers are often used in machine learning applications where it is important to be able to quantify the uncertainty in the predictions. For example, probabilistic classifiers can be used to make decisions about whether to approve a loan, whether to admit a student to a school, or whether to diagnose a patient with a disease.

There are many different types of probabilistic classifiers, and the choice of which classifier to use depends on the specific machine learning problem that is being solved. Some common types of probabilistic classifiers include:

- Gaussian naive Bayes classifiers
- Logistic regression classifiers
- Support vector machines (SVMs)
- Decision trees
- Random forests

MLJ.jl provides a number of probabilistic classifiers as well as several tools for working with probabilistic classifiers. For example, MLJ.jl provides functions for calculating the accuracy, precision, and recall of probabilistic classifiers, and it also provides functions for visualizing the probability distributions of probabilistic classifiers.

The classifier is called **`MyClassifier`**, and it is a subclass of **`MLJBase.Probabilistic`**. This means that it is a probabilistic model that can be used to predict a target variable from a set of features.

The fit function for **`MyClassifier`** ignores the inputs X and returns the training target y probability distribution. This distribution is a **`Distributions.UnivariateFinite`** object, which is a probability distribution for a single variable.

The predict function for **`MyClassifier`** returns the passed **`fitresult`** (pdf) for all new patterns. This means that it returns the probability distribution for each new pattern, based on the training target distribution.

Here is an example of how to use the **`MyClassifier`** classifier:

```
julia> using MLJBase

julia> using Distributions

julia> struct MyClassifier <: MLJBase.Probabilistic
           end

julia> function MLJBase.fit(model::MyClassifier, verbosity, X, y)
             fitresult = Distributions.fit(MLJBase.UnivariateFinite, y)
             cache = nothing
             report = nothing
             return fitresult, cache, report
       end
```

```
julia> MLJBase.predict(model::MyClassifier, fitresult, Xnew) = [fitresult
for i in 1:nrows(Xnew)]
julia> X, y = @load_iris
julia> mach = fit!(machine(MyClassifier(), X, y)
julia> predict(mach, selectrows(X, 1:2))
```

```
julia> predict(mach, selectrows(X, 1:2))
2-element Vector{UnivariateFinite{Multiclass{3}, String, UInt32, Float64}}:
 UnivariateFinite{Multiclass{3}}(setosa=>0.333, versicolor=>0.333, virginica=>0.333)
 UnivariateFinite{Multiclass{3}}(setosa=>0.333, versicolor=>0.333, virginica=>0.333)
```

***Figure 12.1**: Classification example using MLJ functionalities*

In this example, we load the Iris dataset and fit the **`MyClassifier`** model to the training target y. We then use the predict function to predict the probability distribution for two new patterns. The output of the predict function is a two-element array, where each element is a **`Distributions.UnivariateFinite`** object. These objects represent the probability distributions for the two new patterns.

The **`MyClassifier`** classifier is a simple probabilistic classifier that can be used to predict a target variable from a set of features. It is easy to use and it can be used to solve a variety of machine learning problems.

Here is a more detailed explanation of the **`MyClassifier`** classifier:

- The **`MyClassifier`** classifier is a probabilistic classifier because it returns a probability distribution for the predicted value. This means that the classifier can not only tell you what the most likely class label is for a new pattern, but it can also tell you how likely it is that the new pattern belongs to each class.
- The **`MyClassifier`** classifier is simple because it only fits a single probability distribution to the training target. This makes the classifier easy to understand and implement.

The **`MyClassifier`** classifier is versatile because it can be used to solve a variety of machine learning problems. For example, the classifier can be used to classify images, to classify text, or to classify other types of data.

The **`MyClassifier`** classifier is a simple and versatile probabilistic classifier that can be used to solve a variety of machine learning problems.

There are a variety of other methods that are supported by MLJ. You can refer to https://alan-turing-institute.github.io/MLJ.jl/dev/list_of_supported_models/#model_list for using other models.

Fitting a model

When you are training or predicting using a model in MLJ.jl, you need to provide the model with data. The data that you provide to the model needs to be in a specific format. The format of the data that you provide to the model is determined by the scientific type of the data.

`fit` is a method that is used to train a machine learning model. It takes three arguments: the model, the verbosity level, and the training data. The model is the object that will be trained, the verbosity level controls how much information is printed to the console, and the training data is the data that will be used to train the model.

The fit method works by first fitting the model to the training data. This means that the model will learn the relationship between the features and the target variable. Once the model has been fitted, it can be used to make predictions on new data.

The fit method returns three objects, which are as follows:

- The **`fitresult`** object contains information about the training process, such as the loss function, the number of iterations, and the time it took to train the model.
- The cache object contains any data that was used during the training process, such as the model coefficients and the feature importances.
- The report object contains any information about the performance of the model, such as the accuracy, the precision, and the recall.

The fit method is an important part of the machine learning process. It is used to train the model so that it can be used to make predictions on new data.

Predict method

The predict method is a method that is used to make predictions on new data. It takes three arguments: the model, the **`fitresult`**, and the new data. The model is the object that was trained, the **`fitresult`** contains information about the training process, and the new data is the data that will be used to make predictions.

The predict method works by first predicting the target variable for each observation in the new data. It then returns a vector of predictions. The predictions can be deterministic or probabilistic.

In the case of deterministic predictions, the predictions are simply the predicted values for the target variable. In the case of probabilistic predictions, the predictions are a distribution over the possible values of the target variable.

The predict method is an important part of the machine learning process. It is used to make predictions on new data, which can then be used to make decisions.

Here is an example of how the predict method might be used to make predictions on new data:

- We have a model that predicts the price of houses. The model was trained on a dataset of houses that have already been sold.
- We have a new house that we want to sell. We can use the predict method to predict the price of the house.
- The predict method will return a prediction for the price of the house. We can then use this prediction to decide how much to sell the house for.

In this example, the predict method is used to decide how much to sell a house for. However, the predict method can be used to make predictions on any type of data. For example, we could use the predict method to predict the likelihood of a customer clicking an ad, the probability of a patient recovering from a disease, or the number of sales that a company will make in the next quarter.

The predict method is a powerful tool that can be used to make predictions on new data. It is an important part of the machine learning process and can be used to make decisions in a variety of different domains.

Here is a more detailed explanation of the predict method for probabilistic models:

In the case of probabilistic models, the predict method returns a distribution over the possible values of the target variable. This distribution can be used to make predictions about the likelihood of different outcomes. For example, if we have a model that predicts the probability of a patient recovering from a disease, the predict method will return a distribution over the possible values of the probability of recovery. We can then use this distribution to make predictions about the likelihood of the patient recovering from the disease.

The predict method for probabilistic models is a powerful tool that can be used to make predictions about a variety of different outcomes. It is an important part of the machine learning process and can be used to make decisions in a variety of different domains.

Here are some additional details about the predict method for probabilistic models:

- The predict method for probabilistic models can return a variety of different distributions. The most common distributions are the Gaussian distribution and the binomial distribution.
- The Gaussian distribution is a bell-shaped curve that is used to model continuous data. The binomial distribution is a discrete distribution that is used to model data that can take on only two values.
- The predict method for probabilistic models can also return a distribution over a set of possible values. For example, the predict method for a model that predicts the probability of a patient recovering from a disease could return a distribution over the possible values of the probability of recovery.
- The predict method for probabilistic models is a powerful tool that can be used to make predictions about a variety of different outcomes. It is an important part of the machine learning process and can be used to make decisions in a variety of different domains.

Training losses

The **`MLJModelInterface.training_losses`** function is used to get the training losses of an iterative model. An iterative model is a model that is trained using an iterative algorithm, such as gradient descent. The training losses are the losses that the model experiences during training.

The **`MLJModelInterface.training_losses`** function takes two arguments: the model and the report. The model is the object that was trained, and the report is an object that contains information about the training process.

The **`MLJModelInterface.training_losses`** function returns an **`AbstractVector`** of the losses in historical order. The **`AbstractVector`** is a generic type that can be used to store any type of vector. The losses are stored in historical order, which means that the first element of the vector is the loss from the first iteration of training, the second element of the vector is the loss from the second iteration of training, and so on.

If the model calculates scores instead of losses, then the sign of the scores should be reversed before returning them. This is because scores are typically positive, while losses are typically negative.

The following trait overload is also required: `MLJModelInterface.supports_training_losses(::Type{<:M}) = true`. This trait overload tells MLJ that the model supports the **`training_losses`** function.

Trait values can also be set using the **metadata_model** method. The **metadata_model** method takes two arguments: the model and the trait name. The model is the object that the trait values will be set for, and the trait name is the name of the trait.

Feature importances

The **MLJModelInterface.feature_importances** function is used to get the feature **importances** of a model. Feature importances are a measure of how important each feature is to the model's predictions. The **MLJModelInterface.feature_importances** function takes three arguments: the model, the **fitresult**, and the report. The model is the model that you want to get the **feature importances** for, the **fitresult** is the result of training the model, and the report is a structure that contains information about the model, such as the names of the features.

The **MLJModelInterface.feature_importances** function returns an **AbstractVector** of feature importances. The **AbstractVector** is a generic type that can be used to represent any vector, and it is used to store the feature importances in a way that they can be easily accessed. The feature importances are stored in the AbstractVector in a dictionary, where the keys are the names of the features and the values are the feature importances.

The following trait overload is also required: `MLJModelInterface.reports_feature_importances(::Type{<:M}) = true`. This trait overload tells MLJ that the model supports the **MLJModelInterface.feature_importances** function. If the model does not support the **MLJModelInterface.feature_importances** function, then an error will be thrown when the function is called.

If for some reason a model is sometimes unable to report feature importances then **feature_importances** should return all importances as 0.0, as in `[:gender =>0.0, :height =>0.0, :weight => 0.0]`. This is because it is important to be able to get the feature importances of a model, even if the model is not always able to calculate them.

Update! Method

A model can be updated multiple times to improve its accuracy. The "Iterative models and the update! method" refers to a mechanism provided by MLJ to efficiently update or retrain a model without repeating unnecessary computations. It is an optional feature that can be implemented by overloading the update method for a particular model.

The update method is called by MLJ to retrain a model on the same training data when certain conditions are met, such as changes in hyperparameters or the need to increase the number of iterations. The purpose is to avoid redundant computations and improve computational efficiency.

The update method has two variations:

- `MMI.update(model::SomeSupervisedModel, verbosity, old_fitresult, old_cache, X, y) -> fit result, cache, report`
- `MMI.update(model::SomeSupervisedModel, verbosity, old_fitresult, old_cache, X, y, w=nothing) -> fit result, cache, report`

The first variation is used when the model does not support sample weights, while the second variation is used when the model does support sample weights.

If an MLJ Machine is being fit and it is not the first time, the update method is called instead of fit, unless the fit! method has been called with a new rows keyword argument. However, if the update method is not implemented for a specific model, MLJ provides a fallback that simply calls the fit method instead.

The update method is particularly useful for iterative models or learning networks wrapped as models. In the case of iterative models, where increasing the number of iterations only restarts the iterative procedure if other hyperparameters have also changed, the update method ensures that the model is retrained only when necessary. It helps to avoid unnecessary retraining and saves computational resources.

Another use case for the update method is to avoid repeating time-consuming preprocessing of the input data (X and y) required by certain models. By storing the preprocessed versions of the data in the cache returned by the fit method, the update method can access and reuse them, reducing redundant preprocessing computations.

If the **`fitresult`** argument, returned by a preceding call to fit, is not sufficient for performing an update, the author of the model can include any additional information required in the cache return value of the fit method. This additional information can then be accessed and utilized by the update method.

In summary, the update method in MLJ allows for efficient retraining of models by avoiding redundant computations. It is especially beneficial for iterative models, learning networks, and models with time-consuming preprocessing steps. By implementing the update method, model authors can optimize the training process and improve the overall performance of their models within the MLJ framework.

Transform method

A supervised model in MLJ can optionally implement a transform method. The signature of this method is the same as the predict method. The purpose of the transform method is to provide a mechanism for the model to perform feature transformations on new input data. This can be useful when the model has learned feature embeddings or other transformations as part of its training process.

If a supervised model implements the transform method, it should also define a value for the `output_scitype` trait. This trait specifies the scientific type (`scitype`) of the output of the transform method. It assures that the scientific type of the output of `transform(model, fitresult, Xnew)` is always a subtype of the specified scientific type.

One common use case for a transform method in a supervised model is when the model learns feature embeddings for categorical input features during training. The model can then act as a transformer, allowing other supervised models to use it for transforming categorical features instead of applying traditional one-hot encoding representations. This can be particularly useful in scenarios where high-dimensional one-hot encoding is not desirable or practical.

By implementing the transform method and defining the `output_scitype` trait, a supervised model can provide functionality for transforming input data based on its learned representations. This enables the model to be used as a transformer in conjunction with other supervised models within the MLJ framework.

Models with a probability distribution

For models that fit a probability distribution to data, they should be regarded as Probabilistic models with the target variable y set to the data and the feature variables X set to nothing. The predict method for such models should return a single distribution.

Probability distribution models are considered to be a subtype of supervised models in MLJ, where the target variable (y) is the data being modeled, and there are no input variables (X = nothing). These models fit a probability distribution to the provided data. The predict method for such models should return a single probability distribution as its output.

Serialization

Serialization refers to the process of saving a machine (model) object to a persistent storage format and restoring it. The MLJ user can serialize and deserialize machines as they would with any other Julia object.

MLJ allows users to serialize and deserialize models using Julia's built-in serialization mechanisms. However, some models may have fit results that are not serializable, such as C pointers. To address this issue, models can implement a save and restore method to switch between a fit result and a persistent, serializable representation of that result.

The save method takes a model object and a **`fitresult`** object as inputs and returns a persistent, serializable representation of the **`fitresult`**. The restore method takes a model object and a persistent representation of the **`fitresult`** and returns a valid **`fitresult`** object that can be used by the model.

However, there can be a problem when a model's **`fitresult`** (returned by the fit method) is not a persistent object, such as a C pointer that has no meaning in a new Julia session. To handle this, model implementations need to define a save and restore method for converting the **`fitresult`** to a persistent, serializable representation and reconstructing the **`fitresult`**, respectively. The save method takes the model and **`fitresult`** as input and returns a persistent serializable representation of the **`fitresult`**.

The restore method takes the model and the serialized **`fitresult`** as input and reconstructs a valid **`fitresult`** that can be used as if it were returned by the fit method. If a model does not need any special handling for serialization, the fallback implementation of save and restore performs no action and returns the **`fitresult`** or the serialized **`fitresult`**, respectively.

The need for a data frontend for MLJ

The data front-end in MLJ provides a mechanism for models to define how user-supplied data is transformed and represented internally. It serves several purposes and provides benefits in the following ways:

- **Flexibility**: MLJ supports a wide range of data types and formats, such as tables, matrices, and more. By implementing a data front-end, models can define how they expect the data to be formatted and transformed to their specific internal representation. This allows models to be more flexible in accepting different types of data and provides a consistent interface for users to work with.

- **Performance optimization:** The data front-end allows models to perform preprocessing and data transformations once and reuse them during subsequent operations. By defining the reformatting logic, models can avoid redundant computations and improve performance, especially when dealing with large datasets or complex preprocessing steps. This can be particularly important in iterative procedures or when repeated calls to `fit!`, `predict`, or `transform` are made.
- **Memory efficiency**: Some models might require memory-intensive data representations, such as large matrices or specialized data structures. The data front-end enables models to store and operate on data in their preferred format, which can help optimize memory usage and improve overall efficiency.
- **Resampling and evaluation**: The data front-end also plays a role in resampling and evaluation procedures. By implementing the `selectrows` method, models can define how the model-specific data should be subsampled for specific observation indices. This enables efficient resampling of data during tasks like cross-validation or bootstrapping. It also ensures that evaluation procedures operate on the appropriate internal data representation.

Data frontend for MLJ

To implement a data front-end for a model in MLJ, you can follow the guidelines provided. Here's an explanation of the steps involved:

- **Overload the reformat method**: The reformat method is used to transform user-supplied data into the model-specific representation. Implement a reformat method for each form of `args...` that appears in a valid machine construction. This means there should be a reformat method for each possible signature of `fit(::SomeModelType, ...)`. The purpose of reformat is to avoid unnecessary computations when memory resources allow. The fallback implementation returns the input arguments as is.
- **Implement the `selectrows` method**: The `selectrows` method is used to specify how the model-specific data is subsampled for specific observation indices. Implement the `selectrows` method for each overloading of `reformat(model::SomeModel, args...) -> data` that you defined earlier. This allows for more efficient resampling of data during operations like evaluate!
- **Implement other model operations**: Implement operations like fit, predict, and transform, taking into account the reformatted versions of user-supplied data. For example, in the case of supervised models, the

predict function would take the reformatted version of the user-supplied input data. Ensure that the reformatted data is used consistently across the model operations.

By implementing the data front-end, you can optimize the computations and memory usage when working with the model. It allows for efficient transformation, subsampling, and other operations specific to the model's representation of data.

Machines in MLJ

In the context of MLJ.jl, "machines" refer to the primary building blocks used to represent and perform machine learning tasks.

What are machines?

A machine is a type of model in MLJ that is composed of other models. This allows you to combine the strengths of different models to create a more powerful model.

For example, you could create a machine that consists of a linear regression model and a decision tree model. The linear regression model would be used to predict the main effects of the features, and the decision tree model would be used to predict the interactions between the features. This would allow you to create a model that is more accurate than either the linear regression model or the decision tree model on its own.

How to create machines?

To create a machine, you use the Machine constructor. The Machine constructor takes a list of models as input. The models in the list can be any type of model that is supported by MLJ.

For example, the following code creates a machine that consists of a linear regression model and a decision tree model:

```
model = Machine([LinearRegression(), DecisionTree()])
```

How to fit machines?

To fit a machine, you use the **`fit!`** method. The **`fit!`** method takes the machine and the training data as input. The fit! method then trains the machine on the training data.

The following code fits the machine that was created in the previous example:

```
model |> fit!(X, y)
```

How to predict with machines?

To predict with a machine, you use the predict method. The predict method takes the machine and the test data as input. The predict method then predicts the labels for the test data.

The following code predicts the labels for the test data using the machine that was created and fitted in the previous examples:

```
predictions = model |> predict(X_test)
```

How to evaluate machines?

To evaluate a machine, you use the evaluate method. The evaluate method takes the machine, the training data, and the test data as input. The evaluate method then calculates the accuracy of the machine on the training data and the test data.

The following code evaluates the machine that was created, fitted, and predicted in the previous examples:

```
accuracy = model |> evaluate(X, y, X_test, y_test)
```

How to compose machines?

You can compose machines by using the compose function. The compose function takes two machines as input and returns a new machine that is composed of the two input machines.

The following code composes the machine that was created in the previous example with a logistic regression model:

```
composed_model = compose(model, LogisticRegression())
```

`composed_model` is a machine that consists of a linear regression model, a decision tree model, and a logistic regression model. This allows you to create a model that is more powerful than any of the individual models on its own.

Model composition

Model composition is the process of combining multiple models to create a pipeline that can solve a specific machine learning task. The motivation behind model composition is that it allows us to take advantage of the strengths of different models to build a more powerful and accurate model.

The three common ways of combining models are:

- **Linear Pipelines (Pipeline)**: This method is used for unbranching chains where the output of one model is used as the input for the next model. An example of a linear pipeline is dimension reduction (e.g., PCA) followed by a classification model (e.g., `EvoTreeClassifier`). Linear pipelines can also include transformations of the target variable in supervised learning tasks.
- **Homogeneous Ensembles** (`EnsembleModel`): This method is used to blend the predictions of multiple supervised models, all of the same type, but which receive different views of the training data to reduce overall variance. This technique is known as observation bagging.
- **Model Stacking (Stack)**: This method is used to combine the predictions of a smaller number of models of possibly different types with the help of an adjudicating model.
- **Learning Networks**: In addition to these three common methods, there are Learning Networks, which are "blueprints" for combining models in flexible ways. Learning Networks are simple transformations of existing workflows that can be "exported" to define new, stand-alone model types. This allows for more complex model compositions beyond the three common methods mentioned earlier.

Performance measures in MLJ.jl

A performance measure is a way of quantifying the accuracy of a machine learning model. Performance measures are used to compare different models and select the best model for a particular task.

Many different performance measures that can be used to evaluate machine learning models.

How to choose performance measures?

The choice of performance measure depends on the specific machine learning task. For example, if you are building a model to predict whether a customer will churn, you might use the accuracy or the F1 score. If you are building a model to predict the price of a house, you might use the mean absolute error or the root mean squared error.

Built-in performance measures

MLJ provides a number of built-in performance measures. These measures can be used to evaluate machine learning models without having to write any custom code.

The built-in performance measures in MLJ include:

- Accuracy
- Precision
- Recall
- F1 score
- Mean absolute error
- Root mean squared error

Custom performance measures

MLJ also allows you to create custom performance measures. Custom performance measures can be used to evaluate machine learning models for tasks that are not supported by built-in performance measures.

To create a custom performance measure, you use the Measure constructor. The Measure constructor takes a function as input. The function that is passed to the Measure constructor must take two arguments: the predicted values and the actual values.

The following code creates a custom performance measure that calculates the accuracy of a model:

```
function accuracy(predicted, actual)
  sum(predicted .== actual) / length(predicted)
end
accuracy_measure = Measure(accuracy)
```

The **`accuracy_measure`** variable can now be used to evaluate machine learning models.

Model evaluation measures

Model evaluation is the process of assessing the accuracy of a machine learning model. It is an important part of the machine learning process because it allows you to identify areas where the model can be improved.

There are many different ways to evaluate model performance. Some of the most common methods include:

- **Cross-validation:** Cross-validation is a method of evaluating model performance by training the model on multiple subsets of the data and then testing the model on the remaining subset of the data.
- **Holdout sets:** Holdout sets are a subset of the data that is not used to train the model. The holdout set is used to test the model after it has been trained.
- **Bootstrapping:** Bootstrapping is a method of evaluating model performance by repeatedly sampling the data with replacement and then training the model on each sample. The model is then tested on the remaining data.

How to evaluate model performance?

To evaluate model performance, you need to choose a performance metric. A performance metric is a way of quantifying the accuracy of a model. Some of the most common performance metrics include:

- **Accuracy:** Accuracy is the percentage of predictions that are correct.
- **Precision:** Precision is the percentage of positive predictions that are actually positive.
- **Recall:** Recall is the percentage of positive instances that are correctly identified as positive.
- **F1 score:** The F1 score is a weighted average of precision and recall.
- **Mean absolute error:** The mean absolute error is the average of the absolute difference between the predicted values and the actual values.
- **Root mean squared error:** The root mean squared error is the square root of the average of the squared difference between the predicted values and the actual values.

The choice of performance metric depends on the specific machine learning task. For example, if you are building a model to predict whether a customer will churn, you might use the accuracy or the F1 score. If you are building a model to predict the price of a house, you might use the mean absolute error or the root mean squared error.

Evaluating model performance on a hold-out set

The best way to evaluate model performance is to use a held-out set. A held-out set is a subset of the data that is not used to train the model. The held-out set is used to test the model after it has been trained.

The following steps are used to evaluate model performance on a held-out set:

1. Split the data into a training set and a held-out set.
2. Train the model on the training set.
3. Test the model on the held-out set.
4. Calculate the performance metric for the model.

Evaluating model performance over time

It is important to evaluate model performance over time. This allows you to identify any changes in the accuracy of the model.

The following steps are used to evaluate model performance over time:

1. Train the model on the data.
2. Test the model on the data.
3. Calculate the performance metric for the model.
4. Repeat the first two steps for a while.

By evaluating model performance over time, you can identify any changes in the accuracy of the model and take steps to improve the model if necessary.

Model tuning

Model tuning is the process of adjusting the hyperparameters of a model to improve its performance. Hyperparameters are the parameters of a model that are not learned from the data. Some examples of hyperparameters include the number of trees in a decision tree model, the learning rate of a neural network, and the regularization strength of a linear regression model.

How to tune models?

There are many different ways to tune models. Some of the most common methods include:

- **Grid search:** Grid search is a brute-force method of tuning models. Grid search involves creating a grid of hyperparameter values and then training the model on each combination of hyperparameter values. The model with the best performance is then selected.
- **Random search:** Random search is a more efficient method of tuning models than grid search. Random search involves randomly sampling

hyperparameter values from a distribution and then training the model on each combination of hyperparameter values. The model with the best performance is then selected.

- **Bayesian optimization:** Bayesian optimization is a more sophisticated method of tuning models than grid search or random search. Bayesian optimization involves using a Bayesian model to estimate the best hyperparameter values for the model. The model with the best performance is then selected.

Hyperparameters

Some of the most common hyperparameters for machine learning models include:

- **Number of trees:** The number of trees in a decision tree model.
- **Learning rate:** The learning rate of a neural network.
- **Regularization strength:** The regularization strength of a linear regression model.

Evaluating tuned models

It is important to evaluate tuned models to ensure that they have improved performance over the original model. To evaluate tuned models, follow these steps:

- Tune the model on the training set.
- Evaluate the tuned model on the hold-out set.
- Compare the performance of the tuned model to the performance of the original model.

If the tuned model has improved performance over the original model, then you can use the tuned model for making predictions.

What are iterative models?

Iterative models are models that can be updated multiple times to improve their accuracy. They work by starting with a basic model and then making small changes to the model based on the results of the previous update. This process is repeated until the model reaches the desired level of accuracy.

Some examples of iterative models include:

- Linear regression
- Logistic regression

- Decision trees
- Neural networks

How to control iterative models?

There are a number of ways to control iterative models. Some of the most common methods include:

- **Setting the number of iterations:** You can set the number of iterations that the model will be updated for. This is a simple way to control the complexity of the model.
- **Setting the learning rate:** The learning rate controls how much the model is updated in each iteration. A higher learning rate will cause the model to learn more quickly, but it may also cause the model to overfit the data.
- **Using regularization:** Regularization is a technique that can be used to prevent overfitting. Regularization works by adding a penalty to the loss function that is proportional to the complexity of the model.

Common stopping criteria

There are various common stopping criteria that can be used to control iterative models. Some of the most common stopping criteria include:

- **Maximum number of iterations:** You can set the maximum number of iterations that the model will be updated for. This is a simple way to control the complexity of the model.
- **Minimum improvement:** You can set a minimum improvement that the model must make in each iteration before it is updated again. This can help to prevent the model from overfitting the data.
- **Early stopping:** Early stopping is a technique that can be used to stop the model from updating before it has reached the maximum number of iterations. Early stopping is based on the idea that the model will not improve significantly after a certain point.

Regularization

Regularization is a technique that can be used to prevent overfitting. Regularization works by adding a penalty to the loss function that is proportional to the complexity of the model. This can help to prevent the model from learning too much from the training data and to generalize better to new data.

There are a number of different regularization techniques that can be used. Some of the most common regularization techniques include:

- **Lasso regularization:** Lasso regularization adds a penalty to the loss function that is proportional to the sum of the absolute values of the model weights. This can help to prevent the model from learning too many features.
- **Ridge regularization:** Ridge regularization adds a penalty to the loss function that is proportional to the sum of the squares of the model weights. This can help to prevent the model from learning too large of weights.

What are learning curves?

Learning curves are a way of visualizing the performance of a model as a function of the amount of data that is used to train the model. Learning curves typically plot the performance of the model on a held-out set of data as a function of the number of training examples used to train the model.

How to create learning curves?

To create learning curves, follow these steps:

1. Split the data into a training set and a held-out set.
2. Train the model on the training set.
3. Evaluate the model on the held-out set.
4. Repeat the first two steps for a number of different training set sizes.
5. Plot the performance of the model on the held-out set as a function of the number of training examples used to train the model.

Interpreting learning curves

Learning curves can be used to interpret the performance of a model and identify areas where the model can be improved. Here are some things to look for when interpreting learning curves:

- **The shape of the learning curve:** The shape of the learning curve can tell you about the complexity of the model and the amount of data that is needed to train the model. A model with a linear learning curve is a simple model that can be trained with a small amount of data. A model with a quadratic learning curve is a more complex model that requires more data to train.

- **The location of the peak of the learning curve:** The location of the peak of the learning curve tells you about the amount of data that is needed to train the model to its best possible performance. A model with a peak at a small number of training examples is a model that is overfitting the data. A model with a peak at a large number of training examples is a model that is underfitting the data.
- **The spread of the points on the learning curve:** The spread of the points on the learning curve tells you about the variance of the model. A model with a small spread of points is a model with low variance. A model with a large spread of points is a model with high variance.

Using learning curves to improve models

Learning curves can be used to improve models by identifying areas where the model can be improved. Here are some things you can do to improve a model based on its learning curves:

- **Reduce the complexity of the model:** If the learning curve has a quadratic shape, you can reduce the complexity of the model by using a simpler model.
- **Increase the amount of data:** If the learning curve has not reached a peak, you can increase the amount of data to train the model.
- **Use regularization:** Regularization can help to reduce the variance of the model and improve its performance.

Conclusion

MLJ.jl recognizes the importance of data preprocessing and feature engineering, offering a data frontend that efficiently handles diverse data types, missing values, and transformations. It promotes flexibility and reproducibility by providing a wide range of machine learning algorithms for model selection and evaluation. Model composition enables the construction of sophisticated models by combining individual components. MLJ.jl's comprehensive performance measures aid in selecting the best model for a given problem. It supports iterative models, beneficial for large datasets and online learning. Learning curves in MLJ.jl provide insights into model performance as training data size increases, aiding in identifying underfitting or overfitting and informing data collection and model development decisions.

In the next chapter, we will learn about Bayesian statistics. Bayesian statistics is a framework that combines prior knowledge and observed data to make probabilistic inferences and update beliefs. Optimization is the process of finding the best possible solution to a problem by systematically searching for optimal values of variables or parameters.

Questions

- What is the model interface in MLJ.jl?
- What are the benefits of using the model interface in MLJ.jl?
- What are some examples of models that implement the model interface in MLJ.jl?
- Why is there a need for a data frontend in MLJ?
- What are some of the features of the data frontend in MLJ?
- How does the data frontend in MLJ make it easier to work with data?
- What are machines in MLJ?
- What are the benefits of using machines in MLJ?
- What are some examples of machines that can be created in MLJ?
- What is model composition?
- What are some of the benefits of using model composition?
- How can model composition be used to improve the performance of machine learning models?
- What are performance measures?
- What are some of the most common performance measures used in machine learning?
- How can performance measures be used to evaluate the performance of machine learning models?
- What are iterative models?
- What are some examples of iterative models?
- What are learning curves?
- What are the benefits of using learning curves?
- How can learning curves be used to improve the performance of machine learning models?

Chapter 13

Bayesian Statistics and Modeling

Introduction

Bayesian statistics is a method of statistical inference that uses Bayes' theorem to update our beliefs about a hypothesis or parameter in light of new evidence. It is a more comprehensive approach to statistics than traditional frequentist methods, which only consider the likelihood of the data given the hypothesis.

In Bayesian statistics, we start with a prior distribution, which represents our beliefs about the hypothesis or parameter, before we see the data. We then use Bayes' theorem to update our prior distribution to a posterior distribution, which represents our beliefs about the hypothesis or parameter after we see the data.

The posterior distribution can be used to make inferences about the hypothesis or parameter, such as calculating a confidence interval or hypothesis test. It can also be used to make predictions about future data.

Bayesian statistics has several advantages over traditional frequentist methods. First, it allows us to incorporate prior knowledge into our analysis. This can be useful when we have some information about the hypothesis or parameter before we see the data. Second, Bayesian statistics allows us to make inferences about the hypothesis or parameter even when the data is not perfectly informative. This is because the prior distribution can fill in the gaps in the data. Third, Bayesian statistics can be used to make predictions about future data.

Structure

In this chapter, the following topics will be covered:

- Bayesian inference
- Difference between Bayes theorem and frequentist statistical methods
- Basic concepts of Bayesian statistics
- Calculating the posterior distribution
- Making inferences from the posterior distribution
- Bayesian models
- Various Bayesian models
- Manipulating discrete data with Bayesian approach
- Manipulating categorical data with Bayesian approach
- Gaussian Process Latent Variable Model
- Other Bayesian models

Bayesian inference

Bayesian inference is a method of statistical inference that uses Bayes' theorem to update one's beliefs about a hypothesis as more evidence or information becomes available. In Bayesian inference, probability is interpreted as a measure of belief or confidence in an event.

Bayesian inference is a powerful tool that can be used to solve a variety of problems. It is a relatively new technique, but it has become increasingly popular in recent years due to the availability of large datasets and powerful computing resources.

The following are some of the benefits of using Bayesian inference:

- Bayesian inference is a principled approach to statistical inference. It is based on Bayes' theorem, which is a fundamental law of probability.
- Bayesian inference can be used to incorporate prior knowledge into the analysis. This can improve the accuracy of the results.
- Bayesian inference can be used to make inferences about the state of the world based on incomplete or uncertain data. This can be useful in a variety of applications, such as medical diagnosis and financial forecasting.

Bayesian statistics can be used for a wide variety of applications, such as medical research, finance, and machine learning.

The following are some examples of how Bayesian statistics is used in practice:

- **Medical research:** Bayesian statistics is often used in medical research to assess the efficacy of new treatments. For example, a researcher might use Bayesian statistics to calculate the probability that a new drug is effective in treating a particular disease.
- **Finance:** Bayesian statistics is used in finance to make predictions about the future value of assets, such as stocks and bonds. For example, a financial analyst might use Bayesian statistics to calculate the probability that a stock price will rise or fall in the next year.
- **Machine learning:** Bayesian statistics is used in machine learning to train models that can make predictions about new data. For example, a machine learning engineer might use Bayesian statistics to train a model that can predict whether a customer will click an ad.

Bayesian inference can be used to solve a variety of problems, including:

- Classification: Bayesian inference can be used to classify data into two or more categories.
- Regression: Bayesian inference can be used to predict a continuous value from a set of features.
- Inference: Bayesian inference can be used to make inferences about the state of the world based on incomplete or uncertain data.

The following are some of the challenges of using Bayesian inference:

- Bayesian inference can be computationally expensive. This is because it requires the calculation of the posterior probability, which can be a complex function.
- Bayesian inference can be difficult to understand. This is because it requires a basic understanding of probability theory.
- Bayesian inference can be sensitive to the choice of the prior distribution. This means that the results of the analysis can be sensitive to the assumptions that are made about the prior distribution.

Difference between Bayes' theorem and Frequentist statistical methods

Bayesian statistics is different from other statistical methods in a few key ways.

First, Bayesian statistics uses Bayes' theorem to update our beliefs about a hypothesis or parameter in light of new evidence. This is in contrast to Frequentist statistics, which only considers the likelihood of the data given the hypothesis.

Second, Bayesian statistics allows us to incorporate prior knowledge into our analysis. This can be useful when we have some information about the hypothesis or parameter before we see the data. Frequentist statistics does not allow us to do this.

Third, Bayesian statistics can be used to make predictions about future data. Frequentist statistics can only be used to make inferences about the past or present.

Bayesian statistics is a more comprehensive approach to statistics than traditional frequentist methods. It allows us to incorporate prior knowledge into our analysis and make predictions about future data. This makes it a powerful tool for a wide variety of applications, such as medical research, finance, and machine learning.

The following are some additional examples of how Bayesian statistics is different from other statistical methods:

- Bayesian statistics uses probability theory to represent uncertainty, while frequentist statistics uses statistics.
- Bayesian statistics uses priors to represent our beliefs about the unknown parameters, while frequentist statistics does not.
- Bayesian statistics uses Bayes' theorem to update our beliefs about the unknown parameters after seeing the data, while frequentist statistics uses maximum likelihood estimation to find the parameter values that maximize the likelihood function.

Basic concepts of Bayesian statistics

Bayesian statistics is a method of statistical inference that uses Bayes' theorem to update one's beliefs about a hypothesis as more evidence or information becomes available. In Bayesian statistics, probability is interpreted as a measure of belief or confidence in an event.

The basic concepts of Bayesian statistics are:

- **Prior distribution:** A prior distribution is a probability distribution that represents one's beliefs about a hypothesis before seeing any data. It can be based on previous knowledge, expert opinion, or even gut feeling.
- **Likelihood function:** The likelihood function is a probability function that describes how likely the data is under a particular hypothesis. It is calculated by multiplying the prior distribution by the probability of the data, given the hypothesis.

- **Posterior distribution:** The posterior distribution is a probability distribution that represents one's beliefs about a hypothesis after seeing the data. It is calculated using Bayes' theorem, which takes the prior distribution and the likelihood function as input and outputs the posterior distribution.

Bayesian statistics can be used to solve a wide variety of problems, including:

- **Estimating the parameters of a probability distribution:** Bayesian statistics can be used to estimate the parameters of a probability distribution, such as the mean and standard deviation of a normal distribution.
- **Making predictions about future events:** Bayesian statistics can be used to make predictions about future events, such as the probability of rain tomorrow.
- **Testing hypotheses:** Bayesian statistics can be used to test hypotheses about the world, such as the hypothesis that a new drug is effective in treating a particular disease.

Calculating the posterior distribution

Suppose we want to estimate the probability of flipping a fair coin and getting heads. We don't know the true probability, so we need to use a prior distribution. In this case, we can use a uniform prior distribution, which means that we believe that all possible values of the probability are equally likely.

Now, let's say we flip the coin 10 times and get heads 7 times. This new information can be used to update our beliefs about the probability of flipping heads. We do this by using Bayes' theorem, which tells us that the posterior distribution is proportional to the product of the prior distribution and the likelihood function.

In this case, the likelihood function is simply the probability of getting 7 heads in 10 flips of a fair coin. This probability can be calculated using the binomial distribution.

The posterior distribution is then calculated by multiplying the prior distribution by the likelihood function. This gives us a posterior distribution that is centered around 0.7, which means that we now believe that the probability of flipping heads is 70%.

As we collect more data, our beliefs about the probability of flipping heads will continue to update. This is the power of Bayesian statistics: it allows us to use our prior beliefs and new data to make informed decisions.

Now, let us look at another example. Suppose we want to estimate the probability of a patient having a disease, given that they have tested positive for the disease. We don't know the true probability, so we need to use a prior distribution. In this case, we can use a uniform prior distribution, which means that we believe that all possible values of the probability are equally likely.

Now, let's say that the sensitivity of the test is 90%, which means that if the patient has the disease, there is a 90% chance that the test will be positive. The specificity of the test is 95%, which means that if the patient does not have the disease, there is a 95% chance that the test will be negative.

Making inferences from the posterior distribution

A mathematical expression for Bayes' theorem:

```
Posterior = Prior * Likelihood / Normalizing Constant
```

In this expression,

- Posterior is the probability distribution of the parameter after seeing the data.
- Prior is the probability distribution of the parameter before seeing the data.
- Likelihood is the probability of the data, given the parameter.
- Normalizing constant is a constant that ensures the posterior distribution is a valid probability distribution. It is also known as the marginal likelihood or evidence. The normalizing constant ensures that the posterior distribution integrates (or sums) to 1, thereby representing a valid probability distribution.

The prior probability can be any value between 0 and 1. In this example, we will use a prior probability of 0.5, which means that we believe that there is a 50% chance that the patient has the disease.

The likelihood of getting a positive test result, given that the patient has the disease, is given by the following equation:

The likelihood to ensure that the posterior distribution integrates to 1.

```
Likelihood = Sensitivity * (1 - Specificity)
```

In this expression,

- Sensitivity is the probability that the test will be positive, given that the patient has the disease.
- Specificity is the probability that the test will be negative, given that the patient does not have the disease.

Substituting the prior probability, likelihood, and sensitivity into the equation for the posterior probability, we get the following equation:

```
Posterior = (0.5) * (0.9) / Normalizing Constant
```

The normalizing constant is a constant that is used to ensure that the posterior probability integrates to 1. The value of the normalizing constant is not important for this example, so we can ignore it.

Therefore, the posterior probability of the patient having the disease, given that they have tested positive, is 0.45. This means that there is a 45% chance that the patient has the disease, given that they have tested positive.

As you can see, Bayes' theorem can be used to update one's beliefs about a hypothesis, given new evidence. In this example, we use Bayes' theorem to update our belief about the probability of a patient having a disease, given that they have tested positive.

Bayesian models

Bayesian models are statistical models that incorporate prior knowledge or beliefs about a particular phenomenon into the modeling process. They are based on Bayesian probability theory, which allows for the quantification and updating of uncertain beliefs in the presence of new evidence.

In Bayesian modeling, the uncertain quantities in the model, known as parameters, are treated as random variables. These parameters are assigned prior probability distributions that express the initial beliefs or knowledge about their values before observing any data. The prior distributions can be based on expert opinions, previous studies, or other sources of information.

Once the prior distributions are specified, Bayesian models combine them with observed data using Bayes' theorem to obtain the posterior distribution of the parameters. The posterior distribution represents the updated beliefs about the parameters given the observed data. It combines the prior knowledge with the likelihood of the data under the model.

Bayesian models can be used for a wide range of statistical analyses, including regression, classification, clustering, time series analysis, and more. They provide a flexible framework for incorporating prior knowledge, handling uncertainty, and making probabilistic inferences about the parameters and predictions of the model.

One of the advantages of Bayesian modeling is that it naturally accounts for uncertainty and provides a full probability distribution for the parameters, allowing for the quantification of uncertainty in predictions and decision-making. Additionally, Bayesian models can be updated as new data becomes available, enabling iterative learning and refinement of beliefs.

Some commonly used Bayesian models include Bayesian linear regression, Bayesian networks, Bayesian hierarchical models, and Markov chain Monte Carlo (MCMC) methods for sampling from complex posterior distributions. Bayesian models provide a flexible framework for making inferences and predictions. They can be applied to a wide range of problems, including regression, classification, clustering, and time series analysis, among others. By using the full posterior distribution, Bayesian models allow for uncertainty quantification, which is particularly useful when making decisions or performing sensitivity analyses.

Various Bayesian models

Various types of Bayesian models can be used depending on the specific problem and data at hand. Here are some commonly used types of Bayesian models:

- **Bayesian linear regression**:

  Bayesian linear regression extends the classical linear regression. It allows for the incorporation of prior beliefs about the regression coefficients and provides posterior distributions for the coefficients, enabling uncertainty quantification. It allows for uncertainty quantification and provides posterior distributions for the coefficients. For example, suppose you want to predict housing prices based on features like size, location, and number of bedrooms. Bayesian linear regression can estimate the coefficients of these features while considering prior knowledge about their relationships.

- **Bayesian logistic regression**:

  Similar to linear regression, Bayesian logistic regression incorporates prior beliefs about the coefficients, but it is used for binary classification problems where the dependent variable is binary. For instance, imagine you want to predict whether a customer will churn or not based on their demographic and behavioral data. Bayesian logistic regression allows you to estimate the coefficients while considering prior beliefs about their influence on churn probability.

- **Bayesian hierarchical models**:

  Bayesian hierarchical models are employed when data has a hierarchical or nested structure. They allow for modeling both within-group and between-group variability and incorporating prior information at different levels of the hierarchy. For example, consider a study comparing the effectiveness of different treatments across multiple hospitals. A Bayesian hierarchical model can capture the variation within hospitals as well as estimate the differences in treatment effects between hospitals.

- **Bayesian mixture models**:

  Mixture models are used for clustering and density estimation. Bayesian approaches to mixture models allow for estimating the number of clusters, automatic model selection, and uncertainty quantification. Suppose you have customer data and want to segment them into distinct groups based on their preferences. A Bayesian mixture model can identify the number of customer segments and assign each customer to a specific segment, considering uncertainty in the assignments.

- **Bayesian time series models**:

  Bayesian time series models are employed to analyze time-dependent data. They allow for incorporating prior information, modeling complex dependencies, and forecasting with uncertainty. For example, in stock market analysis, a Bayesian time series model can be used to forecast stock prices based on historical data, capturing the uncertainty in the predictions.

- **Bayesian networks**:

  Bayesian networks represent probabilistic relationships among variables using directed acyclic graphs. They allow for efficient inference and reasoning under uncertainty. An example could be a medical diagnosis system that models the relationships between symptoms and diseases. A Bayesian network can incorporate prior beliefs and observed symptoms to estimate the probabilities of different diseases given the symptoms.

- **Gaussian processes**:

  Gaussian processes are non-parametric models used for regression and classification tasks. They provide a flexible and Bayesian way to model complex functions and offer uncertainty estimates in predictions. For instance, in the field of autonomous vehicles, Gaussian processes can be used to model the uncertainty in predicting the trajectory of other vehicles on the road.

- **Bayesian neural networks**:

  Bayesian approaches can be applied to neural networks to incorporate uncertainty in the weights and model parameters. This allows for robust predictions and uncertainty quantification in deep learning models. For example, in image recognition tasks, a Bayesian neural network can provide not only the predicted class for an image but also the associated uncertainty in the prediction.

These examples showcase the application of different Bayesian models across various domains, highlighting their ability to incorporate prior knowledge, handle uncertainty, and provide richer probabilistic inferences.

Bayesian linear regression

Let's consider an example of Bayesian linear regression in the context of predicting housing prices based on features like size, location, and number of bedrooms.

Suppose you have a dataset of houses with the following information:

- Size (in square feet): [1500, 2000, 1800, 2200, 2500]
- Location (categorical): ["Suburb", "City", "Suburb", "City", "Rural"]
- Number of bedrooms: [3, 4, 3, 5, 4]
- Price (in thousands of dollars): [250, 300, 280, 320, 350]

In Bayesian linear regression, we incorporate prior beliefs about the regression coefficients (intercept and slopes) and estimate their posterior distributions given the data. Let's assume a simple linear regression model with the following equation:

```
Price = β₀ + β₁ * Size + β₂ * Location + β₃ * Bedrooms + ε
```

where β_0 is the intercept, β_1, β_2, and β_3 are the coefficients for the size, location, and number of bedrooms, respectively, and ε represents the random error term.

To incorporate prior beliefs, we assign prior probability distributions to the coefficients. Let's assume a normal distribution for simplicity. For instance, we may have the following prior beliefs:

β_0 `~ N(0, 1000)` (prior belief that the intercept is centered around 0) β_1 `~ N(0, 1)` (prior belief that the coefficient for size has a small effect) β_2 `~ N(0, 1)` (prior belief that the coefficient for location has a small effect) β_3 `~ N(0, 1)` (prior belief that the coefficient for bedrooms has a small effect)

To estimate the posterior distributions, we combine the prior distributions with the likelihood of the data. The likelihood is typically assumed to be normally distributed, and we can use Markov chain Monte Carlo (MCMC) methods, such as Gibbs sampling or Hamiltonian Monte Carlo, to draw samples from the posterior distributions.

Using these samples, we can then make predictions and calculate credible intervals that capture the uncertainty in our estimates. The credible intervals provide a range of plausible values for the predicted price.

By incorporating prior beliefs and estimating the posterior distributions, Bayesian linear regression allows us to not only estimate the coefficients but also quantify uncertainty in our predictions, providing a more comprehensive analysis compared to classical linear regression.

Bayesian logistic regression

Let's consider an example of Bayesian logistic regression in the context of predicting whether a customer will churn or not based on their demographic and behavioral data.

Suppose you have a dataset with the following variables for each customer:

- Age: [35, 42, 28, 55, 38]
- Gender: ["Male", "Female", "Female", "Male", "Male"]
- Monthly Income (in thousands): [5, 7, 3, 10, 6]
- Number of Transactions: [10, 5, 3, 12, 8]
- Churn Status: [0, 1, 1, 0, 0] (0 indicates no churn, 1 indicates churn)

In Bayesian logistic regression, we incorporate prior beliefs about the logistic regression coefficients and estimate their posterior distributions given the data. The logistic regression model uses a logistic function to model the probability of churn:

```
P(Churn = 1) = 1 / (1 + exp(-(β₀ + β₁ * Age + β₂ * Gender + β₃ * Income
+ β₄ * Transactions)))
```

where β_0 is the intercept, β_1, β_2, β_3, and β_4 are the coefficients for the age, gender, income, and transactions, respectively.

To incorporate prior beliefs, we assign prior probability distributions to the coefficients. Let's assume a normal distribution for simplicity. For example:

$\beta_0 \sim N(0, 10)$ (prior belief that the intercept is centered around 0) $\beta_1 \sim N(0, 1)$ (prior belief that the coefficient for age has a small effect) $\beta_2 \sim N(0, 1)$ (prior belief that the coefficient for gender has a small effect) $\beta_3 \sim N(0, 1)$ (prior belief that the coefficient for income has a small effect) $\beta_4 \sim N(0, 1)$ (prior belief that the coefficient for transactions has a small effect)

To estimate the posterior distributions, we combine the prior distributions with the likelihood of the data. The likelihood is determined by the observed churn status, and we can use MCMC methods, such as Gibbs sampling or Hamiltonian Monte Carlo, to draw samples from the posterior distributions.

Using these samples, we can make predictions by calculating the probability of churn for new customers and computing credible intervals to capture the uncertainty in our predictions.

Bayesian logistic regression allows us to estimate the coefficients, quantify uncertainty, and make probabilistic predictions. It incorporates prior beliefs and provides a more comprehensive analysis compared to classical logistic regression, taking into account uncertainty and allowing for more informed decision-making.

Bayesian networks

Let's consider an example of a Bayesian network in the context of a medical diagnosis system. Imagine we have a set of symptoms and diseases and want to model the probabilistic relationships between them.

Suppose we have the following variables:

- Chest Pain (CP): [Yes, No]
- Shortness of Breath (SOB): [Yes, No]
- Heart Disease (HD): [Yes, No]
- Lung Disease (LD): [Yes, No]

The goal is to build a Bayesian network that represents the dependencies and conditional probabilities between these variables. The structure of the network can be represented as a directed acyclic graph (DAG) where the nodes correspond to the variables, and the edges represent the probabilistic dependencies.

Let's assume the following dependencies and conditional probabilities:

- CP influences HD: Chest Pain is a symptom that can indicate the presence of Heart Disease.
- SOB influences HD: Shortness of Breath is another symptom that can indicate the presence of Heart Disease.
- HD influences LD: Heart Disease can be a risk factor for Lung Disease.

The conditional probability tables (CPTs) represent the probabilities of each variable given its parents in the network. Here's an example of how the CPTs may look for this Bayesian network:

- P(CP) - the probability of Chest Pain: [Yes: 0.3, No: 0.7]
- P(SOB|HD) - the probability of Shortness of Breath given Heart Disease:
    - HD: Yes [Yes: 0.8, No: 0.2]
    - HD: No [Yes: 0.1, No: 0.9]
- P(HD) - the probability of Heart Disease: [Yes: 0.05, No: 0.95]
- P(LD|HD) - the probability of Lung Disease given Heart Disease:
    - HD: Yes [Yes: 0.7, No: 0.3]
    - HD: No [Yes: 0.2, No: 0.8]

With this Bayesian network, we can perform various types of inference. For example:

- Given observed symptoms, we can calculate the probability of Heart Disease or Lung Disease.
- Given the presence of Heart Disease, we can infer the probability of Lung Disease.
- Given the absence of Chest Pain and Shortness of Breath, we can update the probability of Heart Disease.

By propagating probabilities through the network using the rules of conditional probability, we can make informed inferences about the variables of interest.

Bayesian networks provide a graphical and intuitive representation of probabilistic dependencies and allow for efficient inference and reasoning under uncertainty. They are widely used in various fields, including medical diagnosis, risk assessment, decision support systems, and more.

Gaussian processes

Let's consider an example of Gaussian processes in the context of predicting housing prices based on historical data.

Suppose you have a dataset with the following information:

- Size (in square feet): [1500, 2000, 1800, 2200, 2500]
- Price (in thousands of dollars): [250, 300, 280, 320, 350]

The goal is to build a Gaussian process model to predict housing prices for new properties based on their size.

Gaussian processes (GPs) are non-parametric models that can be used for regression tasks. They provide a flexible and Bayesian way to model complex functions. In the case of housing price prediction, we can assume a Gaussian process prior to the unknown function that maps size to price.

To specify the GP, we need to define a mean function and a covariance function (also known as a kernel function). The mean function represents the prior expectation of the function, and the covariance function characterizes the smoothness and correlation structure of the function.

For example, we can choose a zero-mean GP and use a squared exponential kernel as the covariance function:

Mean function: zero mean Covariance function: squared exponential kernel

Using the observed data, we can compute the posterior distribution over functions, which is also a Gaussian process. This posterior distribution captures the uncertainty in our predictions and provides a probabilistic estimate of the housing prices for new properties.

Given a new property size, we can use the Gaussian process model to make predictions and provide credible intervals that represent the uncertainty in our estimates. The credible intervals give a range of plausible values for the predicted price.

By leveraging the flexibility and Bayesian nature of Gaussian processes, we can model complex relationships between variables and capture uncertainty in predictions. Gaussian processes are widely used in regression tasks, time series analysis, optimization, and other fields where probabilistic modeling and uncertainty quantification are essential.

Bayesian neural networks

Let's consider an example of Bayesian neural networks (BNNs) in the context of image recognition.

Suppose you have a dataset of images labeled with different categories, such as cats and dogs. The goal is to train a BNN to classify new images into these categories while capturing the uncertainty in the predictions.

A Bayesian neural network extends a traditional neural network by incorporating uncertainty in the weights and model parameters. This allows for more robust predictions and provides a measure of confidence in the model's outputs.

In a BNN, instead of having fixed weights as in a standard neural network, we assign probability distributions to the weights and biases of the network. We can use prior distributions to represent our prior beliefs about the weights, and during training, we update these distributions to obtain posterior distributions that reflect our updated beliefs given the observed data.

To estimate the posterior distributions over the weights, we typically use Bayesian inference techniques, such as Markov chain Monte Carlo (MCMC) or variational inference. These methods sample from the posterior distribution or approximate it, respectively.

During inference, we can propagate multiple samples from the posterior through the network to make predictions. Instead of a single output, we obtain a distribution over the predicted categories, capturing the uncertainty in the classification.

For example, given a new image, a BNN might output a distribution indicating that there is a 70% probability of the image being a cat and a 30% probability of it being a dog. This provides a more informative prediction compared to a deterministic neural network, as it allows us to quantify our uncertainty in the classification.

Bayesian neural networks are useful in scenarios where uncertainty estimation is crucial, such as safety-critical systems, decision-making under uncertainty, and active learning, among others. By incorporating Bayesian inference into neural networks, BNNs provide a powerful framework for robust and probabilistic predictions.

Building a Bayesian model

Building a Bayesian model involves several steps, including specifying the model structure, choosing prior distributions, estimating the posterior distributions, and performing inference. Here's a general guide on how to build a Bayesian model:

1. **Define the model structure**:
    a. Identify the variables: Determine the input variables, output variables, and any intermediate variables that are relevant to your problem.
    b. Determine the relationships: Specify how the variables are related to each other. This could be through direct dependencies or conditional dependencies.
    c. Choose the model type: Select the appropriate model type based on the problem at hand, such as Bayesian linear regression, Bayesian logistic regression, Gaussian processes, or hierarchical models.
2. **Specify prior distributions**:
    a. Assign prior probability distributions: Choose prior distributions for the model parameters. Priors reflect your beliefs or assumptions about the parameter values before observing the data.
    b. Incorporate prior knowledge: If you have prior knowledge or information about the parameters, use appropriate prior distributions to represent that knowledge.
    c. Consider the complexity: Select prior distributions that strike a balance between providing enough flexibility to capture the true relationships in the data and preventing overfitting.
3. **Construct the likelihood**:
    a. Determine the likelihood function: Define the likelihood function, which represents the probability of observing the data given the model parameters.
    b. Choose an appropriate likelihood: The choice of likelihood depends on the problem type and the nature of the data. Common choices include Gaussian, Bernoulli, multinomial, or Poisson distributions.

c. Incorporate measurement error: If your data has measurement error or uncertainty, consider incorporating it into the likelihood function to capture the data noise accurately.

4. **Estimate posterior distributions**:

   a. Calculate the posterior distributions: Use Bayes' theorem to update the prior distributions based on the observed data and the likelihood function.

   b. Choose inference methods: Depending on the complexity of the model and the availability of analytical solutions, use appropriate inference methods such as Markov chain Monte Carlo (MCMC) or variational inference.

   c. Obtain samples from the posterior: Run MCMC chains or perform variational inference to obtain samples from the posterior distribution of the model parameters.

5. **Perform inference**:

   a. Make predictions: Use the posterior samples to make predictions for new data points or infer unobserved variables.

   b. Quantify uncertainty: Utilize the posterior samples to compute summary statistics, such as means, variances, or credible intervals, to quantify and communicate uncertainty in the predictions.

   c. Conduct hypothesis testing: Assess the significance of model parameters or test hypotheses by examining the posterior distributions.

6. **Evaluate and refine**:

   a. Assess model performance: Evaluate the model's fit to the data using appropriate evaluation metrics, such as mean squared error, log-likelihood, or classification accuracy.

   b. Refine the model: If the model's performance is unsatisfactory, iterate on the model by adjusting the model structure, prior distributions, or hyperparameters. Consider adding or removing variables, changing the model complexity, or updating prior assumptions.

7. **Interpret and communicate results**:

   a. Understand the model outputs: Interpret the results of the Bayesian model, including the posterior distributions, to gain insights into the relationships between variables, model uncertainty, and parameter estimates.

   b. Communicate effectively: Present the results in a clear and understandable manner to stakeholders, decision-makers, or other interested parties. Highlight the probabilistic nature of the predictions and provide appropriate visualizations or summaries of the posterior distributions.

Remember that building a Bayesian model is an iterative process that requires domain knowledge, data analysis skills, and an understanding of probabilistic modeling. It's essential to consider the assumptions and limitations of the model and continually refine it based on feedback and new insights.

Bayesian modeling in Julia

Turing.jl is a Julia programming language library that provides a flexible and powerful framework for probabilistic programming. It allows users to define and perform Bayesian inference for complex probabilistic models using a high-level syntax.

Turing.jl is designed to enable researchers and practitioners to easily build and experiment with Bayesian models. It offers a wide range of modeling constructs and inference algorithms, making it suitable for various applications such as data analysis, machine learning, and scientific computing.

Key features of Turing.jl are as follows:

- **Probabilistic modeling**: Turing.jl allows you to define probabilistic models using a simple and intuitive syntax. You can express the relationships between variables and incorporate prior knowledge or assumptions about the model parameters.
- **Bayesian inference**: The library provides various algorithms for Bayesian inference, including Markov chain Monte Carlo (MCMC) methods like Hamiltonian Monte Carlo (HMC) and particle-based methods such as sequential Monte Carlo (SMC). These algorithms estimate the posterior distributions of the model parameters given the observed data.
- **Automatic differentiation**: Turing.jl leverages Julia's powerful automatic differentiation capabilities, enabling efficient and scalable computation

of gradients for inference algorithms like HMC. This allows for faster convergence and more accurate posterior estimation.

- **Extensive distributions**: The library offers a comprehensive collection of probability distributions, including common univariate and multivariate distributions, as well as specialized distributions for specific applications. Users can easily define custom distributions as well.
- **Advanced modeling constructs**: Turing.jl provides advanced modeling constructs such as hierarchical models, mixture models, time series models, and hidden Markov models. These constructs allow you to represent complex dependencies and structures in your models.
- **Model checking and validation**: Turing.jl offers diagnostics and tools for model checking and validation. This helps identify potential issues or discrepancies between the model and the observed data, ensuring the model's reliability.
- **Integration with Julia ecosystem**: Being built on the Julia programming language, Turing.jl seamlessly integrates with other Julia packages, enabling users to leverage the rich ecosystem of libraries for data manipulation, visualization, and scientific computing.

Turing.jl is actively maintained and developed by a community of researchers and practitioners. It is continually evolving, incorporating new features, and benefiting from the advancements in the Julia language itself.

Let us solve the coin-flipping example by using the Turing probabilistic programming language to specify and approximate a posterior distribution using samples.

Let us first import the Turing library, which is a probabilistic programming language for specifying and sampling from probabilistic models and the **MCMCChains** library, which provides functions for analyzing and visualizing samples obtained from Markov chain Monte Carlo (MCMC) methods.

```
using Turing, MCMCChains
```

Then, we will define a Turing model called coin flip. It is an unconditioned coin flip model with N observations. The prior distribution for the probability of heads, p, is specified as a Beta(1, 1) distribution. The observations, y, are drawn from N independent and identically distributed Bernoulli distributions with success rate p.

```
@model function coinflip(; N::Int)

    # Our prior belief about the probability of heads in a coin toss.

    p ~ Beta(1, 1)
```

```
    # Heads or tails of a coin are drawn from `N` independent and
identically
    # distributed Bernoulli distributions with success rate `p`.
    y ~ filldist(Bernoulli(p), N)
    return y
end;
```

We can generate random samples from the coinflip model. It returns a tuple with the sampled value of p and an array of sampled values of y.

```
rand(coinflip(; N))
```

We will define a conditioned version of the coinflip model. It takes an additional argument y (an array of observations) and conditions the model on those observations. The `| (; y)` syntax specifies that the model should be conditioned on the observations y.

```
coinflip(y::AbstractVector{<:Real}) = coinflip(; N=length(y)) | (; y)
```

We will create an instance of the coinflip model by calling it with the data argument. The data argument should be an array of observations.

```
model = coinflip(data);
```

We will then create a sampler object for Hamiltonian Monte Carlo (HMC) sampling. The NUTS (No-U-Turn Sampler) algorithm is used here.

```
sampler = NUTS();
```

We will perform MCMC sampling using the specified model and sampler. It draws 1000 samples from the posterior distribution. The progress=false argument suppresses the progress bar.

```
chain = sample(model, sampler, 1_000; progress=false);
```

Let us create a histogram plot of the samples obtained from the MCMC chain. It visualizes the approximate posterior distribution.

```
histogram(chain)
```

You can see that it is much easier to use Turing.jl to evaluate various Bayesian statistical models.

Manipulating discrete data with Bayesian approach

To solve a linear regression problem using Turing.jl, you can follow these steps:

Step 1: Install the required packages: First, make sure you have Turing.jl and other necessary packages installed. You can do this by running the following code in the Julia REPL or Jupyter Notebook:

```
import Pkg
Pkg.add("Turing")
Pkg.add("Distributions")
Pkg.add("StatsPlots")
```

Step 2: Import required packages: Import the necessary packages in Julia:

```
using Turing
using Distributions
using StatsPlots
```

Step 3: Generate synthetic data: Generate some synthetic data for the linear regression problem. Let's assume we have n data points, and x and y are the independent and dependent variables, respectively:

```
julia> n = 100
100
julia> x = rand(n)
100-element Vector{Float64}:
 0.1454876506720857

 ⋮

0.871731039104576
julia> intercept_true = 2.0
2.0
julia> slope_true = 3.0
3.0
julia> noise_std = 0.5
0.5
julia> y = intercept_true .+ slope_true .* x + rand(Normal(0, noise_
std), n)
100-element Vector{Float64}:
 2.985222764640527

 ⋮
```

```
4.1866572131062565
```

Step 4: Define the linear regression model: Define the linear regression model in Turing using the `@model` macro:

```
julia> @model function linear_regression(x, y)
                     n = length(x)
                     intercept ~ Normal(0, 10)
                     slope ~ Normal(0, 10)
                     noise_std ~ Truncated(Normal(0, 10), 0, Inf)
                     for i in 1:n
                            y[i] ~ Normal(intercept + slope * x[i],
noise_std)
                     end
       end
linear_regression (generic function with 2 methods)
```

Step 5: Specify and run the inference: Specify the inference algorithm and run it to obtain samples from the posterior distribution:

```
julia> model = linear_regression(x, y)
DynamicPPL.Model{typeof(linear_regression), (:x, :y), (), (), Tuple{Vector{Float64}, Vector{Float64}}, Tuple{}, DynamicPPL
.DefaultContext}(linear_regression, (x = [0.1454876506720857, 0.49209875397455405, 0.6976075064059876, 0.3139438875546062,
 0.6565478448498397, 0.4643509489078428, 0.39341733797495504, 0.07625720791474044, 0.42006405266254765, 0.748436644324603
 …  0.2977007509631552, 0.9017751841705696, 0.8968453215603662, 0.4973214115087524, 0.21141202878677 3, 0.8931304088232883,
 0.08866350144904234, 0.6026482047451546, 0.885467312917427, 0.871731039104576], y = [2.985222764640527, 3.347246896800883
5, 3.5628741848955148, 2.35566977038332, 4.3670865718408365, 3.8834658864735707, 3.0720361396818436, 1.7694152250612838, 3
.2960643602770197, 4.1866572131062565  …  2.5526672073125107, 4.143135547026115, 5.005564773714585, 2.576648568268848, 2.8
213739059194065, 5.2735357683208814, 2.203008083714879, 3.6041773911638018, 5.058509494861961, 3.7243251698886723]), Named
Tuple(), DynamicPPL.DefaultContext())
```

Figure 13.1: *Bayesian model for linear regression*

Now, let's put our model into the MCMC chain and train our model on discrete data.

```
julia> chain = sample(model, NUTS(), 1000)
┌ Info: Found initial step size
└   ϵ = 0.0125

Chains MCMC chain (1000×15×1 Array{Float64, 3}):

Iterations        = 501:1:1500
Number of chains  = 1
Samples per chain = 1000
Wall duration     = 17.98 seconds
Compute duration  = 17.98 seconds
parameters        = intercept, slope, noise_std
internals         = lp, n_steps, is_accept, acceptance_rate, log_density, hamiltonian_energy, hamiltonian_energy_error, ma
x_hamiltonian_energy_error, tree_depth, numerical_error, step_size, nom_step_size

Summary Statistics
  parameters      mean       std      mcse   ess_bulk   ess_tail      rhat   e ⋯
                                                                               ⋯

   intercept    1.8173    0.0875    0.0043   425.6617   501.6407    1.0017     ⋯
       slope    3.1929    0.1441    0.0070   422.3497   483.8434    1.0023     ⋯
   noise_std    0.4565    0.0319    0.0013   598.6055   551.1876    0.9996     ⋯
                                                              1 column omitted

Quantiles
  parameters      2.5%     25.0%     50.0%     75.0%     97.5%

   intercept    1.6245    1.7615    1.8192    1.8743    1.9907
       slope    2.9189    3.0975    3.1891    3.2935    3.4716
   noise_std    0.4006    0.4336    0.4537    0.4756    0.5320
```

Figure 13.2: *Bayesian chain for linear regression*

Step 6: Analyze and visualize the results: Analyze and visualize the results to understand the posterior distribution of the model parameters:

```
plot(chain)
```

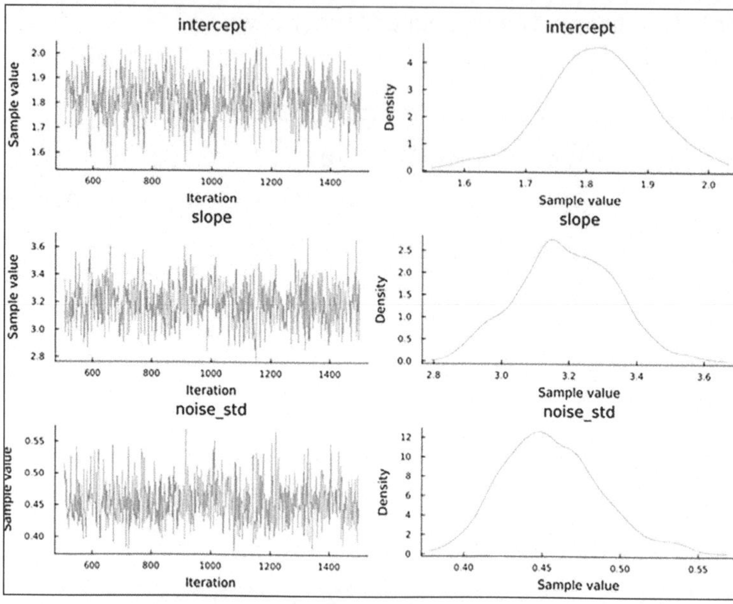

Figure 13.3: Plots and charts specifying the sample value over a standard period and for a certain number of iterations

This will generate plots showing the posterior distributions of the intercept, slope, and noise standard deviation.

By following these steps, you can use Turing.jl to solve a linear regression problem by inferring the posterior distribution of the model parameters.

Manipulating categorical data with Bayesian approach

To solve a Bayesian logistic regression problem using Turing.jl. Bayesian logistic regression allows us to estimate the uncertainty associated with the model parameters and make probabilistic predictions.

To begin, make sure you have Turing.jl installed. You can install it by running the following command in the Julia REPL:

```
using Pkg
Pkg.add("Turing")
```

Once you have Turing.jl installed, you can use it to perform Bayesian logistic regression. Here's an example code that demonstrates the process:

```
julia> using Turing, MCMCChains, Random

julia> # Generate synthetic data
      Random.seed!(123)
TaskLocalRNG()

julia> n = 100  # number of data points
100

julia> x = randn(n)
100-element Vector{Float64}:
  0.8082879284649668
 -1.1220725081141734
  ⋮
  0.14837536667608195

julia> y = rand(Float64, n) .< 1 ./ (1 .+ exp.(-3 * x))  # logistic
regression model
100-element BitVector:
 1
 0
 ⋮
 0

julia> # Define the Bayesian logistic regression model
      @model function logistic_regression(x, y)
                    # Priors
                    β ~ Normal(0, 5)
                    α ~ Normal(0, 5)
                    # Linear predictor
                    η = α .+ β * x

                    # Likelihood
                    for i in 1:length(x)
                          y[i] ~ Bernoulli(1 / (1 + exp(-η[i])))
                    end
```

```
    end
logistic_regression (generic function with 2 methods)
```

In this example, we generate synthetic data with a logistic regression relationship between the input x and the binary output y. We define the Bayesian logistic regression model using the `@model` macro provided by Turing.jl. The model specifies the priors for the parameters β and α, and defines the linear predictor η and the likelihood of the data y. The logistic transformation is done by `p = 1 ./ (1 .+ exp.(-η))` to ensure the probabilities are calculated correctly.

We then use the sample function to run the MCMC sampler (in this case, we're using the NUTS sampler). We specify the model, the sampling algorithm, and the number of samples we want to obtain (in this case, 1000 samples).

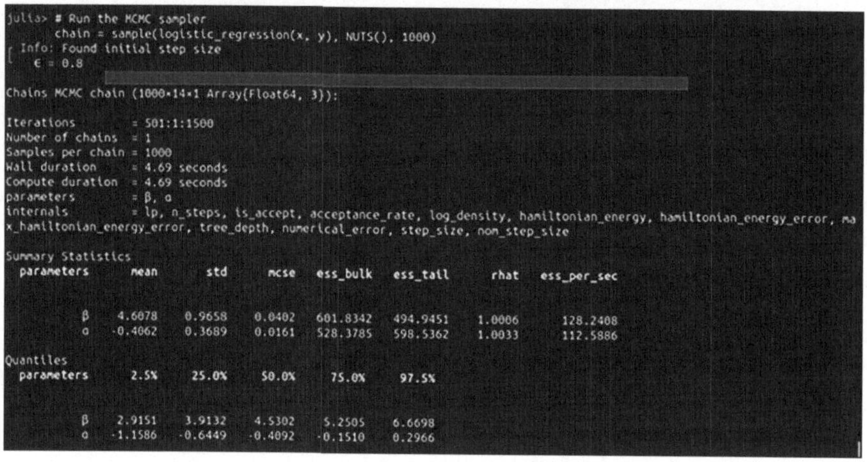

```
julia> # Run the MCMC sampler
       chain = sample(logistic_regression(x, y), NUTS(), 1000)
┌ Info: Found initial step size
└   ϵ = 0.8

Chains MCMC chain (1000×14×1 Array{Float64, 3}):

Iterations        = 501:1:1500
Number of chains  = 1
Samples per chain = 1000
Wall duration     = 4.69 seconds
Compute duration  = 4.69 seconds
parameters        = β, α
internals         = lp, n_steps, is_accept, acceptance_rate, log_density, hamiltonian_energy, hamiltonian_energy_error, max_hamiltonian_energy_error, tree_depth, numerical_error, step_size, nom_step_size

Summary Statistics
  parameters      mean       std      mcse   ess_bulk   ess_tail      rhat   ess_per_sec

           β    4.6078    0.9658    0.0402   601.8342   494.9451    1.0006      128.2408
           α   -0.4062    0.3689    0.0161   528.3785   598.5362    1.0033      112.5886

Quantiles
  parameters      2.5%     25.0%     50.0%     75.0%     97.5%

           β    2.9151    3.9132    4.5302    5.2505    6.6698
           α   -1.1586   -0.6449   -0.4092   -0.1510    0.2966
```

Figure 13.4: *Bayesian chain for logistic regression*

After running the sampler, we can summarize the results using the summary function from the MCMCChains package. This provides a summary of the posterior distributions of the parameters.

Finally, we can extract the parameter samples from the chains using indexing (`chains[:β]` and `chains[:α]` in this example) for further analysis or visualization.

```
julia> # Summarize the results
       describe(chain)
2-element Vector{ChainDataFrame}:
 Summary Statistics (2 x 8)
 Quantiles (2 x 6)
julia> # Extract the parameter samples
```

```
      β_samples = chain[:β]
2-dimensional AxisArray{Float64,2,...} with axes:
      :iter, 501:1:1500
      :chain, 1:1
And data, a 1000×1 Matrix{Float64}:
 2.2379346024854163
 ⋮
3.2173969793645107
julia> α_samples = chain[:α]
2-dimensional AxisArray{Float64,2,...} with axes:
      :iter, 501:1:1500
      :chain, 1:1
And data, a 1000×1 Matrix{Float64}:
 -0.3670272203555585
  ⋮
 -0.0674713027768106
```

Gaussian Process Latent Variable Model

The Gaussian Process Latent Variable Model (GPLVM) is a probabilistic latent variable model that combines the flexibility of Gaussian processes (GPs) with the ability to learn low-dimensional representations of high-dimensional data. It is primarily used for dimensionality reduction and nonlinear embedding.

Here's a step-by-step explanation of the Gaussian Process Latent Variable Model:

1. **Data representation:** GPLVM assumes that we have a dataset of high-dimensional observations, denoted as X, where each row represents an observation and each column represents a feature or variable.

2. **Latent space:** GPLVM introduces a lower-dimensional latent space, denoted as Z, where each row represents a latent variable or dimension. The goal is to learn a low-dimensional representation of the data that captures its structure and preserves important information.

3. **Mapping function:** GPLVM assumes that there exists a nonlinear mapping function that relates the latent space Z to the observed data X. This mapping function is defined as f(Z), where f is a smooth and flexible function.

4. **Gaussian process prior:** GPLVM places a Gaussian process prior to the mapping function f. A Gaussian process is a collection of random variables, any finite number of which has a joint Gaussian distribution. It is defined by a mean function and a covariance (or kernel) function. The choice of kernel function determines the assumptions about the smoothness and characteristics of the mapping function.

5. **Likelihood model:** GPLVM assumes a probabilistic relationship between the observed data X and the latent space Z. The specific likelihood model depends on the nature of the data. For continuous data, a common choice is a Gaussian likelihood, while for discrete data, other likelihood models can be used.

6. **Inference:** Given the observed data X and the model assumptions, the goal is to infer the latent variables Z and the parameters of the Gaussian process, which include the kernel hyperparameters. This is typically done using variational inference or Markov chain Monte Carlo (MCMC) methods.

7. **Dimensionality reduction and reconstruction:** Once the latent variables Z are inferred, GPLVM provides a low-dimensional representation of the data. This representation can be used for tasks such as visualization, clustering, or classification. Additionally, GPLVM allows for the reconstruction of the original high-dimensional data from the learned latent variables by applying the inverse mapping function f^{-1}.

Let us solve a Gaussian Process Latent Variable Model (GPLVM) problem using the Turing.jl package in Julia. Please make sure you have Turing.jl and other necessary packages installed before proceeding.

```
using Turing
using Distributions
using Plots
using LinearAlgebra


# Generate some synthetic data
function generate_data(N)
    x = range(0, stop=2π, length=N)
    y = sin.(x)
    return x, y
```

```
end

# Define the GPLVM model
@model function gplvm_model(x, y, Q)
    N = length(x)
    D = 1

    # Priors
    μ = zeros(N, Q)
    Σ = Diagonal(ones(N))
    Λ = Diagonal(ones(Q))
    σ² = 1.0

    # Latent variables
    z = Vector{Vector{Real}}(undef, N)
    for i = 1:N
        z[i] ~ MvNormal(μ[i, :], Σ[i, i])
    end

    Ψ = Λ * Λ' + Diagonal(ones(Q) * 1e-6)

    # Observed variables
    for i = 1:N
        f_i = Ψ * z[i]
        for j = 1:D
            y[i, j] ~ Normal(f_i[j], σ²)
        end
    end
end

# Set the number of latent dimensions
Q = 2
```

```
# Generate synthetic data
x, y = generate_data(100)

# Set the number of samples and iterations for inference
num_samples = 1000
num_iterations = 10

# Run the inference using Hamiltonian Monte Carlo
chain = sample(gplvm_model(x, y, Q), HMC(num_iterations, 0.01),
num_samples)

# Extract the posterior samples
posterior_samples = get(chain, :z)
```

In this example, we first define a synthetic dataset using the `generate_data` function. Then, we define the GPLVM model using the `@model` macro from Turing.jl. Inside the model, we specify the priors for the latent variables and the observed variables. The latent variables z are drawn from a multivariate normal distribution, and the observed variables y are drawn from a normal distribution with mean `f_i` and variance σ^2. We set up a diagonal covariance matrix Ψ to model the covariance between the latent dimensions.

After defining the model, we set the number of latent dimensions Q and generate the synthetic data. Then, we specify the number of samples and iterations for inference. In this example, we use Hamiltonian Monte Carlo (HMC) as the inference algorithm. Finally, we extract the posterior samples of the latent variables z from the chain and visualize the latent space using a scatter plot.

You can customize this code to fit your specific GPLVM problem by modifying the priors, data generation process, and inference settings according to your requirements.

Other Bayesian models

Hidden Markov Models (HMMs) and Bayesian Networks are both popular probabilistic graphical models used in machine learning and statistics. While they have some similarities, they also have distinct characteristics and applications.

Hidden Markov Models (HMMs)

- HMMs are a type of generative model that models sequential data with hidden states.
- They consist of a set of observed variables and a set of hidden (unobserved) states.
- The hidden states form a Markov chain, where the current state depends only on the previous state.
- The observed variables are conditionally dependent on the corresponding hidden states.
- HMMs are widely used in speech recognition, natural language processing, bioinformatics, and many other domains where sequential data modeling is needed.

Bayesian Networks

- Bayesian Networks, also known as Belief Networks or Directed Acyclic Graphs (DAGs), are graphical models that represent probabilistic relationships among a set of variables.
- They consist of nodes representing random variables and directed edges representing probabilistic dependencies between the variables.
- The dependencies are defined by conditional probability distributions (CPDs) associated with each node given its parents in the graph.
- Bayesian Networks allow for both causal reasoning (explaining how variables influence each other) and probabilistic inference.
- They are used for decision-making, risk assessment, medical diagnosis, anomaly detection, and other domains where modeling complex dependencies between variables is important.

While there are similarities between HMMs and Bayesian Networks, they differ in terms of the underlying assumptions and modeling capabilities. HMMs are specifically designed for modeling sequential data with hidden states, whereas Bayesian Networks can handle more general dependencies between variables in a directed acyclic graph.

It's worth noting that HMMs can be seen as a special case of Bayesian Networks where the graph structure is a linear chain and all variables are discrete. However, Bayesian Networks have a more flexible structure and can capture a wider range of dependencies, including cyclic or feedback connections.

Both HMMs and Bayesian Networks are powerful tools for probabilistic modeling, and their choice depends on the specific characteristics and requirements of the problem at hand.

You can learn about hidden Markov models (https://turinglang.org/dev/tutorials/04-hidden-markov-model/) and Bayesian networks (https://turinglang.org/dev/tutorials/03-bayesian-neural-network/).

Conclusion

In conclusion, Bayesian inference is a statistical framework that allows for updating beliefs and making inferences based on prior knowledge and observed data. It differs from frequentist methods by treating probability as a measure of uncertainty or belief rather than long-term frequency. The key concepts in Bayesian statistics include the prior distribution, likelihood function, and posterior distribution, which represent updated beliefs. The posterior distribution is calculated by combining the prior distribution and likelihood function using Bayes' theorem. Inferences can be made from the posterior distribution, including point estimates and credible intervals. Bayesian models encompass a wide range of techniques, such as linear regression, logistic regression, and Gaussian process latent variable models. These models provide flexibility for modeling complex data structures and relationships, supporting accurate and nuanced analyses. Overall, Bayesian inference is a powerful and intuitive approach to statistical analysis with various applications in decision-making processes.

In the next chapter, we will learn about how code profiling and optimization are essential steps in improving the performance and efficiency of Julia programs. Julia provides several tools and techniques for code profiling and optimization, allowing developers to identify performance bottlenecks and optimize critical sections of their code.

Questions

1. What is the key difference between Bayes' theorem and frequentist statistical methods?
2. What are the basic concepts of Bayesian statistics?
3. How is the posterior distribution calculated in Bayesian inference?

4. What are the different ways of making inferences from the posterior distribution?
5. Can you explain the concept of Bayesian models and their role in statistical analysis?
6. What are some examples of various Bayesian models?
7. How does Bayesian linear regression differ from traditional linear regression?
8. What is Bayesian logistic regression, and how is it different from standard logistic regression?
9. Can you explain the Gaussian Process Latent Variable Model (GPLVM) and its application in Bayesian modeling?
10. Are there any other notable Bayesian models that are commonly used in practice?

Chapter 14
Parallel Computation in Julia

Introduction

Parallel computing is a computing paradigm that involves breaking down a computational task into smaller subtasks that can be executed simultaneously on multiple processing units. It aims to solve problems more quickly by dividing the workload among multiple computational resources, such as multiple processor cores, CPUs, GPUs, or even distributed computing systems.

In a traditional serial computing model, a program or task is executed sequentially, with each instruction or operation being processed one after another. Parallel computing, on the other hand, allows multiple instructions or operations to be executed simultaneously, potentially reducing the overall execution time.

Parallel computing can offer several advantages, including:

- **Speedup**: By distributing the workload across multiple processing units, parallel computing can significantly reduce the execution time of computationally intensive tasks. This is particularly beneficial for tasks that can be divided into independent subtasks that can be processed concurrently.
- **Scalability**: Parallel computing provides a means to scale the computational power of a system by adding more processing units. As the size of the problem or the complexity of the computation increases, parallelization allows for efficient utilization of available resources.
- **Handling large datasets**: Parallel computing can be used to process and analyze large datasets efficiently. By splitting the data and distributing it among multiple processors or nodes, parallel algorithms can process the data in parallel, accelerating the analysis or computations.

Parallel computing can be achieved using different approaches, such as:

- **Shared-memory parallelism**: In shared-memory parallelism, multiple processing units, such as CPU cores, share a common memory space. Threads or processes can be used to divide the workload, and synchronization mechanisms are used to coordinate their execution.
- **Distributed computing**: In distributed computing, multiple independent systems or nodes work together to solve a problem. Each node typically has its own memory and processing capabilities, and communication mechanisms are used to exchange data and coordinate the computation.
- **GPU computing**: Graphics Processing Units (GPUs) are highly parallel processors that excel at performing computations on large datasets. GPU computing utilizes the parallel processing capabilities of GPUs to accelerate computations for tasks that can be parallelized.

Parallel computing requires careful consideration of factors such as task decomposition, load balancing, communication overhead, and synchronization to ensure efficient utilization of resources and avoid potential pitfalls such as race conditions and data dependencies. Modern programming languages and frameworks, including Julia, provide tools and libraries to facilitate parallel programming and make effective use of parallel computing resources.

Structure

In this chapter, the following topics will be covered:

- Parallel computation in Julia
- Asynchronous programming
- Asynchronous tasks in Julia
- Task operations
- Connecting via channels in Julia
- Multi-threading
- Speeding up data science workflows
- Using the power of JuliaHub

Parallel computation in Julia

Julia provides robust support for parallel computation, allowing you to take advantage of multiple cores or distributed computing resources to speed up your code. There are several mechanisms and libraries available in Julia for parallel programming:

- **Shared-memory parallelism**: Julia has built-in support for shared-memory parallelism using multi-threading. The Threads module in Julia allows you to create and manage lightweight threads that can run concurrently. You can use the `@threads` macro to parallelize loops and execute iterations in parallel. Julia's `SharedArrays` package provides a way to create arrays that can be shared among threads.
- **Distributed computing**: Julia has a built-in distributed computing framework that enables parallel execution across multiple processes, either on a single machine or across a cluster of machines. The Distributed module in Julia provides functions for launching and managing worker processes. You can distribute tasks using constructs like `@distributed` and `@spawn`.
- **Parallel computing libraries**: Julia ecosystem offers several libraries for parallel computing. For example, the `SharedArrays` package mentioned earlier provides a way to work with large shared arrays across multiple processes. The `DistributedArrays` package allows you to work with distributed arrays that can be automatically partitioned across multiple processes. The `ParallelAccelerator` package provides automatic parallelization of computations using just-in-time (JIT) compilation.
- **GPU programming**: Julia has excellent support for GPU programming. The **`CUDA.jl`** package allows you to write GPU-accelerated code in Julia, utilizing the power of NVIDIA GPUs. With **`CUDA.jl`**, you can write parallel kernels and offload computations to the GPU, achieving significant speedups for certain types of calculations.

When working with parallel computation in Julia, it's important to consider factors like data dependencies, load balancing, and communication overhead. Julia's parallel programming constructs and libraries provide the flexibility and tools to handle these aspects efficiently and effectively.

Asynchronous programming

Asynchronous programming is a programming paradigm that allows for concurrent execution of multiple tasks without blocking the execution of the main program. It enables programs to initiate tasks, continue with other operations, and handle the results of the tasks once they are completed, without waiting for each task to finish before moving on.

In synchronous programming (also known as blocking programming), each operation is executed sequentially, and the program waits for each operation to complete before moving on to the next one. This can be inefficient if there are long-running operations, such as I/O operations or network requests, that cause the program to wait for a response.

Asynchronous programming, on the other hand, enables non-blocking execution. It allows the program to start a task and then move on to other tasks or operations while the first task is being processed in the background. The program can later handle the results of the tasks once they are completed.

Asynchronous programming is particularly useful in scenarios involving I/O-bound operations, where the program spends a significant amount of time waiting for input/output operations to complete, such as reading from or writing to a file, making network requests, or interacting with a database.

Key concepts and techniques used in asynchronous programming include:

- **Asynchronous functions or methods**: These are functions or methods that are marked or“ designed to be executed asynchronously. They typically return a `promise`” or a “`future`” object that represents the result of the computation that will be available in the future.
- **Callbacks**: Callbacks are functions that are registered to be called once a specific asynchronous operation completes. They allow the program to specify the actions to be taken once the task is finished.
- **Promises and Futures**: These are objects that represent the results of asynchronous computations. They allow the program to retrieve the result of the computation once it is available.
- **Event loops**: An event loop is a central component in asynchronous programming that manages the execution of asynchronous tasks. It continuously checks for completed tasks and triggers the associated callbacks or notifies the program when the results are available.

Asynchronous programming is widely used in various programming languages and frameworks to build responsive and efficient applications that can handle concurrent operations effectively. It allows programs to make optimal use of system resources, such as CPU and I/O, and can greatly improve the performance and responsiveness of applications that involve waiting for I/O or other external operations.

Asynchronous tasks in Julia

Asynchronous programming in Julia is facilitated through the use of Tasks. A Task represents a computation that can be suspended and resumed at any point, allowing for non-blocking, concurrent execution of code.

When a piece of code is designated as a Task, it can be interrupted (suspended) at certain points and switched to another Task, allowing other computations to proceed concurrently. This is different from traditional function calls, where the control must wait for a function to complete before returning.

Tasks in Julia can be created using the `@task` macro or by explicitly calling the `Task()` constructor. Once created, a Task can be started using the `schedule` function or by invoking the `start` function on the task object. This initiates the execution of the Task in the background.

To suspend a Task and allow other computations to proceed, the `yield` function is used. When `yield` is called within a Task, it temporarily pauses the execution of that Task, allowing other Tasks to be scheduled and executed. The `yield` function can be used to explicitly yield control, or it may be implicitly called when certain operations (such as I/O) are performed.

Tasks can also communicate and synchronize with each other using channels. Channels are communication constructs that allow Tasks to send and receive values between each other. By sending and receiving values through channels, Tasks can coordinate their execution and exchange information.

Asynchronous programming with Tasks in Julia enables the execution of multiple operations concurrently, making it useful for scenarios involving I/O operations, network communication, and other situations where waiting for external events is required. It allows programs to make efficient use of system resources and can improve performance by overlapping computations that would otherwise block each other.

It's worth noting that Julia also provides other constructs and libraries for asynchronous programming, such as coroutines and libraries built on top of Tasks (for example, `async` and `await` syntaxes). These constructs offer more expressive and high-level ways of working with asynchronous code.

Task operations

In Julia, Tasks represent units of computational work that can be created, scheduled, and executed asynchronously. Here are the basic operations involved in working with Tasks:

1. Task Creation: Tasks can be created using the `Task()` constructor or the `@task` macro. The `Task()` constructor takes a 0-argument function as an argument, specifying the code that the Task will execute. The `@task` macro is a shorthand for creating a Task with an anonymous function. For example:

```
julia> t = @task begin
       sleep(5)
       println("done")
   end
```

In this example, a Task `t` is created that sleeps for five seconds and then prints "done".

2. Task Scheduling: After creating a Task, it needs to be scheduled for execution. Scheduling a Task adds it to an internal queue of tasks that are ready to run. The `schedule()` function is used to schedule a Task for execution. For example:

```
julia> schedule(t)
```

This schedules the Task `t` for execution.

3. **Task Execution**: Tasks are executed asynchronously, meaning they run independently of the main program flow. The actual execution of Tasks occurs when the Julia runtime system has available resources, such as when the program is idle or waiting for input. The execution of a Task can be interrupted and resumed at any point.

4. **Waiting for Task Completion**: The `wait()` function allows a Task to be explicitly waited upon. When `wait()` is called on a Task, the calling Task blocks until the specified Task completes its execution. For example:

```
julia> schedule(t)
Task (runnable) @0x000000010e3fb850

julia> wait(t)
done
```

In this case, the program will pause for five seconds before proceeding to the next line after `wait(t)`.

5. **`@async` Macro**: The **`@async`** macro is provided as a convenient way to create and schedule a Task in a single step. It is equivalent to calling `schedule(@task ...)`. For example:

```
julia> @async begin
       sleep(5)
       println("done")
   end
Task (runnable) @0x000000010e3a2ef0
```

```
julia> done
```

This creates and schedules a Task that sleeps for five seconds and prints "**done**".

By using Tasks and asynchronous programming, Julia enables concurrent execution of code, allowing for efficient utilization of system resources and handling of I/O operations without blocking the program's execution.

Yieldto function in tasks

In Julia, the low-level primitive `yieldto` is used to suspend the current task, switch to another specified task, and specify a value that the target task's last `yieldto` call will return. `yieldto(task, value)` allows for switching between tasks, enabling task-style control flow. This mechanism is why tasks are referred to as "`symmetric coroutines`," as each task can be switched to and from using the same mechanism.

While `yieldto` is a powerful tool, most uses of tasks in Julia do not directly invoke it. This is because manually managing task switching and determining when to switch back can be complex and require careful coordination. Instead, higher-level constructs such as `put!` and `take!` are provided, which internally handle task switching and maintain state to manage blocking operations like those used with channels.

In addition to `yieldto`, several other basic functions are available to effectively use tasks:

1. **`current_task`**: This function returns a reference to the currently running task. It allows you to access and manipulate properties of the current task, such as querying its state or associating data with it.

2. **`istaskdone`**: This function is used to check whether a task has exited, meaning it has completed its execution. It returns `true` if the task has finished, and `false` otherwise. It helps determine the completion status of a task.

3. **`istaskstarted`**: This function checks whether a task has run yet. It returns `true` if the task has started executing, and `false` otherwise. It helps determine if a task has been scheduled and is currently running.

4. **`task_local_storage`**: This set of functions allows manipulation of a key-value store specific to the current task. It provides a way to store and retrieve data associated with a task. Functions like `get_task_local` and `set_task_local` are used to interact with the task-local storage.

The rest of the functions complement `yieldto` and provide additional capabilities for managing and interacting with tasks. They help in tracking task status, accessing task-specific data, and determining when tasks have completed their execution while `yieldto` is a foundational primitive, higher-level constructs and functions provided by Julia's task system simplify the usage of tasks and manage task switching, making it easier to write code that leverages the benefits of task-based concurrency.

Scheduler in Julia

In Julia, task scheduling and event handling are managed by the scheduler in the Julia Base library. The scheduler keeps track of runnable tasks and executes an event loop based on external events like I/O requests or message arrivals. Most task switches occur when tasks are waiting for events, and the scheduler handles the resumption of tasks once the events they are waiting for occur.

The primary function used for waiting for events in Julia is '`wait`'. Many objects implement the wait function, and when called, it causes the task to wait for a specific event to happen. For instance, wait can be used with a Process object to wait for it to exit, or inside a call to read to wait for data to become available.

Under the hood, wait operates on a Condition object responsible for queuing and restarting tasks. When a task call wait on a Condition, the task becomes non-runnable, added to the condition's queue, and yields control to the scheduler. The scheduler can then choose another runnable task to execute or block and wait for external events. When the awaited event occurs, an event handler typically calls notify on the Condition, which makes all tasks waiting for that condition runnable again, and the scheduler will eventually resume those tasks.

Tasks that are explicitly created using Task are initially unknown to the scheduler. This allows for manual task management using '`yieldto`' if desired. However, even if such a task waits for an event using wait, it will still be automatically restarted when the awaited event occurs. This automatic resumption ensures that the tasks waiting for events can proceed with their execution as expected.

Julia's task and event handling mechanisms, along with the scheduler, make it easy to manage asynchronous operations and efficiently utilize computational resources in applications that involve waiting for external events or handling concurrent tasks.

Connecting via channels in Julia

In Julia, Channels provide a mechanism for communication and synchronization between tasks. A Channel is a first-in, first-out (FIFO) queue that allows multiple tasks to write to and read from it concurrently.

Creating a Channel is done using the `Channel()` constructor, specifying the type of objects that can be stored in the channel and an optional size parameter to limit the number of elements it can hold. For example:

```
julia> chnl = Channel{Int}(32)
Channel{Int64}(32) (empty)
```

This creates a channel named `chnl` that can hold up to 32 elements of type `Int`.

To write data into a Channel, the `put!` function is used. It allows multiple tasks to write to the channel concurrently. For example:

```
julia> put!(chnl, 42)
42
```

This puts the value `42` into the channel `chnl`.

To read data from a Channel, the `take!` function is used. It retrieves the next available value from the channel, blocking if the channel is empty. For example:

```
julia> val = take!(chnl)
42
```

This retrieves the next value from the channel `chnl` and assigns it to the variable `val`.

Channels also support other operations such as `fetch` (retrieves but does not remove the value), `isready` (checks if the channel has a value available), and `wait` (waits until a value is available).

Channels are useful for solving problems where multiple tasks need to communicate and synchronize their execution. For example, in producer-consumer scenarios, where one task produces values and another task consumes them, Channels provide a way for the producer to write values into the channel, and the consumer to read those values.

Channels can be used in conjunction with Tasks to orchestrate complex work distribution patterns. Multiple tasks can be bound to the same channel, allowing them to read from and write to the channel concurrently.

Additionally, channels can be used as iterable objects in `for` loops. The loop variable takes on each produced value until the channel is closed. For example:

```
julia> function producer(c::Channel)
                  put!(c, "start")
                  for n=1:4
                  put!(c, 2n)
                  end
                  put!(c, "stop")
              end;
julia> chnl = Channel(producer);
julia> take!(chnl)
"start"
julia> take!(chnl)
2
julia> take!(chnl)
4
julia> take!(chnl)
6
julia> take!(chnl)
8
julia> take!(chnl)
"stop"
julia> for x in Channel(producer)
              println(x)
        end
start
2
4
6
8
stop
```

In this example, the `producer` function produces values into a channel, and the `for` loop consumes those values until the channel is closed.

Closing a channel is done automatically when the associated task terminates. However, a channel can also be manually closed using the `close` function.

Channels provide a powerful tool for coordinating and communicating between tasks, enabling concurrent execution and synchronization in complex scenarios.

Multi-threading

Multithreading is a programming technique that allows a single process to perform multiple tasks concurrently. It enables a program to execute multiple threads of execution within the same process, taking advantage of modern multi-core processors to improve performance and responsiveness.

In traditional single-threaded programs, instructions are executed sequentially, one after the other. This means that if a task takes a long time to complete (for example, reading data from a slow network source), the entire program will be blocked, waiting for that task to finish before moving on to the next one.

Multithreading overcomes this limitation by creating multiple threads, each of which can execute a separate task concurrently. These threads can run simultaneously on separate CPU cores or logical processors, allowing the program to make better use of available resources.

Here are some key points about multithreading:

- **Threads**: A thread is the smallest unit of execution within a process. It represents an independent sequence of instructions that can be scheduled for execution by the operating system. Threads within the same process share the same memory space, allowing them to communicate and share data easily.
- **Concurrent Execution**: Multithreading allows tasks to be executed concurrently, meaning that multiple threads can execute instructions simultaneously. This can significantly improve performance, especially in applications that perform many independent tasks or require responsiveness to user interactions.
- **Shared Memory**: Threads within the same process have access to shared memory, which makes it easy to share data and communicate between threads. However, this also introduces the challenge of managing data synchronization and avoiding race conditions when multiple threads try to access shared resources simultaneously.
- **Parallelism versus Concurrency**: Multithreading enables both parallelism and concurrency. Parallelism refers to the simultaneous execution of multiple tasks on multiple cores, resulting in increased processing

speed. Concurrency, on the other hand, allows tasks to make progress independently, even if they are not executing simultaneously.

- **Thread Safety**: When multiple threads access shared resources, proper synchronization mechanisms (for example, locks and semaphores) are required to ensure thread safety and prevent data corruption or inconsistent results.
- **Context Switching**: The operating system manages the scheduling and execution of threads. It performs context switching, which involves saving the state of one thread, loading the state of another, and switching execution between threads. Context switching introduces some overhead, so excessive use of threads may lead to diminishing returns.

Multithreading is commonly used in various applications, such as web servers, graphical user interfaces (GUIs), video game engines, and scientific simulations. It allows programs to efficiently utilize modern hardware, which often includes multi-core CPUs, and provides a smoother and more responsive user experience. However, multithreading introduces complexities related to thread safety and synchronization, making it essential for developers to design their code carefully to avoid potential issues.

Multiple threads in Julia

Julia is a high-level programming language known for its performance and ease of use. It has built-in support for multi-threading, allowing users to leverage multiple threads for concurrent execution of tasks. The number of threads can be specified using the `--threads` command line argument or the `JULIA_NUM_THREADS` environment variable. Let's explore how to start Julia with multiple threads and how it affects the number of threads available for computation.

1. **Starting Julia with Multiple Threads using Command Line Argument**:

To start Julia with 4 threads, you can use the following command in your terminal or command prompt:

```
julia --threads 4
```

After starting Julia with 4 threads, you can verify the number of threads using the `Threads.nthreads()` function:

```
julia> Threads.nthreads()
4
```

You are currently on the master thread (the main thread) at this point. To check the ID of the current thread, you can use the `Threads.threadid()` function:

```
julia> Threads.threadid()
1
```

2. **Starting Julia with Multiple Threads using Environment Variable**:

Alternatively, you can set the `JULIA_NUM_THREADS` environment variable to specify the number of threads. For example, in Bash (Linux/macOS), you can use:

```
export JULIA_NUM_THREADS=4


In C shell on Linux/macOS or CMD on Windows:
set JULIA_NUM_THREADS=4


In Powershell on Windows:
$env:JULIA_NUM_THREADS=4
```

Remember to set the environment variable before starting Julia.

3. **Propagating Threads to Worker Processes**:

When you start Julia with multiple threads, the number of threads specified will also be propagated to any worker processes you create using the `-p` or `--procs` command line options. For example, if you start Julia with 2 worker processes and 2 threads each, you can use the following command:

```
julia -p2 -t2
```

This will spawn 1 main process with 2 worker processes, and all three processes will have 2 threads enabled. This can be useful for distributing tasks across multiple processes and threads for parallel computing.

4. **Specifying Auto Threads:**

Instead of specifying a specific number of threads, you can use auto as the value for `JULIA_NUM_THREADS`, starting from Julia 1.7. This allows Julia to infer a useful default number of threads to use based on your system's capabilities. For example:

```
export JULIA_NUM_THREADS=auto
```

Please note that if you are using an older version of Julia, setting `JULIA_NUM_THREADS` to auto will be ignored.

Remember that not all operations and packages in Julia are fully optimized for multi-threading. Some tasks may not see significant speed improvements when using multiple threads, while others may benefit greatly from parallel execution. Always benchmark and test your code to ensure that multithreading improves performance for your specific use case.

ThreadPools

In Julia, `threadpools` are used to manage the execution of tasks in different contexts. By default, tasks are executed in the `:default threadpool`, but you can specify that certain tasks are interactive using `@spawn :interactive` to help improve the responsiveness and interactivity of the program.

Here's an explanation of how `threadpools` work and how you can start Julia with multiple `threadpools`:

1. **Default Threadpool**: The :default threadpool is where most tasks run if not specified otherwise. When you start Julia without explicitly setting the `threadpool`, tasks will be executed in the `:default threadpool`.
2. **Interactive Threadpool**: The `:interactive threadpool` is specifically meant for interactive tasks that require more responsiveness and should avoid high-latency operations. When you use @spawn :interactive, the task is added to this `threadpool`, which can help prevent delays and ensure better interactivity for the program.
3. **Starting Julia with Multiple Threadpools**: You can start Julia with one or more threads reserved for running interactive tasks by specifying the number of threads for each `threadpool`. For example:

```
julia --threads 3,1
```

This starts Julia with 3 threads in the `:default threadpool` and 1 thread in the `:interactive threadpool`.

Alternatively, you can use the `JULIA_NUM_THREADS` environment variable to achieve the same effect:

```
export JULIA_NUM_THREADS=3,1
```

This command sets three threads for the `:default threadpool` and 1 thread for the `:interactive threadpool`.

4. **Using 'auto' for `Threadpool` Threads**: Instead of specifying the number of threads, you can use the word auto for either or both `threadpools`. When auto is used, Julia will choose a reasonable default number of threads for the respective `threadpool`.

For example:

```
julia --threads auto,1
```

This starts Julia with a reasonable number of threads for the `:default threadpool` (decided by Julia) and 1 thread for the `:interactive threadpool`.

To summarize, `threadpools` in Julia allow you to manage different types of tasks effectively. By designating tasks as interactive with `@spawn :interactive`, you can ensure that critical interactive tasks are given priority, leading to improved responsiveness and better user experience. Starting Julia with multiple `threadpools`, with the ability to use auto for the number of threads, gives you flexibility in optimizing performance based on your specific use case.

Communication and synchronization in Julia

In multi-threaded programming, communication and synchronization between threads are crucial to ensure correctness and prevent data races. Data races occur when multiple threads access and modify shared data concurrently, leading to unpredictable and erroneous behavior. Julia provides thread-safe communication channels to facilitate safe communication between threads. However, it is essential to be vigilant and follow proper synchronization mechanisms, like using locks, to guarantee data-race freedom.

The recommended way to ensure data-race freedom in Julia is to use locks around any access to shared data that can be observed from multiple threads. A common pattern to achieve this is to use the lock function to acquire a lock before accessing shared data and release it afterward. There are two common ways to implement this pattern in Julia:

1. **Using the `lock` function with `do` block**:

```
julia> lock(lk) do
           use(a)
       end
```

Using `try-finally` block with lock:

```
julia> begin
```

```
        lock(lk)
        try
        use(a)
        finally
        unlock(lk)
        end
end
```

Here, lk is a lock, like `ReentrantLock()`, and a is the shared data that needs to be protected.

By using these patterns, you ensure that only one thread can access the shared data at a time, avoiding data races and maintaining data consistency.

Furthermore, it is crucial to understand that Julia is not memory safe in the presence of data races. If multiple threads access shared data without proper synchronization, it can lead to undefined behavior and unexpected results. Therefore, always use the lock pattern when modifying data (for example, assigning to a global or closure variable) accessed by other threads.

In the provided example, accessing variable a in Thread 2 and Thread 3 without proper synchronization (for example, without using locks) can lead to data races, making the code unsafe and potentially causing unpredictable behavior.

In summary, when writing multi-threaded code in Julia, always use proper synchronization mechanisms like locks to ensure data-race freedom and maintain the integrity of shared data accessed by multiple threads. Following these best practices will help you write correct and reliable multi-threaded programs in Julia.

@threads macro

The `@threads` macro in Julia is a powerful tool to parallelize loops and distribute work across multiple threads. However, as shown in the example provided, using `@threads` without proper care can lead to data races and incorrect results. To avoid data races, you should use appropriate synchronization mechanisms, like using local buffers or atomic operations.

The example demonstrates how to fix the data race issue in the `sum_multi_bad` function by employing the `sum_multi_good` function, which correctly segments the sum into race-free chunks using local buffers for each thread. Here's a breakdown of the solution:

1. **`sum_single` function**: This function calculates the sum of elements in a given collection (a). It's a basic implementation without considering parallelization.

```
julia> function sum_single(a)
           s = 0
           for i in a
               s += i
           end
           s
       end
sum_single (generic function with 1 method)
```

2. **`sum_multi_bad` function**: This function uses `@threads` to parallelize the loop, but it exposes a data race on the shared variable `s`, resulting in incorrect results.

```
julia> function sum_multi_bad(a)
           s = 0
           Threads.@threads for i in a
               s += i
           end
           s
       end
sum_multi_bad (generic function with 1 method)
```

3. **`sum_multi_good` function**: This function fixes the data race issue by dividing the array into chunks and calculating the sum of each chunk independently. The chunks are then combined to get the final sum. Each thread works on its own local buffer, avoiding data races.

```
julia> function sum_multi_good(a)
           chunks = Iterators.partition(a, length(a) ÷ Threads.
nthreads())
           tasks = map(chunks) do chunk
               Threads.@spawn sum_single(chunk)
           end
           chunk_sums = fetch.(tasks)
           return sum_single(chunk_sums)
```

```
    end
sum_multi_good (generic function with 1 method)
```

By using `@spawn` inside the loop, each chunk of the array is processed asynchronously by a different thread, ensuring that there are no data races. The results from each chunk are combined using `sum_single` to obtain the final result.

Remember, as stated in the note, buffers should not be managed based on `threadid()` because concurrent tasks can yield, causing multiple tasks to use the same buffer on a given thread, introducing the risk of data races. Instead, use local buffers or atomic operations to ensure data-race freedom.

In summary, when using `@threads` or any other multi-threading constructs in Julia, make sure to handle shared data carefully to avoid data races. Proper synchronization mechanisms and data segmentation can be used to achieve correct and efficient multi-threaded code.

Atomic Operations

Julia provides the `Threads.Atomic` type to access and modify values atomically, ensuring thread-safe operations and avoiding race conditions. This allows concurrent threads to modify shared data without causing data races. Here's a summary of how it works:

1. **Creating an Atomic Value**: To create an atomic value, you use the `Threads.Atomic` constructor. The atomic value must be of a primitive type, such as Int, Float64, and so on.

   ```
   julia> i = Threads.Atomic{Int}(0)
   Atomic{Int64}(0)
   ```

In this example, i is an atomic integer initialized to 0.

2. **Using Atomic Operations**: You can perform atomic operations on the atomic value using specific functions like `atomic_add!`, `atomic_sub!`, `atomic_min!`, `atomic_max!`, and so on. These operations ensure that the modification is performed atomically, avoiding race conditions.

In the provided example, the @threads macro is used to perform atomic additions to i. Each thread performs an atomic add operation on i, and the resulting values are stored in the `old_is` array.

```
julia> old_is = zeros(Int, 4)
4-element Vector{Int64}:
```

```
 0
 0
 0
 0
julia> Threads.@threads for id in 1:4
               old_is[id] = Threads.atomic_add!(i, id)
       end
```

3. **Avoiding Race Conditions**: Without atomic operations, race conditions can occur, leading to incorrect results when multiple threads modify shared data simultaneously. The second example in the provided code illustrates this issue when using a non-atomic reference (Ref) for accumulation.

```
acc = Ref(0)


@threads for i in 1:1000
      acc[] += 1
end
```

In this case, the final value of acc is incorrect due to race conditions, and the result may vary on different runs.

4. **Correct Usage with Atomic**: To avoid race conditions and obtain the correct result, you can use an atomic value:

```
julia> acc = Atomic{Int}(0)
Atomic{Int64}(0)


julia> @threads for i in 1:1000
      atomic_add!(acc, 1)
end
julia> acc
Atomic{Int64}(1000)
```

Now, with the atomic value acc, the final value is correct (1000).

Per-field atomics

In Julia 1.7 and later versions, you can use per-field atomics to work with atomic operations at a more granular level within a struct. This allows you to specify atomic operations on specific fields of a struct and control the ordering constraints for reads and writes to those fields. This feature enables you to create more fine-grained atomic operations in your code, providing better control over concurrent access to individual fields.

Here are the key points related to per-field atomics in Julia:

- **Decorate Fields with `@atomic`**: You can annotate individual fields in a struct declaration with the `@atomic` macro to indicate that these fields should be accessed atomically.
- **Annotate Writes with `@atomic` and Atomic Orderings**: When writing to an atomic field, you must use the `@atomic` macro before the assignment operation. Additionally, you can specify the atomic ordering constraint for the write operation. The available atomic orderings are `:monotonic`, `:acquire`, `:release`, `:acquire_release`, or `:sequentially_consistent`.
- **Annotate Reads with Atomic Orderings (Optional)**: You can also specify the atomic ordering constraint when reading from an atomic field using the `@atomic` macro. If no atomic ordering is specified for the read operation, it will be done with the relaxed ordering, which is `:monotonic`.

This feature allows you to have more control over the atomicity and ordering of operations on specific fields within a struct, ensuring safe and consistent concurrent access.

Here's a conceptual example of using per-field atomics in Julia:

```
struct AtomicData
      @atomic field1::Int
      @atomic field2::Float64
end

data = AtomicData(0, 0.0)

# Writing to atomic fields with specific atomic orderings
@atomic data.field1 = 42 :sequentially_consistent
@atomic data.field2 = 3.14 :release
```

```
# Reading from atomic fields with specific atomic orderings (optional)
value1 = @atomic data.field1 :acquire
value2 = @atomic data.field2
```

Side Effects of using threads

When working with multi-threading and concurrent code in any programming language, it's crucial to be mindful of side effects and mutable function arguments. As you mentioned, functions in Julia (and some other languages) that have names ending with ! are conventionally considered to be non-pure functions, meaning they modify their input arguments (in-place) rather than returning new values.

In multi-threaded code, these non-pure functions can introduce unexpected behavior and race conditions. If multiple threads concurrently modify the same mutable data (for example, arrays, dictionaries) without proper synchronization, data races can occur, leading to incorrect results and undefined behavior.

To ensure correctness and data-race freedom, you should follow these best practices:

- **Use Pure Functions**: Prefer pure functions whenever possible. Pure functions are functions that do not have any side effects and always produce the same output for the same input. Using pure functions ensures that you can safely call them from multiple threads without worrying about data races.
- **Avoid In-Place Modifications**: Avoid modifying shared data in-place when working with multiple threads. Instead, prefer creating new data structures or using atomic operations for safe updates.
- **Use Atomic Operations**: When you need to perform atomic updates on shared data, use atomic operations provided by Julia's atomic types. This ensures that modifications to shared data are performed atomically and without data races.
- **Use Locks or Other Synchronization Mechanisms**: For situations where in-place modifications are unavoidable or where more complex synchronization is needed, use locks or other synchronization mechanisms (for example, semaphores) to ensure that only one thread can access the shared data at a time.
- **Be Mindful of Side Effects**: Be aware of functions or libraries that have side effects or modify the global state. When using such functions in multi-threaded code, take extra precautions to ensure that they are called in a thread-safe manner.

- **Test and Benchmark**: Always thoroughly test your multi-threaded code and perform benchmarks to verify that the parallelization improves performance and produces correct results.

When using threads in Julia, there are some caveats and limitations to be aware of. While most operations in the Julia runtime and standard libraries can be used in a thread-safe manner, it's essential to pay attention to potential issues to avoid undesirable behavior in multi-threaded programs. Here are some specific limitations and warnings:

- **Manual Locking for Base Collection Types**: If multiple threads access Base collection types (for example, arrays and dictionaries) simultaneously, and at least one thread modifies the collection, manual locking is required to avoid data races. For example, if multiple threads are pushing elements into an array or inserting items into a dictionary, proper synchronization mechanisms like locks should be used.
- **Non-Deterministic Scheduling for `@spawn`**: The scheduling of tasks created with `@spawn` is nondeterministic. This means you should not rely on the order of execution for tasks created using `@spawn`.
- **Memory Allocation and Garbage Collection (GC)**: Compute-bound tasks that do not allocate memory can prevent garbage collection from running in other threads that are allocating memory. This can lead to memory-related issues and inefficiencies. To allow GC to run, you may need to insert manual calls to `GC.safepoint()` at appropriate points in your code.
- **Avoid Running Top-Level Operations in Parallel**: Running top-level operations like include or evaluating type, method, and module definitions in parallel can lead to unexpected behavior and conflicts. It's best to avoid parallel execution for such operations.
- **Finalizers and Threading**: Be cautious when using libraries that register finalizers (functions that are run when an object is garbage-collected) because they may break when threads are enabled. This is due to the inherent complexities of managing finalization in a multi-threaded environment. As a result, some transitional work may be required across the ecosystem before threading can be widely adopted with confidence.

@threadcall

The `@threadcall` macro in Julia provides a mechanism to avoid stalling the execution of tasks when calling external C libraries that perform blocking operations. When a C library performs a blocking operation, it can prevent the

Julia scheduler from executing other tasks until the call returns, which can lead to poor performance and reduced responsiveness in multi-threaded code.

To overcome this issue, the `@threadcall` macro schedules a C function for execution in a separate thread using a threadpool with a default size of 4 threads. The size of the `threadpool` can be controlled via the environment variable `UV_THREADPOOL_SIZE`. While waiting for a free thread, and during function execution once a thread is available, the requesting task (on the main Julia event loop) yields to other tasks, ensuring that other tasks can continue execution even when a blocking C function is being called.

Important points to note about `@threadcall`:

1. **Blocking Call**: From a user's point of view, `@threadcall` is a blocking call, similar to other Julia APIs. It does not return until the execution of the C function is complete. However, the critical difference is that during the execution of the C function, the Julia scheduler can continue to execute other tasks due to the yielding behavior.

2. **Avoid Calling Back into Julia**: The C function called using `@threadcall` must not call back into Julia, as doing so can lead to segfaults. This is because the C function is executed in a separate thread, which is not managed by Julia's scheduler, and calling back into Julia can cause synchronization issues and undefined behavior.

3. **Future Changes**: As stated in the documentation, `@threadcall` may be removed or changed in future versions of Julia. This suggests that the implementation and behavior of `@threadcall` might be subject to modifications in subsequent Julia releases. Therefore, it's important to keep track of updates in Julia's documentation and release notes.

Task migration

In Julia 1.7 and later versions, task migration was introduced, allowing tasks to move to different threads during their execution. Task migration occurs when a task yields, and it may result in the task being resumed on a different thread than the one it started on. This behavior applies to tasks that have been started with `@spawn` or `@threads`, except for tasks spawned using the `:static` schedule option for `@threads`, which freezes the thread ID.

Due to task migration, `threadid()` should not be treated as a constant within a task. If a task uses `threadid()` to index into a vector of buffers or stateful objects, there is a risk of data races and incorrect behavior. This is because, after task migration, the thread ID obtained using `threadid()` might change, leading to unintended consequences when accessing shared data.

To ensure data-race freedom and correct behavior when working with multi-threaded tasks, it's important to avoid relying on `threadid()` as a constant and to be mindful of potential task migration. Instead, consider using other synchronization mechanisms, like locks or atomic operations, to manage shared data safely.

As a general guideline, when writing multi-threaded code in Julia, it's essential to understand task migration and to design your code in a way that accounts for it. By using proper synchronization and avoiding direct reliance on thread IDs, you can write thread-safe and robust multi-threaded code in Julia.

Use of finalizers

When dealing with finalizers in Julia, it's essential to be cautious due to their potential to interrupt any code and interact with global state. Finalizers are typically used to update global state, which can introduce complications when working with multi-threaded code. To ensure the safe use of finalizers in multi-threaded contexts, you can employ different strategies:

- **Preventing Finalizers During Critical Regions**: In single-threaded code, you can call the internal C function `jl_gc_enable_finalizers` to prevent finalizers from being scheduled inside critical regions. This can be combined with locks to ensure that finalizers do not interfere with critical operations.
- **Delaying Finalizers Until Lock is Acquired**: A strategy used by Base in some places is to explicitly delay a finalizer until it can acquire its lock non-recursively. This ensures that the finalizer doesn't run concurrently with other operations that require the same lock. An example of this strategy is demonstrated in the code snippet for `finalize_ref`.
- **Using Yield-Free Queues**: Another approach is to use yield-free queues to handle finalizers. While Julia's Base library doesn't have a lock-free queue implementation, `Base.IntrusiveLinkedListSynchronized{T}` can be used as an alternative. This approach is suitable for code with event loops. The idea is to avoid performing any explicit work inside the finalizer and instead add the finalizer to a queue to be processed at a safer time. For example, this strategy is employed by Gtk.jl to manage lifetime ref-counting. In this approach, you can define the finalizer to use @spawn and a separate thread to run the cleanup work.

It's essential to carefully consider the impact of finalizers on multi-threaded code, as they can introduce potential race conditions and other issues. By employing one of the strategies mentioned above, you can make the use of finalizers safer in multi-threaded contexts. Remember that finalizers should be used with caution, and it's essential to thoroughly test and verify the behavior of your code when using them in multi-threaded environments.

Speeding up data science workflows

Speeding up data science workflows can be achieved through various techniques, including the use of threads, asynchronous programming, and parallel computation. Each approach has its strengths and is suitable for different scenarios. Let's explore how each technique can contribute to faster data science workflows:

- **Threads**: Julia's multi-threading capabilities (via the Threads module) can be used to execute multiple tasks concurrently within a single Julia process. This can be beneficial for certain data science tasks, such as:
  - **Data Loading**: When working with large datasets, loading data from files or databases can become a bottleneck. Using threads, you can parallelize data loading and processing tasks, reducing the overall loading time.
  - **Preprocessing**: Data preprocessing, including data cleaning, feature engineering, and transformations, can often be parallelized. By distributing these tasks across threads, you can speed up the data preparation phase.
  - **Hyperparameter Tuning**: When tuning hyperparameters for machine learning models using techniques like cross-validation, each evaluation can be independent. Threads can be used to parallelize these evaluations, significantly reducing the tuning time.
- **Asynchronous Programming**: Asynchronous programming allows you to handle multiple tasks concurrently without waiting for each to be completed before moving on to the next. In data science, this approach is useful for tasks, such as:
  - **Web Scraping**: When gathering data from web APIs or scraping websites, requests to different endpoints can be performed asynchronously, improving the overall data acquisition speed.
  - **Real-time Data Streams**: Analyzing real-time data streams, such as stock market data or sensor readings, can benefit from asynchronous processing to handle incoming data in parallel.
- **Parallel Computation**: Parallel computation involves executing tasks simultaneously on multiple cores or nodes of a computing cluster.

It is particularly useful for tasks that can be divided into independent subproblems, including:

- **Large-Scale Machine Learning**: Training complex machine learning models on large datasets can be computationally intensive. Parallelizing the training process across multiple cores or nodes can significantly reduce the training time.
- **Monte Carlo Simulations**: In statistical simulations, or Monte Carlo methods, individual simulations can be executed in parallel, improving the efficiency of the overall analysis.
- **Bootstrapping and Cross-validation**: Bootstrapping and cross-validation involve repeatedly resampling data and fitting models, making them suitable candidates for parallel computation.

However, it's important to note that not all data science workflows will benefit equally from each of these techniques. Some tasks may not be easily parallelizable or asynchronous, and introducing concurrency can add complexity, potentially leading to performance degradation due to overhead.

Careful consideration, profiling, and benchmarking are necessary to identify the specific bottlenecks in your data science workflow and determine the most appropriate techniques to speed up the process. Additionally, the availability of hardware resources and the architecture of the data processing pipeline also play crucial roles in optimizing the workflow's performance.

JuliaHub is a web platform that provides various services for the Julia programming language, including package hosting, collaboration tools, and computational resources. While JuliaHub itself is not responsible for enabling async, parallel, or multi-threaded computations directly, it can certainly be utilized in conjunction with the power of Julia's language features and ecosystem to enhance data science workflows.

Using the power of JuliaHub

Here's how JuliaHub can be leveraged for async, parallel, and multi-threaded computations:

- **Package Hosting and Management**: JuliaHub provides package hosting services, allowing developers to share and distribute their Julia packages. Many packages in the Julia ecosystem are specifically designed to support asynchronous, parallel, and multi-threaded computations. By leveraging these packages, data scientists can easily incorporate advanced concurrency features into their workflows.

- **High-Performance Computing Resources**: JuliaHub offers access to high-performance computing resources, such as cloud-based clusters and servers. These resources can be used to execute computationally intensive tasks in parallel, significantly speeding up data analysis and model training processes.
- **Collaboration and Community**: JuliaHub fosters collaboration within the Julia community. Data scientists can share knowledge, best practices, and efficient code snippets related to async and parallel computing through JuliaHub's collaboration tools. By learning from the community, developers can improve their concurrency skills and optimize their data science workflows.
- **Jupyter Notebooks and Interactive Computing**: JuliaHub supports Jupyter notebooks, providing an interactive environment for data exploration and analysis. With Julia's built-in support for async and parallel programming, data scientists can use Jupyter notebooks on JuliaHub to experiment with concurrent solutions and optimize their code iteratively.
- **Benchmarking and Profiling**: JuliaHub's computational resources can be used for benchmarking and profiling data science workflows. By running experiments on different configurations of async and parallel code, developers can fine-tune their implementations for better performance.
- **Job Management and Scheduling**: JuliaHub may provide job management and scheduling capabilities, allowing users to submit and manage concurrent jobs. This can be useful for running a large number of data science experiments in parallel, efficiently utilizing the available computing resources.

It's essential to keep in mind that Julia is a versatile language with powerful concurrency features built into its core. While JuliaHub provides a platform to support these features, the actual implementation of async, parallel, and multi-threaded computations largely depends on the Julia packages and code written by developers. By leveraging the language's capabilities and the resources provided by JuliaHub, data scientists can efficiently harness the power of async and parallel computing for their data science tasks.

Conclusion

In this chapter, we delved into the powerful capabilities of Julia for parallel computation, asynchronous programming, multi-threading, and leveraging the resources provided by JuliaHub to speed up data science workflows. Through a comprehensive exploration of these topics, we have equipped data scientists with essential tools to tackle computationally intensive tasks efficiently and expedite their data analysis processes.

In the next chapter, we will learn about how distributed computing is a powerful paradigm for tackling large-scale computational problems by distributing tasks across multiple machines or nodes in a network. Julia, being a high-performance and flexible language, offers robust support for distributed computing, making it an excellent choice for parallelizing and optimizing computationally intensive tasks.

Questions

1. What is parallel computation, and how does it differ from sequential computation?
2. How can Julia's Distributed module be used to set up a cluster of worker processes for parallel computation?
3. What are the benefits of load balancing in parallel computing, and how does Julia handle load balancing among worker processes?
4. Explain the concept of remote procedure calls (RPCs) in the context of parallel computation using Julia.
5. What is asynchronous programming, and why is it beneficial for certain data science tasks?
6. How can Julia's asynchronous tasks be used to handle real-time data streams effectively?
7. Give an example of a data science task that can benefit from asynchronous programming in Julia.
8. How does Julia manage asynchronous tasks to avoid blocking and improve concurrency?
9. Explain the concept of tasks in Julia and how they differ from regular functions.
10. How can task operations, such as `schedule`, `wait`, and `remotecall`, be used to manage asynchronous computations in Julia?
11. What are channels in Julia, and how are they used for communication between tasks in concurrent workflows?

12. Give an example of a situation where connecting via channels is beneficial for data processing in Julia.
13. What is multi-threading, and how does it allow concurrent execution of tasks in a single Julia process?
14. How can Julia's Threads module be used to create and manage multiple threads?
15. Give an example of a data science task that can be accelerated using multi-threading in Julia.
16. What are the potential challenges or considerations when dealing with multi-threading in Julia?
17. How can parallel computation, multi-threading, and asynchronous programming contribute to speeding up data science workflows in Julia?
18. Explain how hyperparameter tuning and cross-validation can be parallelized to enhance efficiency in data science tasks.
19. What services does JuliaHub offer for Julia users, and how can it support distributed computing and parallel tasks?
20 .How can data scientists benefit from JuliaHub's high-performance computing resources for large-scale data analysis?

CHAPTER 15

Distributed Computation in Julia

Introduction

Distributed computing refers to a field of computer science and engineering that deals with the design, implementation, and management of systems in which multiple computers or devices work together to achieve a common goal. The goal of distributed computing is to leverage the combined processing power and resources of multiple machines to solve complex problems, process large amounts of data, or provide high-performance services.

In a distributed computing system, the individual machines, often referred to as nodes, are connected through a network. These nodes communicate and coordinate their activities to accomplish tasks that would be difficult or impossible for a single machine to handle efficiently. This approach offers several advantages, including improved performance, fault tolerance, scalability, and resource utilization.

There are various models and architectures for distributed computing, including:

- **Client-Server Architecture:** In this model, there are central servers that provide services or resources to client machines. Clients request services from the servers, which then respond with the required data or results. Web servers and databases often use this architecture.
- **Peer-to-Peer (P2P) Architecture:** In a P2P model, all participating nodes can act as both clients and servers. Nodes share resources directly with each other, such as files or processing power. Examples of P2P systems include file-sharing networks like BitTorrent.
- **Cluster Computing:** Cluster computing involves connecting multiple machines to form a cluster. These machines work together to complete

computational tasks, often for parallel processing or high-performance computing purposes.

- **Grid Computing:** Grid computing extends the concept of cluster computing by connecting geographically distributed clusters to create a large, virtualized computing resource. This allows organizations to share resources and collaborate on tasks that require significant computing power.
- **Cloud Computing:** Cloud computing provides resources and services over the internet on demand. It abstracts the underlying infrastructure and allows users to access computing resources, storage, and applications as needed. Cloud platforms like Amazon Web Services (AWS), Microsoft Azure, and Google Cloud are examples of this model.

Distributed computing systems come with challenges related to communication, synchronization, consistency, fault tolerance, and load balancing. Designing and implementing effective distributed systems require careful consideration of these challenges to ensure that the system performs reliably and efficiently.

Structure

In this chapter, the following topics will be covered:

- Distributed computation in Julia
- Asynchronous Execution and Cooperative Task Scheduling in Julia
- Loading packages in Distributed Computing
- Managing processes
- Data transfer in distributed computing
- Variables in distributed computing
- Maps and Loops
- References and Channels
- Distributed Garbage Collection
- Shared Arrays
- Clusters Managers

Distributed computation in Julia

In the realm of high-performance computing, the demand for faster and more efficient computation has led to the evolution of parallel and distributed computing. Julia, a modern programming language designed for scientific and technical computing, embraces this demand by offering robust support for both multi-processing and distributed computing. This chapter delves into the fascinating world of parallelism, exploring how Julia's Distributed module revolutionizes the way we leverage the computational capabilities of modern hardware.

Harnessing the Strength of Many

In today's computing landscape, a single computer often hosts multiple CPUs, while multiple computers can be combined into a cluster. This abundance of processing power holds the potential to accelerate computations significantly. There are two critical factors that influence performance: the speed of CPUs and their access to memory. Even in multicore laptops, variations in memory access speed and cache capabilities impact performance. An efficient parallel computing environment must enable precise control over memory allocation to each CPU. Julia answers this need by providing a multiprocessing environment founded on message passing, allowing programs to execute across multiple processes with distinct memory domains simultaneously.

A Fresh Take on Message Passing

Unlike traditional message-passing libraries like MPI, Julia introduces a novel approach to message-passing. It employs a "one-sided" communication model, where the programmer primarily manages one process in a two-process operation. This design simplifies the interaction by resembling high-level function calls rather than the classic "message send" and "message receive" paradigm. Julia's distributed programming hinges on two core primitives: remote references and remote calls.

Remote References: Bridging the Gap

Remote references are powerful constructs that enable communication across processes. They serve as handles to objects stored on specific processes. Julia offers two types of remote references: `Future` and `RemoteChannel`. A `Future` represents the result of a remote call, providing a way to access the outcome of an operation on a separate process. The result is obtained using wait on the Future or by fetching it. `RemoteChannels` are dynamic communication channels that allow multiple processes to coordinate their actions by accessing the same shared channel. This opens avenues for synchronized processing among various processes.

Remote Calls: Executing from Afar

Remote calls are at the heart of Julia's distributed computing paradigm. They facilitate executing functions on remote processes. When a process makes a remote call, it immediately receives a **Future** representing the result of that call. This non-blocking approach lets the initiating process continue its operations while the remote call progresses elsewhere. Waiting for the result can be done using wait, and the outcome can be obtained using fetch.

Process Identity and Worker Model

In Julia's distributed environment, each process is assigned a unique identifier. The process controlling the Julia prompt bears the ID 1. Concurrently, processes employed for parallel tasks are known as "**workers**". For single-process scenarios, the solitary process is also treated as a worker (Process 1). However, in true parallelism, all processes except Process 1 are considered workers. This distinction is vital for methods like **pmap**, which effectively parallelizes computations across multiple workers.

Embracing Parallelism: A Practical Guide

Putting theory into action, Julia makes it seamless to harness parallel and distributed computing. Launching multiple worker processes on a local machine is as straightforward as invoking **julia -p n**, where n is the desired number of workers. Typically, matching n with the number of CPU threads (logical cores) optimizes performance. It's important to note that the -p argument automatically incorporates the Distributed module, ensuring access to its powerful capabilities.

```
$ julia -p 2

julia> r = remotecall(rand, 2, 2, 2)

Future(2, 1, 4, ReentrantLock(nothing, 0x00000000, 0x00, Base.
GenericCondition{Base.Threads.SpinLock}(Base.IntrusiveLinkedList{Task}
(nothing, nothing), Base.Threads.SpinLock(0)), (8, 0, 141733920768)),
nothing)


julia> s = @spawnat 2 1 .+ fetch(r)

Future(2, 1, 5, ReentrantLock(nothing, 0x00000000, 0x00, Base.
GenericCondition{Base.Threads.SpinLock}(Base.IntrusiveLinkedList{Task}
(nothing, nothing), Base.Threads.SpinLock(0)), (8, 4572472576,
4883600368)), nothing)

julia> fetch(s)
```

```
2×2 Array{Float64,2}:
 1.18526  1.50912
 1.16296  1.60607
```

Here, you are starting the Julia interpreter with 2 worker processes. The `-p` flag indicates the number of worker processes you want to launch. In this case, you are requesting 2 worker processes.

1. **`remotecall(rand, 2, 2, 2):`**
    - The remotecall function initiates a remote call to a specific function on a particular worker process.
    - In this case, you are calling the rand function remotely.
    - The first argument (rand) is the function you want to call.
    - The following arguments (2, 2, 2) are the dimensions for generating random numbers.
    - The result of this remote call is a **`Future`** that represents the outcome of the operation on the specified worker process.
    - The output **`Future(2, 1, 4, nothing)`** indicates that the result will be available on worker 2, process 1, and the call has a unique ID of 4.
2. **`@spawnat 2 1 .+ fetch(r)`**:
    - The **`@spawnat`** macro is used to initiate a computation on a specific worker process, in this case, worker 2.
    - 2 after **`@spawnat`** indicates the target worker process.
    - **`1 .+ fetch(r)`** is the computation to be performed on the specified worker process.
    - **`fetch(r)`** retrieves the value of the previous remote call's result (stored in the Future object r).
    - **`1 .+ fetch(r)`** adds 1 element-wise to the fetched matrix.
    - The result of this spawned computation is a **`Future`** that represents the outcome of the computation on the specified worker process.
    - The output **`Future(2, 1, 5, nothing)`** indicates that the result will be available on worker 2, process 1, and the call has a unique ID of 5.
3. `fetch(s)`:
    - The fetch function retrieves the value of a **`Future`**.
    - In this case, you are fetching the result of the computation initiated by the @spawnat macro.
    - The result is a 2×2 matrix of floating-point numbers.

In summary, the code demonstrates how to perform distributed computations using Julia›s parallel and distributed computing features. It generates random numbers remotely, adds 1 to the resulting matrix on a specific worker process, and then fetches the final result back to the main process for display. This showcases the power of Julia's distributed programming model and its ability to seamlessly perform computations across multiple processes.

The landscape of computing is evolving rapidly, and the demand for faster and more efficient computations continues to grow. Julia's innovative approach to parallel and distributed computing empowers developers to tap into the full potential of modern hardware. By simplifying message passing and providing intuitive tools like remote references and calls, Julia paves the way for seamless multi-processing and distributed computing. Whether you›re working on a single laptop or orchestrating computations across a cluster, Julia's Distributed module equips you with the tools to conquer the most demanding computational challenges.

Asynchronous Execution and Cooperative Task Scheduling in Julia

In the realm of parallel and distributed computing, Julia stands out not only for its powerful abstractions but also for its thoughtful optimizations. In this chapter, we delve into two critical concepts: Future caching and cooperative multitasking. These mechanisms are designed to enhance performance, improve efficiency, and streamline the execution of complex parallel tasks.

The Magic of Future Caching

Julia's `Future` abstraction is a gateway to a world of parallelism, allowing tasks to execute remotely while main processes continue without waiting. A notable feature of Futures is the ability to cache fetched values locally. When a Future's value is fetched, it is stored locally, minimizing network hops and subsequent fetch calls for the same result. This optimization not only reduces overhead but also promotes smoother execution by eliminating redundant network communication.

Cooperative Multitasking: The @async and @ sync Approach

A significant stride in parallelism comes with Julia's `@async` and `@sync` mechanisms. These tools empower developers to manage tasks in a cooperative multitasking environment, harnessing parallelism while synchronizing execution for seamless coordination.

Feeder Tasks and @async

The `@async` macro functions similarly to `@spawnat`, but it focuses on local execution. It is an essential tool in creating "feeder" tasks, a concept pivotal for distributing tasks across processes efficiently. Each feeder task takes charge of computing a specific index, awaiting the completion of its assigned process before proceeding to the next index. Importantly, feeder tasks don't kick off until the main task enters an `@sync` block.

@sync: Coordinated Synchronization

The `@sync` macro serves as the conductor of Julia's cooperative multitasking orchestra. It governs synchronization among tasks, ensuring the main task patiently waits until all local tasks, initiated by `@async`, are concluded. This approach ensures an organized orchestration of parallel tasks, preventing chaotic clashes and facilitating a well-structured execution flow.

Sharing State and Cooperative Multitasking

Julia's cooperative multitasking model enables tasks to share state, fostering efficient collaboration among parallel processes. As of version 0.7 and beyond, `@async`-spawned feeder tasks can seamlessly access shared resources like the nextidx variable. This harmonious state-sharing among tasks that run on the same process exemplifies Julia's careful design to optimize cooperation in parallel execution.

Mindful Context Switching

Cooperative multitasking also comes with a deliberate approach to context switching. Julia strategically schedules context switches at specific points, such as when using `remotecall_fetch`. This calculated synchronization helps to manage execution flows efficiently, ensuring tasks are not interrupted haphazardly.

Preparing for Future Innovations

It's important to recognize that Julia's cooperative multitasking model and resource sharing represent the current state of implementation. This model is designed to facilitate running multiple tasks on a single process, potentially leading to a fascinating M:N threading approach in future Julia versions. However, this advancement might introduce the need for resource locking, particularly when dealing with shared resources.

Julia's approach to Future caching and cooperative multitasking demonstrates a deep commitment to optimizing parallel and distributed computing. By locally caching Future values, Julia minimizes redundant network hops and improves overall performance. The synergy between **`@async`** and **`@sync`** introduces a cooperative multitasking model that elegantly orchestrates parallel tasks, ensuring organized execution. The capacity for tasks to share state and the thoughtful management of context switching showcase Julia's emphasis on balance and efficiency. As Julia continues to evolve, these principles will likely play a crucial role in shaping the future of parallel and distributed computing in the language.

Loading packages in Distributed Computing

We will understand the concept of code availability and loading packages in the context of parallel and distributed computing using the Julia programming language. Let's break down the main points:

- **Code Availability:** When working with parallel and distributed computing in Julia, the code you write must be available on all the processes that will execute it. Each process runs independently, so if a process doesn't have access to the required code, it won't be able to execute functions or use data defined in that code.
- **Example - Availability Issue:** In the given example, a function called `rand2` is defined. When this function is called on process 1, it runs successfully because the function is defined there. However, when the same function is called using the **`@spawnat`** macro to run on another process (process 2), an error occurs because process 2 doesn't have access to the **`rand2`** function.
- **Loading Packages and Files:** In Julia, you can load code from files or packages. The example introduces a file named **`DummyModule.jl`**, which defines a module named **`DummyModule`**. This module contains a mutable struct **`MyType`** and a function `f`. The **`@everywhere`** macro is used to ensure that the **`DummyModule.jl`** file is loaded on every process.
- **Scope and Accessibility:** Loading the code doesn't automatically bring the module's definitions into the current scope of all processes. You need to use `using` or `import` to make the module's contents accessible. For example, after using **`.DummyModule`**, you can create objects and use functions defined in **`DummyModule`**. If a process hasn't brought the module

into scope, you can still send objects of types defined in the module to that process, even if the type itself is not directly accessible.

- **Preloading Files at Startup:** If you want to ensure that certain files are preloaded on all processes when you start Julia, you can use the `-L` flag followed by the file names. This ensures that the specified files are available on all processes from the beginning. Additionally, you can have a driver script that coordinates the computation across processes.
- **Packages and Scoping:** If your code is structured as a package, using the package with `using` will load the package's code on all processes, but the package's contents will only be accessible on the process where `using` was called. This means that even though all processes have access to the package's code, they don't all have access to its contents unless they explicitly bring it into scope.

The overall message is that in parallel and distributed computing in Julia, you need to ensure that your code is available on all processes that will run it. You can achieve this by loading files using the `@everywhere` macro, or by using the `-L` flag at startup. However, loading the code doesn't necessarily bring the contents into scope, and you need to manage scoping and accessibility explicitly across processes.

Managing processes

We will understand the concepts related to multi-processing and distributed computing in Julia. It outlines the principles behind parallel processing, message passing, and distributed programming in the language. Here's a detailed breakdown:

- **Introduction to multiprocessing and Distributed Computing:** Julia provides support for distributed memory parallel computing through the Distributed module, which is part of the standard library. This is particularly useful for utilizing the computational power of modern computers with multiple CPUs or clusters of interconnected computers.
- **Performance Factors:** Performance in distributed computing is influenced by CPU speed and memory access speed. Local memory access is faster than accessing memory on remote nodes. These considerations hold for both multi-core computers and clusters.
- **Julia's Approach to Distributed Computing:** Julia's distributed programming environment is based on message passing. Processes can run on separate memory domains and communicate through message passing, allowing for concurrent execution.
- **Message Passing in Julia:** Julia's message passing is typically "one-sided,"

meaning that one process explicitly manages communication while the other proceeds with its operation. Communication doesn't necessarily involve direct message send and receive operations but often takes the form of higher-level function calls.

- **Distributed Programming Primitives:** Distributed programming in Julia is built upon two core concepts: remote references and remote calls. Remote references allow processes to refer to objects stored on other processes, while remote calls involve requesting another process to execute a certain function on specific arguments.
- **Using Remote References:** Remote references come in two forms: `Future` and `RemoteChannel`. A `Future` represents the result of a remote call and can be fetched to obtain the result. A `RemoteChannel` is a communication channel between processes.
- **Creating and Fetching Remote Calls:** Remote calls return `Future` objects representing the result of the computation. They return immediately, and you can wait for them to finish using `wait` and obtain the result using `fetch`.
- **Using `@spawnat` Macro:** The `@spawnat` macro evaluates an expression on a specified process. It's similar to a remote call but more expressive. It's used to perform computations on remote processes.
- **Efficient Fetching:** The `remotecall_fetch` function combines fetching and calling a remote function in one step, making it more efficient.
- **Parallel Processing and `@async`:** `@async` is a macro used to run tasks concurrently on the local process. It's useful for creating feeder tasks for each process.
- **Code Availability and Loading Packages:** Code must be available on all processes that use it. Loading code from files or packages using `@everywhere` or the `-L` flag ensures code availability. Using packages requires managing scope.
- **Starting and Managing Worker Processes:** The `addprocs` function adds worker processes, `rmprocs` removes them, and `workers` lists active processes. It's important to load the `Distributed` module on the master process before adding workers.
- **Custom ClusterManagers:** Julia supports various types of clusters, including custom ones. A `ClusterManager` can be implemented to define how Julia interacts with different cluster setups.

Data transfer in distributed computing

We will understand the concept of data movement in distributed programming using Julia and the importance of minimizing data movement for achieving performance and scalability, with examples illustrating different ways data can be moved between processes and highlighting the trade-offs involved.

- **Data Movement Overhead:** Data movement, which involves sending messages or transferring data between different processes, often constitutes a significant portion of the overhead in distributed programs. The goal is to reduce the number of messages and the amount of data moved to improve program performance and scalability.
- **Explicit and Implicit Data Movement:** In Julia's distributed programming constructs, there are both explicit and implicit data movement operations. The `fetch` function is an explicit data movement operation because it directly requests that an object be moved from a remote process to the local machine. On the other hand, constructs like **`@spawnat`** have an implicit data movement aspect that might not be immediately obvious.

Example: Constructing and Squaring a Matrix: The text provides an example involving two methods for constructing and squaring a random matrix in a distributed context.

Method 1:

```
julia> A = rand(1000, 1000);

julia> Bref = @spawnat :any A^2;

julia> fetch(Bref);

1000×1000 Matrix{Float64}:

…
```

Method 2:

```
julia> Bref = @spawnat :any rand(1000, 1000)^2;

julia> fetch(Bref);

1000×1000 Matrix{Float64}:

…
```

- **Distinguishing the Methods:** While the difference between the two methods may seem trivial, it has significant implications due to the behavior of **`@spawnat`**. In Method 1, a random matrix is constructed on the local process, and then sent to another process where it is squared. In Method 2, both matrix construction and squaring are performed on the same remote process. As a result, the second method involves sending much less data between processes compared to the first method.
- **Considerations for Data Movement:** Designing data movement strategies in a distributed program requires careful consideration and often measurement. Depending on various factors, such as the availability of

data on different processes and the computational cost of operations, different approaches may be beneficial.

- If the current process needs the data, local construction might be better.
- If computing the data is expensive and only the current process has it, moving it to another process might be necessary.
- If the current process has minimal work between **@spawnat** and **fetch**, eliminating parallelism could be considered.
- If the random matrix generation is replaced with a more expensive operation, adding another **@spawnat** might be advantageous.

- **Choosing the Right Approach:** The choice of data movement strategy depends on the specific requirements and characteristics of the problem. Optimizing data movement involves weighing trade-offs between parallelism, computation cost, and communication overhead to achieve the best overall performance in a distributed program.

Variables in distributed computing

The provided text discusses the behavior of global variables in the context of remote execution using Julia's distributed programming features, such as **@spawnat** and **remotecall_fetch**. It explains how global variables are handled when used in remote calls and offers guidance on how to manage them effectively. Let's break down the information:

- **Global Variables in Remote Execution:** When executing code remotely using constructs like **@spawnat** and **remotecall_fetch**, you might reference global variables. Global bindings in the **Main** module are treated differently compared to global bindings in other modules.
- **Example:** Referencing Global Variables: Consider the code snippet:

```
julia> A = rand(10, 10)
10×10 Matrix{Float64}:
 0.253969   0.00485857  0.871175  0.692261    0.375655
0.914166  0.488375   0.871096   0.406925   0.68845
…
 0.704127   0.682123       0.185796  0.492256  0.629498
0.526364  0.447056   0.0307264  0.829556   0.42526


julia> remotecall_fetch(()->sum(A), 2)
52.61104291838339
```

Here, `sum` must be defined on the remote process (worker 2). While `A` is a global variable in the local workspace, worker 2 doesn't have a variable named `A` in its `Main` module. However, the act of shipping the closure `()->sum(A)` to worker 2 results in `Main.A` being defined there. Importantly, `Main.A` on worker 2 continues to exist even after the **`remotecall_fetch`** returns.

- **Handling Global References in Remote Calls:** Remote calls with embedded global references (limited to the **`Main`** module) behave as follows:
    - New global bindings are created on the destination workers if they are referenced as part of a remote call.
    - Global constants are also declared as constants on remote nodes.
    - Globals are re-sent to a destination worker only within the context of a remote call if their value has changed.
    - The cluster does not synchronize global bindings across nodes.
- **Example Illustration:** The text provides an illustrative example to demonstrate these points. After calling **`remotecall_fetch(()->sum(A), 2)`** and then modifying `A`, calling **`remotecall_fetch(()->sum(A), 3)`** results in different values of **`Main.A`** on workers 2 and 3, while the value of **`Main.A`** on the master node (node 1) is set to `nothing`.
- **Managing Global Memory on Workers:** While memory associated with globals may be collected when they are reassigned to the master node, no such action is taken on the worker nodes. The bindings for globals continue to be valid. To release memory associated with them on remote nodes, you can use the `clear!` function to manually reassign specific globals to `nothing`. This action will release the memory as part of the regular garbage collection cycle.
- **Best Practices:** The text emphasizes the importance of being cautious when referencing globals in remote calls. It's preferable to avoid using globals in such cases if possible. If you need to reference globals, consider using `let` blocks to localize global variables. This helps avoid unexpected behavior due to global variable bindings on remote workers.
- **Example of Using `let` Blocks:** The text provides an example of using a `let` block to ensure a global variable remains local and doesn't interfere with remote execution.

```
julia> A = rand(10, 10)
10×10 Matrix{Float64}:
 0.414612   0.708716   0.451456  0.0138283  0.714173   0.825522
```

```
0.647969  0.615009   0.0255661  0.857037
…

julia> remotecall_fetch(()->A, 2)
10×10 Matrix{Float64}:
 0.414612   0.708716   0.451456  0.0138283  0.714173   0.825522
0.647969  0.615009   0.0255661  0.857037
…
julia> B = rand(10, 10)
10×10 Matrix{Float64}:
 0.181936   0.866609  0.352039   0.975791   0.847819   0.640851
0.51947   0.206783   0.366583  0.819961
…
julia> let B = B
       remotecall_fetch(()->B, 2)
End
10×10 Matrix{Float64}:
 0.181936   0.866609  0.352039   0.975791   0.847819   0.640851
0.51947   0.206783   0.366583  0.819961
…
julia> @fetchfrom 2 InteractiveUtils.varinfo()
  name              size summary
  ----------- --------- --------------------
  A           840 bytes 10×10 Matrix{Float64}
  Base                  Module
  Core                  Module
  Distributed 1.151 MiB Module
  Main                  Module
  r           216 bytes Future
```

This example shows that A is defined on worker 2, but B is captured as a local variable within the let block, and thus a binding for B does not exist on worker 2.

Maps and Loops

We will understand the concept of parallel map and loops in Julia's distributed programming context, showcasing examples and best practices for performing parallel computations efficiently. Let's break down the information:

- **Parallel Computation without Data Movement**: Many parallel computations don't require data movement and can be executed independently on multiple processes. A common example is a Monte Carlo simulation where multiple processes perform independent trials simultaneously.
- **Defining a Parallelizable Function**: The text introduces a function called `count_heads` that counts the number of "heads" in a sequence of random coin flips.
- **Using `@spawnat` for Parallel Execution**: The @spawnat macro is used to execute the `count_heads` function on different processes simultaneously. The results are then fetched and combined using the fetch function.
- **Parallel For Loop with `@distributed`**: A more generalized approach to achieve parallelism is demonstrated using a parallel for loop implemented with the `@distributed` macro. In this example, multiple iterations of the loop are assigned to different processes, and their results are combined using a specified reduction operation (in this case, +).
- **Parallel Loop Behavior**: It's highlighted that parallel for loops differ from serial for loops. The iterations don't necessarily occur in a specific order, and variables or array writes aren't globally visible since iterations run on different processes.
- **Avoiding Shared Variables in Parallel Loops**: It's cautioned that using shared variables directly within parallel loops can lead to unexpected behavior due to the separate copies of variables on different processes. Shared Arrays are introduced as a workaround for this limitation.
- **Using Read-Only "`Outside`" Variables**: While modifying shared variables in parallel loops can lead to issues, using read-only variables from outside the loop is reasonable. The example demonstrates how a read-only vector can be used within a parallel loop.
- **Asynchronous Parallel Loops**: It's mentioned that the reduction operator can be omitted if not needed. In such cases, the loop runs asynchronously, spawning independent tasks on available workers and returning an array of Future objects. The caller can wait for these futures to complete later.
- **Parallel Map with pmap**: The concept of parallel map is introduced using the pmap function in Julia. This function applies a given function to

elements of a collection in parallel. An example is provided where singular values of multiple large random matrices are computed in parallel using pmap.

- **Comparison between pmap and @distributed for**: The differences between pmap and @distributed for are explained. pmap is designed for cases where each function call involves a large amount of work, while `@distributed` for can handle smaller tasks. Both use worker processes for the parallel computation, and the final reduction is done on the calling process for `@distributed` for.

References and Channels

We will understand the concepts of remote references and abstract channels in Julia's distributed programming framework. Let's break down the information:

- **Remote References and `AbstractChannels`**: Remote references in Julia are used to refer to objects that are stored on remote processes. These remote references are always associated with an implementation of an `AbstractChannel`.
- `AbstractChannel` and Concrete Implementations: An `AbstractChannel` is an abstract type that defines the behavior of communication channels between processes. Concrete implementations of `AbstractChannel`, such as Channel, are required to implement specific methods like `put!`, `take!`, `fetch`, `isready`, and `wait`.
- **Remote Object Storage in Channels**: A remote object referred to by a Future (a type representing a reference to the result of an asynchronous computation) is stored in a `Channel{Any}(1)`. This means that the remote process holds a channel with a size of 1, capable of storing objects of any type.
- `RemoteChannel` **and Rewritable References**: `RemoteChannel` is a type that allows for rewritable references to different types and sizes of channels, as well as other implementations of `AbstractChannel`. This flexibility enables you to refer to various types of remote communication mechanisms.
- **Constructing Remote Channels**: The constructor `RemoteChannel(f::Function, pid)()` is used to create references to channels that can hold more than one value of a specific type. The function f is executed on the process with the given pid, and it must return an `AbstractChannel`. This allows you to construct references to channels with different properties on remote processes.
- **Example of `RemoteChannel`**: An example is provided to illustrate the use

of **RemoteChannel**. For instance, **RemoteChannel(()->Channel{Int}(10), pid)** constructs a reference to a channel of type Int and size 10. This channel exists on the worker process identified by pid.

- **Methods on RemoteChannel**: Methods such as **put!**, **take!**, **fetch**, **isready**, and **wait** can be used on a **RemoteChannel**. These methods are proxied onto the actual channel implementation on the remote process, allowing you to interact with the remote channel as if it were local.
- **Custom Implementations with RemoteChannel**: RemoteChannel can be used to refer to user-implemented AbstractChannel objects. For example, you can create your custom channel types and use RemoteChannel to interact with them on remote processes.
- **Example in dictchannel.jl**: The text mentions that there's a simple example provided in the **dictchannel.jl** file in the Examples repository. This example uses a dictionary as the remote storage for the channel, showcasing the flexibility of remote channels for various use cases.

We will understand the concepts of channels and remote channels in Julia's distributed programming framework. It introduces their usage through an example of parallel computation involving **interprocess** communication. Let's break down the information:

- **Channels and RemoteChannels**:
  - A Channel is a communication mechanism that is local to a single process. It cannot be directly accessed by other processes.
  - In contrast, a **RemoteChannel** serves as a handle to a Channel and allows values to be exchanged across different worker processes.
  - The pid (process id) associated with a **RemoteChannel** identifies the process where the backing store (the actual Channel) exists.
  - Any process with a reference to a **RemoteChannel** can perform operations such as putting and taking items from the channel. Data is automatically sent to or retrieved from the process associated with the **RemoteChannel**.
- **Serialization of Channels and RemoteChannels**:
  - When a Channel is serialized, the data present in the channel is also serialized. Deserializing it creates a copy of the original object.
  - Serializing a **RemoteChannel** involves serializing an identifier that points to the location and instance of the underlying Channel. Deserializing a **RemoteChannel** results in a reference to the same backing store as the original.

- **Parallel Computation Example**: For multiple worker processes to perform parallel computation using channels for `interprocess` communication, we need to follow the steps:
    - Workers are added using `addprocs(4)` to create four worker processes.
    - Two `RemoteChannel` instances, jobs and results, are created to manage communication between the master process and the workers.
    - A function `do_work` is defined using `@everywhere`, making it available on all worker processes. This function simulates the execution of tasks.
    - The `make_jobs` function populates the jobs channel with job IDs.
    - n jobs are created using `make_jobs(n)` and fed into the jobs channel asynchronously.
    - Parallel tasks are started on worker processes using `remote_do` to process jobs from the jobs channel and write results to the results channel.
    - Results are fetched from the results channel using a loop that prints job IDs, execution times, and worker IDs.

Distributed Garbage Collection

When you have objects referenced by remote references in a distributed computing scenario, these objects can only be freed when all the references to them across the cluster have been deleted.

Here's how the process works:

- **Reference Tracking**: The node that stores the actual value of the object keeps track of which workers in the cluster have references to it. Whenever a remote reference, like a `RemoteChannel` or an `unfetched` Future, is serialized and sent to a worker, the node where the value is stored is notified about this addition of reference.
- **Garbage Collection Notification**: Similarly, when a remote reference or an `unfetched` Future is garbage collected locally (on the worker where it was created), the owning node is notified again. This notification mechanism is handled by an internal serializer that is aware of the cluster's structure.
- **Cluster Context**: It's essential to understand that remote references are only valid within the context of a running cluster. You can't serialize and deserialize references to and from regular I/O objects; this is not supported.

- **Tracking Messages**: The notifications are managed using "`tracking`" messages. When a reference is serialized to another process, an "`add reference`" message is sent to the owning node. Conversely, when a reference is locally garbage collected, a "`delete reference`" message is sent to the owning node.
- **Futures Behavior**: Futures are designed to be written once and cached locally. Fetching a Future also triggers an update to the reference tracking information on the node that holds the value.
- **Value Freedom**: The node that owns the value of an object will free it from memory only when all references to it have been cleared.
- **Serializing Fetched Futures**: If you serialize a fetched Future to a different node, the value is also sent along with it. This is because, by the time you serialize it, the original node might have already collected the value.
- **Local Garbage Collection**: The local garbage collection of objects depends on their size and the current memory usage in the system. Smaller local reference objects may not be immediately collected.
- **Explicitly Calling Finalize**: It's a recommended practice to explicitly call the finalize function on local instances of `RemoteChannels` or on `unfetched` Futures that you no longer need. This sends an immediate message to the remote node, instructing it to remove its reference to the value. This is particularly important because the local reference may not be collected immediately due to memory management considerations.
- **Reference Invalidation**: Once you call finalize on a reference, it becomes invalid. You can't use it in any further operations or calls.

Local Invocations in Distributed Computing

When working with distributed computing in Julia, there's an interesting behavior to consider regarding local invocations, which involves how data is copied and manipulated on remote nodes. Let's break down this behavior:

- **Data Copy for Remote Execution**: In distributed computing, when you use `remotecalls` or store data in a `RemoteChannel` or Future on a different node, the data is copied over to the remote node for execution. This naturally results in serialized copies of the objects on the remote node.
- **Local Execution on Same Node**: However, when the destination node for a `remotecall` or data storage is the same as the local node (the node where the call originates), the call is executed as a local call. While it might run in a separate task, there's no serialization or deserialization of data. Consequently, the call operates on the same object instances that were passed, and no copies are created.

- **Demonstrating Local Invocation**:
  - When you create a `RemoteChannel` on the local node and perform put! operations on it while modifying the same object instance between calls, only a single object instance is stored in the `RemoteChannel`. The modifications made to the object instance are reflected across all operations.
  - On the other hand, if the `RemoteChannel` is owned by a different node, modifications between calls result in separate object instances being stored.
- **Local Invocations and Data Copy**:
  - This behavior is generally not problematic. It's a consideration mainly if the object is both stored locally and modified after the call.
  - In such cases, it might be appropriate to store a deep copy of the object to ensure that modifications don't affect the stored version.
- **Applying to `remotecall`**:
  - The same principle applies to `remotecalls` executed on the local node.
  - When a `remotecall` is made to the local node, it behaves just like a direct invocation. The call modifies local objects passed as arguments.
  - However, when the `remotecall` is executed on a remote node, it operates on copies of the arguments passed.
- **Demonstrations**:
  - You can observe this behavior:
    - When invoking a `remotecall_fetch` on the local node, modifications to the input argument affect the fetched result because it's executed locally.
    - When the `remotecall_fetch` is executed on a remote node, modifications to the input argument don't affect the fetched result since it operates on a copy.
- **Considerations and Use Cases**:
  - This behavior is generally manageable and might not be an issue for most scenarios.
  - It becomes relevant if the local node is also used as a compute node and arguments are modified after the call.
  - In such cases, you might need to consider using deep copies of arguments for the call invoked on the local node.
  - Calls on remote nodes always operate on copies of arguments.

Shared Arrays

Shared Arrays in Julia are a powerful tool for distributed computing, allowing multiple processes to jointly access and manipulate the same array data using system-shared memory. Here's a comprehensive explanation of how Shared Arrays work and how to use them effectively:

- **Basic Concept**:
    - Shared Arrays map the same array across multiple processes using system-shared memory.
    - Unlike Distributed Arrays (DArrays), where each process accesses a chunk of data, Shared Arrays allow each participating process to access the entire array.
    - Shared Arrays are particularly useful when large data needs to be shared among multiple processes on the same machine.
- **Module and Loading**:
    - The functionality for Shared Arrays is provided by the **`SharedArrays`** module.
    - This module must be explicitly loaded on all participating workers using the **`@everywhere`** using **`SharedArrays`** directive.
- **Array Indexing and Behavior**:
    - Shared Array indexing (assignment and access) follows the same rules as regular arrays.
    - Operations are efficient due to direct access to local process memory.
    - Algorithms designed for regular arrays can work naturally with Shared Arrays, though they will operate in single-process mode.
    - To work with algorithms expecting regular arrays, you can extract the underlying array using the sdata function.
- **Creating Shared Arrays**:
    - The constructor for a Shared Array follows the pattern:
        - `SharedArray{T,N}(dims::NTuple; init=false, pids=Int[])`
    - This creates an N-dimensional shared array of type T with dimensions dims, across the processes specified by pids.
    - Only processes specified by pids (and the creating process) can access the Shared Array.
    - Note that only elements of bits type (**`isbits`**) are supported in a **`SharedArray`**.

- **Initialization and Parallel Initialization**:
  - You can specify an init function when creating a Shared Array, with the signature **`initfn(S::SharedArray)`**.
  - The **`init`** function is called on all participating workers and can be used to initialize the array.
  - Parallel initialization can be achieved by having each worker run the **`init`** function on a distinct portion of the array.

```
julia> using Distributed
julia> addprocs(3)
julia> @everywhere using SharedArrays

julia> S = SharedArray{Int,2}((3,4), init = S -> S[localindices(S)] =
repeat([myid()], length(localindices(S))))
3×4 SharedMatrix{Int64}:
 2  3  5  6
 2  4  5  6
 3  4  6  6
julia> S[3,2] = 7
julia> S
3×4 SharedMatrix{Int64}:
 2  3  5  6
 2  4  5  6
 3  7  6  6
```

In this example, S is a 3×4 Shared Array of Integers, where each element is initialized to the process ID.

- **Customizing Work Distribution**:
  - The **`localindices`** function provides disjoint one-dimensional index ranges, useful for dividing work among processes.
  - You can define your own partitioning strategy using functions like **`indexpids`** and length.
- **Avoiding Conflicts**:
  - Since all processes have access to the same underlying data, conflicts can arise when multiple processes modify the same element.

  - Care must be taken to avoid such conflicts, ensuring that processes don't interfere with each other.
  - Parallel algorithms should be designed to minimize overlapping work.
- **Parallel Kernel Example**:
  - An example of parallelizing a kernel is provided:

```
function advection_shared!(q, u)
    @sync begin
    for p in procs(q)
        @async remotecall_wait(advection_shared_chunk!, p, q, u)
    end
    end
    q
end
```

  - This function distributes chunks of the array to different workers for parallel processing.
- **Performance Comparison**:
  - Shared Arrays offer significant performance advantages in terms of reduced communication overhead between workers.
  - Compared to parallel implementations using @distributed, Shared Arrays can lead to faster execution times and better resource utilization.

Cluster Managers

In Julia's distributed computing framework, the concept of **`ClusterManagers`** plays a crucial role in managing and organizing the launching, networking, and event handling of worker processes within a logical cluster. Here's an in-depth explanation of how **`ClusterManagers`** function and their key characteristics:

- **Responsibilities of a ClusterManager:**
  - A **`ClusterManager`** oversees several critical tasks within a Julia cluster, including:
    - Launching worker processes within the cluster environment.
    - Managing various events during the lifespan of each worker process.
    - Optionally, providing data transport between workers.

- **Characteristics of a Julia Cluster:**
  - A Julia cluster consists of several interconnected processes, where each process serves a specific purpose.
  - The initial process, often referred to as the master process, is assigned an ID of 1.
  - Only the master process has the authority to add or remove worker processes from the cluster.
  - Communication between processes is direct and seamless, enabling any process to communicate with any other process.
- **Establishing Connections between Workers:**
  - Connections between workers are established through a specific process:
    - The `addprocs` function is invoked on the master process, along with a `ClusterManager` object.
    - The appropriate launch method is called, spawning the required number of worker processes on the designated machines.
    - Each worker process starts listening on a free port and outputs its host and port information to the standard output.
    - The cluster manager captures the standard output of each worker and makes this information available to the master process.
    - The master process parses the output, establishes TCP/IP. connections to each worker, and notifies workers about others in the cluster.
    - Each worker connects to every worker with an ID lower than its own, forming a mesh network where each worker is directly connected to all others.
- **Transport Layer and Customization:**
  - The default transport layer for communication between workers uses plain `TCPSockets`.
  - However, it's possible to replace the default transport with a custom transport to suit specific needs.
  - Custom transport implementations require setting up connections to remote workers and providing appropriate IO objects for message-processing loops.
- **In-Built Cluster Managers:**
  - Julia provides two built-in cluster managers:
    - `LocalManager`: Used when `addprocs()` or `addprocs(np::Integer)` is

called. It launches additional workers on the same host, utilizing multi-core and multi-processor hardware.

  - `SSHManager`: Used when **`addprocs(hostnames::Array)`** is called with a list of hostnames. It launches workers on remote hosts via SSH and can also handle master-worker and worker-worker connections via SSH.

- **Custom Cluster Manager Implementation:**
  - A custom cluster manager must be a subtype of the abstract **`ClusterManager`**.
  - It should implement the launch method responsible for launching new workers and the manage method, which handles various events during a worker's lifetime (such as registration, interruption, and finalization).
- **Worker Configuration with WorkerConfig:**
  - A **`WorkerConfig`** object stores information related to workers and their behavior.
  - Fields include **`io`**, **`host`**, **`port`**, **`count`**, **`exename`**, **`exeflags`**, **`userdata`**, **`tunnel`**, **`bind_addr`**, **`sshflags`**, **`max_parallel`**, and **`connect_at`**.
  - Custom cluster managers can utilize specific fields to tailor worker behavior and connectivity.
- **Cluster Cookie for Authentication:**
  - All processes within a cluster share the same cookie, serving as an authentication mechanism.
  - Workers must be started with the same cookie as the master process to ensure secure connections.
  - The cookie can be passed to workers through command-line arguments or stdin.
  - Cluster managers can retrieve the cookie using the **`cluster_cookie()`** function.
- **Security Considerations for LocalManager and SSHManager:**
  - **`LocalManager`** and **`SSHManager`** are designed for secure environments.
  - **`LocalManager`** binds only to the loopback interface by default, ensuring local connections.
  - **`SSHManager`** uses SSH to launch workers and can be configured for passwordless login.
  - Security measures, such as secure networking and encryption, can be customized using custom cluster managers.

Conclusion

In this chapter, we delved into the realm of distributed computation in Julia, exploring how to harness the power of multiple processes for parallel and cooperative task execution. Through various concepts and techniques, we learned how to leverage Julia's capabilities to distribute workloads across multiple machines or cores, leading to enhanced performance and efficiency.

I want to take a moment to extend my heartfelt congratulations to each one of you for your hard work and dedication in mastering the concepts of Julia for data science and machine learning. I am truly delighted that you have completed your studies and hands-on exercises in Julia successfully. Your commitment to understanding the intricacies of this programming language and its application in the fields of data science and machine learning is commendable. It is through hands-on experience that we truly solidify our knowledge and gain the confidence to apply what we've learned to real-world situations. I trust that these exercises have given you a strong foundation and practical insights that will serve you well in your future endeavors.

Julia is a versatile and powerful language, and your newfound expertise in it will undoubtedly open up a world of possibilities in data science and machine learning. As you move forward, I encourage you to continue exploring and experimenting with Julia, pushing the boundaries of what you can achieve in these exciting fields. Remember that learning is a lifelong journey, and there is always more to discover and accomplish. If you have any questions, need further guidance, or wish to delve deeper into specific topics, please do not hesitate to reach out. I am here to support your continued growth and learning. Once again, congratulations on your achievements, and I look forward to hearing about your future successes in the world of data science and machine learning. Keep pushing the boundaries, stay curious, and never stop learning.

Questions

1. What are the benefits of asynchronous execution and cooperative task scheduling in a distributed computing environment, and how do they contribute to overall performance?
2. How does loading packages in distributed computing differ from loading them in a single process, and why is it important to ensure all processes have access to the required packages?

3. Explain the role of process management in distributed computing. How can you dynamically add or remove processes, and why is this flexibility valuable?
4. What strategies and considerations should you keep in mind when transferring data between processes in a distributed setup? How can you minimize data transfer overhead?
5. In the context of distributed computing, what challenges can arise when working with variables across different processes? How can proper scoping and synchronization mitigate these challenges?
6. How do maps and loops contribute to parallelization and concurrency in distributed computing? Provide examples of scenarios where these constructs can be effectively utilized.
7. What are references and channels in the context of distributed computing, and how do they facilitate communication and synchronization between processes? Provide real-world scenarios where their usage would be beneficial.
8. Explain the concept of distributed garbage collection. How does it ensure efficient memory management in a distributed environment, and what factors influence the process of garbage collection?
9. What is the purpose of Shared Arrays in distributed computing, and how do they differ from Distributed Arrays? How can Shared Arrays optimize data sharing among processes?
10. Describe the role of Cluster Managers in distributed computing. What responsibilities do they have in terms of process launching, management, and networking within a logical cluster?

Index

A

abstract channels
  concept 442, 443
addcounts!() function 163
arguments
  data 176
  edges 176
  weight 176
array
  about 103, 104
  in Julia 88-93
asynchronous execution 432
asynchronous programming
  about 400, 401
  concepts and techniques 401
asynchronous tasks 401, 402
atomic operations 415, 416
attributes
  plotting 277-279
autocorrelation 167
autocovariance 167
autoencoders 326

B

backends
  plotting 281, 282
bar plot 131
Bayesian approach
  used, for manipulating categorical data 388-390
  used, for manipulating discrete data 385-388
Bayesian inference
  about 367
  benefits 367
  challenges 368
  examples 368
  problem solving 368
Bayesian linear regression 375, 376
Bayesian logistic regression 376, 377
Bayesian model

about 372, 373, 394
building 381
types 373-375
Bayesian modeling
in Julia 383-385
Bayesian network 377, 378, 394, 395
Bayesian neural networks (BNNs) 380-383
Bayesian statistics
concepts 369
problem solving 370
versus Bayes' theorem 368, 369
Bayes' theorem
about 183
versus Bayesian statistics 368, 369
blocking programming 400
bound mutable variable
versus copy mutable variable 37-39
broadcasting 108

C

caching 432
categorical data
about 318
consideration 318
handling 319
in DataFrame 253-255
manipulating, with Bayesian approach 388-390
CategoricalVector 253
censored probability distribution
about 196, 197
versus truncated probability distribution 198
channels
connecting 406, 407
channels and remote channels
concept 443, 444
ClusterManagers function
about 449
characteristics 449-451
code structure
managing, in Julia 77-79
columnindex function 129
common stopping criteria 362
compound expression
about 47
functions, defining 48
concurrency
versus parallelism 408
conditional evaluation
about 40-42
exceptions, handling 44, 45
short circuit, evaluating 42, 43
conditional probability 182
context switching 433
contour plot 289-293
control flow
constructing 39, 40
convolutions
in Distributions.jl 204, 205
cooperative multitasking model 433
cooperative task scheduling 432
copy mutable variable
versus bound mutable variable 37-39
correlation
about 153, 165
drawing, from Raw Data 4, 5
counteq() function 161
counting method
about 161
addcounts!() function 163
counteq() function 161
countmap() function 163, 164
countne() function 162
counts() function 162
proportionmap() function 164
proportions() function 163
countmap() function 163, 164
countne() function 162
counts() function 162
covariance 152, 165
cross-correlation 169
cross-covariance 169
cumulative histogram 299, 300

D

data
  accessing, from database 122-124
  acquiring 118-121
  DataFrame, visualizing 131
  fetching 215, 216
  inspecting 117-228
  loading, from CSV file
    into DataFrame 126-128
  manipulating 229, 230
  obtaining 117, 118
  TextAnalysis package 130
  text files, saving 128, 129
data analysis
  features 6
  need for 6
  observational estimation 175, 176
  outlier detection and treatment 156
  statistical function 172-174
data containers 310
DataFrame
  categorical data 253-255
  data joining 255-262
  data reshaping 248
  data sorting 244
  missing data 239
  sorting 245-248
  Split-Apply-Combine (SAC)
    strategy 262-268
DataFrameMacros.jl package 232
DataFrame objects
  constructing 211-213
  data, fetching 213-215
  data, inspecting 213-215
  data, manipulating 213-215
DataFrames.jl package
  about 210
  environment, setting up 210, 211
  functions 255
DataFramesMeta.jl package
  about 230, 232
  examples 231
DataFrames package 142
data frontend for MLJ
  about 354, 355
  benefits 353, 354
  need for 353
data handling
  in Machine Learning in Julia
    (MLJ) 309, 310
data joining
  in DataFrame 255-262
data manipulation framework
  DataFrameMacros.jl package 232
  DataFramesMeta.jl package 230, 232
  in Julia 230
  Query.jl package 232, 233
data-model type mismatches
  addressing 324
  feature engineering 324
  scientific type coercion 324
data preparation
  data-model type mismatches,
    addressing 324
  data splitting 323, 324
data preprocessing
  with MLJ transformers 334, 335
data reshaping
  in DataFrame 248
  in Julia 249-252
  melting 249
  pivoting 248
  stacking 249
data science
  about 2
  defining 2
  machine learning 4
  problem 143, 144
  statistics 3, 4
  task automation, need for 3
data science workflows
  asynchronous programming 422
  parallel computation 422, 423
  speeding up 422
  threads 422

data sorting
  in DataFrames 244
data splitting
  about 323
  partition 323
  unpack 323
data transfer
  in distributed computing 436-438
decision trees 326
descriptive statistics
  about 149
  purpose 149
descriptive statistics measures
  correlation 153
  covariance 152
  entropy 154
  mean 150
  median 150
  mode 151
  overview 149, 156
  quantiles 154, 155
  range 151
  standard deviation 152
  summary statistics 155
  variance 151
  weighted mean 150
  weighted sum 150
deterministic regressor
  about 343, 344
  types 343
dictionaries 104
dimension inspection 194
discrete data
  manipulating, with Bayesian approach 385-388
distance method
  in StatsBase.jl 158
distributed computing
  about 428
  data transfer 436-438
  local invocations 445, 446
  message-passing libraries 429
  modern hardware 429
  packages, loading 434, 435
  parallelism 430, 431, 432
  process identity 430
  remote calls 430
  remote references 429
  variables 438-440
  worker model 430
Distributed Garbage Collection
  about 444
  working 444, 445
distribution function
  about 186
  dimension inspection 194
  parameter retrieval 188
  probability, estimating 192, 193
  sampling 189
  statistics computation 190, 191
  type hierarchy 186, 187
Distributions.jl
  convolutions 204, 205
  mixture models 202-205
Distributions.jl package 185, 196

E

entropy 154
Euclidean distance 158

F

feature importance 350
filter 107
finalizers
  using 421
fit method
  about 347
  objects 347
function-end keyword 51, 52
function name
  about 52
  rules 53
functions
  defining 48

G

Gaussian Mixture Models (GMMs) 326
Gaussian processes 379
Gaussian Process Latent Variable Model (GPLVM) 391-394
gkldiv function 161
GLM.jl 210
Grid search 360

H

hash function 99
hasproperty function 129
Hidden Markov Models (HMMs) 394-396
histogram 131
hyperparameters 361
HypothesisTests.jl 210

I

innovation
  preparing 433, 434
interquartile range (IQR) 157
iterative model
  about 361
  controlling 362

J

joint probability 183
Julia
  arrays 88-93
  Bayesian modeling 383-385
  code structure, managing 77-79
  data manipulation framework 230
  data reshaping 249-252
  data structure, setting 102, 103
  missing values 240-243
  multiple dispatch 73-76
  passing argument 57
  probability package 183, 184
  tuple data structure 94-96
Julia code methods
  with IDEs 19
  with Notebook 19, 20
  with REPL 19
Julia data structure
  operations 103
  setting 102, 103
Julia data structure, operations
  array 103, 104
  broadcasting 108
  dictionaries 104
  filter 107
  map 105
  reduce 106
  sets 104, 105
  tuples 104
Julia functions
  arguments 54
  body 54
  function-end keyword 51, 52
  return statement 55
  revisiting 51
  writing 58
JuliaHub
  using 423, 424
Julia language
  about 6-9
  features 9, 10
  for data analysis 10, 11
  IDEs, working with 18
  installing 17
  limitations 13
  setting up 17
  terminal session, running 18
  use cases 12, 13
Julia package manager
  about 20
  project environment 20-22
  REPL mode, working 22, 23
Julia system type
  about 58-61
  data type 70-73
  hierarchy 62-70

K

key value mapping 97-101
keyword argument
  about 56
  closed 176
  nbins 176
K-means clustering 326
Kullback-Leibler divergence 161

L

L1dist() function 158
L2dist() function 158
language frameworks
  about 234
  dplyr, comparing with 235
  pandas, comparing with 234
Lasso regularization 363
learning curves
  about 363
  creating 363
  interpreting 363, 364
  using, to improve models 364
linear regression 326
line plot 131
Linfdist function 159
local invocations
  in distributed computing 445, 446
logistic regression 326
loops 45-47

M

machine learning
  about 4, 307
  need for 306, 307
  reinforcement learning 307
  supervised learning 307
  unsupervised learning 307
Machine Learning in Julia (MLJ)
  2D data handling 311-313
  about 308
  built-in performance measure 358
  custom performance measure 358
  data containers 310
  data handling 309, 310
  key features 308, 309
  key goals 309
  machines 355, 356
  model evaluation measure 358, 359
  model performance, evaluating 359, 360
  model tuning 360
  performance measure 357
  regularization 362
  scientific types of data 310-315
macroexpand function 84
Macros
  using 80-85
main module 77
Manhattan distance 158
map 105
map and loops 441, 442
matrix-variate probability distribution 200-202
maxad function 160
mean 150
meanad function 160
median 150
melting 249
missing data
  about 239
  handling 139, 140
  in DataFrames 239
missing values
  in Julia 240-243
mixture models
  in Distributions.jl 202-205
MLJ.jl 210
MLJ.jl model interface
  about 338, 339
  feature importance 350
  fit method 347
  model representation 339, 340
  predict method 347-349
  probability distribution model 352
  serialization 353

supervised model 341, 342
training losses 349
transform method 352
update method 350, 351
user-defined model 342, 343
MLJ transformers
used, for data preprocessing 334, 335
mode 151
model composition 356, 357
model loading 331-333
model matching 329, 330
model queries 328, 329
models
about 325
supervised learning model 325
unsupervised learning model 325
model search 327, 328
model tuning
about 360
Bayesian optimization 361
Grid search 360
Random search 360
module subtyping
example 109, 110
msd function 159
multiple dispatch 73, 75
multithreading
about 408, 409
atomic operations 415, 416
Auto Threads, specifying 410
concurrent execution 408
content switching 409
finalizers, using 421
limitations 419
parallelism, versus concurrency 408
per-field atomics 417
shared memory 408
side effects 418, 419
task migration 420, 421
@threadcall macro 419, 420
threads 408
thread safety 409
@threads macro 415
with Command Line Argument 409
with Environment Variable 410
worker processes, propagating 410
multivariate probability distribution 199, 200
MyClassifier classifier 346

O

observational estimation
in data analysis 175, 176
outlier detection and treatment
in data analysis 156
overlaid histogram 298, 299

P

parallel computation
about 399
distributed computing 400
GPU programming 400
parallel computing libraries 400
shared-memory parallelism 400
parallel computing
advantages 398
approach 399
parallelism
versus concurrency 408
parameter retrieval 188
partial correlation 166
passing argument
in Julia 57
per-field atomics
about 417
key points 417
pivoting 248
Plots.jl
about 210
bar plot 131
histogram 131
line plot 131
scatter plot 131
Plots.jl histograms
2D histogram 300-302

about 293-295
cumulative histogram 299, 300
overlaid histogram 298, 299
stacked histogram 297, 298
weighted histogram 295-297
Plots.jl package
about 272-277
installing 273
recipes 286
scatter plot 279-281
subplots 284, 285
PooledVector 253
positional argument 55
posterior distribution
about 371, 372
calculating 370, 371
predict method
about 347-349
example 348
Principal Component Analysis (PCA) 326
probabilistic classifiers
types 345
probabilistic regressor 344-346
probability
about 182
Bayes' theorem 183
conditional probability 182
estimating 192, 193
joint probability 183
probability distribution
fitting 205, 206
probability distribution model 352
probability package
in Julia 183, 184
processes
managing 435, 436
project environment
bound mutable variable, versus copy mutable variable 37-39
compound expression 47
conditional evaluation 40-42
handling 24-26
loops 45-47
numerical data handling, in Julia 26-32
variable names, in Julia 36, 37
variables, declaring 32-35
proportionmap() function 164
proportions() function 163
Python
integration 110-113

Q

quantiles 154, 155
Query.jl package 232, 233

R

random forests 326
Random search 360
range 151
Raw Data
used, for drawing correlation 4, 5
recipes
in Plots.jl package 286
reduce 106
regression data 316-318
regularization
about 362
Lasso regularization 363
Ridge regularization 363
reinforcement learning 307
remote references
concept 442, 443
Ridge regularization 363
R language
integration 113, 114
rmsd function 160

S

sampling 189
sampling method 161, 164
scatter plot
about 131
in Plots.jl package 279-281

scientific types
about 310
examples 310
serialization 353
series types 279
sets 104, 105
shared array
about 447, 448
example 448, 449
Split-Apply-Combine (SAC) strategy
about 262
in DataFrame 262-268
sqL2dist function 159
stacked histogram 297, 298
stack function 251
stacking 249
standard deviation 152
standard score 156
state multitasking model 433
statistical function
in data analysis 172-174
statistics 3, 4
statistics computation 190, 191
statistics module 148
StatsBase.jl
distance method 158
StatsBase module 172
StatsModels.jl 210
Statsplots.jl recipes
examples 287-289
using 286
string
functions 132-134
regular expression 137, 138
temporal data 138
Text File, reading 134, 135
Text String, splitting 135-137
working with 132
subplots
in Plots.jl package 284, 285
subtypes() function 67
summary statistics 155
supertypes() function 65
supervised learning 307
supervised learning model
about 325
decision trees 326
linear regression 326
logistic regression 326
random forests 326
Support Vector Machines (SVMs) 326
supervised model
about 341
types 341
Support Vector Machines (SVMs) 326
Synthetic Data
categorical data 318
categorical data, handling 319
categories, tracking 321, 322
data preparation 323
data scientific type for categorical data 320
data scientific type for categorical data, changing 320, 321
generating 315, 316
regression data 316-318
weights 325

T

task migration 420, 421
task operations
about 402
@async macro 403
task completion 403
task creation 402
task execution 403
task scheduling 403, 405
yieldto function 404
task scheduling 405
taxicab distance 158
temporal data
about 138
handling 140-142

methods 142
missing data, handling 139, 140
packages 141, 142
TextAnalysis package 130
threadpools
about 411, 412
communication
and synchronization 412, 413
default threadpool 411
interactive threadpool 411
multiple threadpool 411
@threads macro 413
time-series data 138
TimeSeries package 142
TimeZones package 142
training losses 349
transform method 352
truncated probability distribution
about 197
versus censored probability
distribution 198
t-SNE 327
tuned models
evaluating 361
tuple data structure
in Julia 94-96
tuples 104
Turing.jl
about 383
key features 383, 384
type hierarchy 186, 187

U

univariate probability distribution 195, 196
unstack function 251
unsupervised learning 307
unsupervised learning model
about 325
autoencoders 326
Gaussian Mixture Models (GMMs) 326
K-means clustering 326
Principal Component Analysis (PCA) 326
t-SNE 327
update method 350, 351
user-defined model
deterministic regressor 343, 344
probabilistic regressor 344-346

V

variables
in distributed computing 438-440
scope 49
variance 151, 165
vector
sorting 244, 245

W

weighted histogram 295-297
weighted mean 150
weighted sum 150
weights
revisiting 333, 334

Y

yieldto function
about 404, 405
current_task 404
istaskdone 404
istaskstarted 404
task_local_storage 404

Z

Z-score 156